D0429593

EXPOSING MYSELF

EXPOSING
MYSELF

Geraldo Rivera

with Daniel Paisner

BANTAM
NEW YORK • TORONTO • LONDON • SYDNEY • AUCKLAND

EXPOSING MYSELF
A Bantam Book / October 1991

All rights reserved.
Copyright © 1991 by Maravilla Production Company, Inc.

The text was designed and the project was supervised by M 'N O
Production Services, Inc.

Library of Congress Cataloging-in-Publication Data
Rivera, Geraldo.
    Exposing myself / by Geraldo Rivera, with Daniel Paisner.
      p. cm.
    ISBN 0-553-07642-6
    1. Rivera, Geraldo. 2. Television journalists—United
States—Biography. I. Paisner, Daniel. II. Title.
PN4874.R537A3 1991
070'.92—dc20   91-17973
[B]   CIP

Published simultaneously in the United States and Canada

Bantam Books are published by Bantam Books, a division of Bantam
Doubleday Dell Publishing Group, Inc. Its trademark, consisting of
the words "Bantam Books" and the portrayal of a rooster, is
Registered in U. S. Patent and Trademark Office and in other
countries. Marca Registrada, Bantam Books, 666 Fifth Avenue,
New York, New York 10103.

PRINTED IN THE UNITED STATES OF AMERICA

RRH   0 9 8 7 6 5 4 3 2 1

To C.C.,
friend to Gabriel,
mother to Spike, Romeo, Connie, and Beulah,
wife, and love of my life.

"Geraldo Rivera should be arrested for exposing himself."
—Reuven Frank
former president, NBC News

ACKNOWLEDGMENTS

I started writing this in 1973, but chickened out fairly early in the process. My first nod is to Jim Griffin, my agent at William Morris, who convinced me in 1989 that the time was right to get it going again, as a combination TV news history of the last twenty years and an autobiography. I began writing it myself, but proceeded in fits and starts, like a cold Chevy. So nod number two goes to Deb Futter, the Bantam editor who convinced me to bring in Dan Paisner to ensure continuity and an unbroken attention span. I wrote, he rewrote the first half; then, he wrote, I rewrote the second. It was a smooth working arrangement, interrupted only by the insanity of my television life, and his wife's refusal to give birth even after ten months of pregnancy. The next most valuable player was Steve North. Steve started working with me more than fifteen years ago, went away, then came back in 1990 to help me research and report this book. Now a reporter/producer on my television talk show, he conducted most of the interviews we sprinkled through the text to provide texture and another point of view. Dan Pepper, my long-time business manager, has added an aspect of stability and continuity to my life. Jo-Ann Torres Conte and my wife C.C. were invaluable in filling in the gaps in my memory. C.C. was also profoundly tolerant. It isn't easy to stand by when your husband is singing, "To All the Girls I've Loved Before." Finally, thanks to the people who agreed to relive their roles in this improbable journey.

EXPOSING MYSELF

PROLOGUE

NEW ORLEANS

For fifteen years the second half of my name had been "ABC News." It would come out as if by reflex: "Geraldo Rivera, ABC News." (It still does, sometimes.) And so, on December 15, 1985, the day I was removed from the ABC News payroll, I also lost part of my identity. It was the first time since I was fourteen years old that I was without a job—a high-paying, high-profile job, in this case—and the day I lost it stands as a dividing line, separating everything I am from everything I was. It marks the first time in my life—professionally and personally—that I was vincible, and afraid. I had lost part of my name and I would have to make a new one.

I left ABC News because I was told to, and because I made some

1

mistakes. One mistake was that I renewed my three-year, three-million-dollar contract on a handshake and not on paper. Another was that I took a very public stand against news management for its hesitation and, ultimately, failure to run a controversial segment reported by my friend and colleague Sylvia Chase, linking the Kennedy brothers, John and Bobby, to Marilyn Monroe near the end of her life. I was also of the mistaken, and perhaps deluded, impression that the network's news division, specifically its *20/20* program, could never absorb the loss of a famous and flamboyant newsgatherer like myself, someone who had contributed valiantly, and often spectacularly, to its broadcasts for the past decade. Surely, I thought, they would swallow whatever they had to swallow to keep me. I also thought, naively, that the people who labored beside me to put *20/20* on the air would rally around to convince ABC News President Roone Arledge and his underlings that they were about to make a hideous error.

The day I left ABC News was the day I began to doubt and redefine everything about myself: work, ethics, truth, power, celebrity, success, integrity, passion, fidelity, love, family. I was overwhelmed by uncertainty. Losing my job the way I did—publicly—made me cherish the people close to me, the parts of me that did not belong to ABC News. But the midlife trauma also led me to question everything I ever knew and believed about broadcast journalism, and about the place I had carved in it for myself.

All of this I kept to myself in the weeks surrounding my departure from the network. I kept it to myself partly because when you're in the middle of something it's difficult to isolate and understand it enough to talk about it. I lacked perspective. Also, I had spent years perfecting a macho image, stuffed with bravado, and there was no place for this uncharacteristic uncertainty. Friends and family could not be allowed to see me this raw and tentative.

So when Jim Griffin, my perpetual-motion, chain-smoking, ex-jockey agent at the William Morris Agency called me to his office to discuss an offer from Tribune Broadcasting to host a live, syndicated special called "The Mystery of Al Capone's Vault," I was all ears. "I am honor-bound as your agent to convey all offers,"

Jim said, with less enthusiasm than it takes to switch channels, "but I have to tell you this is the worst possible idea."

"How much?" I wanted to know, desperate for anything. I wanted to work and I needed the money.

"Twenty-five thousand dollars," he said.

"For what?"

"They want you to host a syndicated special. Two hours, live. They've got some deal with a vault that supposedly belonged to Al Capone. It's been sealed for years. They want to open it on live television."

"What do you think?" I asked. I knew what I thought—even the worst possible deal sounded good to me.

"I think twenty-five thousand dollars is spit. It's syndicated and syndicated shows never do well." He had a whole list of reasons why I should not accept the job, ending with his assessment that my doing this show would not be unlike boxing's former heavyweight champion Joe Louis, at the end of his career, becoming a professional wrestler. "It's beneath you," he said finally.

It was, and so I told Jim to ask for fifty thousand dollars.

I needed to stay solvent. I owed three hundred thousand dollars a year in alimony and child-support payments. I had lost my house in Malibu, my apartment on Central Park West, and a large portion of my other assets in an expensive and bitter divorce a year earlier. I also had expenses on a modest (for Manhattan) penthouse apartment on Ninety-sixth Street and Madison Avenue. I had my parents to support, and a host of others to help out. And then there was my sailboat, the *New Wave*, a graceful forty-four-foot blue sloop with lots of sea-miles under her keel. She consumed about fifty thousand dollars a year—at the time, a passion I could not afford, and one I could not afford to lose.

ABC News had been paying me over a million dollars a year when they cut me loose, and I had always found a way to spend almost all of it. That's an enormous amount of money, I know, and yet I took it for granted. A million dollars was my nut, what I needed to keep everything going.

I don't lay these figures out here to brag, or to cry poor. I know many families who get by—comfortably—on two percent of what

I was earning. I invoke the numbers merely to put things into perspective, to show what I was thinking. I had come to depend on my handsome salary, and at the time I couldn't see my way clear to a withdrawal.

ABC paid me a five-hundred-thousand-dollar cash settlement upon termination, which I wasn't allowed to talk about then, but can now. So, with five hundred thousand dollars in pocket, I told myself I needed five hundred thousand dollars more to make it through 1986. Fifty thousand dollars, I thought, would give me a month to sort through the slow trickle of job offers and figure out my next move. So far, the slow trickle amounted to one offer: a two-hundred-thousand-dollar-a-year gig hosting a talk show for the Cable News Network, where I had been pinch-hitting for Larry King since my departure from network news.

Two hundred thousand dollars was a lot of money then, it still is, but it was not enough for me. Plus, the job itself (a daytime talk show on cable TV?), was not what I had in mind. I needed more—more challenge, money, and exposure. Trouble was, I had no idea where to find these things. They certainly had not come looking for me.

Fifty thousand dollars, for a few weeks' work, was a start. And it bought me a month. "Ask for fifty," I told Jim, "then I'll do it."

"Fifty is still spit," he said.

"Jim, I've got nothing else lined up. Nobody's knocking down my door."

"You realize the vault may be empty?" he tried.

I had not considered this melancholy prospect, but now that he brought it up I did not think it would be a problem. "There's that chance," I said. "But what if it's not?" I gestured to the horseplayer's credo in needlepoint my ex-jockey agent had long ago hung on his wall: "Scared money never wins." "What about that?" I said.

"You'll be standing there on live television, national television, with two hours to fill," Jim said. "You better learn a song, or a couple jokes, just in case."

I convinced myself, and Jim Griffin, that it didn't matter if Al Capone's vaults were empty or riddled with cash and corpses. Whatever we would or would not find in the basement of Chicago's Lexington Hotel, I was sure I could produce a great documentary on an intriguing period in American history—prohibition, and the era of the Chicago mob. It was a chance to tell a story that people seemed to want to hear.

And, beyond CNN, it was the only thing on my plate. I told Jim I wanted the job.

"Fifty?" he asked, making sure.

"Fifty."

Tribune upped the ante and I had a job.

My first order of business was an appearance at the annual National Association of Television Producers and Executives (NATPE) convention. I hadn't counted on this.

The buying and selling of syndicated television programming is, I learned quickly, an unusual enterprise. It seems to have a lot to do with pomp and flash and sirens and bathing beauties and clowns and fresh popcorn. If I hadn't been in the middle of it—literally, right there on the cavernous New Orleans Convention Center floor, with a "Hi, my name is Geraldo Rivera" tag smiling from my lapel—I might have been able to step back and wonder at the scene. Instead, I was (and remain) convinced, people were stepping back and wondering at me.

There I was, battling malignant embarrassment, flanked in the Tribune booth by two gorgeous models, immodestly dressed in Roaring Twenties style. We were set among larger-than-life-size photo blowups of Al Capone, and an authentic seven-passenger 1926 Packard touring car in mint condition. There were also several very large pictures of me.

They really pulled out all the stops, those Tribune people. "The Mystery of Al Capone's Vault" was little more than a high concept, but still they were selling the hell out of it. To them, the bells and whistles of NATPE were the symphony of the cash register. To me, the whole thing made me feel small and humiliated.

But I held up my end of the deal. I always do. I glad-handed the endless swarm of conventioneers—mostly nonnetwork-affiliated independent station managers considering our program for their air. I also shouldered their skepticism and the bubbling curiosity of their wives. Nobody really knew what to make of me and my involvement in a program like this, and these television-station executives were not above asking how it was that my career had come to this.

But my career had come to this. After everything I had done, Al Capone was all I had going, and as distasteful as the whole NATPE circus was, I was determined to make a success of it. I was going to work as hard as I possibly could to make the show as good as I possibly could, and do everything in my power to market it to ensure that as many people as possible watched it.

It was my one chance back.

Enter Judd Rose, until several weeks earlier a fellow traveler at ABC News. He was there with his camera crew, men I had worked with before, on what had become a perennial pick of network assignment editors: the annual trip to NATPE to mock the blatant hucksterism of syndicated television. The reports were widely appreciated at the network for the way they ridiculed the worst aspects of this overtly commercial, highly competitive business. Judd's pieces were particularly on-target. I remembered watching them along with everyone else, laughing.

Which is why his appearance at this particular NATPE convention was my emotional undoing. My heart, and pride, raced each other to new depths. I was horrified at the thought of being found out. Of course, there was little hiding my involvement with the program—it had been announced in the television trade magazines, and the show would, after all, be syndicated nationwide and to a dozen foreign countries—but I did not want to come face-to-face with a recent peer, with myself at such a disadvantage.

Not only was I no longer working in network news, but I was here, at NATPE, pandering.

I actually hid. I found a corner of the Tribune booth set off from the bells and whistles, and stole away for a few minutes while the ABC News crew passed. My only hope was that they would not come looking for me. I played the imagined encounter out in my mind. If Judd approached me, I would put the best face on the situation. I would emphasize the documentary aspects of the program, and play down the opening of the vault. But I knew he wouldn't buy it. I knew that if he spotted me and came by, cameras rolling, I would wind up being laughed at back at ABC News, by people who for fifteen years had been my television family. The prospect was worse than being beaten.

Hiding, I started to wish for my old job, for Judd Rose's job, for anything that would take me off that convention floor. I was willing to start all over again. I would have worked for a local station. I would have taken anything as long as it held the faint promise of getting back onto network television. But I had burned my bridges at ABC News; I had been the object of competitive tension at CBS and NBC for so long, there was no way they would ever hire me; CNN couldn't afford me. Where else was I going to go? What was I going to do? This? Host sensational syndicated specials at fifty thousand dollars a pop? I joked during this time that I was the most famous unemployed person in America, and it may have been true, but the joke burned every time I told it.

Thankfully, Judd Rose didn't see me, but the incident—having been so ashamed of where I was and what I was doing that I actually had to hide from a former colleague—and the emotions attached to it—pride, embarassment, and, mostly, fear—have never left me.

That convention left other scars. The near run-in with that ABC News crew was only one of them. I remember very clearly returning to my hotel room after I was through on the floor each day and looking automatically at the red message light on the phone beside my bed. For the three or four days I was there, the light never once flashed red. Not once. I would open the door and think, maybe Jim Griffin called with a job offer, or, maybe Roone Arledge changed his mind, or, maybe the new management team at Capital Cities/ABC had overruled Roone and wanted me back.

No one called.

Every time I opened the door to my hotel room, it was another hit in the stomach. I found myself hungering for a call, some sign that there was still a place for me in the world beyond New Orleans. But there was none.

CHAPTER ONE

614 NINTH STREET, WEST BABYLON

Aesthetically speaking, growing up on Long Island sucked.

I arrived there with my family, from the seedy streets of Williamsburg, Brooklyn, early enough to watch the last of the scrub pine being shaved from the sandy soil to make room for the tract homes, gas stations, fast food restaurants, and shopping malls that now blanket the thirty miles to the New York City line. In my memory, there wasn't a tree, or a hill, for miles; my feelings of fondness for my boyhood home stem largely from the fact that it instilled a desire to travel.

In the early Eisenhower years, the town of West Babylon, in Suffolk County, was architecturally indistinguishable from the working-class communities surrounding it. It was a bedroom community for the employees of the Island's two big defense plants, Republic and Grumman Aviation, bordered to the north by the predominantly black village of Wyandanch and to the south by Babylon proper, a more prosperous, WASP enclave on the other side of the Long Island Railroad tracks. Our town, with one notable exception, was made up largely of blue collar Irish and Italians.

We Riveras were the grand exception. My father Allen Cruz Rivera worked for Republic. "Allen" was Dad's *nom de mariage*, taken to assuage his Jewish in-laws when he married my mother Lilly Friedman. Cruz, which translates as "cross" in English, was Dad's real first name, but he worried that my mother's family would choke on the Christianity of it. One of nineteen children born to a proud, hard-working Puerto Rican sugar plantation worker, Dad came to the United States as a young man filled with boundless ambition and energy, but his dreams, sadly, eluded him. Throughout my years in West Babylon, he was up at four-thirty each morning, supervising the mostly Hispanic staff in the Republic cafeteria kitchen.

His oldest son struggled, too. I wet the bed, on and off, until I was eight. I was allergic to grass, milk, chocolate, and dogs. I was underweight. I had acne. Worst, I was asthmatic. Fate, I learned early on, was blind and unreliable. I was cornered into developing an engaging, resourceful personality to get people to look past the pimples.

As I sit here, seeking to recreate that long-ago period, my thoughts are bracketed by the loving warmth of family, and by the harsh, judging realities of the outside world.

Some scenes stick out, like the time, shortly after we moved into our new home, when my older sister Irene intercepted a mostly Labrador puppy on its way to the pound to be destroyed. Irene enlisted the enthusiams of her younger siblings—me and my little sister Sharon—and we pleaded with Dad to let us keep the black mutt, whom we called Patty, short for Patent Leather. Patty and I would spend hours tramping through the partially bulldozed pinewoods. Unfortunately, I became asthmatic whenever Patty and I spent too much time together. When the asthma attacks were heaviest, it was like breathing through a thin straw; I grabbed for air in gulps and starts. But I didn't mind the trade-off. Mom, though, decided Patty had to go. She had rushed me to the hospital emergency room for a shot of adrenaline too many times to consider weathering even one more attack for the sake of a dog.

Trouble was, we knew no one who would take Patty in. If we brought her back to the pound, my parents feared the mutt would be destroyed. Dad was assigned the unpleasant task of driving Patty to Wyandanch and urging her out of the car. On the open road, he hoped, the sweet animal had a fighting chance of begging for a new home. Dad came back and told us she had been adopted by a nice family, and we adjusted to life without her. Several days later, on a Sunday, I was sitting in the living room with my family, listening to the radio, when my uncle Louie knocked on the door. He had Patty in his arms. The dog was exhausted and matted with dirt and blood. She had been hit by a car, but had made it most of the way home before collapsing a block away. We built a doghouse in the backyard, off limits to me, and Patty stayed with us for several more years.

At ten, I took my first tentative steps into the world of journalism, as a paperboy. I sold and delivered the *Long Island Press.* It was a hard sell. *Newsday* was the dominant Long Island newspaper at the time (it would later force the *Press* to shut down), so my offering was the neighborhood's second choice. The struggle taught me two things about the news business: It is hard to be number two, and never take a job where winter winds can blow up your pants.

At eleven, our family expanded by two. My baby brother Craig was born, and my cousin Wilfredo came to live with us. The main thing I remember about Craig's arrival is how unimpressed I was by the gurglings and cooings that drove the rest of the family to adoration and distraction. Willie, though, made quite an appearance, and an impression. Willie is the son of my father's brother Juan, who never left Puerto Rico. Pushed by his poverty and bad attitude, Juan told his brother Cruz to care for his boy.

LILLY RIVERA: Willie was actually staying with his aunt Ana in the Bronx, and he was causing her a lot of trouble. He was always out, playing in the street. You know, she just couldn't handle him, he was too much, so his grandpa came up from Puerto Rico to take him home. My husband drove to the airport to see them off because he wanted to see his father. Geraldo went with him and, I think, so did Irene. So they got to the airport, and I was home with the baby and Sharon, and they started talking, and next thing you know Al turns to Geraldo and says, "How would you like another brother?" And Geraldo says, "Sure." And then to Irene, "How would you like another brother?" "Sure." And then he picked up the phone and called me and said, "How would you like another son?" And Craig is just five months old. But, you know, I said, "Sure, there's always room for one more."

My parents' decision to adopt Willie officially left me tentative at first, and bewildered. Outwardly, I was excited, but underneath I was unsure. He was almost exactly my age, and the sudden competition was unnerving. Through no fault of his own, Willie encroached on a world I had spent eleven years building; my friends became his, and his world became mine. I think we all felt a certain honor in rescuing a kid from the clutches of the Third World, but I felt it less than everyone else. Perhaps it had to do with our proximity in age, or the burden of accommodating Willie's untamed personality. More likely, it had to do with my early ambivalence surrounding my own heritage. He was so Spanish-looking, my new brother Willie. I had blended into the neighborhood to where I was just another American kid, and here my brother had trouble speaking English. It was tough enough straddling two dramatically different (both beseiged) worlds.

My mother, for example, wanted her eclectic suburban family to have a religious identity, and to accomplish this we joined the newly established Temple Beth El. The congregation was so small (there were only about a half-dozen families) that my Bar Mitzvah was held in the borrowed North Lindenhurst Volunteer Fire Department hall. Rabbi Ralph Kingsley called me to the makeshift podium, to read in Hebrew from the Torah. The audience, my extended family, recognized the solemn moment and the room became silent. Because my father's side of the family greatly outnumbered my mother's, it was mostly a Puerto Rican crowd. As I began to read, the assembled Rivera clan, unfamiliar with Jewish ritual but wanting to acknowledge the moment with appropriate respect, removed their yarmulkes and placed the skullcaps over their hearts.

My growing up was a strange mix of whitefish and *pasteles.* Despite the occasional oddities of culture clash, the Rivera and Friedman sides of the family got along almost without incident, even if we didn't all speak the same language. What made our strange ethnic combination even more interesting was how stereotypical my parents were. Mother is as Jewish as a knish, while my dark, handsome father could have done those Ricardo Montalban-rich-Corinthian-leather car commercials. Indeed, there was some talk on my mother's side that the shock of Lilly's mixed marriage had driven her parents to an early grave, but I always read those grumblings as Jewish guilt clashing with Puerto Rican pride.

The social tolerance of our West Babylon neighbors surprised me. At least it surprises me now, in retrospect. The aberrations still bother me. One first-taste of racial prejudice came at the hands of a high school girlfriend, a lovely Italian brunette who looked like Annette Funicello. Ida and I were going hot and heavy for a couple weeks, until suddenly she stopped answering my calls. I later heard her parents were afraid our relationship would produce black children.

At the other end of our mix was anti-Semitism, which I was introduced to shortly after my fire hall Bar Mitzvah. Six of us were grouped around Rabbi Kingsley in his borrowed office in the village of Lindenhurst, reading from the Bible. Suddenly, our attention was broken by a heavy pounding at the glass door. Through the glass I could see several menacing junior Nazis, shouting things about Jewish people. In later years, I would react with vigilante indignation, but back then I was only shocked, embarrassed, and afraid. What was there about Judaism that made these strangers so angry? What was there about my family that left me feeling so exposed?

The incident, however fleeting, was a turning point. I started to approach my Judaism the same way I approached acne, as something to cover up, unless I was in the company of fellow Jews. Finding cover, with a name like Rivera, was easy. I was not the

first in the family to seek such assimilation. When I was born, my
mother filled in my birth certificate with the name Gerald Riviera,
adding an extra "i" to my father's surname. She did the same thing
for my sister Irene. Later, she would drop the pretense for my
sister Sharon, only to pick it up again with the birth of my baby
brother Craig. Whenever we asked her about the inconsistencies,
she would shrug shyly and joke her way out of it. "I just forgot
how to spell it," she would say, and leave it at that. Underneath, I
came to realize, she was deeply embarrassed over what was a
clumsy attempt at an ethnic cover-up.

With my parents and younger sister known as Rivera, and with
various documents bearing one spelling or the other, we were all
confused. School officials were also stymied. My high school
yearbook carried one spelling for my graduation photo, and the
other for my team pictures. Over the years, the name-game has
been an absurd humiliation, forcing me into countless and often
contradictory explanations. Once I became a public person, it even
gave rise to the convoluted tale—first spun by a New York disc
jockey in 1973—that I was a Jew posing as a Puerto Rican to cash
in on affirmative action, and that my real family name was Rivers.

At the time, though, Mom's gambit worked. Once out of high
school and at large in the world, access to the alternative spelling
allowed me all the social mobility I could afford. When in doubt
about how people would respond to a New York Puerto Rican, I
would pose as someone more elegantly continental, still vaguely
Hispanic, perhaps the son of a businessman from Spain or
Argentina. Maybe it helped somewhere along the line. Maybe it
didn't. But until the age of twenty-four, I was Gerry Riviera,
Americanized Latin lover in search of greater expectations and
better scenery.

The beauty of the name was in its ambiguity, which also allowed
me to allay any anti-Semitic attacks. In fact, religion almost never
came up in high school or college. The assumption was that all
Latins were Catholic, and in West Babylon I played to that illusion
on all significant Christian holidays, dutifully trudging to church
with my mostly Italian school friends. They taught me the
minimum necessary rituals, with emphasis on the act of contrition.

Mom fought a stubborn rear-guard action in those early days, continuing to insist on the celebration of Hanukkah over Christmas. But just before the Christmas following the verbal assault in Rabbi Kingsley's office, Irene and I swung away from my mother's Jewish influence and marched into the living room rebelliously flaunting our first Christmas tree. Mom was crushed, but not defiant. She didn't have to be. Assaulted by genetic guilt, and unwilling to hurt her further, we dubbed the tree a Hanukkah bush, and mixed "Rock of Ages" with our newly liberated repertoire of carols.

The swing of my ethnic pendulum accelerated during my sixteenth summer, which was spent with my grandparents in Puerto Rico. The visit was a long-due awakening. After years as a field supervisor on a huge sugar plantation, Abuelo Juan was a respected member of the community. In his older years, he was always referred to as "Don" Juan, an honorific roughly equivalent to the English "Sir." Abuela Tomasa was a proud lion of a woman, a loving disciplinarian with sharp, almost Indian features. She ruled the house, a queen crowned with a mane of brilliant white hair, pulled back in beautiful contrast to the worn mocha leather of her face. My grandparents were married for over six decades. Both lived to be ninety-five. They had nineteen of their own children and, in testimony to the island's centuries of colonial domination, buccaneerism, and intermarriage, they ranged in appearance from chocolate-brown to peachy-white. My grandparents also adopted two other kids and helped to raise countless nieces, nephews, grandchildren, and neighborhood waifs.

I was tossed into that Rivera family stew with only a smattering of school-taught Spanish to help me make sense of the comings and goings. It was a magnificent summer, even if I needed subtitles at first. Before the summer was out, I learned how to speak Spanish out of necessity. And, I became close to my father's family for the first time, stirring in me an awareness of my Puerto Rican heritage and pride.

Most significantly, at least to this horny teenager, I discovered women. Back home, the summer before, I enjoyed a short exploration with a loose older girl who played a wicked Wendy to the neighborhood Lost Boys. At fourteen, I ranked last and least in that particular crowd. "Big Beth" would lead two or three of the older boys up a rotting wooden staircase to the second floor of an abandoned house we called the Old Allen House, just a block from my home, then up a drop-ladder to the third-floor attic. I hung around outside, moon-faced, taking in the creaking noises and bawdy laughter above, wanting to be let in. Every other neopubescent kid for blocks around knew something sexual was going on up there, but none was as persistent. I ignored all requests and commands to leave.

Finally, Big Beth let me enter. I walked gingerly up the second-floor stairs, then dashed across to the ladder of happiness. I was most of the way up when she loomed into view. She was so big she blocked out the light. Her hefty, naked limbs straddled the entryway, nearly covering it. She commanded me to strip. When I was finally bones and bare-assed, she barked again: "Climb up."

I advanced awkwardly to the top rung. "Stop there," she said. I stopped. And stiffened. "Now touch my leg," she instructed. I reached for the inside of her thigh. "Jesus!" she cried out, pulling back, "your hand's freezing." She was right. They were.

My hands still get cold at showtime.

It wasn't much of a close encounter—Big Beth was put off by my cold hands and sent me back down the attic stairs—but it promised at future wonder. The next summer, in Puerto Rico, that promise was fulfilled one morning on the muddy orange banks of a tropical river. My newfound bilingualism was beginning to pay great dividends. With a comely, eighteen-year-old distantly related cousin, it assisted in the discovery of passion.

"*¿Geraldito, me gustas?*" my "kissing" cousin said.

"Shhh," I shhhed. "*Estoy buscando el cielo, las estrellas, y mi corazón.*"

The joys I unearthed with my father's family were tempered somewhat upon my return home. In the five years since Willie joined our immediate family, he had grown into an unpredictable kid. He ditched school, took up with bikers and bouncers, and began bulking up. By the time I left home two years later, he would be known as the toughest guy on Long Island. A friction developed between us, and our home became a battleground of tensions. As I shed my ninety-eight-pound-weakling frame, joined the football team, and became a semitough myself, our arguments took a turn to the physical. The tensions came to a head one day on our parent's front lawn. Sharon watched as her big brothers beat the shit out of each other. It was an all-out rumble, made more punishing by our blood ties. I was taller and had the boxer's jab, circling and sticking Willie with my left. He pulled his head down into his shoulders and charged, throwing roundhouse hammers. Sharon cried for us to stop. To her, it must have looked like we would kill each other.

Willie and I were both hurting, but neither wanted to quit. We were brother against brother, and fought with everything we had. As we grew tired, and our punches less forceful, the battle became truly ugly. We turned to words.

"Dirty Jew," Willie cried out, inflicting more pain than the combination of his roundhouse hammers.

"Spic," I jabbed back. A part of me wanted to reclaim the word once I had said it; another part took pleasure in hurting Willie in just this way.

The unspoken prejudices of our mixed traditions had been given voice, and it would be years before the two of us were able to get past that moment to become blood-brother close. Now, we would die for each other. We talk, sometimes, about the old days, and about how easy it is to hurt a tough guy's feelings.

WEST BABYLON HIGH

Like most high schools, mine was segregated by social standing. At the top of the West Babylon High caste system were the jocks, the cheerleaders, and the no-doubt college-bound. These were the all-American Bandstanders, saddle-shoed and letter-sweatered, the dream of every parent and teacher. At the bottom of the ladder were the hapless hoods, incorrigibly blue collar and usually headed to an early exit from academia. These were the Elvis fanatics, the part-time pump jockeys at the corner gas station, all of them dressed in black— slightly pegged pants with pink saddle stitching, and mock-leather jackets—and in love with their cars. And, of course, there was the big, faceless middle, the largest segment of the school population, the kids who were quiet, obedient, ate fatty foods, watched too much television, and shopped in Robert Hall discount clothing stores.

A social diplomat even at that early age, I circulated between the school's top and bottom rungs as cocaptain of the football team and a member of a mild-mannered, little-known street gang called the Corner Boys. My relationship with the school's elite crowd was complicated by my swagger. Despite measured acceptance, I always felt awkward and insecure around those preppy types. I fit in, and I didn't. I was most comfortable at the low end of the scale. As a Corner Boy, it was my duty to sip Knickerbocker beer through a straw, and basically hang out with the other disenchanted pretend delinquents in the group. These days, we would be the punks playing video games and trashing the mall.

Aside from being cool, the Corner Boys' more serious mandate was to protect the town from the would-be delinquents of Amityville and environs. We had one rumble that I can recall, and it had to do with a football defeat, or an insulted girlfriend. Our expeditionary force rendezvoused on a side street around the corner from the Babylon movie theater. We armed ourselves with lengths of chain and weighted sticks, and carried garbage-can covers to use as shields. Fifteen of us piled into a three-car convoy and headed west, for Amityville High. But what I remember most was my secret relief when a patrolling police car pulled up just as our noisy but still nonviolent face-off had begun. Both sides retreated victorious, howling into the night like young apes.

My first car was a 1947 Chevy convertible, purchased with twenty-five dollars earned from an after-school job as a gofer in a rolling steel-door factory. I left the Corner Boys for the Valve Grinders, a car club. We wore black jackets with gold vinyl sleeves and a winged valve emblazoned on the back. I dropped a '54 Corvette six-cylinder engine equipped with three one-barrel carburetors into the Chevy and cut off half the steering wheel so that it resembled an airplane's.

That car changed my life and drove me to my first big trouble. I envied the gaudy spinner hubcaps the other guys had on their cars, but could not afford a set of my own. One night, out cruising, I spotted a set particularly to my liking, and bent to temptation. Before long, stealing hubcaps became a habit. With the right tools, and lightning moves, it was a piece of cake. I was forever trading up; if I saw a new set I liked, I would grab it. I lived the cliche: Even in the suburbs, I was a Puerto Rican stealing hubcaps.

Eventually, I graduated from hubcaps to tires, and from tires to cars. I had my eye on a great-looking bright blue 1955 Olds '88, which was always parked underneath a big tree on a neighborhood street. The tires were like new, and I wanted them. I sized-up the job with my pals and decided the only sure way to remove the tires without being seen was to take the whole car. It would take several minutes to strip the car of its tires, and only seconds to drive it away. My job was to watch the house. Two other guys watched the street, one in each direction, and a third, an apprentice mechanic, hot-wired the car.

Once we eased our first stolen car from the night-shadows of the big tree, we took it on the requisite joyride, leaving rubber at every turn. We tired of the adventure, especially as it began to dawn on us what we had done. Finally, we dumped the car in the woods of Belmont Lake State Park, where we removed the tires, the spare, and the fender skirts. Mission accomplished. The irony of the heist was that the Olds's electric-blue rims did not fit my Chevy, and so the booty went to one of the other guys in on the job.

We were found out a week or so later. My father told me the local precinct captain had just called asking us to go down to the station house. I was filled with awful dread during the silent trip. My worst fears were realized at the police station, when I was confronted with the stolen tires. I will never forget those electric-blue rims. Caught red-handed, our hot wirer had confessed, and given up the names of his coconspirators. The captain let us off with a stern lecture, delivered in front of the assembled parents. Disappointment and hurt washed over my father and spilled onto me, and his shame burned a repentance on my soul. I can't say the incident swore me to a law-abiding future, but I did resolve to die before embarrassing him again.

My closest friends during my last two years in high school were Frankie DeCecco and Vic Furio. The two friendships existed on separate planes, although each would have a profound impact on my young adulthood. Frankie moved to West Babylon from the Greenpoint section of Brooklyn just before our junior year. He shared neither my interest in larceny, nor in sports. The first thing I noticed about him was the way he dressed. He could have passed for Frankie Avalon. We used to wear matching black mohair suits when we went out at night. Frankie already had his when we met; he was with me when I bought mine, at discount, at Howard Clothes, where his mother worked. We wore those mohair suits for our television debut, in 1960, on *Herb Shelton's TV Dance Party,* a local, low-rent dance show, and we wore them on our weekend forays into Manhattan, to places like the Peppermint Lounge in Times Square, where we journeyed to see headliners like Joey Dee and the Starlighters. Whenever we were out on the town, Frankie and I would pretend to be brothers. The pose almost always worked; in those days girls preferred being bad together.

One night, on our way home from the city, we argued over the best way to make it in life. Frankie's ideal was a job like the one his stepfather had, as a salesman for a Chevrolet dealership. My goal was college, which I saw as a means to owning the entire dealership.

"I bet you within ten years I'll be making thirty thousand dollars," I blustered.

"No way," Frankie shot back.

Taking our cue from Cary Grant in *An Affair to Remember,* we vowed that no matter what we were doing or where we were living, we would meet in exactly ten years at the top of the Empire State Building to compare notes. If I was making thirty grand, Frankie would have to buy me a fancy Italian dinner; if I had yet to reach that stratospheric salary, dinner was on me.

When the time came to mark that decade-old wager, both of us were married. I was living in Manhattan and already in the television news business. Frankie was still living on Long Island, selling cars. He conceded the bet and bought dinner at a joint in Little Italy. Dessert was a visit to an Oriental massage parlor on East Broadway. My treat.

Underneath the settling-of-stakes celebration, there was a new tension between Frankie and me. For the first time in our long friendship, there was a burgeoning economic gap between us, a distance that we would never be able to bridge because of everything it represented.

If I wasn't with Frankie during my junior and senior years of high school, then I was usually with Vic Furio, a wiry, red-haired rascal from the next town over. Vic and I discovered the budding East Coast surf scene together. Summers, I would shed my black mohair suit for denim cutoffs and hit the choppy Atlantic breakers off Oak Beach, on Long Island's south shore. Occasionally, we would even get wet. Most of our surfing days were spent roaming the dunes, our boards under our arms, passing ourselves off to the ladies as smooth surf-dudes. Even then, I understood the importance of self-promotion.

I had a craving for the ladies, even in high school. My basic goal was to keep one steady and one on the side, a strategy I would follow well into adulthood. For several years, beginning with the kissing cousin in Puerto Rico, I kept a careful listing of triumphs, and next to each name indicated whether the girl was a "steady" or a "spare."

Mary Pachla was my main steady toward the end of high school, and the first woman I ever exploited. She was the only child of a hard-working Sunrise Highway mechanic and his wife. We started dating in the summer of her sophomore and my junior year. She was a pretty cheerleader, quieter and more thoughtful than the others. Our first romantic encounter was spent under a blanket in the back of the football-team bus, returning home from an away-game.

Lovemaking became our basic entertainment. It was exciting and inexpensive. Mary and I double-dated to my senior prom, with Frank and his steady Jolene. Frank borrowed a brand-new Chevy convertible from his stepfather for the occasion, and we drove up in high-style to a catering hall along Sunrise Highway. Actually, we only drove the last block in style. We took the top down around the corner from the hall, protecting the girls' "beehives" on the way over.

The four of us were slick and removed from the rest of the scene. Our classmates were not a part of our future. No matter what happened later in life, it would happen someplace else, with some other people. We kept to ourselves for the formal part of the evening and then made a quick exit into Manhattan. There, parked underneath the West Side Highway, near the moored S.S. *France*, Mary and I made love, pretending we were on a cruise to Europe.

I had some money stashed away from my summer and part-time jobs, but I almost never spent it on Mary. Our intimacy seemed entertainment enough for both of us, so I used the cash to snare harder game.

Almost thirty years would pass before I saw Mary again. It was my talk show producer's surprise. We were taping a program on childhood sweethearts when out she walked. I was shocked, both to see her, and to realize that she had consented to appear—given the bitter end to our long-ago relationship. Living in Florida and long-married to a NASA official, she is the mother of three.

As a man past the middle of life, I now try to understand why I undervalued women like Mary. Although never analyzed, I claim a Freudian reason, and pin part of the blame for my sloppy love habits on my father. Before evolving as a man, he suffered through what talk show hosts call a "Casanova complex." He was a chronic flirt throughout the first several years of his marriage. He even had a long-term affair with a co-worker from the defense plant cafeteria, a relationship that nearly cost him his family.

I was an unwitting accomplice to the romance. Dad would drop me off at my Little League games, continue on to his dangerous liaison, and return to the field by the end of the game. I never knew of his disappearing act, until one day he lost track of time and returned long after the lights were out and everyone but me had gone home.

Mom looked the other way for as long as she could. Finally, she packed up the kids and took us to stay with my aunt Betty in Brooklyn.

Dad lobbied me to stay behind. "You're the first one to look like my side of the family," he said. "Before you were born, Mama's family looked down on me. Won't you stay?" Although he was not a big drinker, that night he was in his cups. Like most men caught cheating, he felt most sorry for himself.

I went with my mother to Brooklyn.

Happily, we returned to West Babylon a short time later. Dad mended his ways and made himself over to become the world's greatest husband and father. It took me years before I forgave him his transitory weakness of the flesh, but no time at all to copy his moves.

FORT SCHUYLER, THE BRONX

Russell Van Brunt was the principal of West Babylon High. A big, bald, energetic guy with a Teddy Roosevelt grin, he had served as a naval officer on Puerto Rico during World War II. His time on *La Isla del Encanto* instilled in him a special affection for the Puerto Rican people. As the only convenient objects of that affection, he paid attention to the Riveras.

As graduation approached, Mr. Van Brunt encouraged me to trade my strong back and relatively agile mind for a career as a Merchant Marine officer. He arranged for an interview with his alma mater Fort Schuyler, New York State Maritime College. The prospect of a career at sea was thrilling and richer than any postgraduation plan I had formulated on my own. Assuming I could gain admission and graduate, I would earn a college degree, an ensign's commission in the navy reserve, and a license as a third mate in the merchant fleet.

Mr. Van Brunt pulled the strings necessary to get me accepted. I had my one-way ticket off Long Island, with one intermediate stop at a community college in Brooklyn for some remedial courses in English and math.

Fort Schuyler, named for the Revolutionary War fortification that is now its administration building, is a military school much like West Point, although less formal and renowned. I arrived on campus prepared to rebel against organization, flout authority, and generally coast my way to graduation. I went in liking the idea of what the place could give me, but I didn't care for what it was selling. Once there, though, I did an about-face after the very first assembly of the cadet corps, when the commandant addressed the incoming class as men.

Me? A man? At eighteen, the unearned description fit my emerging self-image. Plus, I liked the uniforms and I liked the way my life would look if I managed to complete the four-year program. And so I fell into line and started busting my butt before anyone in authority had the chance to do it for me. I worked and played hard, burying myself in the books and in the fort's extensive intercollegiate athletic program. I started at goalie for the varsity soccer and lacrosse teams and pulled starboard stroke oar for the prestigious rowing team. And, borrowing a page from my mother's book on ethnic obscurity, I assumed the guise of continental Spanish descent. As far as everyone at Fort Schuyler knew, I was Gerry Riviera, son of a well-to-do Spanish merchant.

I became eligible for weekend liberty after Thanksgiving of my first year. On a typical weekend, Frankie DeCecco would drive in over the Throgs Neck Bridge from Long Island. Sometimes he brought my girl Mary with him, along with Jolene; more often, he came alone, and these bachelor visits helped make the weeks seem shorter. It was just like old times when it was the two of us; the only changes to our old routine were our haunts, and my wardrobe. He would pick me up at the fort entrance and we would drive down to the German bars on East Eighty-sixth Street. I no longer wore black mohair; those rathskeller girls loved men in uniform.

I did well that first year, academically and romantically; I tallied up enough "spares" to start a bowling league. The end of the school year was marked by the fort's annual cruise to Europe. To call it a cruise makes the journey sound more luxurious than it actually was. We steamed across the ocean aboard the *John Brown*, a converted World War II troop transport, under the seaworthy eyes of the navy reserve officers and former Merchant seamen on the faculty. As we sailed east out of Long Island Sound, I remember thinking how odd it was that I was about to cross the Atlantic to Europe, before ever crossing the Hudson to New Jersey.

The trip, quite literally, was a rite of passage. The voyage was stormy and breathtaking. I stood night watch at the helm while a gay fourth classman bent over for most of the Filipino galley staff. And I learned to tie knots and various other points of seamanship, under the tutelage of an ancient mariner we called "Pops," who stood before me as a cartoonist's interpretation of a life at sea: corncob pipe, belligerent jaw, and tattoo-embroidered arms.

My closest confidant on board the *John Brown* was a short, barrel-chested Ukrainian named Pete Piachzki. He was both a watchmate and fellow soccer player, but we had almost nothing else in common. He was Eastern European conservative, and I was New York showy. Our friendship was spurred by my first act of heroism. We were both on a scaffold, painting the side of the ship. (Some cruise.) Suddenly, the line holding his side of the rigging snapped. We were fifty feet above the water. Pete was headed for the briny deep when I reflexively dove toward him, barely managing to grab hold of his right forearm with one hand while I maintained my purchase and balance with the other. The platform dipped wildly, but I held fast. Courage or cowardice is usually decided like that, on impulse.

Pete scrambled back up the dangling platform after a few minutes of wiggle and pull, and I had a friend for life. In our off-hours, belowdecks, Pete and I would argue over what to everyone else was a relatively obscure point in ethnic politics: Was a lofty Spaniard (me) genetically closer to a lowly Puerto Rican than a Catholic Ukrainian (him) was to a Communist Russian? The debate would eventually be reduced to playful name-calling: "Commie bastard!" "Paco the Puerto Rican!" Unlike the venomous exchange with Willie some years earlier, these taunts had no cutting edge on them.

We sailed to the Strait of Gibraltar, and then on to Malaga, in the south of Spain, Genoa, Italy, and back out the Mediterranean to Holland, Germany, and the Oslo Fjord in Norway. The days were long, and the vistas incredible. The antiquity of Europe overwhelmed me. It seemed so enduring—but then, I could only compare it to Brooklyn or West Babylon. And the women, even the fallen ones, were unlike any I had known back home. The whorehouses crowding the waterfront red-light districts were reasonably priced, the working girls exciting, exotic, and instructive. Invigorating salt-air, incredible scenery, and reasonably priced sex . . . if this was the sailor's life, then I was ready to make it mine.

Back in the Bronx, though, the bullshit aspects of the military environment changed my plans. I had developed a reputation, not entirely unearned, as a wise guy who did not respect the chain of command. I was not sufficiently deferential to upperclassmen, I was told. I was told this by one upperclassman, in particular, who took it on himself to ride my ass and make my second year a misery. Anthony Russo, my tormentor, was ugly, hawk-faced, and sharp-eyed enough to find any defensible justification for putting me on report, making me ineligible for precious liberty. I plied my various charms in an attempt to win him over, or at least to get him to pay some hateful attention to someone else, but my efforts failed.

Russo knew I would never rat him out to school authorities. He and I became close in the way torturers become familiar with their prisoners. I could read him. Whenever he descended to the "D" deck cabin I shared with three mates, I knew exactly what was coming. I cleaned toilets and swabbed decks at this asshole's whim; the other cadets, disapproving of the harassment, were silenced by the classmate's code and quietly grateful that they were not the targeted sap.

With liberty denied, I would literally slip over the side of the ship and run scared a cold, wet half-mile along the rocky shoreline and meet Frank at the gate. After a couple months of this, I resolved to leave Fort Schuyler as soon as the year ended.

Most of my fellow cadets would go on to serve in Vietnam. Some would lose their lives there. Others would return to broken lives back home. Along with several painful (and expensive) failed marriages, it is one of my life's main regrets that I did not fight in that war. And since 1963, I have been proving to myself, and to anyone else who cared, that I was not scared to fight in Vietnam. I would have welcomed the adventure, and the chance to serve my country. The timing was just wrong.

CHAPTER TWO

TUCSON

When I finally crossed the Hudson River to New Jersey, it was in a 1961 Chevy convertible. The car was in cherry condition; its passengers were not. I was defeated and adrift, going quietly crazy under my parents' roof after the disappointments of Fort Schuyler. Frank DeCecco was running away from Jolene, to whom he was engaged, and a salesman's life of predictable comfort. We were headed for the promised land of California, where we planned on selling cars, or clothes, or going to college. Whatever came up.

We had only three hundred dollars between us, but we had nice wheels, courtesy of Frank's stepfather, and a clean slate. We styled ourselves after Martin Milner and George Maharis in *Route 66,* the hip television show of the moment. Unlike those cool cats on TV, we did our tooling around on the cheap. We stayed in YMCAs, and even those low rates took such a bite out of our budget we hit upon a way to get two sleeps for the price of one. We would arrive right around dawn and not have to check out until the afternoon of the following day.

Our one firm destination, en route, was the University of Arizona, in Tucson. It was on my itinerary for a reason. Doctors had always told my mother that the dry desert air was helpful to asthmatics, and the region had held a kind of healthy appeal to me since boyhood. Before our cross-country odyssey, I had been felled by my first wheezing attacks in several years—spurred, most likely, by the tensions of Fort Schuyler and my uncertain future. As long as I was pulling up stakes, I thought, I might as well give the desert a shot.

Frank and I drove onto the university campus like conquering city-slickers. We had the top down, and the music blaring. I was sitting on top of the backseat, a real cool character. Behind my shades, I took in the scenic splendor, which revealed itself in the form of the lovely young coeds dotting the campus like sun-kissed freckles. As Frank rolled to a stop, I thought, okay, I can go to school here. This won't be a problem.

The school's admissions policies were very open back then, especially when it involved collecting out-of-state tuition, and most especially when the out-of-state student could fill an immediate need as goalie for the school's fledgling lacrosse team. They admitted me on the spot, as a first-semester junior, to begin classes that fall. It seemed so easy, I probably should have asked for a scholarship, or at least some financial aid. Still, I had a new goal, a new direction. I would finish college and make something of myself. And, best of all, I would do these things with palm trees overhead and an assortment of coeds at my side.

Until then, I had a summer to kill, and some money to earn to pay for tuition. The last leg of our journey, after Tucson, passed like a breeze. I was pumped by my new plan to finish school, and what I saw as the last-gasps of wild youth, still to come in California. Driving through the desert near Yuma, Frank and I vowed to head straight to the Santa Monica Beach and baptize ourselves in the Pacific Ocean. It was late, on a chilly, overcast day, by the time we pulled into the beach parking lot. The place was deserted, except for a handful of die-hard surfers. Despite the weather, and the looks of curious contempt we knew would follow, we ran into the water with all our clothes on, making good on our promise to each other and to the gods of the western sea. We splashed in joyous abandon and then raced back to the car before we froze our balls off.

After a week in Los Angeles, we were living in a shady downtown fleabag called The Tartan, down to our last twenty dollars, and desperate. Frank came to me one day all excited about a plan he felt sure would restore economic stability to our vagabond lives: Why not let the hotel's gay residents give us blowjobs, and charge them fifteen dollars for the privilege?

"Come on, Gerry," he urged, "all we have to do is pull down our pants. It's easy money."

I actually gave the idea serious thought, an indication of how dim our prospects were and how easy it is to sink further once you've reached as low as you thought you could go.

We were saved from this particular dishonor by a friendly job counselor at the Los Angeles County unemployment office. There were two immediate sales openings at Foreman & Clark, a local clothing-store chain, and the counselor, an ex-New Yorker, was kind enough to give us the shot. Frank was a lock for one of the jobs; he actually had experience, with a sister chain of stores on Long Island. My chances were less certain. In fact, they were grim. I had no sales experience. The only real chance at the second job, we figured, was to lie.

Frank gave me a crash course on salesmanship and briefed me on the procedures and personalities of the Howard's Clothes stores back East, where he had worked. I passed myself off as a former Howard's employee, and we snared both jobs. I embarked on a short but successful career as a salesman in the men's accessories department. On some weeks, I cleared over two hundred dollars in commissions, a take to match my father's highest salary. It gnawed at me that my painless pushing of socks and underwear were valued on a par with his years of sweat and effort. But I also felt vindicated by these small financial successes, proud.

The work was routine, although my career in sales was not without excitement. Most of the thrills came courtesy of "Loretta," a woman I met who lived near the Foreman & Clark store where I worked as a salesman. The store was in the Lakewood Mall, down near Orange County. After a brief try at public transportation, two and a half hours each way on the bus, I bought a Nash Metropolitan convertible for a hundred and fifty bucks. It was tiny, fuel-efficient, and way ahead of its time. It also burned a quart of oil each day, even if I didn't use it. When it broke down, as it did often that summer, I stayed with Loretta and her roommate.

Loretta was my first woman, although at eighteen she was younger than some of her predecessors. She looked like a Renaissance portrait, all soft curves and mystery. But there was also something glamorous about her. I remember her as being slightly out of focus, like an actress filmed through a gauze filter. She read women's magazines constantly and dreamed of being a lady. When I came over the horizon, filled with tall tales of faraway places, she picked me to love. She liked going on exotic dates to raunchy nightclubs, and was creative at lovemaking, determined to try everything she had read about. With her interest in threesomes and other kinky stuff, she would have made a terrific talk show producer.

That Thanksgiving, when I arrived back at her house on vacation from the university, her roommate told me she was out on a date. Later, when I was steered to the couch to sleep, I figured in my absence Loretta had fallen in love with some other man of the world. When she finally returned and introduced her lesbian lover, I learned the real reason for my displacement. With her arm around the harder-looking, older woman, Loretta explained with quiet intensity how she had gotten pregnant after I had left, how the guy had turned out to be a real rat, not helping to pay for the Tijuana abortion, and how she had sworn off all men as a result, including me. She added that I was free to use the couch for the remainder of the vacation, but that it would be better for everyone if I stayed at Frank's place in West Hollywood. Shaken, confused, and at least half-heartbroken, I left before the lovers awoke the next morning.

*   *   *

My other on-the-job excitement that California summer came one afternoon when three guys bolted out of the store with all the designer suits they could carry, a few thousand dollars' worth of merchandise. I bolted after them, targeting the slowest of the group. I chased him through the Lakewood Mall, finally tackling and restraining him until help arrived. The next day my good deeds were reported in the local paper, under the headline, "Courageous Clerk." I did not save the clip because the paper gave my name as Jim Riviera.

With my salesman's bankroll, a contribution from my parents, and the proceeds from the maximum available student loans, I was able to meet expenses that fall in Tucson. My first order of business was to find a place for myself on that sprawling campus. Finding a place to live was easy; fitting in was hard. I lived in a furnished off-campus apartment on the notorious Speedway Strip, rooming with three other transfer students with funky back-stories. I dressed mine up to compete: I told anyone who cared, and some who didn't, that I was an heir to a restaurant chain back in New York. I bought a used Mercedes—a 1957 220-model, at the distress sale price of five hundred dollars—and kept it buffed and Simonized to lend credibility to my claim.

With more than twenty thousand students on campus, the surest path to the mainstream was to join a fraternity. The Greeks had the best parties, the best seats at sporting events, and the best-looking girls. I was tired of playing the outlaw, the outsider, and so I decided to pledge whatever fraternity would have me. I gave up after my first try, when I was blackballed by Sigma Nu. My unfashionably long hair was at odds with their Young Republican cuts; my black leather jacket clashed with their madras shirts and khaki pants. I was not Sigma Nu material, I was told. If I had been, the rest of this story might be different.

And so, this unaffiliated ethnic found a place just off the mainstream. I joined the school's soccer team and fell in with a group of foreign-exchange students. I was one of two American-born players and began to spend a great deal of time off the field with my mostly Mexican teammates. They were quiet and deferential on the Anglo-dominated campus, but real hell-raisers on more familiar territory. We would drive down to Nogales, the

Mexican city sixty miles south of Tucson, or to Guaymas, a coastal city a couple hours farther south. My pals took me to the best cheap restaurants across the border and showed me the top whorehouses and money changers. And before the end of my first year at Arizona, they also introduced me to marijuana. Pot quickly replaced tequila as my drug of choice, and I spent much of the rest of my college days underneath a sweet swirl of smoke.

It is distressing to me now that I cannot recall a single redeeming act or noble sacrifice during my time at Arizona. I looked on college as a vacation for my morals. I even took advantage of my charmed test-taking abilities to earn extra cash. At a huge university like Arizona, most exams were administered in big lecture halls or auditoriums. It was impossible for the monitors roaming the aisles during exams to match every student present against those actually enrolled in the class. The glitch spawned my first business: I took tests for money. It was a great setup. I would collect the necessary textbooks and class notes from my student-clients a few days before each exam, force-feed myself the material, and spit it back out at show time. I charged sixty dollars for a *C*, seventy-five for a *B*, and ninety for an *A*. Below a *C*, there was no charge. I never worked for free.

Much of my time on campus was spent in a loose haze, but two specific scenes are completely vivid: an epic fistfight, and an encounter with a strange, sad nymphomaniac.

The fight was with Sid Nesbitt, a popular campus con man from Cape Cod, and one of my knockabout roommates. After living together for a few months, Sid and I began to grate on each other. We were both so full of shit that I think we recognized the holes and the bluster in our opposite's character. These particular fireworks were launched over a girl, but the fight was really about who was going to be top dog in the house.

Unlike most normal people, I have had dozens of violent confrontations over the years; some of them have even aired on national television. My ready punches are a function of an inflexible pride, quick temper, and a self-image several times larger than what turns up in the mirror. Most of these violent dances are finished after a punch or two; usually, the guy who hits first wins. If it does not end quickly, a real knock-down-drag-out brawl can be one of the most intense and grueling punishments one body can inflict on another.

What made this battle with Sid memorable, and disturbing, was its length and lack of passion. We were pretty evenly matched and pummeled each other for what seemed an eternity. After a minute or two, we probably weren't even mad at each other anymore. Whatever stood between us had been beaten away and discarded. Still, we kept at it. We were like two fighting cocks, unable to stop until the other had fallen. We flailed to a bloody draw after five minutes. Neither of us had won a thing; both had lost a great deal. I am haunted, still, by the blind fury that allowed me to keep at this guy long after I could recognize what had gotten us started in the first place.

The nymphomaniac was a twenty-two-year-old runaway from a busted marriage to a serviceman. One of my roommates brought her home, after she had spent the previous week servicing an entire fraternity house. I learned these things later. At the time, I had no idea what her story was. As far as I knew, a buddy had brought her home to show her off. She sat quietly on the edge of our old couch and seemed impressed by even our modest quarters. I sat down beside her and started to put on my best moves. We were all drinking, having a good time. She may have been a buddy's girl, but I went after her just the same.

I asked her if I could get her a beer, or if there was anything I could do to make her more comfortable.

"Yeah," her escort interrupted, in a stage whisper, "you can fuck her."

What? I expected the girl to be outraged, or at least flustered. I shot her a look and got back nothing. Not a twitch, not a sound. She just sat there, with a fixed half-smile. Today, I would be filled with rescue fantasies for this creature; then, all I wanted was to outperform my roommates. I announced I would be first up, leading the girl into my bedroom and silently marveling at the good fortune that had smiled on our home. Later that evening, when my turn came up again, I took some time to talk with her. Pat. I think her name was Pat. She was a little on the slim side. Something about her reminded me of the daughter who loses her baby near the end of *The Grapes of Wrath*. Rose of Sharon.

"Why are you here?" I plied. "Why are you letting us do this?"

"I don't know," she said back, her voice flat, dull. "I like it, I guess."

"How did you get here?"

"Some fellas at the University of New Mexico sent me," she said, making it sound like she was a kind of Federal Express package. "I was headin' for California, and they said to stop here. Said they knew some fraternity brothers would take care of me. So here I am."

"And you actually enjoy this?" I said. "This is okay with you?"

"Better 'n being married to my husband," she said. "'Course, I got a little raw, you know, doin' the Sigma Chis like that."

It was demeaning, degrading, and dishonorable, and I was in the middle of it. Any man of conscience would have tried to talk some sense into this girl, but not me, not then. A stiff dick has no conscience.

This incident roared back into memory recently, after watching Jodie Foster's riveting performance in *The Accused,* chronicling a vicious gang-rape at a roadside bar in New Bedford, Massachusetts. I scared myself at the connection. There was no violence in our encounter, but there was little else to distinguish the movie's based-on-fact assault from the drunken party years ago, in our house at the edge of Tucson.

THE EAST VILLAGE

Linda Coblentz was a transfer student from North Carolina, and an artist. We met at a campus party; she stood out like a splash of color in a field of black and white. She was lovely. She had sandy blond hair and blue-green eyes. She wore her eye makeup outrageously thick, her skirts scandalously short. She didn't seem to care what people thought of her, or the way she looked, but I thought she looked wonderful. There was a dreamy quality about Linda that made her seem oblivious to the currents of campus life. She was a "love child" before the phrase was made popular.

When she arrived on campus during my senior year, the men

circled sniffing. I sniffed longer and harder than any of the others and eventually won this great girl as my steady.

"Just don't marry her," joked one of my disappointed rivals, acknowledging his loss. He knew I was graduating, and that Linda would be back on campus in the fall.

He needn't have worried. Marriage was the furthest thing from my mind. Until Vic called.

Vic Furio, my old high-school buddy, had a plan for avoiding the draft. After only two years away from the Maritime College, I had lost all interest in the military. The war in Southeast Asia was in full escalation, and I wanted no part of it. All around me, draft-dodging was becoming the competitive sport of the American college student, and I wanted to play along. I was anxious to hear anything Vic had to say about avoiding the issue.

"Let's get married," he suggested.

I was not exactly sure how this would help, but Vic seemed to think it was a move in the right direction.

"You marry your girl, I'll marry mine," he elaborated.

"What'll that do?" I wondered.

"That gets us an automatic deferral," he said. "Then the four of us will travel, we'll go to Europe to work, or maybe Africa. By the time they catch up to us, the war will be over."

Marriage did, indeed, constitute a deferment from the draft, but only for the remainder of that year, 1965. I also gave serious thought to Vic's casual notion of working in Africa. First, I thought of Stanley and Livingstone. Since there was no money in exploration, I focused on door-to-door sales instead.

VIC FURIO: Geraldo did extensive research on it and found out there was no Hoover vacuum cleaner agent in all of Africa, and there was also no Fuller Brush agent, and so he thought we would open up a franchise in the region, selling the two best door-to-door sales items in the whole world. I think it was pretty down-to-earth and pretty realistic and might have materialized into something. The whole thing was actually quite typical of Geraldo, coming up with ingenious ideas like that. He even went so far as to book us passage.

*   *   *

I was brimming with enthusiasm. I called Vic and told him it was a go. I asked Linda to be my bride, and to travel with me to Africa. I don't recall if I mentioned my ulterior motives. I knew she would say yes. After all, I had given her no reason not to love me, the son of a prosperous restauranteur of Spanish descent, bound for glory and adventure abroad. A beautiful dreamer, Linda accepted my proposal. We decided to marry upon graduation. We then drove one hundred and twenty miles north of Tucson, to Scottsdale, to break the news to her parents. I pulled up in my buffed Mercedes and passed myself off to my soon-to-be in-laws as an heir to a substantial New York City restaurant. They were upscale and educated, gracious and warm. They were also skeptical. Who the hell was I?

Hesitantly, Linda's parents tendered their blessings. They took us out to a fancy French restaurant near Phoenix to celebrate, and I nearly blew my cover at the table.

"If we don't take our napkins, these chaps will never get around to serving us," Linda's father told me gently. Harry, an English-born college professor, reached over, snapped open my napkin, and deposited it in my lap.

I nodded and smiled, and vowed silently to watch Harry closely for the rest of the meal to determine which of the baffling array of utensils in front of me were supposed to be used for which upcoming course.

After meeting Linda's parents, I headed back East for the first time in two years, to tell my family what was going on and to get their blessings. Appropriately, my Mercedes blew up, on Route 80, outside Cedar Rapids. I took a Greyhound bus home from Iowa.

A month or so later, Vic called from Utah with the shattering news that he had changed his mind about the draft-avoidance, marriage-travel scheme, and instead enlisted in the Marine Corps. Great, I thought. Now what the hell am I supposed to do? My wedding was a week away. Linda's parents had arranged a beautiful ceremony. I couldn't back out and probably didn't want to anyway.

The outdoor wedding was held in Scottsdale, beneath Camelback Mountain. The ceremony was performed by candlelight. It was a glorious setting, and a nice party. As I would find out, weddings often are nice parties, warm and optimistic. But I knew almost nobody at this affair. Only my sister Sharon, of my family or close friends, could make the long trip (or really understand my sudden decision to marry). I felt out of place among the ranch-style WASPs who had convened to wish us well.

Africa was out without Vic. California was in. With a hundred dollars, cashed in from our wedding-present take, Linda and I bought a 1954 Chevy and headed West. We settled in a cheap motel on the sand in Huntington Beach, in the shadows of the oil rigs. Our apartment was only one small room, with a bathroom attached; it had no proper closets. But even inconvenient waterfront living had its appeal. And it was cheap. I made up for the lack of closet space by rigging long poles, stretching from wall to wall. We kept most of our stuff in chests, disguised with tablecloths.

We were unlike most struggling young couples in that we had no long-range plans. Until one presented itself, I returned to work at Foreman & Clark, where my weekly commissions soon soared past two hundred dollars. By Thanksgiving, we had saved over one thousand dollars, an unprecedented amount in my young life. We spent the holidays with Linda's parents, which led to an epiphany of sorts. My father-in-law suggested, in front of Linda, that I dip into our savings to buy my bride a new coat. I flushed and stuttered something about the money being our only bankroll for a planned move back East. Harry continued, good-naturedly but also persistently. Finally, he backed off to make room for his second suggestion.

"You have a sharp mind," he told me. "You're fast on your feet. Why don't you go to law school?"

Law school? Why hadn't I thought of that? It seemed like the perfect solution to my career uncertainty; at the very least, it would buy me another three years to figure out what it was I wanted to do.

And so I made hasty arrangements to take the law school boards and did well enough to convince the guardians of the Brooklyn Law School gates to look past my mediocre college transcripts and let me in. Life, once again, was on track. A plan had been handed to me, and it looked like a good one.

I worked through the holiday rush at the store, wanting to

squirrel away as much money as possible for our trip to New York. Finally, just after Christmas, 1965, Linda and I loaded up the Chevy like a scene out of *The Beverly Hillbillies* and left California. Our savings were intact. All of our worldly goods made the trip with us. The ride was prolonged by the need to stop every couple hours to pour a quart of oil into the tired '54. The car got us all the way across the country, only to die in my parents' driveway in West Babylon. I left it there, along with our dog, a lovable shepherd mutt named Ringo. We couldn't keep either where we were going.

Within a week, Linda and I settled in Manhattan, on Seventh Street in the East Village. It was early in 1966, and the neighborhood was just being discovered by young professionals, dope addicts, drifters, and draft-dodgers.

I had come home.

We lived in a one-bedroom apartment in a renovated building facing Tompkins Square Park, just a block away from St. Mark's Place, the epicenter of East Coast anarchism. Now best known for its tent-city housing, a colony of militant homeless, bloody antipolice rioting, and grisly neighborhood murders, during our time the park was a magnet attracting a wide sampling of humanity—a seedier new-world version of the great plazas of Europe. The Puerto Ricans were dominant, having thumped their Eastern European predecessors in a series of rumbles during the late 1950s. Beaten in the gang wars, but not vanquished, the Polish and Ukrainian kids were still there, surly and hanging onto what was left of their turf. So were their parents. From our fourth-story window, Linda and I looked out on stocky women, knitting and wearing babushkas, mingled on the benches with bums, or bare-footed Bohemians playing the flute. Farther off, variously colored kids played hard-top softball, a home run away from rows of somberly dressed European elders sitting hunched over, contemplating concrete chessboards.

Everyone we met came from someplace else, and our lives were soon filled by Kerouac, Dylan, and marijuana-fueled debates on the true nature of man. Aquarius was dawning all around us. On one corner, the university of the streets was offering an alternative education to a wild combination of characters. Sidewalk cafes and storefront services sprang up alongside the borscht pubs and *cuchifritos* stands that predated them. To remind the newcomers that this was still a heavy-duty fringe neighborhood, every so often one of the sleepy-eyed heroin addicts would snap awake long enough to slit someone's throat.

With tuition looming for law school's September start, I answered a Help Wanted ad in *The New York Times,* under the heading, "Wanted: Junior Executives." The job turned out to be a ninety-five-dollar-a-week assistant manager position in Alexander's department store, in the South Bronx. Ladies' cottons. This time I didn't have to lie about my experience to get the job, and I intended to keep it as long as possible as a hedge against the real possibility of failure at Brooklyn Law.

My younger sister Sharon came to live with us for a time during those East Village days. My parents wanted to get her away from a bad boyfriend. We were glad to help. Plus, she was a rent-paying subtenant, and her financial contribution made it possible to afford a park view. A couple of months later, the creep who was after her got drafted. She went home and married a nice guy just back from Vietnam.

For Linda and me, Sharon's departure had the immediate effect of making our one-hundred-forty-dollar-a-month rent prohibitive. I was obsessive about living within our means and decided we had to make a move. With the help of our neighbors, we pushed, pulled, and carried all our belongings from the renovated building on East Seventh to a roach-infested sixth-floor tenement walk-up on East Fifth. In those two blocks, the neighborhood took an extreme turn for the worse. Here, white faces were rare, and poor people were plentiful. The rent on our new, tiny one-bedroom was just thirty-five dollars a month, but it proved very expensive. Before summer was over, our apartment had been robbed four times. Everything we had was gone. On the last pass, the thieves had even taken my homemade birdcage and pet finches; I later found the cage and the birds, crushed at the bottom of a stairwell.

Ironically, this was the golden period of my marriage to Linda. She attended classes at the Art Students League, and waitressed in her downtime, while I made the long commute to Alexander's, located in the dreary shadows of the Bronx Third Avenue el. We seldom argued, and she never complained about our hardships.

One extremely important event did occur during that time: I was at my post at Alexander's, dispensing cheap cotton-shifts to a throng of bargain-hungry women in the store's basement, when my aunt Ana, Dad's favorite sister, came up to say hello. She lived in the area and shopped for the ninety-nine-cent specials run in my department.

"Why you use this name?" she said in her broken, thickly accented tongue, and pointing a hard finger at the Riviera on my name tag. "You ashamed to be Puerto Rican?"

I had no answer. Skating through the last few years at Maritime and on the West Coast, this was the first I had been confronted by someone who knew the whole story.

"I'll get a new name tag," I said, fumbling to remove the damning tag from my shirt. In New York, the name game was not going to fool anyone. In one of those flashes of personal discovery, I resolved then and there never voluntarily to use the bastardized spelling again, and as soon as I could afford to, to change it legally.

AL'S MIDWELL DINER

I was, as usual, a misfit at Brooklyn Law, a dark hippie cowboy among bloodless accountants and bookish clergy. Despite my casual appearance, I hit the books hard. If I was going to fail at this law school business it would not be for lack of trying. Perhaps because I looked so odd in that sea of conformity, I was called on in class more than most. William Shakespeare Herman, my contracts-law professor, who resembled a pit bull in appearance and demeanor, seemed to relish gnawing on me in front of his class. Another professor, an elegant, easily irritated property-law professor named Nightingale, made it a running gag in his class to ask me surprise questions.

Despite their challenges, or maybe because of them, I earned two *A*s and two *B*s that first semester, my best academic showing since grade school. The performance won me a partial scholarship for the second term, which enabled Linda and me to stop borrowing against our future, but did not spread far enough to change our immediate financial picture. We still lived in low-rent squalor on East Fifth Street, ever mindful of the burglars' busy schedules.

As a condition of the scholarship, I had to take attendance, a chore that led to a near fistfight, and also to close friendships with two fellow oddballs. One morning, just before class, one lug indicated me and my attendance-taking clipboard, and said, loud enough for all to hear, "Look at this. The rebel without a cause has become a brownnoser."

"What did you say, you fat piece of shit?" I challenged.

We exchanged a few more barbs, and before I knew it I tossed down my clipboard and jumped over the first row of students, lurching for my tormentor, who stood at least six-three, and two hundred and twenty pounds. Like most other law students, however, he was also pale, flabby, and unathletic. Fights in usually civilized surroundings are always big spectator events, and this was no exception. The proper, probing minds turned licentious and bloodthirsty, and before either one of us could land a respectable blow, the place resembled a dog track more than it did a classroom.

I was winning the fight and blind to its consequences, when I was grabbed from behind by a nodding acquaintance named Daniel Goldfarb, a Penn State graduate still living with his parents on Long Island. "Easy, Riv," he said, pinning my arms to my sides. "He's not worth it. Professor'll be here in a second."

I would have won the fight, but lost my scholarship in the aftermath. I might have even been booted out of the program; as a rule, law schools don't look too kindly on classroom brawls.

Danny and I struck up an instant friendship. Like me, he'd also started law school with an academic inferiority complex. And, also like me, he looked out-of-sync, with his leather jacket and tough-guy exterior. Despite his relatively upscale roots, he spoke like a Damon Runyon head-knocker, hid piercing blue eyes behind dark prescription glasses, and invariably spoke with a Marlboro hanging from the side of his mouth.

DANNY GOLDFARB: It didn't take long to figure out that Geraldo was a real swashbuckler, Errol Flynn playing Captain Blood. That's what he always was, and he carried it off. We were in a cab one day, and the cab turned up the ramp at the U.N. building, to get on the FDR Drive, when somebody mugged a woman, right? So Geraldo gets the cab driver to pull over and he gets out and goes after this mugger. He goes leaping after him. And, of course, I go leaping after Geraldo. And he captures the guy and brings back the woman's purse. All through law school, we had adventures like this. Every week.

As we walked out of that class together, my scholarship intact, Danny and I were joined by the third member of what would become our unbreakable law school trio, Captain Joseph Allen, N.Y.P.D.

"You should have broken that jughead's jaw," Joey said.

Joey, at forty-something, was the oldest student in the school. He smoked Camels incessantly, drank too much whiskey, had gray skin, and carried a bowling ball around in his belly. He had been one of the youngest officers to ever make captain in the history of the New York City Police Department. He was still on active duty and attended law school in what amounted to his spare time. His current duty was as a "fly-captain," which meant he substituted nights on a rotating, regular basis among five Brooklyn precincts, on the regular commander's day off. Despite his hectic schedule, and the pressures of police work, he managed to keep up with the rest of his class.

The son of an Irish cop and an Italian woman from an East Harlem family with alleged mob ties, Joey was as confused as his background. A decorated police hero, he also relished the skim of the job. He would frequently take Danny and me out to dinner "on the muscle." He picked up our tabs without real money, in those days just before the 1970 Knapp Commission destroyed careers and changed at least obvious police ethics in the city.

After that classroom fight, the loner cop took us under his wing. The three of us would often spend time studying in Joey's rotating offices throughout Brooklyn. Night after late night, Danny and I would set aside the books and soak up the real-life crime, poverty, fear, and frustration of those hurly-burly precincts. Those study sessions instilled an affection for the thin blue line that I will never lose, regardless of the moral frailty of cops like my pal Joey.

With my newfound interest in fighting crime, I sought and won an internship with the Manhattan District Attorney's office following my first year, working underneath the city's legendary mob-buster Frank Hogan. The job didn't pay much, but it was a prestigious placement, and an eye-opening experience. Our offices were attached to 100 Centre Street, the huge criminal court building. It seemed the capital of the macabre, the Joker's stronghold in Gotham City. Even in those precrack days, this place burst with melancholy. Cops, crooks, and clerks jostled each other in grimy corridors painted putrid yellow. The lowest of the legal profession, lawyers hungry for dirty money in small increments, hung out in the shadows. Like dope dealers outside a schoolhouse, they would "psst" to passing relatives of the recently incarcerated in hopes of scarfing some greasy cash. Even then, the majority of the defendants were minorities, principally black and Puerto Rican.

My philosophy back then was simple. Cops don't lie. If one of New York's Finest arrested someone, that person was guilty. My friendship with Joseph Allen would change that perspective, but in that summer of 1967, I was a twenty-four-year-old, born-again crime-stopper. I was assigned to the complaint division of the prosecutor's office, under a deputy D.A. named Mel Glass. Now a state judge, Mel was a no-nonsense guy with a much more restrained approach to criminal justice than the one held by his young intern. Our divergent philosophies surfaced in the arrest of a Brooklyn scumbag who admitted his guilt to two detectives assigned to our office. The problem was the bad guy did his confessing before the dicks had read him his Miranda rights, rendering his statement of guilt inadmissible.

I hit upon the enterprising idea of going up to this guy, pretending at naïveté, and asking him out of apparently harmless curiosity what had really happened. Mel explained patiently that prosecuting crimes was not like playing sports, that justice was not only about winning and losing. He suggested that I wanted to win too much and that maybe I should seek another legal specialty. I was stunned by the implication that extremism in the defense of law and order might be a vice.

I took my boss's advice to heart; with my zeal to crush the criminal element chastised, I would soon become Rivera for the defense.

The criminal element expressed its thanks by driving Linda and me out of our home and up to a small, rent-controlled two-room apartment on East Seventy-eighth Street, a half block from the East River. It was a great neighborhood, but the place was closet-size, and another sixth-floor walk-up. Our double bed took up 95 percent of the available floor-space in the bedroom; our bathtub was in the kitchen, next to the sink. Still, it was a relief to live outside the East Village war zone.

I started my second year at Brooklyn Law near the top of my class, and confident that I could comfortably juggle the academic load and part-time employment at Alexander's. I developed a routine that would have exhausted a less resilient man. I slept five hours a night and stuffed my waking hours with classes, study, work, and the considerable commute among school, home, and store. In-between, I found time to mix in weekday soccer practices for the Greek semi-pro team I played with, out in Astoria, Queens, and for games on weekends. Linda kept me anchored at home, well-loved and well-fed. She continued to work as a waitress, in-between art classes, and her subsistence income mixed with mine to leave us somewhat solvent.

The relative equilibrium of our lives was battered by a call from my parents soon after my second year began. They were in deep financial trouble. After fifteen years working in Republic's cafeteria, Dad was fired in 1965, when the defense plant's food concession was sold out to a national restaurant chain. The takeover team had decided that, at two hundred dollars a week, my dad was earning too much money, and, at fifty years, he was too old. With the few thousand dollars my parents had managed to save, plus loans from friends and relatives, they opened a tiny coffee shop in a small shopping center east of our hometown. To the surprise of everyone except Dad, the coffee shop was a modest success. Two years later, he sold it for a profit and leveraged the proceeds toward the purchase of a twenty-four-hour joint called Midwell Diner. He called the new place Al's Midwell Diner, because he did not want to spend the money to add anything more than his name to the neon sign out front.

That diner came close to killing him. Dad worked the place like a man possessed, putting in eighteen-hour days, seven days a week. The diner was only ten miles from the house in West Babylon, but he kept a cot in the diner basement rather than lose the precious time commuting. Despite his best efforts, he was losing a war of attrition. The place wasn't a complete bust, but the income was never enough to service his debt.

My parents did what they could to keep their ordeal from me. They knew that law school, and my tight newlywed budget, were weighing heavily on my mind. I was their last resort when they called asking me to take over as the diner's nighttime short-order cook. Pop was exhausted, his health beginning to fail because of a developing diabetic condition. There was no money to pay another cook's salary. They would not have asked if they did not need me, and now that they had, I could not say no.

Within a couple of days, I was behind the grill, Linda was waitressing, and Danny Goldfarb was manning the cash register. What we lacked in specific skills we more than made up for in charm and enthusiasm. My eager smiles belied my true feelings. Being a short-order cook stunk. It was tougher than law school, and far more frustrating. I had to keep track of twenty orders at a time, and cook them all to order, without benefit of a pencil to keep things straight. The grill splattered hot grease, the egg yolks stubbornly broke when I flipped them, and the frozen-solid burgers either cooked too fast or too slow.

Despite the infusion of talent, the diner and my father continued to fade. When he finally had to close the place, the proud man was crushed. Humiliation conspired with exhaustion to make him instantly old. The financial situation was worse than he let on. He had put the house up as collateral when he purchased the diner, and it was to be sold by the bankruptcy court to clear up his debts. None of the other kids was in any position to help. Irene was going to college and feeding her four kids on her army husband's junior lieutenant's pay. Willie was working two construction jobs to support his new wife and two stepchildren. Sharon's marriage to her ex-soldier-turned-supermarket clerk was already on the rocks. Craig was an adolescent, not old enough for even minimum-wage employment.

That left me, and I had next to nothing. As a second-year law student, however, I did have sufficient expectations to borrow what it took to save the house from the Grim Reaper. The house cost just four thousand dollars at auction, but even that proved to be a huge, nearly unobtainable amount. Thankfully, Mom had not

signed the encumbrance papers, so all the court could sell was
Dad's undivided half-interest.

The house was saved. Willie still lives there with his wife
Maryann and their teenage daughter Patricia, my goddaughter.
Thirty years after Pop planted them, the trees have grown enough
to make the neighborhood seem more permanent.

With the bankruptcy behind us, my family experienced rapid change.
I came to understand how people become shadows of their former
selves. The only job Dad could find was night watchman at a shopping
center. It was an outdoor job in the middle of winter, for next to no
money. I could cry remembering his disappointment and shame. The
job began a fast decline. By early 1968, I was de facto head of the
family, dispenser of advice, small favors, and limited largesse. We spoke
about Dad, often in his presence, as if he wasn't there.

Linda and I broke up a short time later. The end had nothing to
do with the bankruptcy, or the added family responsibility. I just
wanted to screw other women. It began with the girls who hung
around the soccer team. After I started coming home smelling of
dirt, sweat, and sex, my wife got wise.

In my broken relationships to come, there would be enough
money and property to quiet my conscience and mitigate guilt.
There wasn't any of either during those lean law-school years.
Linda got the tiny apartment on East Seventy-eighth Street, and
the absurdly frugal furnishings, but that was it. I hadn't even
gotten around to buying her that new coat her father was on me
about. There was no money to pay off my troubled mind. Worse,
we had dipped into two thousand dollars worth of savings bonds,
left to her as an inheritance, during the many minicrises that
confronted us along the way. It would be over twenty years before
I found the courage to contact Linda, apologize to her and her
caring family, and repay at least my financial debt with interest.

ALPHABET CITY

Free of the charade of fidelity, my second year of law school ended
with a series of wild passions. My relentless promiscuity steered

me into a tremendous jam that summer: One of my several conquests, a stewardess, was pregnant. Her name was "Sally," and she assured me the child was mine. We were faced with a decision, and it was an easy one; carrying out that decision was another matter.

Sally wanted to move on and keep flying, and I wanted nothing to do with a wife and child; abortion was the only alternative. Trouble was, in 1968, it was also illegal. Pal Joey stepped in to bail me out. He arranged for us to use an abortionist favored by his mob cronies, a gypsy woman from the Bensonhurst section of Brooklyn. He also helped me pay for it. There was no way I could afford the three-hundred-dollar fee on my own. Joey, my benefactor, didn't have that much cash on him, either, so he made a few calls.

He sent me to Fulton Street to meet one of his buddies, a black police detective.

He smiled as he presented a shopping bag full of cash. "Go ahead," he said, holding the bag open by the handles, "take as much as you need."

I took exactly fifteen twenty-dollar bills. Obviously, the cash he was handing out was not his own. I later learned that the money had come from an A&S department store robbery committed shortly before. The rogue cop and three other bandits reportedly maced two armored-car guards in an elevator of the store, making off with approximately $350,000 in cash. The gypsy abortionist's fee came from the detective's quarter share.

I brought Sally by subway out to the gypsy lady's eerie ground-floor apartment, heavily draped and smelling of incense and antiseptic. A crazed Doberman barked violently, announcing our arrival and suggesting at second thoughts. The abortionist looked like a cartoon-witch, but she was gentle with Sally, almost mothering. "Come, darling," she said, escorting Sally to her chamber, "let's take care of you."

She injected Sally with some strange fluid and told us she would abort later that night. When she didn't, I called Joey in a panic.

"You gotta go back," he urged. "If you don't finish it, that girl's gonna give birth to a monster."

And so, one week later, we went through the whole wretched

episode all over again. The kind and crazy gypsy explained that the first procedure had been premature. Her work, she boasted, was guaranteed, and there would be no charge for this follow-up visit. She administered the same fluid and cautions. This time, thankfully, they worked.

"We just aborted your son," Sally told me on the long, quiet subway ride back to Manhattan.

As I sit here now, resurrecting that moment, it is startling to me that I cannot place myself back in my young man's shoes. It's not that I think we did the wrong thing. Honestly, I am more angry that the laws of the time forced us on that hellish ride to see the gypsy. The whole business was so dangerous for Sally, and distasteful—a dirty abortion, paid for with dirty money—that the only way to get through it was at some distance, numb. To have been made to skulk about on the fringes in order to terminate an unwanted pregnancy was ugly and stomach-turning. Sally, a small-town girl, kept a brave face throughout the hideous ordeal, but we never talked about it, not really. We went through the motions together. Underneath, there was nothing to say, and everything, and soon it was over between us.

During that same summer of 1968, I moved into my first bachelor pad, a railroad apartment at the bulge of the Lower East Side now known as Alphabet City, so-named because the north-south avenues are lettered A through D. The neighborhood gets progressively worse as you head east from Avenue A. When I lived down there, I used to say the civilized world ended at Avenue B. I lived between C and D, on Seventh Street.

This was my black period. My bedroom had no windows, and the floors, walls, and ceilings were painted in black enamel. "Abandon all hope, ye who enter here," was written above the bedroom entrance. Even my bedspread was black. And, in my first bloom of ethnic consciousness, most of my girlfriends were also black. Or Puerto Rican. These were not Howard University coeds, or Ebony covergirls. My house was a haven for dark-skinned hookers, my bedroom a turnstile to a succession of working girls in search of a different beat and some free legal advice.

I met most of my young ladies at work. I had taken a summer job as a legal assistant for Harlem Assertion of Rights, an antipoverty organization sponsored by the local Democratic club. Our office was in a converted, storefront church on 116th Street and Eighth Avenue, surrounded by endless rows of the city's worst housing for its poorest citizens. From the heavily barred front picture-window, I looked out on a grim landscape devoid of good news. The neighborhood was terrifying; the work was exhilarating. I gained confidence with every apartment saved, or kid snatched from trouble. The pay wasn't enough to buy pizza, but I discovered the heady air around the moral highground. My crusader's heat made me the match of any landlord, judge, cop, or jury.

I found my niche. Rivera for the defense. Rivera for the people. It sounded good, and it made me feel good.

Despite my saintly professional calling, I moved through women with ravenous delight. Romantically, this was a sloppy time for me—find 'em, fuck 'em, forget 'em—but I computed my divine balance sheet against my daytime heroics and still came out ahead. There was one woman from this period who stands out. Her name was Carmen, a young lawyer from Puerto Rico. She had been assigned to New York by the U.S. Office of Economic Opportunity, to compensate for the lack of homegrown Hispanic lawyers available to serve the city's Spanish-speaking poor.

Carmen looked like a Goya painting—red lips, dark eyes, and tango dresses. She wanted to marry me almost as soon as we met. She insisted on meeting my parents immediately and she charmed my father to his Latin core. She was delightful, smart, and good-looking. And—this part threw me—she was a virgin. Carmen was saving it for her husband. This presented a problem. At first, she stopped my heavier advances. When she sensed I was cool to the idea of marriage, she threw herself dramatically across my black bed and said, "Take me anyway."

In a rare act of romantic integrity, I passed on the loaded offer.

Although our relationship was never consummated, my affair with Carmen caused far more than blue balls. She helped sharpen my sense of self as an Hispanic man proud of his heritage. At her urging, I joined New York's Puerto Rican Bar Association (there were only ninety members at that time), and became much more visible at Hispanic political events. This brown consciousness had been building since my return to New York, but had suffered a temporary setback following Israel's smashing victory the year before in the Six Day War. Stoked by my coreligionists' triumph, I had a Star of David tattooed on my left hand, at the webbing of flesh where the thumb meets the index finger. It is still there. (The tattoo, elected in haste, would later cause near-deadly embarrassment when I covered the Middle East for ABC News.)

Carmen never acknowledged my ethnic ambiguities. She called me Geraldo. Gerry did not exist for her, and her influence began to make Gerry more obsolete.

"The world is changing," she would tell me. "It is time to step up and be a leader of our emerging race."

She really talked like that—our emerging race!—and I loved to hear it. Under her influence, I decided that I was a Puerto Rican first and a Jew second. It was the first time I had prioritized my identities in just this way, and the thinking has held. Being a Jew was a fine thing, I resolved, like belonging to a cherished club or secret society. But the Jewish people were strong and prosperous enough to survive without me. My tattoo and my circumcised dick would always mark me, but after Carmen, I would present myself as a Puerto Rican who, if asked, happened curiously to be also Jewish. The Puerto Rican people, my people, needed me.

I remember the Sunday morning in 1968 when I decided to grow my moustache. I was thumbing through a box of old photographs and came upon a 1945 shot of my handsome dad in his army uniform. I had never focused before on the pencil-thin moustache he wore in those days, before he bent to assimilation, and shaved it off. He looked dashing, and exotically foreign. I inspected the stubble on my own face and determined there was enough potential, if properly cultivated, to cover most of my upper lip.

That moustache has stayed with me, in one form or another, ever since, and has become both a professional trademark and a personal symbol of my ethnic rebirth.

The condition that we marry is what killed off the relationship with Carmen, but there was something else that contributed downward momentum. It was ironic in someone so fiercely proud of her heritage, but the longer Carmen stayed in New York, the more North Americanized she became, all blue-jeans and Bloomingdale's. She transformed herself from a fabulous, exotic example of Latin culture into an imitation of a white woman, and I already had plenty of those.

My new Puerto Rican pride returned with me for my third and final year at Brooklyn Law. I had a hard time concentrating on my studies; I was distracted by the front page. In the fall of 1968, the world was spinning out of control; the assassination of Bobby Kennedy hit me especially hard. I also felt a flash of guilt, because I had been supporting RFK's opponent Eugene McCarthy in his long-shot bid for the Democratic presidential nomination. Coming just months after the Memphis murder of Martin Luther King, Jr., the death of this Kennedy was the final straw, and convinced me to cast my lot with "The Movement," the radical/liberal political and ideological alliance that was sweeping together the old left, minority activists, and their allies—half the white population under thirty.

Anarchy, upheaval, and fundamental change seemed inevitable. Draft resistance was escalating faster than the war itself. Bombings and inner-city riots were becoming nightly fixtures on the evening newscasts. Richard Nixon appeared the likely next president of a fractured nation, while his running-mate Spiro Agnew vowed to limit civil dissent. The established political and economic order was everywhere in retreat.

By early 1969, anger was the preeminent force in the land. Rioting near Berkeley had just been dispersed by tear gas and shotguns. A Jersey City police station was sprayed with machine-gun fire. East Seventh Street veterans viewed love-ins and flower children as quaint, naive indulgences for well-to-do children. The Black Panthers were the new ideal: militant, impatient, and in-your-face. Twenty-one of them were indicted that spring for planning to blow up Macy's. I did not quite grasp the connection between the world's largest department store and the oppression of black people, but I took it on faith that the two things were related.

As I coasted through my last year of law school, I became firm in my decision to become a lawyer of and for the people. Watching lawyers like William Kunstler and his young protégé Gerald Lefcourt reinforced the convictions born in the district attorney's office, and cemented at Harlem Assertion of Rights. Like Kunstler,

I would use the law as my instrument to bring about fundamental social change; unlike anyone else, I would toss my Latin passion into the mix. Of course, I was still unsure exactly how to go about doing this. The practice had yet to supplant the theory.

Fate answered my uncertainty in the form of two University of Pennsylvania Law School recruiters. The school administered The Reginald Heber Smith Fellowship in Poverty Law, a federally funded program designed to train and sponsor poverty lawyers to advocate for the poor. The recruiters, a Penn Law School professor and an aide, came to Brooklyn in search of minority attorneys willing to work in our indigent communities for a ten-thousand-dollar annual stipend, the poor leading the poor.

They looked to me, and I looked back. Both sides liked what they saw—I was graduating nineteenth out of 330 students in my law school class; they were offering a ground-level chance to serve my people—with some reservations.

"Are you sure you're brown?" the aide asked timidly at the conclusion of our interview.

"What the hell kind of question is that?" I shot back, openly outraged at this putz and silently fuming that I wasn't brown enough to let my skin answer for me.

"It's just, you know, your name," the putz fumbled, "Riviera." He spelled it out for me, in case I might be hearing it for the first time. "Riviera," he said again. "What kind of name is that?"

"I'm Puerto Rican," I said proudly, defiantly. "My real name is Rivera. Riviera was my slave name."

The night after our graduation, Joey threw a party for himself, Danny, and me. It would be the last time our misfit trio partied together. It was a generally depressing occasion. The party was held in the dimly lit second-floor room of an Irish pub on the Upper West Side. The room was filled with old people—Irish cops, mostly—and smelled of stale beer. I remember thinking I did not belong in that room, on that night, with these people. I no longer fit. I had been offered, and accepted, Penn's Smith Fellowship, and in my head I was already the brown brother from another planet, eager to remake the world according to my ideals.

Danny and I would remain close—indeed, our lives and careers would dovetail with the years—but I distanced myself from my police captain friend on that night. Joey Allen was under investigation for alleged police corruption, haunted by an Internal Affairs inspector named John Walsh. Joey died fifteen years later, disgraced and disbarred. True, he had shown himself to be a good and trusted friend, but he was a discredit to the field of law enforcement. I could no longer forgive one for the sake of the other. Even his kindnesses were tainted by the skim. Despite our friendship and shared triumph, Joey was a rogue cop.

He was part of the problem; I was part of the cure.

CHAPTER THREE

PHILADELPHIA

In the summer of 1969, we talked relevance but lived well. I was as guilty of the liberal chic maxim as anyone else, although not always by choice.

Classes in the Reginald Heber Smith Fellowship in Poverty Law, though administered from the University of Pennsylvania campus, were actually taught at nearby Haverford College, a serene and lovely liberal arts school located on the Main Line, that necklace of suburban privilege strung out to the west of Philadelphia. For five weeks, we were housed in comfortable dormitories as far removed from the gritty streets as Managua is from the moon.

Fewer than fifty of that year's crop of 250 "Reggies" were minorities, and our subgroup was overwhelmingly black except for a Cuban from Florida, a Chicano from New Mexico, and me. We "browns" immediately allied ourselves with our black brothers and sisters. We found much to rail against. The fellowship organizers had assembled an impressive faculty to complement the fine legal minds of Penn—including Harvard's Charles Nesson and Stanford's Anthony Amsterdam—but they neglected to make even one minority appointment. Worse, the Penn-Haverford setting undermined the program's best intentions, and our emerging minority coalition rallied for a more appropriate school, like Howard University, to house the program in the future.

Like many students of that inflamed era, we unleashed our radical agenda on the easiest targets: our teachers and administrators. Why Haverford? we demanded. Why not more minority fellows? More black and Latino faculty members? And, most egregiously, why were certain white fellows being paid more than most of the minorities? I became one of our group's leaders, aggressively articulating our demands for just compensation and more balanced representation. During this intense period of racial polarization, I somehow managed to avoid mention that my mother was Jewish, or that most of my mean-street stripes had been earned in suburban Long Island. These pieces of information, I told myself (and nobody else), were not germane.

After a short time, our informal group coalesced into an ad hoc organization, the Black and Brown Lawyers Caucus, which I cochaired. I still carry that credential on my resume. Our immediate goal was to increase our fellowship stipends to where they matched those paid to our white colleagues. We vowed to press our demands beyond the five-week classroom portion of the fellowship, to stay together to watchdog the white-dominated Legal Services program, and to ensure it remained sensitive to the needs of the mostly minority poor it was designed to serve.

What Carmen had started with her entreaties to "lead our people" was now utterly and absolutely complete. I had gone through an extraordinary metamorphosis. It was like my first ethnic awakening several years earlier, during that high-school summer in Puerto Rico, when I became so fluent I began thinking in Spanish—at Haverford, I did not have to remember what I was, or who I was. I was transformed to where I would even admonish my black and brown colleagues at caucus meetings with heated cries of "C'mon, niggers!" I was permitted even that taboo word, allowed only by the brother oppressed; my racial makeover was complete.

Typically, for me anyway, my black and brown pride did not obscure the program's pool of gorgeous white women from view. The best-looking Reggie was a woman whom I will call Julia Sorenson-Cunningham. Julia was my first hyphenated acquaintance. She was tall, with a pale and beautiful face. She was bony, but with surprisingly big tits and an incendiary smile. Her hair was usually pulled back in a casual ponytail. The only makeup she wore was lipstick. She was also married.

After Haverford, Julia was headed for a Legal Services office in California.

I was immediately attracted to her. Julia later admitted she was also attracted to me, and to the radical/racial noises I was making. (This was our selective liberal chic at work.) Still, she resisted my initial advances, until one day when she announced plainly that her husband was three thousand miles away in California and that it was illogical for a thoroughly modern young woman to deprive herself of physical passion on a technicality. She assured me she would remain emotionally faithful to her beloved husband, but said she saw no reason not to pursue a casual affair.

Sounded good to me.

By the time we left Haverford, we had fallen in love. Our affair was suspended, though, by our geographically opposed careers, and our pending bar exams. We decided to figure out our relationship after we each passed the bar in our respective states. I emerged from the fellowship program with an assignment to the Community Action for Legal Services office, located on Worth Street in lower Manhattan, two blocks north of city hall. Known as CALS, we were the local Legal Services braintrust and headquarters for the regional field offices; we prepared appeals, devised overall strategy, and mollified local political interests. CALS was where the federal suit against New York's antiabortion statute was conceived, truth-in-lending legislation proposed, and mountains of ideologically motivated litigation prepared.

For the first time in my life, I had a perfect job in a perfect setting. Our bright, sprawling loft offices were run by an elegant and very formal black attorney named John De Witt Gregory. My first efforts involved the new truth-in-lending laws. At that time, retail lenders were not required to inform customers of their precise credit terms, and people were often made to pay two to three times the purchase price of various items in usurious interest. Our office was preparing a class-action suit against some of the city's biggest offenders. The work was tedious and exacting, but it affected virtually every poor family in New York whose cars, furniture, and appliances had been purchased on an installment plan.

When I could find the time, I would accompany our already-licensed attorneys into court to listen to their oral arguments. I put myself in their shoes. I told myself I was born to litigate, to stand in front of a judge and jury and argue my client's case with fire and eloquence. I daydreamed while watching John De Witt Gregory argue the abortion suit in federal court. I wanted to be in his position. In my arrogant folly, I even thought I could do a better job.

JOHN DE WITT GREGORY (former executive director, Community Action for Legal Services; currently Distinguished Professor of Family Law, Hofstra University): As a lawyer, Geraldo was very bright, and very, very committed to representation of the poor. I always liked him as a person, but there is one story I tell that I found kind of amusing. Later on, when he had an opportunity to become a television reporter, he came up to me and said that he liked what he was doing at CALS and that he hadn't made up his mind and that he might be willing to stay on if I would appoint him deputy director. And I told him at the time that I couldn't do that. He was just out of law school, and what it represented to me was that he was somebody who had supreme confidence in his abilities, and I think it's been demonstrated that that wasn't misplaced confidence, but at the same time I felt it amusing that he would have, if you'll pardon the expression, the chutzpah to be asking me to appoint him deputy director.

My evenings were given over to the Marino Bar Review course, in preparation for the biggest academic hurdle of my life. In my day, the New York State Bar Exam was a four-part ordeal, spread over two days. It was given in the Commodore Hotel, adjacent to Grand Central Terminal. In recent years, the hotel has been refurbished by Donald Trump, and rechristened The Grand Hyatt, but back then it was a dump. The grand ballroom where the test was given was not air-conditioned, and I dreaded the midsummer heat in the weeks leading up to the exam. Thankfully, judgment day dawned just right; it was neither too hot nor too humid; in fact, my hands were freezing as the proctors signaled us to begin—my old performance anxiety, hidden to all but me.

I quickly glanced at the essay questions and sighed in deep relief. Every single topic had been covered in the bar review course, and I tackled the exam with brio. By the end of the third segment, lunch of the second day, I knew I had totally nailed the exam. I answered each question with the confidence born of absolute preparation. I glided through that fourth segment knowing this would be my last academic trial. My family and my old pal Frank DeCecco could no longer ride me about my professional-student status. I was finally through with school.

Life, I decided, was school and test enough.

Months later, I hung around the newsstand at Seventy-second Street and Broadway late one evening to buy the first edition of the next day's *New York Times*. I grabbed a still-hemped copy from the vendor as the fresh bundle hit pavement, then hurried across Seventy-second to a bench in "Needle Park." There, under a bright streetlight and surrounded by the park's resident junkies, I scanned the long list of examinees who had passed the bar. My heart leapt when I saw the name Rivera, only to sink when I noticed that the first name attached to it was not my own. Then, in a flash of recognition, I looked farther down the list, to Riviera. I smiled. I had come to hate that bastardized name with a passion and was soon to have it legally changed, and yet I was never so glad to see it as I was on that night.

With successful exams behind us, and worthwhile careers underway, Julia and I turned our thoughts to reunion. My budget, on my Legal Services stipend, did not extend to California, and Julia's marriage inhibited her out-of-town travel, and so I finagled a government-sponsored trip West. I arranged a working visit to our Watsonville office, and a meeting with union leader Cesar

Chavez, and I left the rest of my time free for Julia. I was crazy about her, and turned on by the daring of a bicoastal romance with a married lady.

The trip was to be the first of several, including one weekend trip to the Big Sur Inn that comes happily to mind. There was particular sweat and urgency to our lovemaking on that outing, and for the first time we talked of building a lifetime together. On another visit, I was pulled over for making an illegal left-hand turn, while driving Julia's car. My New York State license had been revoked, thanks to a collection of speeding tickets earned on my motorcycle, and Julia rescued me from the highway patrolman by passing me off as her absentminded husband. This last has stayed with me, I suppose, because it suggested at the easy, almost domestic familiarity the two of us enjoyed for a short time.

By my third visit, Julia and her husband had separated. She was not a person who could long endure deceit. We made plans for her to come East after her fellowship obligation was over, perhaps to set up a storefront law office together. In the meantime, she rented a small house, nestled in a grove of eucalyptus trees. In that part of the country, we should have read significance in the fact that our new love nest was located on San Andreas Road.

115 Avenue C

Beyond West Babylon, 115 Avenue C was my most permanent home.

The address belonged to a three-story brick building built cheaply at the turn of the century. A Puerto Rican restaurant occupied the ground floor and specialized in grease-fried pork dishes, bad coffee, and cockroaches. Most of the clientele were welfare recipients with charge accounts settled bimonthly, on check day. The two apartments above the restaurant had been converted into one high-style duplex, renovated by the previous owner. He had spent thousands of dollars fixing the place up, before he realized the Lower East Side was a dangerous place to live. He was looking to dump the building, but prospective buyers had become scarce.

Living around the corner on East Seventh Street, I was unafraid of the troubled neighborhood, and tired of paying rent. I wanted a base of operations and a long-term investment. The building seemed to offer both. Also, the city had announced construction of a new subway line to run under Second Avenue, cut east on Fourteenth Street, then back down Avenue B to service the area. With the coming of a modern transportation system, I thought it was only a matter of time before Alphabet City rebounded. Of course, the subway was never built, and the neighborhood continued to deterioriate. But then, I was never very good at investments.

I debated the purchase with myself, over the space of several weeks. One of these deliberations took me right to my decision. I was walking home from the Lexington Avenue subway stop on Astor Place. I had come from court and was wearing a suit and tie, and my father's wing-tipped shoes. I was carrying a briefcase. I meandered past Cooper Union College, headed east along St. Mark's Place, past the tie-dyed hippies and espresso houses; I cut around Tompkins Square Park, by the apartment building I had shared with Linda, and then over the ethnic borderline to home, across avenues B and C. At the corner of C and Seventh, I looked left to the building I was considering buying. In my mind, I cleaned up the restaurant and painted the facade. Then I unpainted it, worried about the display of relative affluence on that desperately poor block. Still unsure of the move, I walked the rest of the block home.

There, in the mantrap vestibule of my building, I was accosted by three young thugs. One had a knife; another, an empty bottle. The third twisted the briefcase out of my left hand. I held my keys in my right.

"Open the fucking door, man," barked the thug with my briefcase.

I did and let myself be shoved down the long first-floor corridor, surrounded. My apartment was on the first floor, about halfway down the hall. I stopped in front of it.

"Let us in," the knife-wielder demanded.

I knew if these guys got me inside, it would be all over. There were too many of them. And so, on an impulse, I bolted past the trio and down the hallway, pounding on apartment doors as I passed, hollering for help. My scared neighbors stayed inside. My only hope was that one of them would call 911. Meanwhile, I had backed myself into a corner. I turned to face my attackers. There was an alcove to my right that housed a broom, mop, and bucket. I reached for the broom, and brandished it like a housewife's spear. And then I charged. I knocked over the guy with the knife, but I could not get past the other two. The asshole with the bottle smashed his weapon on the back of my head and then cut me with what remained in his hand. I registered the blows, but did not feel them. I continued to fight back; I jammed the bristled edge of my ridiculous weapon into the face of my assailant and pushed violently. The other two fled, apparently realizing they had picked the wrong guy to jump. The third finally pushed past and ran from the building. I reached up to touch my wet, throbbing forehead and came away with blood.

It would take more than a half-hour for police to respond to the scene, and thirty-six stitches to close my wound. The response time to calls of violence in the ghetto is only slightly quicker than the healing time of a broken-bottle gash. The jagged scar has faded with time, but it is still visible at my hairline, a permanent reminder of the way I used to live, and the place I used to live.

The incident was the push I needed to buy the building. I took it as a kind of signal. Plus, I thought the new place offered a more defensible space. I purchased it with a borrowed down-payment, and a mortgage extorted from Manufacturers Hanover Bank. Then, as now, commercial banks "redlined" ghetto neighborhoods. The term refers to the illegal (but widespread) practice of refusing mortgages in high-risk areas. After the bank's initial refusal, I stormed into their quiet, wood-paneled offices on Park Avenue. I threatened the supercilious junior loan officer with a variety of civil rights and conspiracy violations. I pointed out that because of my position at Legal Services, I had virtually unlimited legal resources to make his life miserable. I could sue his bank on behalf of myself, and all others similarly mistreated.

After I scared the arrogance out of this guy, I suggested that I would go quietly out of his life if he just gave me the paltry mortgage. He agreed, and for $27,500 I owned a building in Manhattan, my first-ever home. Over the next half-dozen years, I would be visited there by Mayor John Lindsay, Mick Jagger, John

Lennon, Rudolf Nureyev, assorted European royalty, various high-powered politicians, left-wing radicals, Hell's Angels, Black Panthers, Young Lords, desperadoes, junkies, models, hookers, and an eclectic cast of thousands.

I was a streetwise homeowner, and big-league party-giver, living on the hard edge of the world.

One of my closest associates at CALS during this time was another Smith fellow, Marcia Robinson Lowry. My friend Marcia eschewed femininity for feminism, even before activist women were so-labeled. She was sharp, smart, and attractive, but she wasn't coy about it. In those days, it was impossible for me to deal with women in a nonsexual way; their sexuality was always relevant. It was only after Marcia and I went through our ritual coupling that our relationship deepened considerably.

Marcia was estranged from her husband John Lowry, a Freedom Rider who was twice arrested for his civil rights activities. In my only (albeit uncontested) divorce case, I represented Marcia in her divorce from her activist husband. In return, Marcia became my political mentor, teaching me the ideas and jargon of the New Left. Through her, I came to understand how Martin Luther King, Jr. had envisioned ending the war in Vietnam—by fighting attempts at political repression in this country, and battling racism as a piece of the same puzzle.

We did some excellent work at CALS, both together and separately. Marcia prepared the winning case to legalize New York abortions, which John De Witt Gregory had argued, and later specialized in cases alleging racial, religious, and gender discrimination. My most frequent work was in housing court, winning damages on behalf of poor tenants against rent-control–violating landlords; in criminal court, representing left-wing demonstrators accused of harassment, obstruction of justice, or trespass; and in civil court, on behalf of exploited consumers. Together, Marcia and I represented workers illegally discharged from public employment, usually because of their politics. We were tweaking the nose of the Nixon establishment and we loved it.

Part of my rebellion was drug use. Despite sworn testimony to the contrary, I doubt there are more than a handful of politicians, media personalities, or big-business tycoons in my generation who did not at least experiment with a joint or two. I had been smoking marijuana off and on since Nogales, although I was leery of extending my experimentation to the hallucinogenic drugs that were then widely popular. Until one snowy night in Woodstock, New York, when a guru-type friend provided my first and only hit of acid. It was an unnerving experience. I remember making love to Marcia and exploding (literally, I thought at the time); my body felt like it belonged to someone else, and that I would never reclaim it. I remember walking naked onto a pristinely beautiful snow-covered field, and urinating my initials in the fresh snow. I remember having sex with a huge oak table. I am a person who prides himself on being in control, and I never returned to the uncontrollable folly of acid. It frightened me.

Early in November 1969, the members of the Black and Brown Caucus descended on the Office of Economic Opportunity in our nation's capital. There were forty-five of us, from all over the country, and we were joined by about a hundred black law students from Howard University. Our complaints had been filed two months earlier with Legal Services National Director Terry Lenzner, and they were essentially the same as they had been at Haverford: the all-white staff of the Reginald Heber Smith Fellowship Program was not sensitive to the problems of minority groups. We wanted equal stipends for minority attorneys, and the transfer of the four-million-dollar program to a more appropriate institution—namely, the black-run Howard University in Washington, D.C.

Lenzner, a former college football player who would later gain prominence as a Watergate prosecutor, seemed shocked and embarrassed by the large and aggressive turnout. He was expecting a small meeting with the leaders of our group, during which he would have found some way to placate and send us packing. He was not at all prepared for the confrontational circus we had staged. Still, he sat through a heated two-hour meeting with our group and appeared to be swayed at least by our relocation proposal. We refused to leave until we had a firm answer. As we continued our sit-in, he took the proposal upstairs to his boss Donald Rumsfeld, the conservative ex-congressman and future CIA head who was then serving as OEO director.

In a closed-door meeting, Rumsfeld ordered Lenzner to rescind his tentative agreement, and issued the following statement: "The work of the Office of Economic Opportunity will not be conducted under threat, coercion, duress, or intimidation by any group of individuals." Lenzner tried to convince us of his sincere interest in relocating and improving the program, and pleaded with us to leave the office before the situation got out of control. We declined. Next, Rumsfeld stumbled in and tried his belligerent hand. We blocked the door and refused to let either Rumsfeld or Lenzner out.

When the police finally arrived, they pushed their way through our token resistance, and warned that everyone not leaving immediately would be arrested for illegal entry. We urged all of the students to leave, along with the fifteen Caucus members who had not yet been admitted to their respective bars. We did not want their admissions to be complicated by an arrest. The remaining thirty of our group—twenty men, ten women—were arrested and charged.

It was my first run-in with the law since I stole that car in West Babylon. Back then I was scared and humbled; this time I was exhilarated. As a battle for civil rights, it may not have amounted to much, but to the thirty fingerprinted members of the Black and Brown Caucus, it was a triumph. We had put ourselves at risk for an ideal, and to fulfill a pledge made to each other back at Haverford. And, the risk paid off: The program was transferred to Howard University the following year and remained there until it was phased out in 1985.

Marcia accompanied me to Washington the following week, for a massive antiwar demonstration. The D.C. cops, at the time, had a reputation for brutality matched only by the troops of Chicago's Mayor Daley, and many activist attorneys—from Legal Services, the National Lawyers Guild, and Legal Aid—were dispatched to the capital to serve as legal observers. The thinking was that our presence, complete with armbands proclaiming our status, would have a mitigating effect on police behavior.

It didn't.

The Mall, underneath the sweeping majesty of the Washington Monument, was crowded with tens of thousands of demonstrators. When the throng refused an order to disperse, the police moved in with swirls of tear gas. Next, they made a mounted charge, and when that didn't seem to do the trick, they unleashed a phalanx of club-swinging officers on foot. Marcia was at my side as we watched one cop swing his club like a woodsman's ax, down onto the skull of a young female demonstrator.

MARCIA ROBINSON LOWRY: We were sort of at the edge of the crowd when we saw that, and I remember Gerry and I running to the scene. He had a temper, and the cops were very, very abusive, and I think he was starting to yell at one of the cops, which was clearly the wrong thing to do. This was not the time for reasoned discourse. I remember pulling him back, away from this one cop, because even though what the cops were doing was outrageous, it was clear that all that was going to happen was that Gerry was going to get clubbed as well. It really was frightening. I think it was one of the most frightening physical situations I have been in.

With Marcia pulling me from behind, and the panting, excited cop pushing me roughly on the chest, we watched as the wounded demonstrator was arrested and taken away. She looked like a beaten rag doll.

SPANISH HARLEM

In the fall of 1969, I began hearing about a Puerto Rican activist group called the Young Lords, operating out of a tiny, ramshackle storefront office in El Barrio, Spanish Harlem.

Their movement fascinated me. Up until that time, the only Puerto Rican activists were those involved in demanding that the Commonwealth of Puerto Rico become an independent nation. Those *"independentistas"* were invariably born and based on the island, primarily Spanish-speaking, and not otherwise interested or involved in mainland politics. The Lords were a different complexion: younger, darker, primarily English-speaking, and mainland-born. They were the next generation of Puerto Rican activists, as involved in fighting economic and social injustice and the war in Vietnam, as they were in the island-independence movement.

The Lords crept into my consciousness over a period of weeks, as the young militants disrupted services at the First Spanish United Methodist Church, on 111th Street and Lexington Avenue. They demanded that the church become more involved in helping to ease the temporal as well as spiritual needs of the neighborhood. The First Spanish congregation was made up mostly of prosperous Cubans who had migrated to more middle-class areas over the years, returning to El Barrio only for Sunday services. For the rest of the week, the safe, sound, three-year-old church facilities were unused.

The militants sought to put the building to better use by establishing a day-care program, a free-breakfast program, a lead paint poison-testing program, and an emergency shelter for displaced neighborhood families. For several weeks during services, the Lords had been taking over the podium to outline their plans. The issue came to a head one Sunday in early December when the entire cadre of Young Lords marched to the front of the church in midservice. Resplendent in their trademark purple berets, they attempted to take over the church. Just then, in anticipation of these fireworks, ten plainclothes police officers, hidden among the congregation, stood to quiet the room. They asked the pastor, an elderly pro-Batista Cuban exile named Humberto Carrazana, if he wanted the demonstrators arrested. He nodded yes, and all hell broke loose. When it was over, a dozen Young Lords and several cops had been injured, none seriously. Thirteen Lords were arrested.

Word of the incident reached me at CALS the next day, Monday morning. With the advice of the National Lawyers Guild, the most radical of the movement legal organizations, the Lords had already retained the services of three attorneys, Bobby Lawyer, a black man, and Daniel Meyer and Dick Ashe, both white. I was furious at this last and most recent development. How dare the first, modern, mainland-based Puerto Rican activist group not hire the first, modern, mainland-based Puerto Rican activist attorney?

That night, I took the subway uptown to the Lords' office, on Madison Avenue, between 111th and 112th streets, the heart of the Latin ghetto. The storefront office was narrow and deep, in the railroad-style of most neighborhood buildings. The space nearest the street was a makeshift reception area, separated from the back room by a thick curtain. The officer of the day sat at the front desk, answering the frequent telephone rings with the message, "Free Puerto Rico now!" There were benches laid out for supplicants, applicants, and visitors. The walls were lined with posters of Ché Guevara, Fidel Castro, Marx, Lenin, and Pedro Albizu Campos, the slain Puerto Rican *independentista*. Banners proclaimed, *"Hasta la victoria siempre"* and "When one of us falls, one thousand will take his place."

The offices were dimly lit but buzzing with activity, even at this late hour. I barreled in off Madison Avenue, introduced myself to the officer of the day, and was told to wait while the Central Committee members were in conference. I sat down on one of the benches with a grand display of impatience.

"Who are they in conference with?" I demanded, after no more than a minute.

"Our lawyers."

The reply triggered something in me. I went crazy and responded in a rage. "I'm their lawyer," I shouted, and I marched past the OD, pushed aside the curtain, and stormed into the back office. There, hunched around a smoke-shrouded card table, I saw four members of the Young Lords' Central Committee in deep conversation with their three attorneys.

PABLO GUZMAN (former member, Young Lords' Central Committee; currently, general assignment reporter, WNYW-TV, and *New York Daily News* columnist): There was a commotion out front. We didn't know what it was and a lot of us thought, you know, some kind of an attack was happening or something. And it was Gerry pushing his way past the security guards in the front and insisting that he be allowed to participate. The other attorneys apparently knew him. He pretty much pushed his way in and introduced himself to the committee members and then he and the other lawyers started right away yelling and stuff, arguing, and then we shut everybody up. We wanted to hear what he had to say. Especially back then, the way to win our hearts was to be brash, you know. I mean, this was a classic marriage, the way Gerry just pushed his way in and we saw him arguing with his colleagues, you know, and giving them hell, and at the same time stopping and turning, trying to challenge us. We were like looking at each other like, yeah, let's see what he's like, let's give him a shot, and also like, you know, who the hell does this crazy motherfucker think he is?

By the end of that evening, I was one of the principal lawyers for the Young Lords; by the end of the week, I was even wearing one of their purple berets.

The event that propelled our group to mainstream prominence took root following services on the last Sunday of 1969. In a fitting capstone to the turbulent decade, 150 Lords occupied the Methodist church just after Pastor Carrazana led his congregation from the building. They used sheets of plywood to cover the windows and sealed off the doorways. The chosen symbol of the takeover was nailed to the big wooden door of the gray stucco building: a hand-painted picture of Jesus, the prince of peace, with a rifle slung across his back.

The next morning, the main entrance was opened on the rechristened People's Church. Over the next few days, the atmosphere inside the church was, alternately, like a besieged wagon train and street bazaar. Free breakfasts were served to mothers and children. Beret-wearing Lords lectured neighborhood youths in small groups on the main floor and in the basement. Documentary films were shown, one of them featuring the pre-1968 Olympics riot in Mexico City in which scores of students had been killed. Volunteer doctors gave free physicals and administered lead-poisoning tests to the very young.

The First Spanish congregation was reeling from the takeover, but chose not to call in the police. Instead, they brought a civil action to command the militants to vacate the premises. As we lawyers pushed papers, the occupied building became the focus of wide, even international, media attention. The photo opportunity was irresistible: squads of heavily armed police staking out a ghetto church protected by stern-faced, beret-wearing militants and their numerous supporters. I was among several spokesmen, granting interviews that drew attention to the real needs of the community, and the positive efforts of our clients.

As the standoff moved into its second week, the church became the social center of the entire East Harlem community. Welfare mothers in need of milk, the elderly in need of various assistance,

even junkies in need of detoxification all waited patiently in line to
be admitted to the revolutionary utopia within.

Mayor John V. Lindsay was no Richard Daley. He wanted the
confrontation settled peacefully. With the Lords' social-action
programs receiving generally sympathetic coverage in the press, the
occupation of the church was a story with no bad guys. Lindsay
assigned three of his principal deputies to negotiate a settlement:
deputy mayors Sid Davidoff and Dick Aurelio, and personal aide Barry
Gotterer.

This was big stuff, but the Lords were not buying into it. Their
position, I informed the mayor's team, was nonnegotiable. They
were not going to vacate the People's Church.

Enter Herman Badillo, the man widely regarded as the founding
father of the mainland Puerto Rican community.

HERMAN BADILLO (former Bronx borough president and
congressman, unsuccessful New York City mayoral candidate):
What happened was I got a call from a judge one day (I was then
working in the private sector), assigning me to mediate the case of
the church elders against the Young Lords. I called Geraldo and
arranged to have a committee of the Young Lords come into my
office on Saturday, to begin negotiations. So Saturday, in come
Geraldo and Felipe Luciano and Pablo Guzman and all the others,
and they start running up and down the stairs, and hanging from
the chandeliers and making a mess of the whole office. We were
not getting anywhere. Eventually, I came to agree with the Young
Lords, about what they were trying to do. And we got to be friends.
We had a much tougher time with the church elders. They would
not budge at all, so I finally called down to Washington, to the
church council, and I basically said, look, if you guys don't come
to an agreement with these people then I'm going to join Geraldo
and I'm going to become cocounsel for the Young Lords, and we're
going to try this case. And I'm going to go before a jury and I'm
going to say, yes, the Young Lords are guilty. They're guilty of a
terrible crime. They're guilty of trying to ensure that the poor kids
of East Harlem get a free breakfast. How many juries do you think
are going to convict them?

*   *   *

Slowly, perhaps sensing the loss of both the sympathy and interest of the media, the Lords began the process of compromise that ultimately led to their vacating the church several weeks later. By then, the organization had become a household name; Felipe, Yoruba, David, and Juan, flanked by their attorneys (one of them dressed for action in a purple beret), had become fixtures on the evening news.

With the standoff settled, the Lords were the darlings of New York's New Left. Herman Badillo hosted a cocktail party at the spacious Park Avenue apartment of philanthropist Eleanor Guggenheimer, a wealthy activist who had just run unsuccessfully for the presidency of the city council. Felipe and I were the evening's speakers. I spoke first and urged all people of good conscience to get off their asses and get involved in helping the poor, before the poor came to their neighborhoods to help themselves. Felipe was even tougher and warned of an inevitable class war. Our upscale audience listened with the rapt attention of liberal chic, interested but untouchable.

My association with the group caused me some trouble at CALS, but not much.

"This is not the service to the poor contemplated in your fellowship," John De Witt Gregory told me one day, his voice thick with concern. He argued that my highly publicized actions were attracting negative attention from the OEO in Washington, fueling administration criticism that Legal Services attorneys were just a bunch of effete pinkos, working hard to sow dissent and disorder. I argued that the Lords were doing more to help the poor than a hundred class-action lawsuits.

JOHN DE WITT GREGORY: I was faced with two things. Here I was, with this new, and at that time very controversial, Legal Services program, and although I sympathized with and applauded what Geraldo was doing in East Harlem, there was another part of me, as a bureaucrat, that was kind of hoping it wouldn't come too much to the attention of the people on our board. My recollection is I was always thinking, Where is Geraldo? Will he come to the office today? Even though I knew he was doing something very valuable. I just did not want the distraction of having somebody question what we were doing.

*   *   *

The high-water mark for the Young Lords came later that winter, when they organized a march from Spanish Harlem to the United Nations Plaza, on Forty-seventh Street, to protest what they called the colonial status of Puerto Rico. For the desperately poor people of El Barrio, the issue was very likely of secondary concern, but the turnout was nonetheless impressive.

For reasons having nothing to do with politics, I led the procession in my first city car: a battered, five-year-old blue Volkswagen beetle convertible. Initially, there were to be no vehicles allowed in the parade, but when several of the young women in the Lords' hierarchy complained of female problems, handicapping their ability to walk the planned distance, I was asked to drive them. With the top down, and the girls sitting on top of the backseat—me, honking; them, waving—we rolled from 125th Street, past the still-guarded doorway of the nervously restored First Spanish United Methodist Church; our movements along the entire route were closely monitored by the FBI, and state and local police.

As our procession reached the crest of the hill at Ninety-ninth Street and Lexington Avenue, I turned and saw an inspiring sight. From those heights, the long chain of people marching shoulder-to-shoulder stretched clear back to 125th Street, a city mile. It was the largest political assembly of Puerto Ricans in mainland American history.

As I became more identified as the lawyer for the Young Lords, my emergence was challenged by other movement attorneys, all white radicals, on the grounds that I was not Puerto Rican enough. Central Committee members were frequently reminded, by supposedly well-meaning "friends" of the organization, that I had spent most of my early years on Long Island, and that my mother was Jewish. There was no denying my background, and I struggled to shed light on my foreground. To further quell the backstabbing talk, I applied formally to be admitted to the Young Lords, not as an attorney but as a brown-blooded member.

I was refused and crushed by the rejection. I thought about resigning as the group's counsel, but stayed on because I still believed in what they were trying to accomplish. Several nights later, sitting around that back office card table and sipping cheap red wine with the Central Committee members, I finally mustered the courage to ask about my vetoed membership. "Is it because I'm a half-breed?" I asked.

"No fucking way, man," Yoruba replied. "We love you. But somebody has to be the warrior and somebody has to be the attorney."

PABLO GUZMAN: We knew from the beginning Gerry was half Puerto Rican and half Jewish. It was never an issue with us. All of us had taken different paths to get to Latino consciousness and awareness. His background always seemed more of an issue with people who really had the least to say about it. But when he wanted to join the group, we just felt that his role was as a lawyer. There was a process that took place in the group that was very different from what he had been used to. Gerry was a fighter. He wanted very much to be at the forefront of things. There were a number of things that we did, demonstrations, where we had police lines set up and we had our legal observers, wearing armbands so the cops could identify them, and the next thing we knew he was in the middle of some melee, swinging. It was very hard for Gerry to observe.

Gradually, I began spending almost all of my time in criminal court, constantly defending the Lords on charges ranging from assaulting an officer, to criminal trespass, to loitering. The cops were engaged in a holy war against a group they perceived as anti-American, or at least antigovernment. We were operating in an atmosphere of conflict and confrontation, and our methods changed with our circumstances. Like the Black Panthers and other radical groups, the Young Lords drifted toward violence. Weapons were no longer taboo, nor were alliances with other, more militant organizations. The resources and energies of the organization were being diverted from positive community action programs; we were spending all of our time, and money, defending ourselves.

The war between the cops and the Lords escalated over the next months. The showdown came over the issue of the quality of medical care available to the impoverished residents of the South Bronx. At the time, the area was being served by only one major medical center, the original Lincoln Hospital, now torn down. An aged, decrepit, and already-condemned physical plant, staffed haphazardly with the least and the worst, the hospital was a health care nightmare. Incidents of postnatal deaths and hospital-caused infections were the highest in the city. There were more rats running around the emergency room than hospital staff. The place would have been a scandal in Addis Ababa, or Bombay, but it was quietly tolerated in the urban wasteland of the South Bronx.

Over the years, the city had frequently allocated money to build a new Lincoln Hospital, but the funds were always redirected and the project put on hold. Finally, the Young Lords were approached by members of the neighboring community and by much of the hospital's nonprofessional staff, seeking help. The resulting hospital takeover was the last straw in the tense relationship between the Lords and the police. Surrounding the facility, the cops were in no mood to heed the mayor's admonition to go easy; their union, the PBA, had declared the Lords a public menace, and the mayor a fool for not dealing with them more decisively.

One evening, during the standoff, Yoruba slipped out of the hospital, past the police barricades. He was headed down to Manhattan, to see to other business at organization headquarters. Along with Felipe, he was easily the most recognizable of the group, and the most wanted by the police. He was the subject of a popular movement poster that showed him wearing his dark shades, safari jacket, and purple beret, sitting stone-faced in front of a Puerto Rican flag with the inscription, "Free Puerto Rico Now!"

Predictably, he was followed by a carload of detectives, and arrested. I was called in to bail him out, but not before he was given a serious working-over.

PABLO GUZMAN: I was up in a second-floor holding cell, with all these white cops and one black cop, who I guess was trying to show off to his buddies that he was the nastiest son-of-a-bitch in the precinct. He had four guns strapped to him, this guy, and he had this whole thing about how he was going to do me in, and what bones he was going to break, and all of a sudden there was this commotion downstairs. And everybody, all the detectives who have been hassling me, everything stopped. And there was this roar that kept building, it just kept getting louder, and then Gerry came flying into the room, he jumped over this railing, and it was like broken-field running, and he came over and said, "You okay?" That was the first thing he did was check to see if I was okay. I was like, oh, man, am I glad to see you. And then he turned to the detectives and hollered, "I'm a lawyer and this is my client and if you touch him again I'll have all of your badges." And they froze. It was like their fists were hung in midair. It was like that close. It was like when you're tied to the railroad tracks and the train is coming down upon you in the movies. He saved me from a serious ass-whipping.

That evening, in night court, all charges against my client were dropped. Although construction on the new Lincoln Hospital began shortly thereafter, the event furthered my disenchantment with the practice of radical law. The movement, I still felt, was right and good, but it was getting away from us. Someone was going to get hurt. Or killed.

I found myself thinking of another line of legal work. These second thoughts surprised me, but they made sense. My commitment to CALS was about to expire, and I was through stretching my two-hundred-dollar weekly paycheck to cover my mortgage, student loan payments, and various out-of-pocket expenses. I was through with revolution. Of course, I knew I would miss my association with the Young Lords. We were friends. We had partied together, laughed and cried together, accomplished great things together. Hanging around with the group's proud and swaggering leaders had helped me to define myself. Various pieces of the personal puzzle had been around, but it took the Young Lords to put it all together. I was finally satisfied with the man in the mirror: a street-fighting brown Romeo who loved his people enough to sacrifice or die for them.

Others, I realized, might have seen a different reflection, but I liked what I saw.

Where to go? I wondered. Wall Street was out. So was chasing ambulances. And I could not think of one big city-firm that would have me as an associate. One year out of law school, I was at my first professional crossroads.

Chance, blessed chance, stepped in once again to rescue me from my uncertain future. Gloria Rojas, one of the many local television reporters who had interviewed me during the occupation of the church, called to tell me that WABC-TV was interested in talking to me about a job.

"Doing what?" I wondered.

"Being a reporter," Gloria said.

"The only reporters I know are Clark Kent and Jimmy Olsen," I said. (This was essentially true.)

"You could learn," she tried. "Just think about it. If you're not interested, maybe you'd know some other P.R. who would be."

Within a week, I had an appointment with Al Primo, news director for WABC-TV, Channel 7, the ABC Television Network's flagship local station. He was looking for a Puerto Rican to complement his already ethnically diverse on-air team. Aside from Gloria, who worked for the rival CBS affiliate, New York's million-plus Latino community was not represented on any of the major local news programs. Apparently, Al Primo was out to change that. He caught me mouthpiecing on the air for the Young Lords and thought he saw the makings of a newsman, and so he asked Gloria for an introduction.

He was seated behind his desk when I entered his windowless office, a dimly lit oasis of quiet on the edge of the bright and noisy newsroom. "Hi," he said, rising to shake my hand. "I'm Al Primo."

"I'm Gerry Rivera." I shook back.

"You're taller than you looked on TV," he said, checking me out like a merchant appraising goods.

"And you just think we're all under five-five," I retorted, trying to sound tough, confident, and friendly, all at once. We both laughed.

I relaxed and listened to his pitch. He told me how television would help me to help my people, in ways bigger and better than I could have ever imagined. He told me not to worry that I did not know the first thing about the television news business; the station would send me to a crash course in broadcast journalism at Columbia University. I wondered, out loud, why I should leave the legal profession after I had worked so long and hard to get through law school. He asked how much money I was making.

"About two hundred a week," I replied.

"I'll give you three hundred a week to start, and I'll raise it fifty a year for the next five."

Deal.

"By the way," he said, shaking on our new relationship, "what's Gerry short for?"

"Gerald."

"Gerald?" he tried. "It's not very Puerto Rican, is it?"

"No," I said, "I guess not, but it's better than Sidney."

"Sidney?"

"That's what my Jewish mother wanted to call me."

He laughed politely at the exchange, but his smile seemed forced. I sensed he was disappointed. After all, he was going to some trouble to hire a Puerto Rican reporter; surely, he wanted to at least get his money's worth.

"If you want something more Latin," I suggested, "my father and his side of the family call me Geraldo."

"Geraldo?" he said, and this time his smile was genuine. "Geraldo Rivera." He tested the sound, rolling the *R*s and learning what millions were about to, that the *G* in Spanish is pronounced *H*. "That's better," he said finally. "Let's go with Geraldo."

CHAPTER FOUR

77 WEST 66TH STREET

The broadcast news business was pretty much a conservative, establishment enterprise in the spring of 1970, when I was hired by WABC-TV as part of that station's effort to more adequately address the ethnic mix of its viewership.

At the turn of the decade, station management was making aggressive minority hires in hopes that Channel 7 would make its mark on the New York market by better reflecting its diversity. This was a considerable break from the way things were done in the television news business. Up until then, local newscasts all looked alike and sounded alike—tight-lipped and buttoned-down—from one city to the next: an inoffensive WASP male, sitting at the center desk in a conservative suit and tie, objectively reading the news. Occasionally, the anchor would throw to one of his field reporters—also male, also inoffensively WASPish, also conservatively dressed—for a location piece.

It was the same all over—the same news, wrapped in the same package—and if you weren't tight-lipped and buttoned-down yourself, there was no compelling reason to tune in. Other than to get the news, of course, but there were other ways to get the news.

My first substantive encounters with television news came when I was being interviewed by local reporters in connection with my work with the Young Lords. These interviews occurred often; for a time there, whenever the Young Lords were in the news, so was I. But even then, I would rarely watch the broadcasts when they subsequently aired. (I didn't have a television set in the bedroom, so the late news was lost on me.) Local news, to me anyway, was not relevant. It did not matter. It was not a part of my world, not even when I was making some local news of my own. In a city like New York, where conservative WASPs rode the crosstown bus in equal numbers with blacks, Hispanics, Italians, Jews, and Asians, television's white-bread, establishment formula no longer made sense. I don't know that it ever did, but by 1970 most people I knew could not tell a television newsman from a game-show host.

With the rest of the business comfortably white bread, Channel 7 decided to become seeded rye. The station was starting to make itself an exception in the way local newscasts were built and delivered, and I was signed on to be part of that exception. Al Primo, a glad-handing sort of guy with a sharp mind and shrewd instincts, had been brought in to do for WABC-TV in New York what he had done for KYW-TV in Philadelphia: to serve up, as news director, a local broadcast tailored to the needs and concerns of the local viewers, and delivered by a news team that reflected the ethnic and economic diversity of the viewing population.

I never thought of Al Primo as a champion of social change and equal opportunity (I don't think he thought of himself this way either), but his hiring practices undeniably made him one. He combed out a shiny new coat for a tired old horse; he had made a business decision that ran counter to the way things were done, and he was willing to back that decision with the station's money and his own reputation. *Eyewitness News* was his invention, his concept—his baby—and it has been his lasting contribution to the business of local television news. You can see his stamp in every television market in the country, even today. (Almost every local news broadcast is presented by a "family" of on-air talent, chatting it up, and laughing at each other's jokes underneath the credit roll, another of Al's innovations.)

Before Primo, the prevailing strategy was to seek the middle ground, to make their on-camera reporters seem as much like the plain vanilla network correspondents as possible. He tilted things to where local anchors and reporters suddenly looked as much like their viewers as possible, to where broadcast journalists could exchange opinions with each other on the air, between stories, to where their personalities, backgrounds, and differences were allowed, and encouraged, to emerge.

I think Al was a pragmatic idealist in this sense, but he was a pragmatic idealist who knew when to make his move. And Channel 7 knew when to hire him. Channel 7 had the third-rated local newscast, and it was not even a competitive third, so the station had nothing to lose in adopting his idealism. Remember, WABC-TV was a lot like its network parent in those days: underdogged and overmatched by its competition. A standard industry joke was that ABC's call letters stood for the Almost Broadcasting Company. It was a line I never heard before I met Al Primo, and then heard all the time after I started work in the newsroom. The joke rankled management because it was on-target: it hit home on the network and local levels. Nationally, ABC was still producing a fifteen-minute newscast, long after CBS and NBC had gone to the half hour. The network had no recognizable anchor, no Huntley, no Brinkley, no Cronkite. No identity.

There were no prime-time stars either. When I interviewed for the job at Channel 7, ABC had only one program ranked in the top fifteen: *Marcus Welby, M.D.* Before *Welby*, the lone highly rated show at the network had been *The Lawrence Welk Show*. There was nothing Al Primo could do about the network's fortunes nationwide, but he could turn things around at home, at the flagship owned and operated station. His challenge, and it was significant, was to overcome the weak prime-time schedule leading into his eleven o'clock newscast. Initially, he played to his immediate strength, which amounted, essentially, to the lead-in audience provided on Tuesday nights by *Marcus Welby*. With the *Welby* audience in mind, he would launch his special series and multipart reports a day later than the traditional Monday, and otherwise pack his Tuesday night newscasts with the kinds of stories people would talk about the next morning on the crosstown bus. Over time, he realized that the way to win viewers seven nights a week was not to lure them away from other local news broadcasts, but to bring new viewers into the mix and win them over. The only way to accomplish that, he thought, was to appeal to minority viewers, like myself, who were becoming a majority in New York and who were getting their news from sources other than television.

His strategy fit in neatly with the tenor of the times. By 1970, there was a mounting pressure in all workplaces to accelerate minority hirings, particularly in such visible industries as communications, particularly into such high-profile jobs as the ones in front of local news cameras. Broadcast media outlets had been under pressure to integrate ever since the Kerner Commission issued its strongly worded findings in the wake of the riots of 1968. Al Primo recognized that pressure, but he also thought the impulses behind it made sense, and he set out to build a newscast that would feature something or someone for viewers in every neighborhood in New York City.

That's what *Eyewitness News* really was, a neighborhood newscast—a bulletin from the backyard fence—and before long our reporter/neighbors were familiar faces throughout the metropolitan area. As with most teams, Channel 7 had its starters and its second string.

Milton Lewis was most prominent among the latter group. One of the first recognizably Jewish reporters on the local scene, there was something about him that reminded me of Edward G. Robinson, in appearance and attitude: tough-talking, feisty. He covered city hall like he was in a B-movie, and his pieces gave the broadcast a real and gritty texture. "Now listen to this, . . ." he always began.

Doug Johnson represented the great white middle. He's a big

guy, built like a guard or blocking back. Doug has always been a no-nonsense, no-bullshit reporter, and he had that reputation back then, too. He was the one who'd be sent in for the tough, down-and-dirty stories. And he'd always come out with something. He's still at Channel 7, still a pro, and still a friend.

Gil Noble was the only black male reporter there at the time. He also anchored the weekend newscasts. He'd been a black studies professor at City University when he was hired by Al Primo. Most news directors at that time held the 1950s belief that only certain black men were acceptable to the viewing audience. (The view still holds, to a large degree.) The type was invariably soft-spoken, affable, articulate, preferably lighter-skinned and unequivocally nonthreatening. Michael Jackson, yes; James Brown need not apply. Although darker than most who made it, Gil Noble made the team. He was a good, caring reporter, who over the years hosted a number of award-winning public affairs programs and documentaries on the black community. I later made my talk show debut when teamed briefly with Gil on a little-watched Sunday afternoon public affairs show called *Like It Is*.

Duke Wade was a very blond, very sharp-faced general assignment reporter. He was pushing forty when I signed on, a career beat-reporter who left no lasting mark and eventually moved on.

Bob Miller was a dark-haired journeyman reporter who'd work anywhere, any time. He'd always get the story, sometimes three or four a day, and still find time to crank out a radio piece. He was the kind of reporter every station needs to stay on the air: Someone who'll deliver the goods, never yell, embarrass anyone or get sued, and who'd work for relative peanuts.

Roger Sharp was tall, pale, and competent. He was also a skilled, articulate reporter who lacked the charisma to make him a star. Through him I learned that good work is not enough to get you noticed on television.

Bill Aylward was a tired, cynical veteran reporter in his middle forties. He was a silver-haired fixture on the New York scene, a holdover, really, from the early days of local news. He'd worked his way out of and up from smaller stations, and eventually landed here.

John Shubeck was the society/show-business specialist. An ex-athlete turning toward fudgy, he was still good-looking in his late thirties and always escorting a recognizable woman about town. He'd worked previously on the anchor desk, without success, and shouldered his demotion without complaint. He would leave New York in the coming months for an anchor position in California; there, he enrolled in law school and drifted out of the business.

Melba Tolliver was the first black female reporter to grace the New York scene. (In fact, she was also one of the first female beat reporters of any race in the market.) She'd been a secretary when she substituted as an on-air reporter during an American Federation of Television and Radio Actors (AFTRA) strike in 1968, and then she stayed on. Melba was exceptionally bright and very attractive (she was slender and wore her hair in a big Afro); at the time she was becoming one of the most attention-getting stars in local news. She now anchors the prime-time newscasts on *News12 Long Island.*

Tex Antoine was the first of the character weathermen. He was something of a character himself, but he also created a character, Uncle Wethbee, and he'd do things like put frown lines on Uncle Wethbee's face if it was going to be cold, or rainy. He'd slap a smiling sun on his magnetic weather map if it was going to be a nice day. He wore an artist's smock and did the weather basically as an artist. He'd actually create a forecast, he used to say. He'd stand before the weather map and it would just come to him. His shtick made him one of the few true local superstars. He was huge. For a time there, Tex was the most popular man in New York.

The unhappy sidebar about Tex Antoine is that he was a diabetic and a drunk. By the time I joined the scene, he was already losing out to the ravages of those diseases. His six o'clock newscasts were usually smooth, but more often than not he'd go on a bender during his dinner breaks and come back to do the eleven o'clock show almost sloppy drunk. He'd miss his cues and flub his lines, but the station kept him on the air because of his tremendous popularity. He eventually lost his job when he commented—shockingly, stupidly—that if rape was inevitable, victims should just sit back and enjoy it; he made this comment on the air, after one of the anchors had read a rape story.

I remember one strange incident that was very typical of drunks, and of Tex. Just after I started at Channel 7, I had my family over to the apartment on Avenue C. I had asked Tex to join us. My sister Sharon brought her then-infant son Charles, who is now a six-foot-five, hard-working, and educated young man. Tex was like a television god to my very naive parents—they worshipped him— and they could not have been more thrilled if I had invited the mayor. During dinner, Tex just started crying. Sobbing. Right at the table. It was an uncomfortable scene. "Tex," my mother said, "what's the matter? What's the matter?" Everyone else expressed their concerns. In response, Tex grabbed my nephew and took Charles on his lap and began to rub his head, petting him. "This child is retarded," he said. My family was horrified. In his drunken stupor, this icon had diagnosed a perfectly healthy child as being mentally retarded.

Rounding out the team:

Howard Cosell, who in the next few months would be launched onto the national scene with the introduction of ABC's *Monday Night Football* and who was then a dominant radio personality in the New York market. His brash, opinionated, overblown, and always ad-libbed sportscasts were a highlight of the early *Eyewitness* newscasts.

Frank Gifford, a local hero, then awaiting his crack at a national audience, was another of our sports reporters; he drew the old-line conservative males, who remembered him from his standout football career with the New York Giants, and their wives, who loved his grace and manners.

Jim Bouton, a local hero of more recent vintage, fresh off an all-star, twenty-victory season with the New York Yankees (and resulting shoulder trouble), filled out the sports desk. The author of *Ball Four*, one of the first (and, still, the most sensational) baseball exposés, he was out there and outspoken, and he appealed to the younger, more political male viewers.

Something for everybody.

Bill Beutel and Roger Grimsby, the anchors, were at the head of this heap. Beutel is still anchoring the news at Channel 7, twenty years later. He took to New York and New York took to him. Actually, the city needed a second helping before it made up its mind; Bill had a failed first shot at anchor in the 1960s. He retrenched from that failure as a foreign correspondent, before he returned to local, and for a long time that network gig was his claim to fame. When he returned for his second try, in the early 1970s, the era of the activist anchorman—rolled-up sleeves, hands dirty from digging—was still a few years away, and Bill was very much the gentleman news-reader. He wrote all his own wrap-arounds, as I recall, and he even wrote a daily radio broadcast, but he did very little in the way of real reporting. Plus, he had a very distracting personal life—he up and married more times than gossip columnists could count—and as a second banana he was always content to come in, read the news, and go home.

Roger Grimsby was the star of the show. Al Primo hired him from an anchor position in San Francisco, where he was also managing editor and wildly successful, and he came to New York ready for more of the same. Things didn't exactly happen for Grimsby here the way he thought they would (he never got to call the shots the way he wanted to, the way he was used to), but he was still a news heavyweight in New York for a long time. Roger Grimsby was this very sarcastic, caustic, sometimes arrogant Korean War vet, a real hard guy to know and to work with. There were more rough edges to this guy than there are in a buzzsaw. There was also a bizarre kind of integrity about him, which viewers came to appreciate and admire. Grimsby had his share of problems. He was known to belt back a few between the six and eleven. Like Beutel, he wrote his own copy and left the reporting to others. His slogan, which he used to introduce each newscast, was "Here now the news," and the running gag in the newsroom was no one ever knew whether it was "Hear" or "Here," because he never wrote it down. He was the biggest thing going in New York in the 1970s and he still wound up in San Diego.

COLUMBIA UNIVERSITY

Al Primo had assembled a tremendous pool of talent. The sports desk alone was enough to make a news director drool. (Cosell,

Gifford, and Bouton!) The mix, though, was what got Al Primo all excited, and it's what eventually made *Eyewitness News* the top local newscast in New York. He had a former foreign correspondent and a tough-talking Korean War vet to sit as anchors. He had a Jew, two blacks, and a woman, and he was looking to make more minority hires. (He would go on to hire several more minority reporters, including John Johnson and Roseanne Scamardella, to cover all the bases.)

I was going to fill the Puerto Rican slot, but not before I learned the ropes. I got a fast (and formidable) education. In 1968, the Ford Foundation heeded the Kerner Commission's call to integration and established a minority training program at Columbia University's Graduate School of Journalism. The idea was that every student in the summer-long program would be recruited by a sponsoring media outlet—print or broadcast— which would then offer that student a job upon graduation. (I think there were about thirty students in the program, probably 90 percent black.) Channel 7 sponsored a slot at Columbia, and that's where I was sent to learn how to stand in front of a camera and talk into a microphone and, after I figured that out, how to shoot, write, craft, and edit a news story.

But first, I had to clean my plate of the encumbrances of the life I was about to leave behind. Almost immediately after accepting Al Primo's offer, I began dismantling my law practice, and disengaging with Julia, who had recently decided to leave the West Coast and move to New York to be with me. She made this decision on her own. She also decided we were going to open up a storefront law practice together—she had had stationery printed up, with both our names on it—and she didn't take the news of my career change too well. She had just reinvented her life, and cast me in a major role. Julia came from a fine, respected family. How I fit into her long-term plans—or why—I'll never know, but she built things up in her head (with the help of my romantic bullshit) to where she needed me and our relationship in place to help her make the adjustment to New York, at least for the next while.

I was looking to cut this new life of hers—ours, she thought— out from under her. She could not accept it. One of the things she had a great deal of trouble with was my decision to go by the name

With my father Allen Cruz Rivera, at Lake Ronkonkoma, 1949. *(Courtesy Geraldo Rivera collection)*

The young Riveras: (left to right) Irene, Sharon, and me.Williamsburg, Brooklyn, 1951. *(Courtesy Geraldo Rivera collection)*

Gerald Rivera

G. Riviera

What's in a name? Yearbook photos from West Babylon High (left) and the University of Arizona reveal Mama's uncertain attempts to "continentalize" the family name. *(Courtesy Geraldo Rivera collection)*

(Left) *With high school steady Mary Pachla, dressed for the senior prom, 1961.* (Courtesy Mary Pachla Silipo) (Right) *Mary Pachla Silipo reappeared in my life thirty years later, as a surprise guest on my show's segment about childhood sweethearts.* (Courtesy Geraldo Rivera collection)

With Linda Coblentz, on my first wedding day, August 20, 1965. (Courtesy Josephine Coblentz)

With lifelong friend Frankie DeCecco, 1972. (Courtesy Mary DeCecco)

*My first summer home and second bride. With Edie Vonnegut, Shelter Island,
New York, 1972.* (Courtesy Geraldo Rivera collection)

With Eyewitness News *colleague Melba
Tolliver at our One-to-One festival in
Central Park, 1972.* (Courtesy Geraldo Rivera collection)

*With Terrence Cardinal Cooke,
Central Park One-to-One festival, 1972.*
(Courtesy Geraldo Rivera collection)

At the 1972 Washington, D.C., party celebrating publication of my Willowbrook book hosted by my secret flame Marian Javits (left to right): father-in-law Kurt Vonnegut, Edie's sister Nanette, Marian, society pal Louis Martinz, Edie, and Senator Jacob Javits.

With John Lennon and Yoko Ono in a San Francisco hotel, 1972. It was sometimes difficult to separate the personal from the professional.

On stage at Madison Square Garden for the second One-to-One benefit concert, with Richie Havens, Rita Coolidge, Kris Kristofferson, Denise Nicholas, and Bill Withers, 1973. *(Courtesy Geraldo Rivera collection)*

With my driver and pal Frank Reardon and the champ Muhammad Ali, at Ali's training camp in Pennsylvania. *(Courtesy Geraldo Rivera collection)*

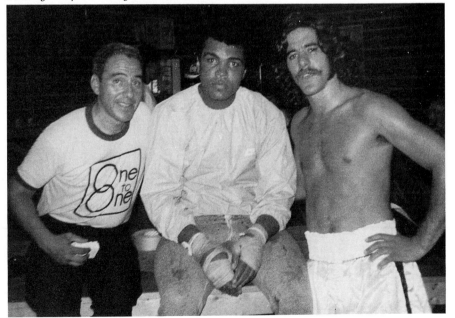

On the Good Night America *set, with super-agent Jerry Weintraub and singer, activist, and friend, John Denver.* (Courtesy Geraldo Rivera collection)

With Bette Midler and Marty Berman at the Friar's Club, 1973. (Courtesy Geraldo Rivera collection)

Doing a stand-up on farm worked by New Jersey migrant workers for the award-winning local news series, "Migrants: Dirt Cheap," 1973. (Courtesy Geraldo Rivera collection)

Cross-promoting the network's Monday Night Football *broadcast, with announcers Howard Cosell, Fred Williamson, and Frank Gifford,* Good Night America, *1974.*
(Courtesy Geraldo Rivera collection)

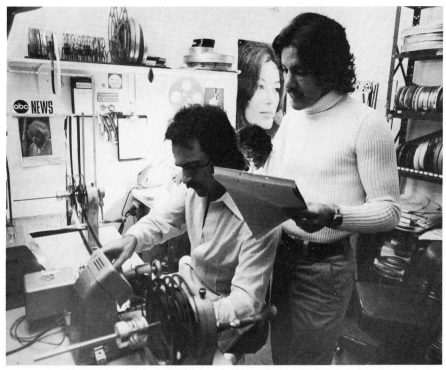

In one of the Eyewitness News *edit rooms, with Marty Berman.* (Courtesy Geraldo Rivera collection)

With Marty Berman, accepting Emmys for "Migrants: Dirt Cheap" and "Working Class Heroes," 1974. (Courtesy Geraldo Rivera collection)

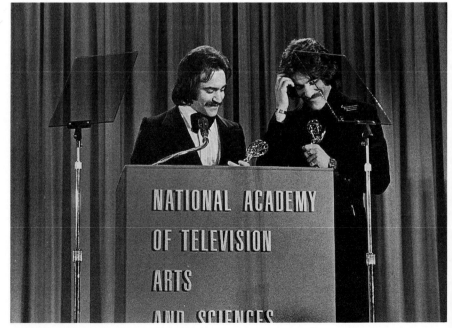

of Geraldo. It may seem like a small thing, now, but it was an indication of how things were between us. And at the time, it was an important change for me, an affirmation of my roots and a signal of the person I had become, but still she resisted it. I remember very clearly telling her not to call me Gerry anymore—on our stationery she had written Gerald Rivera—and she spent the whole rest of the day making fun of the name Geraldo. She'd draw out the name, exaggerating and tripping over the syllables. Mocking. Condescending. I guess she thought it was okay to live with a Puerto Rican and to sleep with him, as long as he did not want to appear to the rest of the world to be too Puerto Rican.

I pushed Julia further and further away. She helped. Or, at least, she didn't do anything to draw close. Her difficulty in accepting my decision to switch careers and to embrace the name Geraldo (and everything that went with that) confirmed that we had no future together. I encouraged her to see other people, which was pretty much a standard tact of mine in breaking things off with a woman. I suppose that by inviting my about-to-be-ex-girlfriends to pursue other relationships, I was hedging against the guilt I would be expected to feel after I was caught in another relationship of my own. She recognized that, and threw it back at me. "When you say freedom for me, what you really mean is freedom for yourself," she'd hurl during one of our suddenly common knock-down-drag-outs.

I would have no response.

We continued to live together, though, and sleep together, which was convenient enough for me, until it led to our biggest complication: Julia got pregnant. Having the baby was never even considered an option, by either one of us. I had walked this block before. By this time, though, in the summer of 1970, abortions had become legal in New York, thanks, in part, to the work of Marcia Robinson Lowry, John De Witt Gregory, and others in my old Community Action for Legal Services office. We all helped to make abortions legal in New York before the Supreme Court ever heard *Roe v. Wade*.

And so, in the early stages of Julia's first trimester, I checked her into the hospital for a safe, clean, legal abortion. I flashed back to that horrible scene out in Brooklyn two years earlier. This time,

Julia was treated like a patient and not a criminal; her health was never in jeopardy. As for me, I did not let myself dwell on the fact that I was losing a child. Mostly I looked on the procedure as an obstacle to get past, an ordeal; I saw it as something that was happening to Julia, and not to me; the abortion, and everything else attached to it, didn't register for what it was.

The last piece of our separation came when Julia left the hospital. I had found a nice apartment for her, at a reasonable rent, and moved her out. Actually, physically, moved her out. I put up the money for the deposit and the security and the moving expenses. It's funny, a little bit, and also sad, and also, maybe, indicative of how things were with us then that I can no longer recall which of us paid for the abortion. I remember I paid to move her out of my apartment, but I don't remember whether or not I paid for the abortion. This strikes me as telling, that I can remember the one and not the other.

I know my recounting here makes me sound like scum, but it was the only way I knew how to deal with things, to break things off with Julia and get on with this new life of mine. I was a different person then; I saw the world through different eyes, acted on different impulses.

And then there were my clients. Severing with them was another thing entirely. Harder, in some ways. Or at least more uncertain. With Julia, I wanted to let go and move on; with my practice, I wasn't so sure. I saw some cases through, and I passed many more on to other lawyers, through CALS, through some colleagues who were looking for extra work, and through some of the major firms who had their younger associates working pro-bono cases. Some of them I even carried with me through the first few weeks of my time at Columbia. A few of the instructors there accused me of double-dipping—drawing my paycheck from WABC and attending classes, while at the same time collecting fees from my fare-beating clients—and they were right. I was having some trouble shutting off one valve for the sake of the other, and, beyond the ambivalence, I was always finding ways to need the extra money the legal work provided. The hundred-dollar fees to appear in court and get a turnstile-jumping client off with a scolding were hard to turn down.

Eventually, though, I settled into the program, and it wasn't too long before Columbia became a kind of haven for me—it was a winding down and a gearing up, both—a much-needed break from the harsh realities of my law practice, of police brutality in the South Bronx, of the stillborn efforts of my militant friends up in Spanish Harlem, of endless poverty and paperwork. The Upper West Side streets enclosing Columbia University were an exciting, revolutionary place to be in the summer of 1970. The campus was in a kind of shambles. The riots of two years earlier were over, but sheets emblazoned with antiwar slogans and minority demands still draped the campus's wrought-iron fences, and hung from dormitory windows. The air was thick with protest, reefer, Black Power, and free love. I suppose it was a lot like most major college campuses in 1970, but it was a long way from my days at the University of Arizona.

The program at Columbia was an accelerated course of study in broadcasting and journalism. I had no background in either, but I quickly developed a flair for both. Actually, what I quickly developed a flair for was the style of the business; the substance came later. The program was under the direction of Fred Friendly, the former president of CBS News who had once served as Edward R. Murrow's producer. In 1971, he was a feisty industry icon and elder statesman. Our instructors were all accomplished members of the press. Alphonso Narvaez wrote obituaries for *The New York Times*; J.J. Gonzales worked for the local CBS television station; Gary Gilson was a fixture in public television; Harry Arah was another CBS refugee from the golden age of Murrow.

My favorite instructor was John Parsons, who became my direct, day-to-day, hands-on advisor. John was a big, round-faced redhead who had changed his name from John Perdito years earlier to gain acceptance in an industry that had not yet embraced ethnicity as an asset. Still, he had an unfailing instinct for almost everything else, including tabloid television, long before the term was even coined. He quickly had us out on mock story assignments, learning by doing. I don't think we were there more than a day or two before we were out covering a breaking story. Our first class assignment was to travel down to Asbury Park, New Jersey, which was then a waning resort city on the Jersey Shore, and the site of a series of riots that summer. The tourist industry there went from waning to finished in what turned out to be a week of disturbances. Half the city and most of the boardwalk were burned by an unexpected uprising of the town's historically complacent black community.

We covered the event as working press, with the chief difference being that our material was seen only by other students, instructors, and, in some instances, by our future employers. We shot footage of the charred amusement area, and of the lingering demonstrations and protests; we interviewed anyone who would talk to us. We did not have enough film to do stand-ups (the industry term for the part of the story where the reporter stands before a relevant backdrop and offers up an intro and outro to the piece), but there was footage of many of us—on-camera, doing interviews—and I remember going back to Columbia and reviewing the material and collecting my share of criticism.

JOHN PARSONS (instructor, Columbia University summer program; former news director, WNEW-TV): Geraldo came to me with certain handicaps. He had a very high, squeaky voice. And he was thin. And I said to him, "Geraldo, you're gonna have to be forceful and powerful," and I gave him tips on how to do that. Close-ups. To unbutton his shirt. Not to wear a tie. To have the camera shoot him low-angle so that he dominated the screen. I thought his appeal would be to women, and he should imagine that he was talking to a woman when he did a report. Let the wind blow in the hair. Be casual. But it was a kind of studied casualness. Remember, these were the first minorities going out there, so it was important that he come on strong. It's like Jackie Robinson. He had to be outstanding, and so I stressed that. And I stressed being original. And looking for causes.

Julia was quickly replaced in my heart, and in my bed, by a beautiful black woman named Michele Clark, a fellow student in the Columbia program who went on to become a correspondent for CBS News. Michele was light-skinned and almost frail-looking, with dark, almond eyes and chiseled features. Her jet-black hair was combed soft and worn long and she walked with a dancer's grace. Michele was from Chicago, and I fell in love in the first hour. To be honest about it, things with Michele started to heat up before Julia moved out of the house; the overlap was only a few weeks, at most, but it seemed like a lot longer at the time.

Michele Clark was probably the brightest student in the Columbia program that summer, certainly the one with the brightest future. I set my sights on her from the very first—after one look at her, it would have been impossible not to—and by the end of that first week there was something going on between us. That was the way I was back then; I saw something I wanted and I went after it.

And so I put myself again into a completely black frame of mind, which in those days of Black Power was an easy, even accepted thing to do. That the majority of my fellow students in the minority program were also black merely meant it was easier for my posturings to go unnoticed. Or, at least, to be quietly tolerated.

In my head I was totally black. I mean, I was as black as Lew Alcindor. Well, at least I was off-black, or near-black, with racial spurs earned over the last three years of street fighting. In truth, I was overwhelmed by racial consciousness. It was us against them, and I made sure Michele Clark saw me as one of us. She had a roommate, Gail Christian, who was from Los Angeles and who was also black, and I took it on myself to show them the town. Gail presented a much tougher image than Michele's, but inside she was as naive about big-city ways as her roommate. I played on their fears and uncertainties, used them to build myself up in their eyes. I would take the ladies any place, at any time. I was fearless. We'd go up to the clubs in Harlem, or down to the Lower East Side. I took them on tours of the red-light districts and the shooting galleries. Anywhere, it didn't matter. The whole city was my turf.

GAIL CHRISTIAN (classmate, Columbia University summer program; former reporter/anchor, KQED-TV San Francisco; KNBC-TV, Los Angeles; PBS documentaries): Geraldo was the cutest boy in the class, with no doubt. And he had this little blue Volkswagen convertible, which absolutely made him the star. This was the first time I had lived in New York, and I remember Geraldo taking us down to what was to me the rattiest neighborhood I had ever laid eyes on in my life, to show us where he lived. And when you opened the door, you know, here was this chic, upscale apartment, with some tree growing out of the center of the floor, if I'm not mistaken. He could always say he lived downtown, with the people, but when you walked inside, it was quite an apartment. And he already had a deal with the local ABC station. I remember he had this ABC blazer, with a seven on the pocket. We all knew that we were going to get jobs, but at that point nobody had actually reported to the place they were going to work. Geraldo was already on the payroll, so he was kind of the class star because of that.

My family didn't say much to me during this time about my choice of relationship. (Come to think of it, they didn't say much about my career change, either, other than to worry that my legal education had been a waste of time and money.) As far as Michele was concerned, I think my father could relate to what I was going through (he did, after all, fall for my mother, a nice Jewish girl), and my mother had the good sense to keep quiet. She knew I was going through a lot of changes in my life, and probably thought that this Black Power kick would pass. (It's likely she also thought I'd soon return to being a lawyer.)

Michele Clark and I were all over each other that summer. We went to classes together and took our meals together and edited stories together and studied together. We even lived together, sort of, as together as circumstances allowed.

JOHN PARSONS: They were very close, and she was so talented that she was a challenge for him. I would play Michele off Geraldo. I would always say to Geraldo, "Michele's going to be a star. You're going to have to struggle." I was always pitting her against him. And I think, because he was so competitive, that it was natural for him to want to shine, to want to be the best coming out of that class.

By the end of the program, we were so caught up in each other that Michele was prepared to walk away from her prospective job at WBBM-TV, the CBS-owned and -operated station in Chicago, just to stay in New York to be with me. I couldn't believe it. That kind of thinking was so foreign to me then. Here she had this marvelous opportunity unfolding in front of her; it was the choicest job offered to anyone in the program. *CBS Morning News*—the network!—also wanted her, and she wanted to chuck it all to marry me. She told me she didn't care if she was a housewife, as long as we could be together. It was hard to fit those emotions to the strong-willed and competent young woman I had fallen for just three months earlier, but this is what she wanted. Or, at least, what she said she wanted.

"You can't do this," I told her. "You have to go, you have to go back." I promised her I'd write her, reminded her that New York and Chicago were only short plane-rides apart, that we would both be earning enough money to see each other frequently. But I didn't write her; once she'd gone, I didn't even call. We never saw each other. What was the sense of it? was how I thought things out at the time. What was the point? When I started at Channel 7, I knew, I'd be onto something, someone else. Women were fun to me then. I'd move from one to the next. Those were the days of free love, and my attitude was you did the best you could for your partner as long as she was your partner. That was where the obligations ended. A failed marriage had taught me that to restrict yourself in some kind of synthetic way was unnatural and stupid.

I was a weak person when it came to women, especially in the summer of 1970, when the prevailing moral code let you screw around with anyone you wanted to. But Michele was by no means one of the interchangeable women in my life. Not at all. She was special, just not special enough that I would pledge long-distance fidelity. No one was that special. We hadn't even said good-bye when I was already looking around for her replacement.

Michele Clark took the job in Chicago and began to blaze a remarkable career of her own, a career that came to a tragic end before it ever had a chance to really get started. Two years later I was married again and living with my wife Edie in a duplex apartment on the top two floors of a West Village brownstone. On Saturday, December 9, 1972, as was my weekend custom, I woke up early and walked the long block to the nearest newsstand, on Seventh Avenue and West Eleventh Street. I bought a copy of *The*

New York Times and a container of coffee and then I walked home and sat on the front porch of my building and flipped open the paper. What I read hit me like a kick in the nuts. There, on the front page, was news that Michele was presumed dead, along with forty-five other people (including Democratic Congressman George W. Collins, and the wife of E. Howard Hunt, one of the seven men indicted in the Watergate break-in several months earlier), in the crash of a United Airlines jet on Chicago's Southwest Side.

I was absolutely devastated by the news and I read the front page again hoping it would tell me something else, something different. With my current marriage already in shambles, Michele's death caused lingering feelings of loss. She would have been bigger, better, and more beautiful than any of today's crop of top female reporters. She could have been the one to shake me from the infidelity and instability of my romantic relationships. I flipped to the continuation of the story and found a picture of Michele, my Michele, smiling back at me. I let myself be devastated all over again. I sat there on my porch, on that cool West Village morning, and cried.

CITY COLLEGE, SOUTH CAMPUS

I had to borrow my father's overcoat, and one of his old sharkskin suits, for my first day of work at WABC-TV. My wardrobe was completely unprepared for a life on the public stage of television; I was only slightly better prepared. My father's coat and suit were all the way out of fashion. Plus, the sharkskin suit shined ridiculously under the studio's bright lights. Basically, I looked like a kid who had borrowed his dad's clothes for his first day of work.

The first story I covered for Channel 7 was on the Tuesday after Labor Day, my first day on the job. It also happened to be the day of the Democratic primaries in New York State. I was assigned to interview the losing candidate in the race for the attorney general nomination, a typical rookie assignment. I asked the guy all the right questions, and stood and listened as he gave all the pat, expected answers. Then I did a stand-up, and a fancy wraparound, and sat around and waited to see how I looked on television.

If I was waiting on that piece, I never would have found out. They wound up cutting me out of the story, and excerpting a couple of sound bites from the losing (and soon to be forgotten) candidate. One of the anchors read a lead-in, which I did not write, and then there were a couple quotes from this guy, and that was it. I had spent the better part of a day at campaign headquarters, waiting around for my interview, and most of what we shot ended up on the editing-room floor. This, I was told, was the way things worked. It might take a while for my face, and my voice, to actually get on the air.

Thankfully, I did not have to wait too long. I was assigned to do a story on truancy later on during my first few weeks, and the way I chose to do it was to sit down on a stoop in front of a tenement building with a bunch of truants and ask them why they weren't in school. Simple. Direct. Clean. We found a group of kids almost right away who were willing to sit down for a few minutes and talk. There was a stretch of Sixty-seventh Street, between Broadway and Amsterdam Avenue, that was a holdout in the gentrification of the surrounding neighborhood. It was only a block away from our offices at 77 West Sixty-sixth Street, and it was there that I chose to do the stand-up (or, more accurately, sit-down) portion of the piece.

It never occurred to me to do the story any other way. I mean, if the viewer was going to come away with any kind of sense of what these kids were about—what frustrated them about the system, what excited them, what drove them away—then the reporter had to be down with them, relating to them, without the false walls put up by a suit and a tie and the conventional newsgathering techniques that went with them.

So I rolled up my sleeves and sat down. These kids just opened up to me, and what we came away with was tough, emotional, and honest. It was real, and it was unlike anything I had ever seen on television dealing with street kids, poverty, and related subjects, but keep in mind I had not seen much. I did not know a thing about what made good television, but this was good, I thought. It was also natural for me, easy. I came away from the interview thinking, I'm gonna do okay.

Al Primo was ecstatic when he saw the cut piece. He had never seen a reporter get involved like this before. The way I actually sat down with these kids, on the stoop there, just floored Al, and his enthusiasm extended to the rest of the newsroom brass. I couldn't look up from my desk in the bustling newsroom without catching some congratulations from news management. I also caught my share of jealousies and resentments from my new colleagues. (This was to mark the beginning of a lot of personal tension in the newsroom.)

I'd made my first splash, and it was a cannonball. I still don't fully grasp how revolutionary this approach must have seemed to my bosses. My approach was just the obvious, natural way to go about getting the story. If I had solicited opinions before I went around the block to Sixty-seventh Street, somebody would have tried to talk me out of what I had in mind. It just wasn't the way things were done. It was too involved. In 1970, reporters were still judged by their objectivity, by their ability to remain detached, cool, even superior to a story and its subjects. The ideal was still the WASP network correspondent, expert-seeming with some knowledge hidden in his three-piece suit, dispassionately collecting information and passing it on to the viewer.

But I didn't make a conscious decision to reinvent the wheel. I had never studied any reporter at work, nor plotted a way to distance myself and stand out from the other beat reporters. I just looked at the problem—how to get the story—and this is what I came up with.

BOB ALIS (former WABC-TV cameraman): I learned, after a while, that Geraldo was willing to gamble. He would extend himself more than most reporters. I remember we went to Spanish Harlem and we were doing a thing on drugs and we walked into an abandoned house where there were some junkies and he goes over to one of them, with the cameras rolling, and he says, "Show me your track-marks." And with that he takes the guy's arm and lifts up his sleeve. And in those days you just didn't do that. Most reporters would not walk onto a junkie's turf. But Geraldo had a theory. We used to talk about this. You can walk into Gestapo headquarters, with the camera rolling and the light on, and you've got a minute, maybe two minutes to get in and get out before they realize you're on their turf and they can take you. Geraldo didn't know how things were being done. He was just going by his instincts.

* * *

Instinct got me through those first assignments, and I was lucky enough to have an on-target gut. I recently looked at tapes of some of my earliest work and came away surprised (and somewhat embarrassed) at how similar it was to my work today. I was brand-new at the job, and yet fell right into a way and feel that was right for me, natural. I never looked for a style, or a signature, but in just being honest and straightforward I found the foundation for a career.

But instinct, alone, does not make a career. It doesn't even make a good story. You also need luck. Occasionally, the good luck runs bad, and I've had my share of both. (Bad judgments, too, also mixed with the good.) Curiously, that same block where we shot my talked-about truancy story was a few weeks later the site of my first professional humiliation. The two locations could not have been more than a hundred yards apart. On the same side of the street even. And what happened to bring me down a few slats happened for the same reasons that made my truancy story such a runaway success: I didn't know any better.

I had spent the better part of a day in the Bronx on a housing story—it was something about the razing of a tenement, if I remember—and I interviewed the landlord, and the demolition company, and the people who were being evicted. I talked to everybody and covered everything. I had only been on the job for three weeks, but my footage, I knew, was complete. The one thing I didn't return to the newsroom with was stand-up footage with me posing in front of the targeted building. We didn't always do stand-ups in those days—film was far more expensive than videotape has become—and nobody told me to bring back anything other than the interview footage. My understanding was the piece would have a lead-in from Roger Grimsby or Bill Beutel, and that would be it. Every stand-up I had done on previous assignments had been specifically requested.

At about four-thirty in the afternoon, just an hour and a half before air, the assignment editor decided we were going to give the story more play than originally thought. The truancy story had generated a lot of positive response on my behalf, and management must have seen this housing story as a chance to generate more of the same. (It was probably also a slow newsday, and they needed to fill more time.)

Whatever the reasoning, we needed a stand-up, I was told, but we didn't have time to send me, with a crew, all the way up to the Bronx and return with the film in time for the broadcast. The editor suggested I go around the block to one of the tenement buildings on Sixty-seventh, and do the stand-up in front of a high-rise there. They told me not to say, "This is Geraldo Rivera, reporting from the Bronx," or anything to identify my location, just to introduce the story and go into the packaged material.

This I did.

The story wasn't on the air five minutes before the residents of that stretch of Sixty-seventh Street called the station complaining. Loudly. One older woman actually spotted herself on our broadcast, leaning out her window and looking on at the crew. The callers were appalled by the implication that they lived in condemned Bronx tenements, and they had every right to be. I was too young, too green, and too stupid to know any better.

Obviously, in retrospect, what we did showed an incredible lack of integrity and journalistic ethics, but at the time, I just figured if this guy on the assignment desk told me to do this then it must be standard operating procedure. What did I know? The incident was not about staging, or deceiving the audience, at least not from my perspective. From where I sat, it was about a young, green kid doing what he was told without stopping to think about it.

Nevertheless, the fallout from this piece was painful. Dozens of callers lambasted me, and the block committee wrote an angry letter of condemnation. With Congress already investigating charges of rigged news coverage throughout the industry, management could not have been more embarrassed if I had been caught pissing in Central Park. The outside press never picked up on the gaffe, but the in-house criticism was severe. I tendered my resignation. I still had a legal case or two kicking around my desk at home, and I was only a few months removed from what could have become a thriving (or, at least busy) law practice. I figured I could start things up again there without much problem. Maybe I wasn't cut out for this journalism business, I started to think. I had never really been formally trained. We never covered this at

Columbia. What I learned at Columbia was mostly technical; it was a fast how-to course and what I now needed to learn was how-come.

And so I offered to resign. Maybe I'd made a mistake, I thought, maybe it wasn't too late to double-back and pick up where I left off as a lawyer. I was, for the first time in a long time, completely unsure of myself and the decisions I'd made.

Al Primo would not accept my resignation, but he did suspend me—though, it wasn't for more than a few days. It was just a slap on the wrist, really, but at the time it was like a multiple compound fracture. "Stick it out," he said, "you've only been in the business three weeks. Give it a year."

The guy on the assignment desk wound up taking most of the heat for what happened; his suspension, I think, ran a little bit longer. I remember a long conversation with Al Ittleson, who at the time was the executive producer of the broadcast, which consisted mainly of me wondering if I should go back to being a lawyer, if I'd acted too quickly in giving up my practice. I didn't understand all this, I said. The world of broadcast journalism was still as foreign to me as it was when I didn't watch television. He told me to calm down, go home, use the suspension time to just take a breather, and then come back and forget it ever happened. "Just remember," he said, "we don't do that around here."

It was quite a lesson. In just three weeks at the station, I'd gone from a rising star to a fallen one, and the stories that led to each, turned on the same block, on the same side of the street, and on the same impulse.

There was another story, early on, that almost cost me my job. I was sent out to do a piece on the increasingly widespread use of heroin among the white, middle class. To show how easy it was to buy heroin, I took a crew to the south campus of City College and purchased two-dollars' worth of the stuff from a street pusher. On camera. The piece made quite a stir, and it also made its point: Heroin had reached down to where we could not look away from it. To my mind, it was an effective and telling use of the medium. Management saw things a little differently; I was suspended for committing a felony, even though I was never charged by the city for the same offense. The standards of my new profession were tougher than the criminal code.

After these two fiascos, the assignment desk started to send me out on softer stories. Most of the pieces I had done up until then had a kind of edge to them, a grit, and it seemed to me that news management had a sudden rethinking on what my role would be. Already nervous about my radical political history, I think they began to see me as too much of a loose cannon, too unpredictable. Over the next weeks, I gradually became a kind of lifestyle reporter. I bounced on a waterbed with some scantily clad models. I reported from the car show at the New York Coliseum. I covered the birth of a bear at the zoo. I rode an elephant in the procession announcing the New York arrival of the Ringling Brothers Circus.

It became clear to me what they were doing: keeping me as far away as possible from anything that was potentially controversial. They were defusing me. Everything "hard" went to someone else; everything "soft" had my name on it. I don't remember thinking that I was being sold out, or feeling any kind of righteous outrage at the directions my career was taking. I don't even remember feeling then that the botched tenement stand-up had directly led to this sidetracking of my career.

What I do remember, very clearly, is telling myself, hey, this is a good-paying job, just cash their checks and keep your mouth shut. I still had great expectations for myself, and thought I could still accomplish these things through television, despite this loss of momentum. Also, I convinced myself I could still be as relevant as I wanted to be in real life.

THE TOMBS

It wasn't always easy to separate real life from television. Real life came close to bumping me off the air, on several occasions. The first came in October of 1970, just a month after I'd started at Channel 7. Mayor John Lindsay appointed me and five other community leaders (including William J. vanden Heuvel, a former assistant to Attorney General Robert Kennedy, to serve as chairman) to fill six Board of Corrections slots that had been left vacant for up to five years.

The Board of Corrections had essentially been dormant for the better part of a decade, and the mayor was responding—somewhat belatedly—to heated cries of overcrowding and mistreatment in city jails. Toward the end of the summer of 1970, there had also been a series of riots and uprisings in the Manhattan House of Detention—The Tombs—and other city jails, and these incidents also led the mayor to wake the board from its slumber.

Mayor Lindsay knew me mainly through my work with the Young Lords. He had actually come to my apartment on Avenue C the previous year. It was shortly after I'd bought the apartment and renovated it, and he was taking one of his tours of the Lower East Side. He often did that. And somehow my decision to live in the middle of this urban wasteland had worked its way up through his administration to where he wanted to stop by to see for himself how I was singlehandedly performing a redevelopment miracle on Avenue C.

He came unannounced, surrounded by the press, his hyperactive aides, and top police department officials, and I literally had to race out back ahead of them all to place a garbage can over a marijuana plant I had growing in my backyard. I opened the door, and then I remembered about the plant and thought, "Oh, shit!" I was sure they'd see it and recognize it for what it was. I was frantic, but trying to act casually. Now, this was 1969, and I knew many in Lindsay's administration smoked dope, but there I was, frantic that the charismatic and popular mayor of New York would see my pot plant. It was a pretty funny scene. I really thought I'd be found out, and disbarred, or sent to jail; worse, I'd be held out to ridicule. There was a part of me that said I was being ridiculous, but there was another part that was afraid for my career and reputation.

I chose to accept the nonsalaried Board of Corrections position, with considerable misgivings. I knew I was tapped at the militant urgings of the Young Lords to advocate for the large Hispanic population in the city prison system, and because of that, I felt a great deal of responsibility to my people. I thought I might be able to use the position on the board to bring about some positive change. I was honored to have been asked and felt a certain call to duty to meet the challenge.

I was also concerned that there might arise a conflict with my new position as a television newsman. The conflict, as I saw it, was twofold. The first: There might arise an issue that commanded the board's attention at the same time it commanded my assignment editor's. The second conflict was more relevant to me than any potential clash between journalistic ethics and public service. I was deeply concerned that the more public my involvement on the board became, the more I would seem to viewers as a part of the very establishment I was railing against as a newsman. This was a self-centered view, I know, but it was how things looked to me then. There were a lot of problems in New York City, and I did not want to be seen as a part of any one of them, even if I might have been able to help alleviate it. I was building a new image, and a new career, and they were each tied up in the same thing: my emerging reputation as a people reporter.

Nevertheless, I went forward, over the objections of station management and against the advice of some of the people I had come to trust during my short tenure at WABC-TV. I also went against what would have been my own better judgment. One of my first public stands as a member of the board, curiously, was on behalf of black activist Angela Davis. The board had jurisdiction over the Women's House of Detention, a brick high-rise in the heart of Greenwich Village. Davis was being held there in November 1970, on murder and kidnapping charges. She sued the city over her being placed in solitary confinement (where she was kept, ostensibly, for her own safety), and I stepped in and supported her demand to be let out into the general prison population, or released on reasonable bail. I toured the facility the day after she filed suit and interviewed the guards and inmates there and found no good reason why the notorious radical had to be separated from the rest of the prison population. "None of the inmates expressed any animosity or hostility toward Angela Davis," I stated in my affidavit.

I also argued in court against Davis's multimillion-dollar bail. It was an excessive amount then (as it would still be today), and I argued bitterly and vehemently for a lower figure. The Young Lords, members of the Black Panthers, and a corps of white radicals filled the courtroom to echo their disapproval. Ultimately, our pleas were heard, and Davis was released on bail. I don't know how instrumental I was in freeing Angela Davis, but I did succeed in creating a circus in that courtroom. And I relished the role of ringmaster, even though my actions overstepped the privilege afforded by my position on the Board of Corrections, just as it overstepped my position as a newsman.

WILLIAM J. vanden HEUVEL (former chairman, New York City Board of Corrections): Geraldo was concerned about the television reponsibilities that he had, and he was also concerned about being identified with the prisons, or with the government, at all. He felt that he had to take an outside position, even though he felt that we were doing a fantastic job, confronting the establishment and bringing about reforms. He was only a member of the board for a few months, as I recall it.

I resigned not long after I signed on. I was too conflicted to stay and give the board the attention and enthusiasm it deserved. My resignation letter was published in *The New York Times*, and one of the things I wrote about, and protested about, were the conditions of The Tombs, which I had inspected as a member of the board. The facility has since been closed, but The Tombs then was almost a medieval place. A Depression-Era relic, the high-rise prison adjacent to Manhattan's Criminal Court Building was thick-walled and heavily barred, and painted in this horrible, institutional green. The living conditions were abominable, and often inhumane. The cells were six feet by eight feet, with three and sometimes four prisoners to a cell. Inmates were locked in their cells for at least twenty-two hours a day. The wards were potentially explosive.

"For a hesitant moment, the lid on the garbage can is lifted," I wrote. "We look inside, see and smell the muck we've probably known was in there all along, experience the appropriate shock, revulsion, and shame, and then move on to the next garbage can, changing nothing. . . . I take that back. One thing has changed. We can no longer pretend that, like the good Germans of another era, we don't know what is going on inside The Tombs. Now we know—but we'll forget."

I was also slow to recognize that my position at *Eyewitness*

News could not shake me from my activist roots, but it could (and should have, and finally did) reshape the manner and method of my activism.

THE GREENWICH HOTEL

Television was a role I was playing, and a good-paying gig. In real life, I knew, I could still effect change, or shed light on injustice and indignity, even if, on television, all I could seem to do was ride elephants and jump on water beds.

But instead of defusing me by assigning me to soft, feature-type stories, the assignment desk gave my career a jump-start. These lifestyle stories started to bring a kind of fame that my first street and political pieces did not. I didn't plan on it, but I began to develop a persona. It was a lightweight persona, true, but it was more noticeable than any I'd ever had before. I felt sure it had to lead to something. People began to recognize me on the street. I started to get fan mail. Within about three months, by December 1970, I was the most popular street reporter on the *Eyewitness News* team.

The routine was basically the same from one day to the next. I would usually do two different stories for the six o'clock news, and then a third story for the eleven o'clock broadcast. If a six o'clock story was big enough, we'd recut it for the eleven. I kept my apartment on Avenue C, but I basically lived in and around the newsroom in those first months. I used to get to work by subway in those days, and later, by motorcycle. (I had replaced my old Ducati with a 500-cc Honda that was small enough to fit in my hallway.) My workday started at about ten in the morning, and ran until about eleven-thirty at night, after which I'd go out partying until early morning. In those days before disco, I'd either be at a private party, or one of the neighborhood's many jazz and blues clubs. I was coming and going at all hours, and the neighborhood I lived in was still the pits, a real contrast from the new places I'd found. On the way to my high-profile, high-paying job, I'd have to pass by the poorest people in America, and I would pass them again on my way home from a hot night-spot or after-hours party.

I kept the apartment, I think, because it kept me grounded; as long as I lived on Avenue C, I would never forget how low I had been or lose sight of how high I was climbing.

My world was in tremendous flux. I had gone from being a young activist attorney, to a would-be advocacy journalist, to a short-term member of a civilian review board monitoring the city's criminal justice system, to a society-page personality in the space of a few months. I had a lot to figure out, and at the same time I had to find a place for myself in the soap opera of the newsroom. I've never been too great about fitting in, and the Channel 7 newsroom became a clear and telling example. Almost as soon as my popularity began to eclipse that of my colleagues, I began to experience a kind of resentment in the newsroom. Some of the reporters, like Bill Aylward and Duke Wade, would literally turn their backs if I asked them a question. Help and advice that were here and there offered when I arrived in the newsroom were now offered grudgingly, or not at all.

The cold shoulders even extended to the anchor desk. Roger Grimsby would regularly try to trip me up during the broadcasts. He would change a scripted lead-in, or ask me a bizarre or tangentially related question he knew I would have a tough time answering, just to see me squirm in living color. He was notorious for this with every reporter, but he seemed to kick it up a notch when it involved me. Others commented that it seemed like he was out to get me, show me up. Over time, though, as I grew more comfortable on camera, I actually came to enjoy this sparring with Roger. It kept me on my toes and alert, and I took it as a challenge. I began to see it as something different from the cold treatment I received in other parts of the newsroom, because I thought I could detect a trace of respect coming from the other side of the duel. With the others, it was more like I was stealing their spotlight, or making them look bad. With Grimsby, it was a high-wire sword fight, and the wily veteran seemed to enjoy the matchup.

I did develop good working friendships with some of my colleagues. Melba Tolliver and Gil Noble became friends, partly, I suspect, because we all wore the same minority stamp. We were in the same boat and all needed help paddling against the current. Among the white establishment, only hard-working Doug Johnson was smart enough to see that my lightweight successes were in no way a threat to his career. But these friendships were very much the exception. For the most part, I kept to myself. Maybe it was emotional self-defense, but I began to look on this unhappy band of Geraldo-haters as mediocre underachievers. I no longer cared what they thought of me.

AL PRIMO: I tried very hard to establish a team spirit, a family environment there. But we had a lot of rules. I mean, everybody had to wear jackets with sevens on them, and everybody had to have a shirt and a tie. Roger Grimsby, and others were critical of that, but it was Geraldo who did away with it. One day Geraldo showed up, you know, in a turtleneck or something, and he looked very good in it. It looked right on him. And so we just bent the rules a little bit. And of course, there was some resentment about that. They were all like, "Oh, why do I have to wear a shirt and a tie if he doesn't?" And I'd say, "At *Eyewitness News* everybody is equal, and some are more equal than others." They knew what that was all about.

The bigger I got, the more I got paid. My salary, when I started out, was three hundred dollars a week. My five-year contract called for a fifty-dollar-a-week raise at the end of each year. The catch— and I didn't know this when I signed, but figured it out soon enough—was that three hundred dollars a week was less than the union minimum. In working for scale, I received a per-story fee on top of my weekly salary. I think I earned an extra twenty-seven dollars for every story that carried my voice; if my image was on camera, in a stand-up or interview, the story was worth a few dollars more.

This came to a lot of money, particularly with the kind of volume I was cranking out. I was nearly doubling my salary with these on-air fees. The six o'clock show had only recently been expanded to an hour, and filling it was a daunting challenge to the assignment editors. They saw it as a pound of program to deliver everyday, even if it was a slow newsday. I saw it as another eighty bucks.

Being on the air as often as I was paid other kinds of dividends. It led directly to a chance story that pulled me by the short hairs right off the lifestyle beat. In February 1971, I was sent out to cover a denim fashion show at the Greenwich Hotel on Bleecker Street. It was a typical assignment for me at that time. It was a Friday night, and I remember thinking ahead to my plans for later in the evening, and for the weekend. The story was just a routine chore, a detail that stood between me and the end of my week. I had gotten to where I could do these by rote.

I was with Edgar Price, one of my regular cameramen. There was also a lighting man with us (in those days, we always traveled with a lighting man), and a sound man. Edgar had been in Vietnam as a combat photographer, before he landed at Channel 7. This guy was built like a brick shithouse. He needed all that heft and muscle, because in those days he had to tote around two cameras: a sixteen-millimeter Auricon, with big film magazines, mounted on a big, heavy wooden tripod; and a Filmo, a crank windup sixteen-millimeter silent camera. Edgar walked with the Filmo in his right hand, and the Auricon on its wooden tripod in his left, and the load wasn't near enough to make him grunt.

A crowd was gathered there on Bleecker Street. People were pointing up, riveted to the roof of the hotel. It didn't take too long to figure. Someone was about to jump. I stammered something to Edgar, but he was already filming with the silent camera. And just as the camera started to roll, the guy jumped. Edgar caught the whole thing, right down to where the guy smacked the pavement, just a few yards in front of us.

It was horrible, but it was also news. Edgar had the kind of footage you lead broadcasts with, a big story. Then, another remarkable thing happened. The jumper's twin brother came running out of the hotel. He recognized me immediately. I was someone familiar, comfortable, and he grabbed me by the lapels and started telling his story. He trusted me because of the intimacy and immediacy of television.

Edgar started rolling with the big camera, the sound man plugged in. The kid was frantic, and it was not yet clear that his brother was dead, but still he kept babbling. He told me that his father was a Marine Corps colonel, that he and his twin brother were heroin addicts, that they'd been holed up in the hotel for a few weeks. He said they'd worked their way east from Southern California on a cross-country odyssey, ripping people off whenever they needed money to buy drugs to make the next leg of the trip. I learned later that many suicide victims travel west, and jump off the Golden Gate Bridge, but these brothers were heading to the flip side for the same dark reason. After two weeks in a New York hotel room—shooting up, watching television, whatever—these guys were so strung out, out of touch, and desperate that one just said, "Fuck it."

The brother was holding tight to my shirt as he talked, gripped by the heroin and by the emotion of what he was going through. He was sweating, shaking. At times it seemed he was all there and lucid, and at times it seemed like he was not. His words came fast, and then slow. Everything about the unfolding scene was hellishly dramatic. I was torn between trying to keep him talking—it was, I knew, an incredible story—and directing his attention to his brother. I wanted to shake him from his ramblings and yell, "Go to your brother, man. Don't talk to me." But I didn't. I just let him talk, and when he stopped I asked questions to fill up the pause.

Paramedics arrived at the scene, and then the kid shifted his attention. We followed them to the hospital, without a thought for the denim fashion show. When the jumper was finally pronounced dead, the brother came out and talked to me some more. This time I put my heart into it, and my head. I had no real experience interviewing someone under these kinds of circumstances, but I knew junkies, and I knew how to get them to talk. I asked this kid everything: Where were you getting the dope? How much were you taking? How much were you spending? Who were you ripping off? Did you rip off your own family? Did you hurt anybody? What did your brother say to you before he jumped? I surrounded his story. I'm sure a more experienced reporter could have also gotten a story out of this kid, but he might have gotten a lesser story: less raw, less true.

During the interview, I kept thinking of something John Parsons had drummed into me at Columbia. Throughout the summer program, Parsons constantly stressed the importance of making the most of your opportunities, of not letting a story get away. To illustrate, he would tell a story about Adam Clayton Powell, a charismatic black ex-congressman from Harlem.

Powell slandered a woman in his district, calling her a bag lady (before the term referred to homelessness), and linking her to neighborhood drug pushers. The woman sued, and was awarded $250,000 in damages. Powell never showed up to defend himself and refused to pay any attention to the verdict. He tried to ignore the whole thing, hoping it would go away. He was ultimately held in contempt of Congress, impeached, and thrown out of office. Powell eventually went into hiding on the island of Bimini. A young CBS reporter tracked him there and secured an interview. It was developing as the biggest story in the country at the time, and a tremendous scoop. But not in the hands of this reporter, who asked Powell three or four questions and then left.

What John Parsons told me was that if I ever found my Adam Clayton Powell, if I ever got an opportunity like that, I had better seize it. Be prepared. Don't blow it. Don't just ask three or four questions and leave. Ask everything. Forget nothing.

That's what I kept thinking when I was interviewing this kid: Ask everything. Seize it. Don't blow it. It kicked right in. I was asking questions, and listening, and underneath it all I was thinking, "Don't let this kid get away."

This was my Adam Clayton Powell.

I knew in my heart I was too big for the hole they'd put me in at *Eyewitness News.* I was ready for something else, and I knew that something else was coming. If it wasn't this story for me, it would have been another. I also believe that in the hands and heart of another reporter, this same set of circumstances would have resulted in an entirely different story. The old-guard television reporter would have booted it, because his approach would have been textbook and predictable. This kid needed someone to hear him, someone to bounce off. He needed me. He started to pour his heart out, and I pulled the rest.

The story led the eleven o'clock newscast that night. I knew it was special, but Gil Noble was the first to tip me to how special. The next day was Saturday, and I had the day off, but Gil was assigned to do the follow-up story. He looked at the footage and then he called and said, "Take that story and put it in your hat. Treasure it. They don't come around like that too often."

The newsroom was nearly empty when the story aired on Friday (as it always is for the eleven o'clock broadcast, particularly on Fridays), and so Gil's was one of the few voices of genuine enthusiasm and congratulations. I also heard from Bill Aylward, fast becoming my leading newsroom nemesis. He took Gil's sentiments and twisted them around to where you could hardly recognize them. "You'll never have a story like that again, pal," he challenged. "You got lucky."

The story created a major stir, but it was diluted by the time I got back to work on Monday. That is not to say the piece did not have a major impact on my career; it did, but by Monday it was basically old news. Gil was never able to find the brother for his follow-up, and the story died. That's what happens in the television news business. Great stories are like perfectly blown smoke rings: For a few seconds they hold their shape, and their grace, and then they start to dissipate and disappear.

But the smoke ring held long enough to change the way management saw my role at *Eyewitness News*. My career just metamorphosed. Literally overnight. I was transformed from the denim fashion reporter, the elephant-riding, water-bed-bouncing feature guy, into the hard-core ghetto reporter. It was that sudden, and dramatic; the story had as profound an impact on my career as any other I would ever cover. From Al Primo and Al Ittleson on down to the assistant assignment editors, it was thereafter acknowledged that the street was my turf. No one in the newsroom could go out to the frontlines and come back with what I could. No one in the city could deliver the same goods.

I was made roving ambassador to this new, uncharted territory. It's not only that I got different assignments, but the assignment editors began to yield to my judgment. I was suddenly allowed, and encouraged, to do original reporting, to go out on stories that I dug up and felt passionate about. If there was a drama unfolding that I wanted to document, or if there was a wrong I wanted to try to set right, I was given a crew and time on the newscast to tell the story. Keep in mind, in those days, the only time cameras were sent into ghetto areas was when something extraordinary was happening (riots, fires, mass murders), and usually only when some white authority figure (cops, firemen, National Guardsmen, city administrators) had established temporary jurisdiction. The New York City that was typically covered in the early 1970s ran from Ninety-sixth Street to the Village, with exceptions made to include the highways and airports. There were huge, densely populated areas of the city that were being ignored—the East Village, Harlem, the outer boroughs.

And so I was set loose on the city's vast nonwhite population, on its meanest streets. I had found my beat and I was out to change the world.

CHAPTER FIVE

EAST 100TH STREET

One of the first stories under my new hat of ghetto reporter was a three-part series called "Drug Crisis in East Harlem," which later ran as a half-hour special. It was a signature story for me. The idea came to me through my old law school friend Danny Goldfarb, who was working as a parole officer while trying a second and third time to pass the New York State bar exam. The fourth try was the charm for Danny, but his second and third tries were the charms for me. One of his paroled clients was this small-time drug dealer named Charlie, who ultimately gave us the first real look at the world of young addicts.

"Drug Crisis in East Harlem" was a series of day-in-the-life profiles of Charlie and two other junkies. The three of them lived on the same block on East 100th Street, between First and Second avenues—at the time, the single worst block in New York City— and I wanted to shine a light on this particular darkness.

Each of the junkies was eighteen years old, and we followed them like shadows. We followed them around the tenement hallways and stairwells, when they were shooting up. We followed them up to the tenement rooftops. We followed them buying dope. We followed them at home. We saw the world through their eyes, at least for a little bit. It was gripping. We used long lenses and shot through the darkened windows of a van, trying to give viewers a sense of a typical day in the lives of these kids. A report like this is pretty standard today (particularly with the low-cost availability of hidden microphones and cameras), but in 1971, nobody had eavesdropped so closely on the hard-core drug scene; in fact, nobody had ever attempted to bring viewers, up-close and personal, into a world so completely removed from their own.

The keys to the story, though, were the three kids. They really talked. The pictures weren't anything without the words to go with them. These were some of the first in-your-face interviews I ever did, and they would eventually become a speciality. I was wearing my tough-guy clothes and chewing gum, and I pushed these kids until they broke and gave me what I wanted. I remember everyone was so afraid of junkies in the early 1970s. There was all this talk about how they would kill their own mothers to get money to buy dope, about how they were violent, subhuman, and heartless, and a lot of that was true. But I walked into this story the same way I walked the streets of the city: I put on a head that told me there wasn't a junkie in America who could stand up to me.

I was very aggressive with these kids. I pushed, probed, and bullied them into revealing something of themselves, something of why they lived the way they lived. I tried to get them to tell me where their lives were going, and how they thought they were going to get there. I actually, physically, pushed these kids on camera to get them to open up; I had my hands on them constantly during the interviews, in a manner that was challenging and confrontational. A part of me thought it was my job to beat a confession out of them.

What we came away with was a great piece of illuminating journalism. It was a call to the people of New York to take a hard look at their own neighborhoods, their own children, to find the core of the emerging and devastating drug problem. It was good television and it was a classic example of the type of people-reporting that nobody else was doing.

People responded. The authorities overreacted. That block of East 100th Street was completely razed shortly after the series aired. We might not have made the drug problem go away, but we made that block go away. And we won awards, among them the prestigious Columbia DuPont Award (bestowed at a black-tie affair at my recent alma mater), and the New York State Associated Press Broadcasters Award for General Excellence in Individual Reporting. The citation for the A.P. award called the series "a moving account of disillusionment, hopelessness, and degradation of not only the addicts themselves but the very slum conditions that encircled their lives."

The success of "Drug Crisis in East Harlem" led to the second of my many contract renegotiations with the station. (The first was after the jumper story at the Greenwich Hotel.) Actually, this story led first to a brief, one-day walkout and then to a raise. I saw the way people were responding to me and to my work, and I got it in my head that my weekly salary was less than I deserved. True, it was more money than I'd ever made—particularly with the per-story fees tacked on—but it wasn't enough. I wanted Al Primo to tear up my contract and write me a new one. Again. He was appalled, but I counted on that and figured he'd come around. I didn't have an agent at the time. Nobody had agents then. I didn't even have a lawyer. The contracts were all about fifteen pages thick, and I wouldn't even read them. The only thing I was concerned with was the last page, where all the numbers were. Just show me the money and I'll sign. I think I came away from the impasse boosted up to about eight hundred dollars a week. By the end of my first year at the station, I was making fifty thousand dollars a year, and from what I gathered, I'd unbalanced the entire salary structure of the newsroom. Only Bill Beutel and Roger Grimsby were making more, and I'd pass Bill before the next year was out.

If the hard side to my new career was making me rich, the soft side was about to make me famous. The new soft side was the show business beat I inherited from John Shubeck, who'd been replaced as Channel 7's anchorman by Roger Grimsby and stayed on as a kind of culture reporter. John's was a protracted, graceful exit, and I suppose his continued appearance on the air as a contributor helped to create a sense of transition for the audience, from one anchor to the next.

John Shubeck took the change in stride, and he quietly covered the culture beat with grace and aplomb. There was no spontaneity to his work, though, no spark. He interviewed artists, writers, movie stars, fashion designers, and society dames as if they were interchangeable. He was dispatched to charity balls and auctions, and covered them like straightforward news stories. He dipped into the world of New York celebrities and came back with a series of predictable profiles and reports. For all his personal flair, his pieces were pedestrian.

In early 1971, John Shubeck took another job on the West Coast, and the culture beat became available. I was reluctant to take it at first, having so recently made the successful shift back to hard news, but there was something about the glamorous aspects of John's world I found hard to resist. I was becoming, I'll admit, somewhat addicted to the lifestyles of the rich and famous (another phrase that had yet to be thought up), seduced by them, and the idea became less distasteful the more I thought about it. To be honest, I started to crave the particular pieces of limelight this new beat had to offer. I thought I could find room for it alongside the hard-core, down-and-dirty stories I was already covering. I still prided myself on my social mobility, on my ability to fit in as easily with a junkie on the streets as with a rock 'n' roll singer, or a fashion designer. It was the one lesson I'd taken with me from West Babylon High School, the way I had of fitting in with the jocks, the collegiates, and the punks. I could play both ends of the field, a kind of Renaissance man.

John continued on long enough to make his contacts mine, and after a few weeks comparing notes, I was set loose on the stars. The first celebrity I interviewed for Channel 7 was Englebert Humperdinck, who was appearing at the Americana Hotel's Empire

Room. Englebert Humperdinck, for those who can't quite recall
the man with the hard-to-forget name, was a wildly successful,
mildly entertaining middle-of-the-road singer and middle-aged sex
symbol. Women whose daughters went crazy for the Beatles went
crazy for him, the same way they went crazy for Tom Jones. I
knew who he was, but I'd never seen him perform.

Celebrity profiles, at the time, consisted mainly of footage of the
celebrity in performance, with a couple of backstage or dressing-
room questions thrown in to round out the piece. The interviewer
was always cordial, and deferential, as if all of these pieces came
off the same assembly line. I wanted to try something different,
and so we took a walk. No big deal. Englebert and I simply took a
stroll on the streets, and rolled the cameras.

But it was a big deal. I got all kinds of heat from the rest of the
newsroom for what was seen as an attempt to put myself on a level
equal to Englebert Humperdinck. Walking with a celebrity? It was
unheard of.

It seemed like a good idea at the time. I wasn't intimidated by
this guy—he wasn't a politician, a nuclear physicist, or an oil
tycoon—and I wasn't intimidated by the expectations of my
newsroom colleagues. I didn't see any reason for the interview to
be formal (and deferential) and like every other celebrity interview
that had preceded it. Englebert Humperdinck had a sense of
humor about himself. I teased him about the way his female fans
would throw their underwear up on the stage to him, and then he
laughed and teased me about my bushy moustache ("You look like
Pancho Villa," he joked), and then things loosened up to where we
put together an entertaining and intimate profile. I had never
seen a celebrity story done like this but, again, I hadn't seen much.

The succession of celebrity interviews that followed all featured
a good deal of chummy reporter involvement. The technique
became a staple for me. For an interview with Johnny Mathis, in
the early part of 1971, we set up a basketball hoop in the Waldorf-
Astoria Hotel and filmed the two of us playing some one-on-one.
In between baskets, we talked about his athletic aspirations—he'd
been an all-star athlete in high school—and made little or no
mention of the fact that he had one of the greatest voices of our
time. It was a given, his voice, and I thought we could use the
time to better, richer effect by telling our viewers something they

didn't already know. The resulting piece was successful because it was different and insightful, and because in putting the reporter on the same level with the celebrity, it made the viewer feel like he was being let in on something. The technique made the story, and the celebrity, more accessible.

The airing of the Mathis story, incidentally, marked one of the many times Roger Grimsby tried to pull the rug out from under me. I was extremely sensitive to the fact that Mathis was a well-known homosexual. My fear was that Roger would make some inappropriately snide remark about me and Johnny spending all that time together, running around in shorts. Instead, Roger tripped me up with an obscure fact he remembered from his days as a reporter in San Francisco; he abandoned his scripted lead-in and introduced me by saying, "Now, here's Geraldo, with a profile of a guy whose brother used to be a toll-taker at the Golden Gate Bridge."

I actually froze and mumbled something that sounded a lot like, "Er, er, er." A stage-frightened Ralph Kramden would have handled the situation better than I did. I eventually managed to work my way into the taped portion of the piece, but its impact had been mangled by my flustered lead-in.

Score one for Roger, who must have been delighted.

I inherited something else from John Shubeck, other than the celebrity beat. I inherited his film editor Marty Berman, the only editor from the Channel 7 ranks who was even close to my age, and who shared my sensibilities. Marty was a Jewish hipster, Brooklyn-born and -bred, the first kid on his block to abandon the traditional Mickey Mantle haircut in favor of long sideburns and platform shoes. Our meeting was another chance encounter that transformed my career. Marty and I—save for some stops and starts along the way—have worked together ever since. Early on, before Marty assumed the roles of lifelong friend and partner, he helped me to shape the way I conceived, wrote, and edited my stories for air. He toned down my knee-jerk liberal reactions to social problems with healthy doses of his Jewish skepticism and calm. Also, he helped me to define my own personal style; at his urging, I dumped my dad's overcoat and old wing-tipped shoes; I began to emphasize my hair, and my physique.

Marty Berman did much more than edit my pieces and tell me

how to dress; he became my friend, advisor, and confidant, what my nonsectarian police buddies refer to as "a rabbi." He became a constant reminder to me of my Jewish half. He was always encouraging me to acknowledge my Jewish heritage, which I eventually did at his urging. I resisted at first because I thought the Puerto Rican community desperately needed role models—the Jews had plenty—but Marty convinced me that a full disclosure would broaden my appeal, and would enable me to be more honest with myself and my viewers. "Believe me," Marty would argue, "with twenty-seven syllables in your name, nobody's going to forget you're a Puerto Rican."

In 1971, Marty was not only the youngest of the *Eyewitness News* film editors (the others were fifty- or sixty-something), he was also the most enthusiastic. Most everyone else seemed jaded, and bored. Their attitudes were reflected in their work. Marty's work was different because his attitude was different. He was bright and energetic, and approached each story as though it were his first, or his last. He'd only been at Channel 7 a short time (before that, he worked as an ABC page), and already he'd carved out this little niche for himself, through John Shubeck, doing cultural and celebrity stories and lifestyle pieces. It gave him a chance to be creative and different. He'd recently won an Emmy for his work, and because he was so young and successful, some of the same resentments that started to build toward me were also being directed at him. We were going through the same motions, and it seemed natural that we would eventually work together. Yet Marty resisted our pairing at first—he thought having to work with this brash young Puerto Rican would upset the good thing he had going—and he even asked the supervising film editor to reconsider the assignment.

We overcame Marty's initial reluctance and developed an almost immediate rapport, one that has lasted for nearly twenty years. We'd sit in the editing room, going over our footage, and we'd come up with complementing ideas on how to make the stories work. There was a great fit there, and there still is. It was Marty who worked with me to reinvent the celebrity profile. We both ignored the old ways of gathering and editing footage, of building a feature piece or a hard-news story, in favor of something new.

*   *   *

MARTY BERMAN (former film editor, *Eyewitness News*; currently executive producer, *Geraldo*): I remember one day, going to meet the crew, I forget what the story was. But we met the particular crew, and it was early, so we went into a luncheonette that had big windows facing the avenue. And as we were having our lunch, and talking about nothing special, we were looking at this construction worker. This guy had a hard hat on, and no shirt, and he was using a jackhammer. And it occurred to us, wouldn't it be a great idea to do a series about working? One day Geraldo could be a construction worker, and a short-order cook, and whatever. You know, a walk-a-mile-in-my-shoes kind of thing. We thought up the whole promotion right there: Next week, Geraldo goes to work for a living. And then we did that series, which was called "Working-Class Heroes." We used the John Lennon music. People are still doing that series.

Marty and I also pioneered the first-person, participatory pieces that are now standard fare on every local newscast. In those days, nobody had yet hit on the idea of turnabout in broadcast journalism. Feature pieces and profiles, at that time, were invariably straightforward and matter-of-fact; in print, reporters could stretch convention to where they became a part of the story, to where their emotions and experiences were welcomed by their readers, but for some reason there was less elastic to the broadcast end.

DAVE WEINGOLD (former sound man, *Eyewitness News*): I remember Geraldo decided he wanted to do a story with him jumping out of an airplane, parachuting. And we said, "Okay," you know, "let's do that." He didn't have to check with anybody, we just set it up ourselves and went ahead and did it. It was one of the sidebar stories we used to do. And I remember going over to Radio Shack and buying a tape recorder, a cassette tape recorder, which was brand-new back then, and strapping it to his emergency chute and putting an external microphone in his helmet, so we could hear him all the way down. So he did all the preliminary training, and then he went up in the airplane, and he jumped out of the thing. And I remember, we listened to the recording, and we couldn't use any of it, because all he was saying, all the way down, was, "Oh, shit! Oh, shit! Oh, fuck!"

One of the entertainment stories Marty and I did was a profile of a member of the corps de ballet of the New York City Ballet. We basically plucked our ballerina at random from the corps. This girl was blonde, fetchingly beautiful, and aching to break out of her background role. I talked to her about her life, her career, and her aspirations to go on to be the prima ballerina. It was a combination celebrity-profile and working-class hero story, and to give it an extra spin, I convinced her to dance with me in the Lincoln Center plaza. I don't know what Marty and I were thinking when we thought this one up, but we operated on a pretty loose leash, almost from the very beginning.

Our ballerina was a good sport about it. I got dressed out in tight jeans, and we put together this whole fantasy sequence, which we shot in front of the big fountain. I wasn't any kind of dancer, but I was a good athlete and in good-enough shape that I didn't embarrass myself any more than the conceit of the piece required. We had our cameras up on the balcony, looking down, and I basically stood still and watched as she did her pirouettes.

The dance portion of the profile didn't run more than ninety seconds or so. We took it back to the studio, and Marty scored it and turned it into a dreamy, slow-motion sequence. It worked because it was fun, and more personal than a typical personality profile. We listened to this young woman's hopes and set them to dance. And we gave her a chance to shine, even if it was only for ninety seconds on a local news show, and even if she had to do it alongside the only Puerto Rican in Manhattan who couldn't dance. The spotlight was on her, and on that night she was a star. She danced, and that's what people took away from the story. That's what they remembered.

I took a lot of shit for that piece—there goes Geraldo, stunting for the cameras!—but I didn't mind it. I was convinced that most of my colleagues were bitter and resentful of my success; they were looking for things to criticize. But I'd always get the story, and in this case I also got the girl.

ELAINE'S

In a final gesture before he shoved off for the coast, John Shubeck brought me along to a party at Elaine's, the celebrity hangout on the Upper East Side. The evening would have a considerable effect on the rest of my life. The party, which was given by George Plimpton, was packed by the literary set—Tom Wolfe, Kurt Vonnegut, Norman Mailer—and by chic fashion designers like Giorgio di Sant'Angelo, who would become my great friend.

I was strictly a middleweight in a crowd like this, but people seemed to know who I was. I was an odd kind of ghetto pet to New York's jet set, and I was invited to a lot of parties like this at the time; I knew the streets, and real people, and how the other half lived. I also knew that these were the things—bulletins from the front—I was expected to bring with me to the party. I was a kind of otherworld fascination to these people, and they were fascinating to me.

The party was a particularly heady gathering. Elaine's was filled with great-looking women. At one point, Giorgio di Sant'Angelo, who was an elegant Argentinian-born designer, a flamboyantly gay charmer with European good looks, approached me from across the room. He had on his arm a beautiful waif of a girl, with long straight blonde hair and doelike eyes, and he walked over to me and announced, "Geraldo!" and he started speaking to me in Spanish, loud enough for the whole room to hear. I'd never met him, but he clapped me on the back like a good, old friend, and then he went on about this and that. What he really wanted was to introduce me to the waif.

Edie Vonnegut was about twenty-two years old. I was about to turn twenty-eight. Of course, she wasn't a waif at all, but she did look a little out of place. She was wearing a big sheepskin coat that was all wrong for the room, if not the season. She was, I learned, an artist and she'd just returned from a long stay in Adelphi, a backwoods town in the interior of the island of Jamaica. She didn't have anything else to wear and looked every bit the innocent flower that she was.

I was, at first, taken by the name—her father, Kurt Vonnegut, was the biggest thing in contemporary fiction, and his books had just recently become important to me—but I was also completely taken with her. The great-looking women of Elaine's all blended into the background after one look at Edie. She was small, and lightly proportioned, and there was something fairy-goddesslike about her. We were attracted to each other almost immediately, physically and spiritually. As soon as we could make our exit without raising too many eyebrows, we left the party in my Volkswagen convertible.

We went to her father's apartment to collect some of her things, and then back to my place on Avenue C. Within twenty-four hours, we were living together. It happened that fast. That's the way things moved in those days. Edie and I took up in the back bedroom of the apartment, overlooking my tiny backyard. (I had a roommate at the time, an intense, neoconservative lawyer friend of mine from Alabama, named Leo Kayser, and he had the smaller bedroom, facing the street.) In an instant I went from making my own splash on New York's jet-set scene, to squiring Kurt Vonnegut's daughter along the same fast lane. The society pages started reporting about our relationship. It was a sudden and wonderful turn.

I was a little bit awed by Edie's father, not so much by the man as by what he represented. *Slaughterhouse Five*, out for a year or so, had reached the top of the best-seller lists, and was still the most widely read book on American college campuses. *Sirens of Titan* and *Cat's Cradle* were also out, and talked about. Kurt would never be as hot as he was at that moment. Everyone I knew had read at least one of his books.

Meeting Kurt Vonnegut—like this, through Edie—threw me, at least at first. I'd met some heavy hitters in my first few months in the television news business, but never on such intimate, almost equal, terms. It offered me a close (and advantaged) perspective on fame, my first. I liked the way it looked on him. In this strange light, Kurt struck me as a very unusual guy, a lot like the characters he wrote about: unhinged, awkward, out of place on this planet. He always seemed to see the bizarre aspects of everything, the benignly twisted. He was almost like an eccentric professor, or inventor. He wore a constant half-grin, and saw the absurd in everything. There was nothing cynical about the way he saw the world; actually, he was almost childlike in that way.

My relationship with Edie moved on fast-forward. I was overwhelmed by her family and allowed myself to be absorbed into the rhythms of their big, rambling house on the edge of a salt marsh in Barnstable, Cape Cod. Kurt would write there, and that alone was enough to give the place a certain poetry for me, a charm. His life was in a kind of transition then. He was just beginning to break away from the Cape and move toward the New York literary world—he'd just taken an apartment in Manhattan— but I did catch the tail end of the Vonnegut family traditions and gatherings. Edie's mother Jane was decidedly WASPy, but she was also a warm, down-home, earth-mother-type, and her household reflected that. In addition to Edie, there was also a brother Mark, and a sister Nanny, and she also had three cousins—the Adams boys—who were raised as stepbrothers. Their parents had died in a terrible train wreck, and Kurt and Jane adopted them after the tragedy.

I was enthralled with Edie and her family, and the scene that went with them. Her father and I would spar intellectually. Her brothers and I would spar athletically. And Edie and I would spar romantically. We were crazy about each other, and I was crazy about the whole package. The romance, it seems to me now, was partly about Edie and partly about everything else.

The Vonneguts took me in like I was one of their own, and I began to cherish my visits to the Cape, both for the warm, good times I had there and for everything the visits represented about my professional success and my emerging personal life and social stature. Every year, I learned, Kurt would lead the clan on something called The Marsh Tromp. He'd stand on the edge of the salt marsh there and he'd pick out a point off in the distance—a mile or so away—and then the entire family would make a beeline for that point. Kurt would lead the way. The idea was you couldn't deviate from the straight line, as you tromped your way through the salt wallows and the muck. They were in this stuff up to their knees. It was slow, hard-going, and they loved it.

The tromp was a dear memory from Edie's childhood, and I made it to the scene in time for the last full-scale adventure. It was a huge, big deal to them all, and I was honored to have been a part of that, and saddened, in retrospect, that it was to be the last such outing for Edie and her family. There was pure, exhilarated joy on their faces as we made our way across the marsh, the kind of happiness that comes from family tradition and energy. And love. It also comes, I suppose, from a bit of creative weirdness. I was both a part of it and an outsider to it.

But it was the last of how it was. Kurt would soon leave his wife Jane and fall for a well-known New York photographer named Jill Krementz (they later married and started a new family), and the atmosphere of the big house on the edge of the salt marsh was forever changed. My relationship with Kurt changed as he changed. But I liked Edie's father a great deal, particularly when he was surrounded by his entire family, and I think the admiration and affection were mutual. Newspapers and magazines would call to ask Kurt about me all the time, because of my relationship with his daughter, and he would say I was the most innocent man he'd ever met. We never talked about it, but I think it must have been my idealism that he found innocent. (I can't imagine anything else about me that he might have seen in that way.) Roger Grimsby, in one of his menacing modes, seized on Kurt's description of me as innocent in a profile in *New York* magazine, and responded in a letter to the editor: "Kurt Vonnegut is a great writer of fiction."

I fell face-first in love with Edie. I called her Pie, short for Honey Pie. The more involved we became, the less interested I was in other women. (I never became totally disinterested, but I was on my best behavior during the first months of our courtship.) We were quite a contrast, the two of us. I was urban, gritty, dark, and skeptical, and she was rural, soft, light, and trusting. Innocent, too, to borrow her father's phrase. She'd gone from Cape Cod to art school and then to Jamaica, where she painted and lived with her brothers on a farm where one crop was marijuana. She was extremely talented; there were times when I admired her artistry as much as I admired her father's. Her art was like herself: dreamy and otherworldly. Her paintings were filled with angels and goblins and winged horses. One of her pieces—of an angel riding a winged horse—still hangs in my home, over the mantel.

*   *   *

MARTY BERMAN: In the middle of Avenue C, in the worst area of the city, was this flower child, living with Geraldo. I can see this image of the two of them in bed, on Avenue C, with all her long curly hair, and Geraldo lying next to her. It's a very odd picture, and the camera pulls back, and beyond this bed are these gang members and knives and dope dealers and stuff like that. It's like that image of John and Yoko in bed, in Canada, with all the reporters. That's what I see. I see Edie in bed with Geraldo and he's got this kind of silly look on his face, and I widen out and I see the whole world, this sick, crazy world around them.

As the summer of 1971 progressed, and our relationship deepened, we began to talk about marriage. I remember one conversation, which for some strange reason also included my roommate, Leo Kayser. Leo stayed on in the front upstairs bedroom even after Edie moved in with me at Avenue C, and the three of us were having dinner one night in the apartment's main-floor room. Leo, who did pro-bono work for one of the city's larger law firms, had a privileged background—his investment banking family had underwritten the initial public offering of Coca-Cola—but you'd never know it judging by the gray suit he always used to wear. He wasn't quick to part with his coin, but he was very generous with his advice. Leo had one of the sharpest minds I've ever encountered—then or since—and he wasn't afraid to speak it if he had something he wanted to say. That night, as he saw his good friend hurtling toward the altar, something boiled forth. There, right in front of Edie, in his untempered Alabama drawl, he said, "Geraldo, I know you're planning to marry this girl and I also know that you have this feeling that she's this big deal, and she's the daughter of this famous author, and you feel pretty good about being associated with these people."

I stared him down, but he kept on. There was no stopping Leo once he got going. "I got news for you," he said. "She's not going to outgrow you. You're going to outgrow her in no time. You'll see. What is she? She's a hippy artist, and she can't paint worth a damn anyway. Who cares about these damn angels and goblins?"

Edie just sat there, not saying anything. I never saw her get angry in our entire time together. Not at me, not at her family, and not at Leo. (We all gave her plenty of opportunity.) She was too soft and sweet for that. Too innocent. She just looked across the table at this insulting little man—her new roommate—and suffered him quietly.

I was furious at Leo. How dare he say such things in front of Edie? What the hell was he thinking? I let passion fly, grabbing the table and throwing it over on him; he went falling down the three stairs leading up to the raised dining area. The table fell on top of him. There were dishes and broken glasses and food all over the place. I jumped the stairs after him, and Leo scrambled to his feet and ran down the full staircase and out of the apartment, all the time yelling, "You'll see I'm right, you'll see I'm right, you'll get tired of her in no time."

It was quite a scene: the seething, macho man chasing the tiny, libertarian lawyer with a Southern-fried accent. I pursued him to the door, but didn't follow him to the street. What was the point? Besides, I wanted to get back to see how Edie was doing. I needn't have worried. My Pie was already cleaning up the mess, and I helped her, silently. I don't think we ever talked about what Leo said that night. We just let it hang in the quiet apartment, evaporating.

BANK STREET

In the summer of 1971, former Beatle George Harrison sponsored and hosted two benefit concerts at Madison Square Garden for the people of Bangladesh. He assembled a powerhouse group of musicians to join him onstage, including Bob Dylan, Eric Clapton, Ringo Starr, Leon Russell, and Ravi Shankar. It was the biggest thing in the city that summer, and I managed to get exclusive access to the concert for Channel 7. All of this was arranged through a man named Allen Klein, a cigar-smoking, heavy-bellied Jewish guy who ran Apple Records.

Before the concert, Allen had orchestrated a party at his gaudy mansion in the affluent Riverdale section of the Bronx—all done up in lavendar and lace—for me to meet George and Ringo. I'd been traveling the celebrity beat for a few months by this time and

I'd been involved with Edie's family and the literary and society trappings attached to them, but this was something else. This was The Beatles. They were like gods to me, the prophets of my generation; they were unapproachable, unbelievable.

Pinch me.

That summer was only a year or so after the Beatles had officially broken up, and they were still the biggest stars in the business. Their albums remained on the charts, and everyone still hoped for a reconciliation. (It was too soon to call it a reunion.) Radio stations carried news of their comings and goings as if they were royalty. Their breakup was reported like a death in the family, or at least a divorce. And two of those former Beatles, George Harrison and Ringo Starr, had descended upon this purpled Bronx mansion to attend a small party, to meet me. Me? I couldn't believe it. These guys actually knew who I was—they'd been living in New York during the ongoing Apple Records litigations over the legal dissolution of The Beatles—and had seen my work and wanted to meet me.

There were about ten of us there that afternoon, on the lawn at Allen Klein's. I remember pointing down to the Hudson River and explaining to George Harrison how it was that I had seen Europe before ever crossing the river to New Jersey. He could not understand this. Later, he asked me if this was the river across which Washington had thrown his legendary silver dollar. He was charming and engaging, absolutely without attitude. He had always come across as the quietest onstage and in his public guises, but in personal conversation he was almost gregarious. He was also genuinely curious about my life and passionate about his own interests, which at that time included his guru, transcendental meditation, the problems in Bangladesh, and other aspects of Eastern life.

Ringo was different—less serious, but also delightful. He struck me right off as funny, and not at all as daffy as he was made out to be in *A Hard Day's Night*. He didn't take anything too seriously; he didn't talk politics, or anything heavier than music. Everything was cool to Ringo.

The concert, which ultimately raised close to eleven million dollars, was a tremendous success. It was also the most incredible concert I had ever seen. Bob Dylan, another idol, showed up as an unannounced guest, and Billy Preston was there, and Eric Clapton. And I was there with my camera crew taking it all in—from backstage and from the concert floor—the only camera crew allowed in during the show (other than the documentary-film makers). It was an incredible coup for *Eyewitness News*, and we were able to broadcast pieces of the two concerts and backstage interviews for our viewers who couldn't squeeze into the sold-out Madison Square Garden.

My new friendship with George Harrison led—indirectly, I think—to an invitation to meet John Lennon. Meeting George and Ringo was one thing; meeting John was something else entirely. Yoko Ono actually sent for me to meet John.

Apparently, I had first come to Yoko's attention during the Angela Davis/Board of Corrections incidents the previous November. There was something about the stand I took there that stayed with her. Perhaps she'd seen my letter of resignation in *The New York Times*, or the news accounts of my impassioned efforts to help Angela Davis. Whatever it was, I was told that after I'd developed a small friendship with George Harrison, through the Concert for Bangladesh, she was reminded again of my work and wanted to meet me. And if Yoko wanted to meet someone, then so did John.

They summoned me to their basement apartment on Bank Street in the Village. It was smack in the middle of their give-peace-a-chance phase. The apartment was a duplex occupying the ground floor and basement of a nice old brownstone. They were both in bed the first time we met. I remember being surprised by this, though I might have expected it.

I rang their doorbell at the agreed-upon time and was met by a big, burly guy who led me into another room where I was met by a less-big, less-burly guy, who led me into another room where I was met by a woman, who wasn't big or burly at all. Actually, it may have been May Pang, who was working for Yoko at the time. I had to go through three or four layers of people, and through three or four rooms, before I was led into the master bedroom.

And there he was. John Lennon. The only bigger kick would have been meeting Elvis Presley on such intimate terms, although by that time Elvis was gaining weight and selling out in Las Vegas. John Lennon was it for me. He was rebel, poet, artist, feminist, working-class hero, and antiwar advocate. He wore fairly thick, rimless glasses, and pajamas. His hair was cut short, and he was clean-shaven; the long, flowing hair and bushy beard of the year before were gone, casualties of the mounting immigration problems John would face over the next few years.

The bedroom looked like it belonged to a prosperous hippie. There was a guitar by the side of the bed. (There was always a guitar around John.) Their big television set was on, although I don't recall what they were watching. It seemed like background music, white noise. John and Yoko loved to watch television, at a time when nobody in our generation was watching television; if my visits, and our conversation, were any indications, they liked the local news most of all. To them, the television was a kind of window on the world. The rest of the room was in disarray—clean, but untidy. It also seemed shut off from the rest of the world, all dark, quiet, and warm; I remember thinking it was like a womb.

I sat down on their big bed and we rapped about world peace and poverty and Nixon and everything else we could think of. It seemed like the easiest, most natural thing in the world to them, to be entertaining a visitor in their bedroom—in bed, in their pajamas—and it seemed the same to me. Of course, John could have done almost anything and it would not have seemed odd to me. I remember drinking a lot of wine at that first meeting. And we talked for hours. The bedroom was jammed with an eclectic mix of very modern art—some pieces of Yoko's, some Japanese pieces—and several posters protesting the Southeast Asian war or urging compliance with the grape and lettuce boycotts. It was a happening house that had turned its back on irrelevant rock 'n' roll affluence to embrace the great issues of the day.

Finally, I offered to take them out to dinner, and they lit up at the idea. They got dressed, moving about the room without a thought to my being there. Modesty was not the first thing on their minds, and I could not help but notice Yoko's unexpectedly ample breasts. She was, I noticed for the first time, an exotic and attractive woman. In everything that's ever been written or said about Yoko Ono, no one has ever mentioned what a hot ticket she was, and as our friendship developed I became convinced that sex was the great, true hold she had on John. Yes, she was political, intelligent, and artistic, but she was also sexy. They were very clingy together, like teenagers. John could not keep his hands off her.

John got dressed in a T-shirt, baggy fatigue pants with lots of pockets, and an old army jacket. Even though he was passionately opposed to the war, he almost always wore fatigues during this period. And then we went out, just the three of us, to a local place in the West Village. Nothing fancy, just dinner. John was able to walk around the Village with impunity in those days. The whole world was hip. Of course, people noticed John, but they didn't bother him. In fact, I was stopped and bothered by more people than he was on the way to the restaurant.

When the bill came, I grabbed it without even hesitating. The bill came to about a hundred bucks, with wine and tip. I paid for it with my (relatively) newly acquired American Express card, and John told me it was the first time since he had been in America that someone else had picked up a check. There was something sad about the way he said this, and I was reminded that he had spent almost all of his adult years surrounded by bodyguards and sycophants. I think it put me over the top in his eyes, paying for dinner like that. We became fast friends and dropped in and out of each other's lives for the next few years.

You couldn't be friendly with John Lennon in those days without also being friendly with Yoko. I don't think I ever saw him without Yoko at his side. I didn't mind. I'd never known him without Yoko, so I didn't know anything different. We'd see each other several times a week, sometimes daily, and she was always around.

It was a struggle to me, at first, not to let on how much this budding friendship with John meant. I still held tremendous feelings of awe—a fan's adulation, I suppose—but I was careful not to let them show. He was also charming, funny, and smarter than I've ever heard anybody give him credit for. The parallel relationship that was developing with Kurt Vonnegut and the literary set was different in that I was basically an illiterate person growing up. I was drawn to Kurt's work, and fascinated by it, but it was new to me, fresh; his work, for me, had yet to make it from the surface to the core. John's work was a part of my history. I had even ripped off his hairstyle during college.

But I played it cool. I had to, I thought, or John and Yoko wouldn't want anything to do with me. Remember, I saw myself the Mau Mau in the Promised Land. I had an edge on everyone else and I wanted to keep it. I could travel and mix where John and Yoko couldn't. I was streetwise and plugged-in, the only television newsman held in high regard by the Young Lords, the Black Panthers, and other denizens of the radical left. I'm sure that's what attracted John and Yoko to me in the first place. John was totally into the antiwar movement, and other causes, and I guess he thought being with me would bring him closer to that edge.

At the tail end of 1971, we hung out, partied, and went places together. Most times, we stayed home, at their place or mine. John and Yoko were so political that virtually every one of our conversations had to do with some profound issue. Every dinner had an agenda; every outing a goal. John deferred to Yoko about everything—where to eat, what to wear, what to think (or at least what to think about). She became a kind of translator between John and me. If there was something I did or said that he didn't quite understand, because he didn't have that bundle of experience, then Yoko would put things in perspective for him.

I remember driving them around town in my old VW beetle, with the top down. I was very good on the history and geography of Manhattan and would take them on little tours. John was immersed in the city in those days and he was hungry for a ground-up view (he was working on material for the album *Some Time in New York,* which he recorded with the band Elephant's Memory), and so I took him to the Heights across the Brooklyn Bridge, and down to the Battery and the Fulton Fish Market, and up to the scary cool of Harlem. Until he met me, he'd seen the city through a kind of filter. Through me, he saw the city as it was, and as it could be.

We talked about the Beatles, but I was always careful not to push. He was very disparaging about his brilliant career with the group, and about that period of his life. He seemed to dismiss his work as irrelevant and childish; he'd snicker about it, as if he really thought he'd gotten away with something. He felt very strongly that the work he was doing as a solo artist was really representative of him as a poet and musician. The Beatles, to him, were silly and superfluous. I never pushed him because these were things I didn't necessarily want to hear, and also because I never wanted John to feel that I was reporting on him, prying. I wanted him to feel, absolutely, that he could trust me, tell me anything, without wondering if I was taking notes.

He pushed me about my work, though, all the time. I loved the attention and welcomed his criticisms. I'd do a piece on the eleven o'clock newscast and my phone would be ringing with a comment from John by the time I got home. He and Yoko watched the news all the time; they were genuinely and passionately interested in what was happening, and in whether or not people were talking about them. They courted the press, but they were also fearful of it. Yoko and John were two of the most paranoid people I'd ever met. When John did a benefit concert in Michigan for a guy named John Sinclair, an antiwar protestor who'd been jailed for possession of an insignificant amount of pot, there was a consensus in the house on Bank Street that the phones were being tapped. ("It ain't fair, John Sinclair, in the stir for breathing air.") Yoko always had the feeling they were being watched. There was a kind of siege-mentality beginning to brew, a feeling not just that the Beatle-fanatics were on the loose, but also, and more important, that the federal government was somehow mobilizing its huge forces to hurt them in some way. Even before John's immigration problems started, he was always conscious of the fact that he was just a guest in this country and not a citizen.

BARNSTABLE, CAPE COD

My friendship with John and Yoko barely extended itself to include Edie. We rarely double-dated during this time. Mostly, Edie stayed home. She had her friends, and I had mine. She also had a new job, drawing shoe ads for a company called Capezio, up near Columbus Circle, and that took up a lot of her time, even if it didn't take up all that much of her talent. The times the four of us were all together, though, resonate for the way Yoko would talk around Edie, never to her. She'd talk about her as if she weren't there, or she wouldn't talk about her at all. Yoko Ono, circa 1971, may have been a feminist, but she was also a chauvinist.

By fall, as I was doing more celebrity-type stories, I started getting an aggressive physical response from some female viewers. Groupies. I had broad demographic support in those days, but teenage girls and young women apparently started to see me as a kind of rock 'n' roll newsman, and their reactions, when I passed on the street, or in a restaurant, reflected that. Edie grew insecure, and one of the reasons we decided to get married was my desire to show her that she could be confident in me, that she could trust me to handle the temptations that came with being a celebrity.

We drove up to tell her parents, and they were somewhat surprised at our decision. "I didn't know that people did that anymore," her earth-mother mom said when we announced our plans to marry. Everything started to move very fast. Wedding plans were set in motion, and handmade invitations were sent out to friends and family.

We were married in the first week of December 1971, at the Vonnegut house in Barnstable, Massachusetts, on Cape Cod.

MARTY BERMAN: I was sort of in charge of the ceremony, and there was this wonderful song by Johnny Mathis that Geraldo loved at that time. It was from *Jacques Brel Is Alive* . . . and it was called "If We Only Have Love." I was so nervous. I remember bringing two LPs, 'cause I was so nervous that one of them would have a scratch in it. I brought two brand-new copies of this album, and for hours before the wedding I was cuing it up and timing it, trying to figure how long it would take for everybody to walk in and to be at the right point where I could bring the music up full. I remember it being really very, very impressive, and the music was terrific, and there was a window behind the person performing the ceremony, a French window with small panes, and the corners had snow in them. It was like a painting. It was very beautiful and very touching, and I don't know if anybody else did, but I know Geraldo was crying and I was crying. It worked for us. I don't know if they got it at all. I mean, I think Kurt and all those people, they just didn't get it at all. Johnny Mathis didn't make any sense to them.

MELBA TOLLIVER (former reporter, WABC-TV *Eyewitness News*): It was in the winter, very cold. I remember Marty playing some

Johnny Mathis, he's crazy about Johnny Mathis. He was sort of back there with the music and the hi-fi, producing the wedding. That's what I remember, and I just remember it also being extremely cold that night. Now that I think of it, it's kind of interesting that I was there because I never considered Geraldo an intimate friend of mine. I liked him and I also got frustrated with him at times, but I never had the feeling that you could ever be close to him. And then here was a guy who was this real ladies' man and real tough guy and all of that, and yet he apparently had a very soft, sort of sentimental romantic side of him. It was a very sweet wedding.

There were candles everywhere, and the old colonial house looked like a postcard from winter wonderland. Edie looked like an angel, all dressed in innocence and lace. The ceremony was short and essentially nonsectarian, performed by a Universalist minister. There were prayers for peace on earth, mutual love, respect, and fidelity. I said my vows with vigor and optimism, pride and affection. Edie was great, from an exotic and fun family, and I took her hand knowing she would be a perfect wife.

My old friend Frankie DeCecco stood as my best man in what was to be the last great moment of our long friendship. We had grown apart in recent years, a separating that was accelerated by the high-life I'd embraced since signing on at *Eyewitness News*. The gap between his world (he still sold cars on Long Island) and mine was widening, but there was still enough of a bridge that I wanted him there beside me when I took this important step.

Of course, my family was there, and they were bursting with pride. They were also overwhelmed by the whole scene. The house, the people, the lifestyle . . . everything was big, new, and different to them. This was how the other half lived, and though they were proud, they were also intimidated by it all, my parents especially. To be honest, I was embarrassed by them in those days. My parents were like Ma and Pa Kettle, and I'd look to deflect attention from them at every chance. They were so incredibly provincial compared to the new life I was leading, and I still wasn't sure enough of my own footing to just let them be themselves.

But, God bless them and damn me, my family couldn't have been more loving or proud. An unconditional, unadulterated pride flowed from West Babylon to wherever I was and whatever I was doing. I could tan by its warm glow, and when I stopped long enough to appreciate it, I felt sheepish and ashamed at the way I'd let myself be embarrassed by them at other moments. At these times, I'd want to return to my parents some of the things they'd always struggled to give to me, and the easiest way I could think to do this was to spread some of my new wealth. My father had grown infirm in the months surrounding my wedding to Edie. He became increasingly ill with diabetes and he wasn't able to do any kind of physical work. He'd taken a job as a night watchman at an A&S, until I finally encouraged him to give it up and retire and let me take care of them. I bought them their first motor home, and they hit the road in their new hobby. One of the things they said they missed most when they started to travel in their RV was the chance to watch their son on the news every night, at six and eleven. If I could have, I would have invented them a VCR.

I'm sure my rapid and public success distanced me in many ways from my family in those early years. What I'm not sure about is how they were all affected by what was happening to me. My visits home became less frequent, and less focused. My mind was always someplace else. On the surface, nobody seemed to mind, or to notice, but they began treating me too deferentially, jumping nervously to fulfill my every real or imagined need. Are you hungry? Want a nap? You look tired. Skinny. Give me those shoes. Take my seat. My mother became almost a shrine-keeper, storing the hundreds of awards and citations I'd begun receiving; she would actually lead tours through my old bedroom. The room was as much mausoleum as museum; it was a memorial to her son, the star who had taken flight and moved up and away.

The wedding was a signal of all this. Yes, my family was there with me, but in another, deeper sense, they were someplace else. They were open-eyed and openmouthed at the spectacle and by my new life. It would be a journey of several years before I had enough self-confidence and perspective to shed the jet set and the glitterati, and return to their always-loving, never-judging arms.

It was a pretty wild ride, as I turned the corner into 1972. There was something happening all the time: with Edie, with John Lennon, with Giorgio di Sant'Angelo, with *Eyewitness News*. I was filled with energy and ambition. Back then, it was a relatively easy thing for me to work all day, get off work after the eleven o'clock news, and then party until the middle of the morning. I was built differently. I was in good shape, or at least I was benefitting from having been in good shape when I first took the job. I could grab a couple hours sleep and get up at nine the next morning and start the whole thing all over again.

The period from late summer 1971 through 1972 was marked by the most rapid evolution of my life. In many ways, I peaked during those months. There has never been a time—then or since—when I was more original or creative. I was constantly probing, constantly experimenting. I would have felt as at home with the president of the United States as with John Lennon in the basement on Bank Street. I was filled with confidence and passion, and I felt totally invulnerable; if someone shot at me, I often thought at the time (and still do, to a degree), I would have been winged, getting both a Purple Heart and a good story out of the experience.

I had the city figured out to where I even proposed a strategy to revivify the predominantly Puerto Rican, desperately poor Lower East Side neighborhood where I lived. I wrote an article for *The Village Voice* in which I put forth my plan to establish an apolitical, grass-roots organization to fill in the cracks left untended by government bureacracy. "The basic, overriding philosophy of the organization would be practical," I wrote, "even cynical. It is difficult to label its philosophy; the closest, easiest tag is 'radical-pragmatism.' It would have the ability and desire to do anything, get along with anybody, and be anything it had to be, to exist, to function effectively, and to accomplish its goal: a minimal level of dignity and a decent existence for those within its geographic area of responsibility. It would be a mean and angry bully; it would be a catalyst."

The shadow government I proposed never took root in any real or substantive way, but I continued to practice my own brand of radical pragmatism in my work at the station. That took root, and it flourished. I made myself into a bully for change, a catalyst. I was making a big impact in New York. Not just in terms of popularity, but in terms of effectiveness. My work effected change. It made things happen, or not happen. Almost all of my noncelebrity stories had a moral; I wasn't reporting so much as I was pointing out examples of problems, and preaching. Through frequent news stories and the station's public affairs program, *Like It Is*, which I cohosted on the weekends with Gil Noble, I was able to shine a new and powerful light on the problems facing our community. I would almost always demand corrective measures, and often got them: a home for the family who had no home; heat for the family who had no heat; relief from oppressive landlords, or dishonest merchants, or drug pushers loitering on the block. I was on the side of the underdog, and I got results.

I was inventing television activism and motivating the docile, self-interested community to get involved. The sixties' banner of idealism had in me its first celebrity flag-carrier, film at six and eleven.

On November 21, 1971, *The New York Times* did its first story on me, and it signaled my arrival on the New York television scene, at least as far as the establishment media was concerned. "The secret of Rivera's success?" John J. O'Connor asked in the piece. "He knows New York City and he knows what he is talking about. Unlike many newsmen who have difficulty telling the difference between a drunk and a heroin mainliner, he is knowledgeable about all aspects of the city jungle. He is not an outsider relying on 'official sources' for a story; he sees the story at the level that it happens.

"Television news is part of television show business," O'Connor continued, "and Rivera is not the least bit shy about becoming a star, about instant recognition off-camera. Besides boosting his own ego, he points out, it is an essential development for the Puerto Rican community. For one thing, New Yorkers can get to see that the stereotype of the Puerto Rican as some sort of threat is nonsense. For another, Puerto Ricans get a sense of pride and personal identity in his own success. . . .

"Rivera himself refuses to be typecast. If he is outraged at certain social conditions, he is equally outraged when a policeman is shot in the back—and gets threatening letters when he says so on televison. If he is a first-rate 'activist' reporter, he also throws himself into celebrity interviews that bring 'some entertainment and a change of pace' to the program. . . . Directly and emotionally involved, he has tapped an area that has been given, if anything, superficial and Establishment-oriented coverage on television. The awards, I suspect, are only just beginning."

The story validated and legitimized me. It also stroked me in a way that mounting celebrity, contract renegotiations, or my pending marriage to Edie Vonnegut, could not. It told me that the work I was doing was righteous and good and on-target. (It also described my appearance and manner of dress as "super-cool swinging," which was the kind of phrase even *The New York Times* could get away with in 1971.)

I was going places, but I didn't have a clue where I'd turn up. Of course, the standard progression for a television newsman was to make the move from local to network. That's the way the career ladder worked in the television news business. But *Eyewitness News* was a very different creature than ABC News at the national level. At Channel 7, we were happening, the news team was the most creative thing in television. At the network, they were trying to look like the other guys, at CBS and NBC, and they were failing at it. They were small and shriveled, and we were sexy and thriving.

And we were New York. That was key. We were this polyglot, integrated, unpredictable family. Al Primo had made his vision of a true neighborhood newscast a reality. In less than a year we had grown from a dismal third in the local-news ratings to a competitive second. Some weeks we finished at the top. Before long we'd pull more viewers than the local CBS and NBC stations combined. I remember we did an on-air promo during this time that became a classic local television news campaign, one of the most memorable spots ever done for a broadcast news organization. It was directed by Jerry Della Femina, who went on to become an advertising industry heavyweight. The commercial was set at a traditional Puerto Rican wedding, and the script had me bringing the entire *Eyewitness News* family as my guests. Roger, Bill, Melba, Tex, the whole clan. We were greeted at the reception by this big Hispanic woman, who was supposed to be an older relative of mine. And then the camera followed us inside, to all my "relatives," and then we all started dancing and whooping it up with the rest of the guests. And then came the tag line to the spot: "The *Eyewitness News* Family. Bringing You the News, at Six and Eleven." Fade to black.

That's how we saw ourselves in the fall of 1971. And that's how the city perceived us. Moving on, at that time, to national television, would have been like a demotion for me. I had the best contacts one could possibly have. I was making a ton of money (far more than most network newsmen). I was connected. It's impossible to work in this business without an ego, but mine wasn't smart enough (or neurotic enough) to worry that no one knew me in Indianapolis. They knew me in New York, and that was all I cared about. The city was the absolute center of my universe. I never wanted to be president of the United States. I grew up wanting to be mayor.

CHAPTER SIX

Tina's Diner, Staten Island

On Monday afternoon, January 3, 1972, Marty Berman and I were sitting in his tiny editing cubicle in the Channel 7 newsroom, putting polish to a piece about an old man forced to live in his car after his tenement was razed to make way for a luxury high-rise apartment building. It was the kind of piece we did well, and often—the little guy, bumping up against the system or big business, and losing. This particular story, for all its heartbreak, had the smell of a dozen before it, and Marty and I were having some difficulty mustering our indignant enthusiasms. The piece was to be shown on that night's six o'clock newscast, and as we stitched the last of it together, we were also kicking around ideas for our next report.

We were looking for the giant story that would break routine. We had divorced ourselves from the assignment desk in the months since our collaboration began, and it was not uncommon for us to have two or three stories in the works. On this day, though, we had nothing. We were just thinking out loud. Marty's editing room was eight feet by ten feet, and our ideas would bounce off the walls of the cramped, close space like in a pinball machine. I tossed out the idea of getting a camera crew and going to Puerto Rico to do a profile of my father's vast and disparate family. Not a bad idea, but Marty rejected it as being too personal. Also, he had a second, more compelling objection: There was no way Al Primo would free up the funds (and the manpower) we needed to make a story like that work.

We thought big, this reporter and editor, but we were tethered to reality by a shoestring.

Eventually, we hit on the idea of doing a series on victimless crimes: drug use, prostitution, gambling. . . . It was a good idea—workable, promotable—and so we kicked it around some more. It wasn't a giant, but it was enough to keep us going. As we talked, the series took shape and we lost track of time to where we had to scramble to get that night's story ready for the six o'clock broadcast. The scene was typical of the way we worked at the time: We would barely finish one thing before we were onto the next. It was almost like the idea of the story, the concept, was more interesting than the story itself, than the telling.

And so we wrapped the piece on the old man living in his car, gathering up the right amounts of outrage and condemnation, and then we tidied things up for the night. The next day, Tuesday, we'd give the victimless-crimes series our full attention. I was no longer doing two stories for the six and another for the eleven. I was working longer, more elaborate stories, or multipart series. I had the chance to give things some depth and perspective. Marty had the chance to be creative in the editing room. It was a nice (and unusual) luxury in a business that had long been known for its haste and churn.

But that Tuesday was slow-going. I had a tough time getting any momentum on the victimless-crimes idea—maybe it wasn't the series to shake the cobwebs from our day-to-day—and there wasn't anything else happening in the city that grabbed my attention.

Wednesday I played hooky. I called in sick and stayed home with Edie. I knocked around the apartment, paid some bills, read a book, tried to get things organized for the new year. I think we went out to lunch, or maybe to a movie. I was still wound-up from the wedding and the holidays, and I needed a breather.

The phone rang at about ten o'clock that night. It was a rare and good thing that I was home, because it would turn out to be the single most important phone call I'd ever taken. It changed my life. It changed a million lives. There is no exaggeration here. This one call set in motion a series of dramatic events that would have a deep, lasting, and positive impact on the millions of mentally retarded people in New York and throughout the country.

A doctor friend named Mike Wilkins was on the other end of the line. I'd known Mike since my days with the Young Lords, when he was a radical doctor and I was a radical lawyer. In January 1969, he ran the clinic in the Young Lords' church, to test youngsters in Spanish Harlem for lead poisoning and anemia. For the next several years, we bumped into each other here and there, because we knew the same people and had the same passion for the same causes. One of the last cases I ever accepted as an attorney was at Mike's urging. He'd taken a job at the United States Public Health Service Hospital on Staten Island, to fulfill his military obligations, and discovered there that the government had been recruiting young Native American women from reservations out West, training them as licensed practical nurses, and then paying them substandard wages to work in public health facilities. I was retained to bring suit against the hospital on behalf of the nurses.

We won the case, and Mike and I went our separate ways. Until he called on that Wednesday night with the news that he and a like-minded social worker named Elizabeth Lee had just been fired from the Willowbrook State School on Staten Island, the nation's largest facility for the mentally retarded, operating under the jurisdiction of New York's Department of Mental Hygiene. They were fired, he said, for encouraging parents with children living at the school to organize so that they could more effectively advocate for improved conditions there.

Willowbrook State School was not really a school at all. It was a human warehouse. Over the previous year, Mike Wilkins and another doctor, Bill Bronston, began to talk to parents about the horrible living conditions inside the state-run institution. Willowbrook was overcrowded and understaffed; its budget had been repeatedly slashed by the Department of Mental Hygiene, whose own budget had been repeatedly trimmed by then governor Nelson Rockefeller. The conditions on the wards, which housed more than six thousand patients with varying disabilities and levels of intelligence, were unhealthy, unsafe, and inhumane. Efforts at education and physical and occupational therapy were minimal at best; the overwhelming majority of Willowbrook's "patients" spent their days heavily sedated, poorly fed, and largely ignored.

Also, the staff was scandalously underpaid (attendants earned an average of $115.48 per week), working conditions were abominable, and turnover was widespread. The administration, strapped for state funds and unable to stanch the attrition, welcomed it instead. The patient-to-attendant ratio, which should have been about four-to-one, had dropped to about forty-to-one. Those parents who continued to visit their children in the facility (most, incidentally, did not) were never allowed on the wards to see firsthand how their children were living; rather, children with visitors were dresse' (others, often, were not) and brought out to the lobby areas to meet their guests.

If the country was aware of Willowbrook at all, it was because of a 1965 visit by Robert F. Kennedy, during his senatorial campaign, when he toured the facility and declared it a snakepit. He was genuinely and emotionally appalled at the conditions there; he had a retarded sister, Rosemary, and I'm sure the indignities the patients suffered there struck him on a deeply personal level. But Robert Kennedy never made any pictures of Willowbrook's horrors available to the general public, and his vivid description and righteous indignation were not enough to sustain prolonged outrage or a call for reform.

If the city was aware of Willowbrook at all, it was by name only, and not by reputation. The school, at the time, was the largest employer on Staten Island; almost everyone who lived in the city's most suburban borough had a friend, neighbor, or acquaintance who was somehow connected to the facility. Others knew the place by its deceptively lovely name, or by its spacious and pastoral setting on three hundred and eighty rolling green acres. The grounds, also deceptively lovely, were a bucolic and familiar landmark. From the outside, Willowbrook looked like an exclusive golf club or college campus; from within, it was just as Robert Kennedy had described—a snakepit.

All through 1971, Mike Wilkins, Elizabeth Lee, and Bill Bronston had been quietly working to make Willowbrook a better place. Their successes were small, but mounting. In Building Six, where Mike and Elizabeth were based, they organized wienie-roasts and lectures for the parents and siblings of their patients, and at these gatherings they would discuss ways to humanize the facility. They brought in mental health experts to explore new models for care and treatment. Attendance at these meetings gradually grew. The three also spoke to Staten Island community groups, giving voice and heart to the plight of Willowbrook's mentally retarded population.

The Willowbrook administration, headed by a gray-haired, portly doctor named Jack Hammond, was, predictably, unresponsive to these efforts. Dr. Hammond was actually ousted from one meeting, as parents grew angry at his unwillingness to address their concerns. A protest was held outside the Willowbrook gates one Sunday afternoon, and Jane Kurtin, a reporter for a local newspaper, *The Staten Island Advance*, took notice and wrote a series of articles about the substandard living conditions and lack of educational programs at the facility. The articles, like Robert Kennedy's condemnation five years earlier, generated a ripple of public protest. *The New York Times* quoted a local politician describing the school as a "horror show." But the words alone were not enough to raise an eyebrow in a town jaded by an endless Asian war, rampant crime, recession, and every other conceivable unpleasantness.

The story of Willowbrook State School, when it was covered at all, was reported strictly from the traditional point of view, with visuals of concerned parents and citizens demonstrating outside the walls of the facility, but showing nothing of what was inside. Without images to support those cries for help, the accounts were not able to capture the city's attention. The horror was vague, ambiguous, the indignities hinted at, but not known. More, there was a synthetic balancing to all the reports of Willowbrook's deplorable conditions: The parents would say one thing, and then the administration would deny the parents' claims and say another. Back and forth. Back and forth. Most reporters will tell you there are two sides to every story, and most times they'd be right. But on some stories, as Edward R. Murrow once said, there is no other side.

In late December 1971, Mike Wilkins and Elizabeth Lee were fired from their positions at Willowbrook. (Dr. Bill Bronston, who'd been in place long enough to enjoy permanent civil service status, was kept on.) Administrators told Wilkins and Lee their dismissals were due to a hiring freeze, that because they were both still in the probationary period of their contracts, they would have to be let go. Their jobs, which for the first time were described as "provisional," were being eliminated.

MIKE WILKINS (former attending physician, Willowbrook State School): I don't watch a lot of television, but I knew Geraldo had been working as a reporter. I was aware that he was leading this semicelebrity life. We still saw each other, off and on, mostly when he'd get sick or something. And so I called him and said, "Let me run this by you." And I told him the story of how we were fired, and how we wanted to get some licks in at these people. We thought that they were condoning inadequate care there, and a large part of it was that no one knew how bad the conditions were. We were in the backwaters of New York City, and no one knew what was going on.

I didn't hear any bells and whistles when Mike Wilkins called. It sounded like a good story—the firing of an idealistic young doctor struggling to improve conditions on his wards—but it did not signal anything extraordinary. This was unfamiliar territory. I did not know the first thing about mental retardation. I did not know anybody touched by it in any way. Today, we have a young actor with Down's syndrome starring in a network television program, but back then there were no Special Olympics, no telethons, no celebrity-sponsored charity drives. Nothing. No one talked about mental retardation. Families with mentally handicapped children were generally too embarrassed to talk about it, and that embarrassment was encouraged by administrators at state-run facilities such as Willowbrook, where parental involvement was discouraged. The children were institutionalized at a young age and, too often, forgotten.

Initially, then, I was not as outraged at the situation Mike Wilkins described as I should have been. I was operating out of ignorance. But I knew enough to be aware there was something here worth pursuing, and so I told Mike to call me back the next morning and I would see what I could do. If I thought about the story at all that Wednesday night, I thought about it as a quick hit, the kind of piece we could turn around in a couple hours and move on to the next one. It wasn't the giant Marty and I were looking for, but it was solid. I actually called in to the assignment desk from home on Thursday morning, and asked for a camera crew before I heard back from Mike, but was told there weren't any available.

Mike's next call set off sirens. When I asked him to describe the conditions at Willowbrook, he told me that in the building where he worked there were sixty mentally retarded children, with only one attendant to take care of them. He told me that most of these kids walked around naked all day (there weren't enough clothes to go around), and that many of them were so heavily medicated that they would lay about in a kind of stupor, sometimes smeared with their own feces.

MIKE WILKINS: Geraldo said, "Well, can you get me into the place, to film it?" And I thought, Whoa. Hold on a minute. It had never occurred to me, to take him in there with a camera crew and all. I didn't think that far. I didn't know if it would be legal or otherwise approved of. But, as a matter of fact, after I'd gotten fired, no one had bothered to take my key. And one opened all at that place. There were something like thirty buildings and all you needed was one key, because you'd be on call some weekends and have to be able to get into every building. And I still had my key, and so I told him, "Yes, we can get in."

The story about kids lying in their own shit got me a crew. It also sparked my activist fury. I made arrangements to meet Mike Wilkins at a joint called Tina's Diner, on Staten Island, about a mile from the school. By the time I got there with my crew, it was two o'clock in the afternoon; we had to be out of Willowbrook with the film by three if we wanted to get it back to far-off Manhattan in time for the six o'clock broadcast. Mike was waiting for us. He hadn't changed much. His short, dark hair had thinned and receded, but he was still fired by idealism and rebellion. We embraced in the parking lot, and he thanked me for coming. I was concerned about the time and I told Mike we had to move things along if we wanted to get the film on its way back to the station in time for air. Outside, in the cold, leaning against our cars, we formed a loose plan of attack, operating under the assumption that any institution allowing retarded children to exist under the sordid conditions Mike was describing would do whatever it could to discourage picture-taking. We decided that we would storm the building, shoot what we could, and get out before anyone in charge could confiscate the footage or make our lives difficult for showing it.

BUILDING SIX, WILLOWBROOK STATE SCHOOL

I drove—I always drove, when we were out on a heavy story—and Mike sat up front, giving directions. The crew sat in back and prepared on the fly: Bob Alis, the cameraman, tinkered with his newer, lighter version of the Auricon sound-on-film camera; Dave Weingold, the sound man, connected his audio lines to the camera; Ronnie Paul, the lighting man, got his portable sun-gun ready. We drove past the guard at the gate at high speed. Willowbrook, seen for the first time, looked so pretty as I careened onto the grounds in our big black Chevy sedan that I took a split second to wonder if Mike had taken us to the wrong place, or, worse, if his shocking descriptions were embellished. It was possible, it occurred to me, that his firing had clouded his perspective. Willowbrook looked too pastoral a place to house the horrors he'd described.

I jumped the curb in front of building six and took the Chevy right up onto the grass. I wanted to get as close to the building as possible. We poured out of the car and raced inside, cameras rolling. Mike Wilkins led the charge and Bob Alis filmed from behind. I was in a kind of warrior trance, my commando mode, and all I could think was to get inside, get the footage, and get out. I had a mission and I didn't stop to wonder about what we'd see, or feel, or what it would all mean, just as long as we could document it on camera.

I was totally unprepared for what would happen next.

We bounded up the steps and into a washroom area; the smell hit us before we reached the empty room, but it was bearable. I thought to myself, this is nothing. There's no story here. But we kept on. Mike knew where we were going. Next, he turned and opened a heavy metal door with a small glass window. We barreled in after him. There we saw about sixty profoundly retarded children living on a drab, cold ward that looked like an unfinished basement. There were wooden benches and straight-backed chairs scattered randomly about the floor. Exposed pipes ran the length of the room. Chunks of plaster were peeling from the dirty cement walls, which at one time had been painted in institutional green. A store-bought sign with the message "Merry Christmas" hung on one wall. The other walls were bare.

The residents bore only a passing resemblance to children. Some, as Mike had warned, were naked; others wore fragments of clothing; others wore straitjackets. Their heads were swollen; their bodies, bent and twisted, and their eyes were blank or rolled back. Their movements were either wild and jittery and unpredictable, or slow, almost somnambulant. Some of the children were lying on the floor or on benches; some sat and rocked back and forth, as if they were davening; others staggered aimlessly about the room. A few ran from Ronnie's light; most were attracted to it.

It has been twenty years since I last looked at the unedited footage from that first visit, but the images are clear and haunting.

I can still see myself from behind, long hair and black leather jacket, pointing out the atrocities I wanted Bob Alis to capture, saying, "Shoot this, shoot that."

I can see a child drinking water, like a dog, from an open toilet bowl.

I can see a small black and white television set, turned on but not tuned in; and in the glow of the cathode, I can see several children watching the blurry screen and listening to the static.

I can see a boy of about eight or ten, lying on the cold floor, curled in the fetal position, his pants pulled down around his ankles, waiting for an attendant to come and clean the shit from his ass.

I can see a large black woman struggling with several children in the middle of the room; she is holding one child under her arms, like a parcel; two or three other children—moaning, flailing—are clinging to her from behind. I can see the look on this woman's face: a sheepish shrug, which seemed to say, "This isn't my fault."

A chorus of wails and moans that sounded more electronic than human accompanied the images. And the rank odors of shit and piss and vomit mixed together left the room smelling of institutional stench.

I later wrote, "This is what it looked like. This is what it sounded like, but how can I tell you about the way it smelled? It smelled of disease and it smelled of death."

At first, I was so filled with adrenaline that what I was seeing didn't really register. I took it all in, but didn't recognize any of it for what it was. I was still thinking, okay, let's get this on film and move on. I had a tactical job to do here. Get the story, I kept telling myself. Get the story. But after only a few seconds—it started to hit me.

It was almost as if the air had thickened. My movements became more difficult. I stopped barking out directions to Bob Alis and to the rest of the crew. I became almost paralyzed, gripped by what I was seeing. I couldn't move from the bathroom, where I'd wandered, my eyes fixed on the row of toilets without seats and caked with filth, here and there a small child curled around the rotting porcelain bases. I thought I'd seen everything at that point. After a year and a half reporting from the trenches of New York City, I'd seen mass murder victims, fire victims, drowning victims, drug overdose victims, horrible crash victims. I had seen what I thought were the pits of human misery and despair. But this, all of this, was the most horrific, nightmarish thing I had ever seen.

I was snapped back into action by the need to get out of there. I knew we were running out of time. Going in, we expected about a two-minute window in which we could film before the authorities were alerted to our presence. We were pushing things. Any minute now, I felt sure, a building supervisor, or the police, would descend on Building Six. Mike Wilkins, on the lookout, had so far seen nothing. Still, it was time to move.

I stumbled from the bathroom and found Bob Alis in the dayroom. "Let's go, Bob," I said. "That's enough. We have to move."

"Just a minute," he said, "I've got to get some more shots."

'No," I said, "let's go. We've got enough."

BOB ALIS: This is news, you haven't got a second chance at it. So you've got to be keyed up to do it right the first time. Nobody's going to do it again for you. When you've been doing this for a long time, you realize you can take anything. As a cameraman, as long as you're looking through a viewfinder, as long as you're concentrating on your job, then the discomfort, to put it mildly, comes later. The weight of the camera, you had to concentrate on that, in those days. And there were technical things you had to concentrate on. There's no other way to do it. I can look at bodies through a camera differently than when I look at a body when I haven't got a camera.

We'd been in there less than five minutes. We left the same way we came in. We loaded back into the sedan, and I tore out of there like we were in a bad movie. I skidded and bumped and fishtailed back onto the campus road and stomped on the gas. On the way to the exit, we passed two Department of Mental Hygiene police cars heading in the opposite direction. Their lights and sirens were on. We left rubber and roared past. Once we were off the grounds, I knew there was nothing anyone could do to keep this story off the air.

Mike gave me directions to Elizabeth Lee's apartment. No one else spoke. I don't know what the others were thinking. I don't even know what I was thinking, not exactly.

My mind raced. What if the film didn't come out? We always worried about that in those days, before videotape; you never knew whether you would get a picture. Also, what if the state came down on station management and prevented us from using the film? Surely, Willowbrook administrators would attempt to block the showing of our illegally obtained footage. I was all over the place with worst-case scenarios, but then at some point I started telling myself there wasn't anything anybody could do to keep me from telling this story. If the film didn't come out, we'd just go back and shoot it again. I'd find a way. If there was some kind of legal hassle, I'd find a way to ignore it, or overcome it, and move forward. I was so outraged there would be no containing me. They'd given the wrong person the wrong ammunition, and I was going to make them regret it.

As I drove the mile or so to Elizabeth Lee's apartment, underneath the shell-shocked silence that filled the car, I vowed that I would close Willowbrook down. The conditions there were so inhumane, so outrageous, so far beyond the realm of human decency, there was no way they could be allowed to continue. I knew that once the story broke, once I showed those pictures, I would humble whoever was responsible. I would punish them.

And I would liberate those children.

ADMINISTRATION BUILDING, WILLOWBROOK STATE SCHOOL

I was still reeling when we arrived at Elizabeth Lee's apartment a few minutes later. To this point, all I'd gotten were the pictures to the story. Here, now, I was after the rest of it.

Mike Wilkins filled in some of the blanks. On-camera, he told me that the ward we had just seen housed some of the most severely and profoundly retarded children in Willowbrook. He also told me that conditions there were comparable to conditions in most other buildings. He told me that there were thousands of children like the ones we had just seen, not going to school, sitting on the wards all day, not being talked to or cared for by anyone. He told me that one hundred percent of the patients at Willowbrook contracted hepatitis within six months of being in the institution. And he told me that during his eighteen months on staff, there had been approximately three or four preventable patient deaths every week that could be directly attributed to neglect, malnutrition, and diseases spread from unclean living conditions.

He was articulate and thorough, his steady tone belying what he was saying.

We were joined at the apartment by a group of parents who came to show their support for Mike and Elizabeth, and to protest the conditions at the school. I interviewed some of the more-vocal parents who explained to me, through tears, how it was they'd come to place their children at the school, and how now, after so many years, they saw no viable options for alternative care. They told me of their struggles with the administration, and applauded the efforts of Mike Wilkins and his emboldened colleagues.

Our story—giant, explosive, shocking—was starting to take shape, and at three-thirty we met a motorcycle courier back at Tina's Diner and dispatched the first film to the newsroom. "Tell them what we've got," I told him before he roared off, but in fact, it would take a while before we knew what we had—at least a half-hour for the drive into Manhattan, and another forty-five minutes in the lab, developing the film.

We still had some reporting to do.

As I've stated, this was a classic example of a one-sided story, and I was expected by the conventions of broadcast journalism to at least look for another side. With the footage safely on its way to the lab, I decided to return to Willowbrook to interview its director Dr. Jack Hammond. I knew there was nothing Hammond could say to lessen the horror and impact of our film. There was no way he could explain away what we'd just seen. All he could do was to seek some legal means to try and prohibit its airing. (A temporary restraining order was not without precedent, or possibility.) He had, by now, most likely been informed of our earlier visit to building six, but there was a chance that he had not. I was concerned that by returning for the administration's point of view we would tip him off to our story, but I felt it was a chance we had to take.

Jack Hammond had been the director of Willowbrook since the summer of 1965. Upon his arrival, he was heralded as a quiet reformer, and he may have been, but as his tenure dragged on, and he sat and watched his budget and his staff shrink every year, parents began to complain that he was too quiet. He began to be seen as an old-line bureaucrat, and to take on that look and

demeanor. I had him figured for the enemy. I blamed him for what
these kids were being made to suffer. I wanted to take him down.

Mike Wilkins told us how to get to the administration building,
and we walked in with the camera rolling. Hammond's secretary
seemed to panic under the lights, and she returned with her boss
in less than a minute. "Dr. Hammond," I said, introducing myself
and gesturing to the crew and the rolling camera, "in view of the
school's severe staff shortage, why were Dr. Wilkins and Mrs. Lee
fired?" I made no pretensions at playing the cool, dispassionate
reporter; I blasted with everything I had.

"I have no comment about Dr. Wilkins," Hammond replied, his
manner brusque, official.

He was the calm, and I was the storm.

"Well," I shot back, "he claims that the conditions in some of
the wards here are pretty bad."

"The conditions here are deplorable," he allowed, "but they are
no better or worse than those in any other facility for the mentally
retarded in the state."

"What can be done about it?" I demanded.

"Have the legislature restore the budget cuts."

He had a practiced, patient answer for every challenge I hurled.
We went back and forth like this, and we were getting nowhere.
After a few minutes, I realized I had all I needed from Hammond,
all I was going to get, and so I gestured to Bob Alis to kill the
camera.

When Bob and the rest of the crew left the room, Hammond
turned to me and said, "I understand you were inside building
number six this afternoon."

I knew where he was headed the instant he started in, and I
immediately regretted waving off the crew. I wanted a record of
this exchange.

"We were near there," I said.

"No," he insisted, "you weren't near there. You were inside."

"I'm just going to tell you this," he warned, "if you broadcast
the face or any recognizable feature of any resident of this facility,
you will be in serious trouble. I have already called your station
and so informed them."

His attempts to restrict our broadcast were less prohibitive than

I had feared, and offered a clue to why no one had been able to blow the lid off this wretched place. The administration had kept the world away by hiding behind the shield of the patients' rights to privacy. The way I saw it, though, the issue wasn't privacy; it was the patients' rights to basic human dignities, and our rights (and obligations), as members of the press, to expose their situation. I left there not knowing what to make of his warning, or if I would honor it.

It was after four o'clock when we finished with Jack Hammond, and we were up against airtime. We really had to tear out of there to get back to the newsroom in time for the six. We didn't have two-way radios in those days, or cellular phones, so we did not communicate with the newsroom that we were on our way. The assignment desk had come to rely on me, and to trust me, to get back to the newsroom in time for the broadcast. I drove like a lunatic through the beginnings of rush-hour traffic and made it back to West Sixty-seventh Street with only about forty-five minutes to write and edit the story. It would have to be enough time. I took over the newsroom. I announced—loudly, to all in earshot—that this was the biggest story this station, this city, had ever seen.

77 WEST 66TH STREET

Word of what we had reached the newsroom before we did. Steve Skinner, the producer of the six o'clock news, alloted us more than ten minutes of airtime, without commercial interruption, about four times longer than the typical news story and the longest story *Eyewitness News* had ever run. Marty was busy on another project, so I commandeered another editor, Don Liebert, to load the uncut film onto the movieola. There was still the chance that nothing came out, and I was anxious to see what we'd brought back. I needn't have worried. Looking at the footage over Don's shoulders brought back all the revulsion. It came in a rush. It was like revisiting the same bad dream. There were moments when I caught myself looking away from the editing screen. Bob Alis had captured all of it, and then some. He'd been busy filming in the dayroom while I was frozen by the scene in the bathroom, and so there were new horrors to turn from.

As I watched, and didn't watch, I kept hearing Jack Hammond's warning. I don't know why, but it gnawed at me. I knew that in buying into his threats and not showing the faces of these children, I would diminish the impact of the material. I knew that unless we could make the story human and personal, these horrifying images wouldn't even dent the city's hardened consciousness. And yet I also knew that the threat of a lawsuit from the state's Department of Mental Hygiene, or from some of the parents, could easily derail our efforts at shutting down the place.

I was ripped apart by indecision, but we were hurtling toward deadline. I had to make a choice and I made the wrong one. I punked out. I told Don Liebert to edit the footage so that none of the kids were recognizable. He accomplished this by using wide- and rear-angle shots, and by keeping each scene extremely short, to about a second in length. It was the safe way to go, but it was gutless.

Strangely, Don Liebert's staccato jump-cuts and quick flashes didn't hurt the story or lessen its impact. Instead, they added a surrealistic dimension, one that perhaps best captured the sad chaos on those wards. The children appeared on the screen as unrecognizable, yes, but also frightened, vulnerable, and helpless. Their plight hit home. I'd made the wrong decision, for the wrong reasons, but it turned out okay. You could even argue that the fast cuts and anonymous horrors made the piece more disturbing than it would otherwise have been. After that first night, though, I never mentioned Hammond's warning to anybody else at the station; nobody mentioned it to me, and that would be the last time I abided by it.

By the next day, it seemed that all people could talk about was Willowbrook. Doug Johnson told me it was the biggest local story he'd ever seen. The entire city, it seemed, was galvanized by it. The thinking, caring viewers of the metropolitan area all had the same reactions—shock, outrage, anger—and almost immediately we began to see a bitter and widespread censure of the Willowbrook administration.

It was as if some muckraking broadcast journalist stumbled upon Hitler's concentration camps, with cameras rolling. (That's how it registered for others, too; at one of the subsequent protests, on the school grounds, I saw a parent carrying a placard announcing, "Remember Dachau, Remember Willowbrook.") In many ways it was just as unacceptable—what was happening to these kids, what was going on out there on Staten Island—just as hideously wrong as the concentration camps of World War II.

By midnight, the station had received more than three hundred telephone calls from viewers outraged at what they had seen. This was an enormous response. Typically, we'd hear from a couple dozen viewers, tops. Before Willowbrook, for example, one of our biggest audience responses stemmed from a report on the cruel and violent treatment of dogs and cats in a privately run local kennel; having gotten such a heated reaction by exposing those kinds of conditions for animals, you can just imagine what we'd tapped into here. Those were our pets; these were our children.

GENE MARCIONA (former assignment editor, *Eyewitness News*): It was just fantastic. Al Primo had often said, if we ever find a story that we feel we can get our teeth into, then we got to stay with it and stay with it and make that story the focus of our news show for weeks and weeks. We needed a story like this one, and this was obviously the one. When Geraldo came back with this story, we knew this was the one, and we knew we were going to keep with it 'til the end.

By the next morning, when I logged back in at work, we'd heard from another seven hundred viewers. We'd struck a chord—the numbers were extraordinary—and it became quickly apparent that we had to have another piece ready for Friday's six o'clock newscast. Trouble was, I had been asked by the assignment desk to cover what could have been (literally) an explosive story. This often happens in the news business: You get going full-steam on one story, and then along comes another breaking story to get you going in a completely different direction.

Federal agents had been tipped to the planting of nine time bombs by antiwar radicals in banks around the country. Three of the targeted banks were located in New York, and I was to spend the early part of the day following the bomb squad from bank to bank. It was a tense and heady assignment, and on any other day I would have welcomed it. This was the kind of down-and-dangerous trench reporting I loved and did well. On this day, though, my mind was someplace else. All morning long, tracking the city's bomb squad, my thoughts wandered back to Staten Island, to the children. Already those images had burned into my memory; the echoed wails and moans drowned out the frenzied activity in the targeted banks.

I was able to concentrate enough to get the reporting done on the bomb-squad story, but I didn't have the head for the editing. As soon as I returned to the newsroom late that afternoon, I told Steve Skinner, our producer, that I wanted off that bomb-squad story and back onto Willowbrook. Steve was more than accommodating, but there was no time to return to Staten Island for a follow-up in time for the six o'clock newscast. While I was out on the bank job, we continued to get calls from angry viewers, and so it was clear that we had to put together something for the six, but what?

Marty and I put our heads together and restitched the previous day's footage with his fresh perspective. We restored some of the material I had asked Don Liebert to delete the day before—the faces of the children—and then I wrote a script that made prominent mention of the number of phone calls we'd received since last night's broadcast. The pictures were largely the same; the words were new, and improved. It had taken a day, but I'd finally found the words to adequately express what I was feeling when I'd walked onto those wards. I'd been up against it the night before—and, also, in the middle of it—and the right words simply didn't come. I was thinking too much about the mechanics of the story and ignored the emotions behind it leaving the piece something less than the indictment it should have been.

Time dragged. I wanted to get this follow-up story out there, and I wanted to get it right. If last night's piece was the set-up punch, tonight's would be the knockout blow. Six o'clock couldn't come soon enough.

The bombs were the lead story, and on any other day I would have been all pumped up about it. Twenty minutes into the broadcast I did the Willowbrook follow-up, my own private lead story. I did live intros and outros to both pieces, which was not unprecedented but unusual. (In the days when I did two stories for the six o'clock, one or both of them was on film, with no live studio lead-in.) I don't know how I managed the bomb story lead-in, because all I could think about was the Willowbrook piece.

The orchestrated chaos of the studio seemed to come to a halt when the piece came up on the monitors. Everyone watched, frozen. The same thing had happened the night before, but on this night my colleagues knew what to expect. They'd seen this stuff already, and yet they were riveted to their screens for a second look. I couldn't watch those scenes again—I'd spent the afternoon with them, in Marty's editing cubicle; they were already a part of me—and so I watched the others as they took them in. I saw the same look on the face of almost every reporter, cameraman, and stagehand: their lips bit-back in disbelief, their eyes tortured and wanting to look away, but held by the drama of what they were seeing. The studio—off-camera, off-mike—is almost never still and silent, but it was at 6:20 P.M. on Friday, January 7, 1972.

I closed the piece, live, with these words: "We showed you that film again, because it comes with the promise that we're not going to let this story die. We're going back to Willowbrook. Again. We're going to talk to the parents. Again. And look at those horrible wards. Again. And show them to you. Again and again and again. Until somebody changes them. Even with your help we probably won't be able to change the world, but we just might be able to make life a little more bearable for some kids living at the outer edges of society."

I left the studio and made for my desk. I sat down, and the rest of my emotions caught up with me. I cried the tears that wanted to come since I'd first stepped into Building Six. I sobbed into my hands, at my desk in the newsroom. I didn't have an office—in those days, none of the reporters did—and I sat out there, head in hands, and let the tragedy of those children wash over me.

I didn't know it then, but this was the zenith of *Eyewitness News* as a philosophy; this was local television news at its best; this was advocacy reporting in its purest sense. This was what I'd been put here to do—on this earth, and in that newsroom. My coverage of those Willowbrook stories would shine as the triumph of emotion over procedure, passion over objectivity, the outsider over the establishment. It was important, and it was right and true. I will always remember that moment—that Friday, in the newsroom, after the knockout-punch-of-a-follow-up—the way a football player might remember a winning touchdown, a Romeo a great conquest, or a politician the election that he pulled from the fire. I was spent—emotionally and physically—but this was my glory.

GREAT GORGE, NEW JERSEY

Edie and I went on a press junket that weekend, to the Playboy Club in nearby Great Gorge, New Jersey. It was one of those public relations perks we probably weren't supposed to accept. In those days, all reporters were blanketed by invitations to nearby (and not so nearby) vacation spots or nightclubs, with all expenses paid. The deal was you'd be brought out to some hot-shit establishment trying to make a push for itself, and there be spirited and dined and shown a good time, all on the house. In return, it was hoped that the junketed reporter would find a way to make favorable mention of the place—in his newspaper, or on his newscast—at the first reasonable opportunity.

That's the way those things worked. I worked a little differently. The only thing I ever agreed to do at those P.R. junkets was to eat their food and enjoy their accommodations. That's all. Whenever I was invited to one of those things, I'd explain that there was no way I would ever mention their resort, or their restaurant, or whatever it was they were trying to peddle, no matter what kind of VIP treatment I received. Invariably, they'd tell me to come anyway.

And so, this time I went. It was free. Plus, it was conveniently located ("less than an hour and a half from midtown Manhattan," brochured the flak who extended the invitation). Mostly, it was a chance to ski and hot-tub and forget, in little bits, the horrors I had seen across the river, on Staten Island. Willowbrook State School and the Playboy Club at Great Gorge were probably no more than fifty or sixty beeline miles apart, but they might as well have been on different planets.

But I needed the contrast, welcomed it. I needed to get away. I'd been unable to shake the sights and sounds and smells of Willowbrook since my visit two days earlier. I found myself unable to enjoy a simple thing like listening to music, or taking a shower, or reading a magazine. I felt guilty for even thinking about enjoying myself, or relaxing. I couldn't get my own life back without first winning theirs back for these children. My thoughts were everywhere polluted by the ugly footage that ran through my head, unedited, on some kind of unending loop.

Edie and I could not leave the city fast enough. Through me, the sudden strains of Willowbrook had reached her, even in the day or two after the first report aired. We both wanted to get away from it, and so we packed up my Beetle and made for the George Washington Bridge to New Jersey. It didn't matter where we were going, just that we were going. I'll ski all weekend, I thought, until I'm too tired to do anything else, until I'm too worn out to even think.

The downside to our going was that the Willowbrook story continued to unravel, without me to pull at it. I knew this would happen, but knowing it and experiencing it were two different things. Overnight, the story had become bigger than just me, and I expected that. Other stations were covering it, the local newspapers were covering it, it was only logical that *Eyewitness News* send out a reporter to keep pace with the other guys. Still, it troubled me. It wasn't that I was possessive of the story, I don't think. Rather, I did not like that the fate of those children suddenly rested with someone else. I did not trust another reporter—any other reporter—to deliver the kind of story I knew I could deliver, the kind of story that would shut down Willowbrook and help to find a better way of life for the children who lived there.

Robert Miller was assigned to do the follow-up story for our newscast that Saturday. I didn't trust the story in his hands. He and I rarely saw things the same way, and even a one-sided story like Willowbrook would look different to us. He was taken on an official tour of the facility by Dr. Hammond, along with other members of the local press. This time, the news cameras were shown only what the administration wanted them to see. This time, the wards, were cleaned up; the children, dressed. Higher-functioning patients from Building Seventy-eight were trotted out to demonstrate that, indeed, some of the school's efforts were positive and goal-oriented and making a difference.

When we arrived at the Playboy Club, I was thankful that Great Gorge was still in signal-range of WABC-TV; I would not have to miss the station's Willowbrook coverage in my absence. But when Edie and I sat in our room and watched Robert Miller's report on the Saturday edition of *Eyewitness News,* I wished we were in Vermont, or Switzerland, or someplace far beyond the station's reach. I wished I hadn't seen it; more than that, I wished it never aired. I was furious with Robert Miller and with station management. And I was furious with myself.

Saturday's piece was nothing more than a counterpoint to my first pieces on Thursday and Friday. It was the flip side to a one-sided coin. Not only did Miller miss the story, but he made me look bad in the bargain. The credibility of our first pieces was immediately thrown into question. People who had been aghast at what I had shown would now think the situation not as bad as it really was. They'd think I trumped-up the tragedy as some kind of play for ratings, or popularity. By letting Hammond show-and-tell him around the premises, Miller had undermined the work of the previous two days.

Worse, he'd let the air out of an extraordinary display of public support. I didn't think we'd ever get it back.

ROBERT MILLER (former reporter, *Eyewitness News*): It was a Saturday, and I happened to go out to Willowbrook. I got the assignment. A lot of channels, not just seven, went out to Willowbrook to get corroboration of these awful things that were going on. The man who was the head of the institution at that time said to us, "Yes, yes, these things do go on. We don't have enough people to take care of these profoundly retarded, because it practically requires a one-on-one situation. However, we also have this." And he took us through an area where people were educable, where they were feeding themselves, and they were neat and clean. And they didn't require as much care as the others required. And I put that on the air that night, the Saturday night following the first Geraldo explosion. And we never saw that side of the story again, because it didn't sell. As a matter of fact,

Geraldo said later that I was duped. I was not duped at all. I mean, the guy said, "Look, you want to see this stuff again, I'll show it to you. But I'll also show you this." There was no duping at all. It was just a matter of what you wanted to put on the air.

On Sunday, Duke Wade was sent out to interview Dr. Bill Bronston. Bill's candor won us back a good deal of the momentum we'd lost the night before; he was as outraged as I was that the attention had been deflected from the abject mistreatment of those children, and onto something else.

"There are nearly six thousand people here," Bill said, trying to mitigate against Jack Hammond's whitewashing. "There are approximately one hundred and thirty youngsters in Building Seventy-eight, which was shown yesterday. There are one hundred and twenty-five more in another fairly good building, and about one hundred and fifty females in one more building who are getting a decent, minimum program. But what we're saying is that the overwhelming majority of this thing is what counts, and you can't look at a token program or a building that's been especially cleaned up and say that this is the essence of Willowbrook or the essence of the strategy of the state of New York in caring for the handicapped."

Duke Wade, despite the fact that he was no friend of mine, gave Bill Bronston plenty of time to make his point.

BUILDINGS 23, 25, AND 27, WILLOWBROOK STATE SCHOOL

The two weekend reports effectively cancelled each other out, which basically put me right where I'd left off when I returned to the story on Monday, January 10. The assignment desk gave me free reign on the follow-up, and unrestricted use of a crew, and I had two things to accomplish. First, I went back to Willowbrook to prove a point. I returned with Mike Wilkins to the B ward of Building Six. The children there were almost exactly as we'd left them, despite the mounting controversy. The differences were subtle, and not for the better. The children were quieter than the week before, more dazed and glazed over, and Mike explained that many of them had likely been sedated with Thorazine, the most widely dispensed drug at the school; sixty or seventy undrugged patients, he elaborated, would be too much of a burden on the single attendant assigned to the ward.

On this visit, I felt a right to be there, and so I instructed the crew to move about the building as if we owned the place. I wanted to overstay my welcome and I wanted Bob Alis to film any confrontations with Willowbrook officials. I thought the story needed that kind of heat to get us going again. With impunity, then, we wandered onto the adjacent ward, A ward, where the children were being fed. I learned that their basic diet consisted of corn, bread, a green vegetable, and milk, which was all mixed together in a kind of gruel. I also learned that with no solid food to chew on, the gums of most young patients eventually weakened to where their teeth would fall out or rot. The average feeding time per child—it had been timed, Mike Wilkins told me—was three minutes.

Imagine feeding your own child a full meal in that time. I watched as an attendant fed one small boy, who seemed to be about ten or twelve. The child's head was tilted back, his mouth hung open like a giant baby bird's, and the attendant ladled the mushlike substance from bowl to mouth in a rhythmic motion. The spoonings seemed timed, like a metronone. Most of the gruel wound up on the child's chin; some of it was spit back against the too-frequent spoonings; what was swallowed was taken in gulps and starts. The scene, which was repeated three times a day, everyday, struck me as one of the cruelest, most inhumane things I'd seen on these wards.

Mike Wilkins told me on-camera that this kind of force-feeding was dangerous to the children in two ways: The food can clog in the windpipe and choke the child to death; and, more likely, the food can work its way into the lungs and trigger pneumonia. (More children at Willowbrook died from pneumonia than from any other cause.) Eleven Willowbrook patients had choked to death on their food in 1971, and Mike Wilkins estimated that the actual number was several times greater than the official count. Even Jack Hammond admitted to *The New York Times* that such deaths by force-feeding were a fact of life at the institution, but he said those incidences were rare. Asked to define rare, he answered, "Perhaps three or four deaths a month."

The second stop on my agenda was a noon press conference called by State Assemblyman Andrew Stein. He had toured Willowbrook a month earlier as a member of the Assembly Committee on Health and he'd been trying to contact me since Friday. Now New York City Council president and a perennial aspirant for mayor, Stein was well known by newsmen even then for his ability to generate publicity. I didn't return any of his calls; I had no intention of giving him a free ride on this one. It was my story, not his, and to be honest, I didn't care what Andrew had to say on this issue. As far as I was concerned, if he was so passionate about the odious conditions at Willowbrook he should have done something about it in December, when he first became aware of them.

His press conference today—we were told he would have comments on the firing of Mike Wilkins and Elizabeth Lee—wasn't going to help these kids. It was just another example of a local politician doing too little, too late, for the wrong reasons. I attended his press conference because I wanted to interview some of the parents (I spoke to one mother who told me, disturbingly, that her child would be better off dead than in Willowbrook), and because I was on an ego trip of my own. I wanted to film other local news crews filming Stein. I wanted to show how the thing we had started was growing. I felt very strongly that the only way to close Willowbrook down—or at least improve conditions there— was to generate a media frenzy, a circus played out in our tent.

To Stein's credit, he did more in those early stages to heighten public awareness on the conditions at Willowbrook than any other local politician. After the press conference, he marched the news media to the downtown offices of the Department of Mental Hygiene, where he joined Mike Wilkins, Elizabeth Lee, and concerned parents in confronting Deputy Commissioner Dr. Frederic Grunberg. We filmed Stein asking Grunberg if he would join him in a statement declaring Willowbrook "a disgrace, a disaster, and in desperate need of federal help."

"I am prepared to join you right now," Grunberg replied, in a thick German accent. "And I am sure that I will have complete backing from Dr. Miller [New York State Commissioner of Mental Hygiene Dr. Alan Miller]. The conditions at the Willowbrook State School are absolutely deplorable, just as they are in most of our large institutions."

It was a small victory. We had met the enemy and (in public, anyway) he agreed with us.

Because of our Willowbrook reports, we were suddenly the most watched, most talked-about newscast in New York. The six o'clock show that Monday night scored a nineteen rating, representing over forty percent of the viewers. It was the highest rating *Eyewitness News* had ever received and it was equal to the combined total of our rivals WCBS and WNBC. There was a lead editorial, under the heading "Spotlight on Willowbrook," in the next morning's *New York Post*, crediting us with breaking the story and leading the way. There was a front-page story in *The Village Voice*.

Other reporters assigned to the story by competing news organizations were looking to us to see what we had next. *Eyewitness News* had become almost a part of the story. We dominated it. We were so integral to the effort to expose the conditions in Willowbrook, and to liberate its children, that a planned rally in front of the school, originally scheduled for eight o'clock Tuesday morning, was pushed back to noon to ensure that I would be on hand with our camera crew. It was as if the rally wasn't worth staging if I couldn't be there to record it for our newscast.

I couldn't be there because I had other plans for the morning. While the rest of the reporting pool waited like lemmings for the scheduled protest, Mike Wilkins and I made unannounced visits to the cluster of three buildings located farthest from the main entrance. These "raids," with cameras rolling, were the way this story had been built, and we weren't finished. The rest of the news media waited for developments to drop into their laps, while we were out looking, digging, exposing. The differences in approach were telling, and they would turn up throughout my career.

This time we didn't drive through the main gate, but approached on foot, through the woods behind the school grounds. We hid behind bushes and trees, like something out of an old Warner

Brothers cartoon. It was real cloak-and-dagger stuff, with Bob Alis filming the whole approach from behind. It would have been funny if the stakes weren't so serious. Once on the grounds, we ran across a field to Building Twenty-seven, which housed two wards of young girls. The drama was probably unnecessary, I realize now. (I might have realized it then, too, and gone ahead with it anyway.) There were only two security men patrolling the Willowbrook grounds, and they would have been too conscious of the cameras to interfere. I was swept away by the crusading excitement of it all and charged, when a walk through the front door might have produced the same results.

But even if it was superfluous, our dash made exciting footage, and added an element of drama to what I was consciously structuring as the quest of two young idealists—Geraldo Rivera and Mike Wilkins—for truth and justice. Whatever our dash may have been, Buildings 23, 25, and 27 were for real. These were our first visits to the girls' wards, and for me they were the worst of all. The young women in Building Twenty-seven were grotesque. Their moanings and wailings echoed the sounds in Building Six, but there was something sadder about these voices, something more innocent. Many of the girls sat nude against the cold, hard walls of the ward, and there was something sadder, too, about their nakedness. (Over the years, many had been sexually abused by sick members of the school staff, who were often hired without background checks.) Some of the girls in Building Twenty-seven were clothed, and Mike Wilkins pointed out that school officials had been busy with a kind of makeshift makeover, dispensing new clothes to all the wards likely to be visited by the press. Giving these children new clothes was a lot like giving a Band-Aid to a rape victim.

One older woman held the only toy I'd yet to see in the institution: a hard plastic doll. The doll was naked and missing an arm or a leg. The poor woman stroked it in a kind of elaborate distraction, cooing like a mother.

Later that morning, I was introduced to Bernard Carabello, a young man with cerebral palsy who had spent virtually his entire life inside Willowbrook's walls. He had been misdiagnosed as mentally retarded at the age of three, and it had stuck. He had cerebral palsy, which meant his mind wasn't giving the right commands to the rest of his body. His wiring was frayed, but his mind was sharp. The cerebral palsy left Bernard without full control of his muscles or his movements; if he got excited or agitated, his hands would flail around. He drooled constantly. His speech was dysarthric, which made it difficult for him to talk and to make himself understood. Difficult, but not impossible.

Bernard had become a friend to Mike Wilkins, and Mike held him out to me as a kind of light, an example of what Willowbrook could accomplish if its head and heart were in the right place.

Our interview, which took place in Bill Bronston's apartment, put our evolving story over the top.

BERNARD CARABELLO (former resident, Willowbrook State School): I remember my mother taking me to Willowbrook. I'll never forget that day, at all. I was three years old and it's still a picture in my mind. She handed me into the arms of this woman, all dressed in white. I'll never forget that. I didn't know what was happening. I just remember the picture of it and I remember not liking the way this woman looked. And I was there for eighteen years. I don't try to block it out, because I can't pretend that it didn't exist. There's nothing I can do about it. I didn't think I would ever leave. I always thought Willowbrook would always be my home, for the rest of my life. That was my life. My whole day was, like, sitting on the ward. That's all. I did not look at TV and I did not read. I just sat in the corner and tried to sleep. When we got hungry, we had to wait until the next meal. We didn't have access to the refrigerator, or anything like that. I used to have to drink water from the toilet bowl or else I would go thirsty. I couldn't button my shirt, I couldn't tie my shoes, I couldn't button my pants. I couldn't wash myself. I wasn't given the opportunity to learn. We were bathed everyday, but they washed us out of this dirty pail that they used to scrub the floors with. And they used the same rag on everybody. I'd seen people die from choking on their food. I saw a person get tied to the bed and get hung. I watched that, and I watched it get covered up also. And then, after eighteen years, I just got tired of getting the shit beat out of me, and I got tired of having people kick me in the stomach and the head. It was random, and sometimes it wasn't random. And then I met Geraldo. I think I would have been dead today if it weren't for Geraldo.

I expected Bernard's words to match his body. I was as surprised as any viewer when they did not. Before Willowbrook, I had no experience with the mentally retarded or the physically handicapped and, frankly, I was unsettled by this sudden proximity to it. I didn't know to look past the disabilities and embrace the capabilities. I focused on what a young man like Bernard couldn't do, and not on what he could. I went into our interview with small expectations. In my ignorance, I assumed from his physical disabilities that he would also be retarded. Surely, an intelligent, feeling (and delightful) human being would not have been made to endure the cruelty and hardships of those wards for his entire life. Knowing that Bernard was made to live like the other young people in the wards I'd seen, and judging from his appearance, the most I thought I could pull from him in our interview was some emotion, some feeling.

I was happily astonished. Bernard struggled to get the words out—every sentence was a fight—but he got the words out. When they came, they were powerful and moving.

I saw Bernard as the happy ending. He was hope. I saw in him the potential for virtually all of those children. Through him I came to understand that every one of them had some degree of potential. Each life could be made better, richer, by degrees. Here was Bernard Carabello—happy, bright, smiling in the face of it all—proving that if we just slowed down the system and paid some attention, we would find sparks of humanity all over that godforsaken place.

BERNARD CARABELLO: I was scared. I never did anything like this before, like this interview. They had to sneak me out of the building to Dr. Bronston's house. I had no idea who the hell Geraldo was. I'd never watched the news. I was twenty-one years old, and I'd been at Willowbrook since I was three, and I was scared about what was going on because, don't forget, I had to go back to Willowbrook. I had to live there after all this. They could have beat the shit out of me, they could have taken a stick and cracked it over my head, or they could have taken a belt buckle and whipped my butt, like always happened. So you can see why I was scared, and Geraldo could see that I was scared, and he even told the director of Willowbrook, Dr. Hammond, he told him, "If anything happens to Bernard, I'm holding you personally responsible."

He was spunky, he was courageous, and he was frightened. He was willing to risk everything, not merely to help himself, but to help the other patients there. I sat there and listened to Bernard, and I fought back anger and tears. They must have known this. They must have known that there was this person inside that body. More, they must have known the varying human potential in all of those six thousand patients.

I had never met anyone like Bernard. We clicked, and we've been good friends ever since. For everything he'd been through, and he'd been through a lot, he was a fighter, politicized, and willing to lay it all on the line. The institution hadn't managed to kill him, it hadn't managed to stifle his soul. And it hadn't quashed his sense of humor. (After a later, anticipated visit to one of the school's wards for young men, it was Bernard who pointed out that the patients had all been given new sneakers, in yet another administration effort to make cosmetic changes where only sweeping changes would suffice. "Their sneakers are so new, they squeak," Bernard said.)

Bernard hadn't lost his heart, and he would come to be the most eloquent symbol of our effort.

LOS ANGELES REGIONAL CENTER FOR THE MENTALLY RETARDED

The rest of the Willowbrook story has all rolled together with the years. I remember slices of it, but I'm missing whole chunks. I covered it for several weeks more, as the lead reporter, on virtually a daily basis. There were big days, and not so big days, and days where there wasn't much happening at all, but we always managed to come up with a related piece. If there were any official developments to the story (such as the twenty million dollars Governor Rockefeller restored to the Department of Mental Hygiene's previously slashed budget), I was there to report them. If there were any unofficial turns the story could take (such as unearthing the Robert Kennedy "snakepit" footage and putting it on the air), I took it there, too.

Soon, I moved off of the Willowbrook campus and widened the scope of the piece to the area's various programs and facilities for the mentally retarded. I found good things and bad, and I let them balance each other out. I even traveled with a crew to California. In those days, this was an unheard-of expense for a local news operation, but we had a point to make. We wanted to show that there were model programs, functioning effectively and efficiently in a state beset by problems of the same type and magnitude as New York's. I profiled the Los Angeles Regional Center for the Mentally Retarded and held it out as a shining alternative. All over California, large Willowbrook-like institutions were being phased out in favor of smaller, community-based programs; state dollars were directed to providing programs to encourage parents to keep their children at home.

I also made my first national television appearance, when Dick Cavett devoted the entire ninety minutes of his late-night talk show to a discussion of Willowbrook and the care of the mentally retarded. As his last guest, Cavett brought out my new friend Bernard Carabello, who revealed one of the more frightening bits of information to ever surface around this story. Bernard told how he'd been summoned to Willowbrook's administration offices shortly after his interview appeared on our *Eyewitness* newscast. There, two staff doctors had questioned him about his relationship with Mike Wilkins. The two doctors had actually encouraged Bernard to confess to a homosexual relationship with Mike and threatened him with seclusion—the state-school version of solitary confinement—if he refused to do so. It was a shocking revelation, one that not only confirmed Bernard's earlier fears of reprisal, but also invalidated every single thing a Willowbrook official had ever said about wanting to do right by the school's children.

Finally, I prepared a half-hour prime-time special on the story. "This place isn't a school," I denounced in the special. "It's a dark corner where we throw children who aren't pretty to look at. It's the Big Town's leper colony." The special aired on Wednesday, February 2, 1972. I watched it in the bedroom of our apartment on Avenue C. Edie cooked a TV dinner, and the two of us watched. Two and a half million New Yorkers did the same thing. The show was the highest-rated local news special in the history of television, a distinction it held until the following year, when another documentary of mine, "The Littlest Junkie," achieved the same status.

The Willowbrook special put a cap on the most extraordinary period in my young career, although the cap wasn't twisted on too tight. I would continue to visit Willowbrook over the next ten years, both as a follow-up reporter and as an outraged citizen. Too, those first stories sparked what has since become a lifelong concern for the mentally retarded. In the months after the day-to-day story went away, I established the One-to-One Foundation, a money- and consciousness-raising group formed with the expressed intention of closing down the huge state-run institutions for the mentally retarded. I also wrote a book, my first, for Random House, a detailed account of the evolving story called *Willowbrook: A Report on How It Is and Why It Doesn't Have to Be That Way.*

The giant story Marty and I had been looking for ended up changing my life, and the lives of countless others.

MIKE WILKINS: I really believe that without Geraldo, we wouldn't have made news at all. And I don't think it was just the film that did it. It was his approach and his style. When you go in that room, in those buildings, you feel very sick at heart about what's going on. I had brought people in there, to show them where I worked, and they would cry. You know. And they wouldn't want to leave. They'd want to adopt one of these kids, you know. And Geraldo related to it like that, and he was able to make the people of New York City see that. I don't know if anyone else would have been as tenacious as he, but I know that they wouldn't have made it explode on the scene the way he did. We had been trying to get some attention for months, and nobody cared, and then Geraldo came, and he presented it, and all of a sudden the whole city cared. It was in everybody's face. He does that. He puts things in your face.

*   *   *

The state's Department of Mental Hygiene began almost immediately to reduce overcrowding at the institution. From a high of around sixty-five hundred residents when it was the world's largest, the population dwindled to just a few hundred. The process would take fifteen years. Social change, however necessary or popular, takes time.

CHAPTER SEVEN

HOTEL DES ARTISTES

Willowbrook humbled me. It made me a different journalist and a different person. It also made me a celebrity.

Everything that had been happening when the story hit—the parties, the independence in the newsroom, the street notoriety— was heightened as a result of Willowbrook, and by the time the story quieted down, I was left with a new life.

It was a complete and sudden transformation, and I relished it. I loved the attention and everything that came with it. My days and nights were a constant, invigorating stroke. I was twenty-nine and the city was mine.

To understand what I was going through during this time, what

171

my life was like, I think it's important to understand how others saw me. Television critics, after Willowbrook, were still unwaveringly kind to me; they would turn later, but not yet. "If WABC's nightly *Eyewitness News* were a newspaper," *Life* magazine wrote at the time, "Rivera would be its feature writer, its parajournalist. . . . Right now, Geraldo Rivera is a local New York boy, but that won't last long. New York has a way of nationalizing those who charm it." Hardly a week would go by without some mention of my work, or exploits, in one of the local newspaper columns; movie companies were calling, seeking rights to my life story; a documentary was in the works, intended for a Spanish-speaking audience, tracking my life and career. Soon, profiles and reviews started to appear in publications like *Time, Newsweek, New York* magazine, and *Harper's Bazaar*.

My colleagues were as cool as ever, perhaps more so in the shadows of my new spotlight. An aggressive jealousy, a tension, followed me around the station like a dark cloud. Several weeks after Willowbrook, things deteriorated to where I actually, physically, separated myself from the rest of the newsroom, in a gesture I thought appropriate to my growing stature and new independence. There was a basement in our building at 77 West 66th Street, used over the years to store film and files and the detritus of the television news business. I took it on myself to clean the place out, and move my office downstairs. I didn't clear the move with anyone, I just did it. I had two or three volunteers at the time, and we cleaned the place out, brought desks down, and set up shop. We made the basement over into our own little headquarters. The next day, when Al Primo and the rest of the management team came to work, I informed them that I would be operating out of the basement. That was all there was to it. Once I'd made the move, I had very little contact with the other on-air reporters; our working relationship became confined to the set, on the air, where it was, by necessity, cordial and removed.

DOUG JOHNSON (reporter, *Eyewitness News*): There was a lot of jealousy. Of course there was. Because this guy, this kid, who had come from no place, was rapidly on his way to being a superstar and nothing would stop him. You could tell from the people on

the street. I can tell to this day, just from the questions you get
from people on the street, who's hot and who's not. Geraldo was
hot. The truth is, there's nobody in television news anymore that's
that hot.

I was mobbed by viewers (young girls, mostly) wherever I went;
like a rock star with a hit record, I would stop traffic, turn heads,
and start a crowd. I had unpaid interns whose job was to go
through the sacks of fan mail that accumulated in my basement
office every week.

My family looked on at these various developments from afar.
There had been a distancing ever since I'd taken the job at WABC-
TV. My marriage to Edie seemed to put a kind of fence along this
new expanse; Willowbrook, and the roughage that came with it,
turned the fence into a wall. None of us could see our way clear to
the other side. I became so far removed from my parents—and, to
a lesser degree, from my siblings—that we had almost no
relationship during this time. It's not that we didn't speak or visit
(we did, often); it's just that when we did get together we had
nothing substantive to say. They were all as proud of me as ever,
and I know I was filled with the same love and respect for them I'd
always felt, but one hand no longer knew what the other was
doing. If I'd stopped long enough to think about the turns our
relationship had taken, it would have made me incredibly sad;
when I did stop, years later, I turned things around to where they
used to be.

My good, old friends saw me as pretty much the same, when
they saw me at all. I started to spread myself so thin I never had
time for anybody. My social life was muddied by new acquaintances,
by people hoping that something of what was happening to me
would rub off on them. I'd begun to shed lifelong pals like Frankie
DeCecco, and good friends of more recent vintage, like my Alabama
lawyer roommate Leo Kayser, and supplant them with socialites
like Giorgio di Sant'Angelo. I didn't do these things willfully, or
even consciously; they just happened, and I suppose I let them
happen because I wanted to see where these new associations
would take me. It was as if I'd gotten swept up in a strong and
strange current, and I didn't have the ability—or, frankly, the

desire—to look for a low-hanging limb and pull myself to firm ground.

JOHN JOHNSON (reporter, *Eyewitness News*): It all started, with Willowbrook. It was the right time and the right place. We were going through a very, very revolutionary era, where the antihero, in a way, was in, where someone who had Geraldo's charisma was very attractive to the jet-setters. Here he was, almost an outlaw type, who also had the soulfulness to care about the children who were being mistreated at Willowbrook, but who also could get down and boogie. It all fit together.

There was no room for Edie in this new world of mine. At least, I didn't make room for her. This was my one great moral failing during this period: I started to leave Edie behind, to separate. I justified this behavior by telling myself that most of the society invitations did not include her, that it was me (and only me) the swells wanted, and I was too intoxicated by the attention to risk my welcome by bringing her along. I could have, and should have, but I chose not to.

I had been relatively faithful to Edie since we'd gotten together, and entirely faithful during the first two months of our marriage, but the dam broke after Willowbrook. It broke in a big way, and once it did, I was too weak to stem the rush of opportunities. There were a couple people instrumental in pulling my finger from the dike. One was my great new friend Giorgio di Sant'Angelo; another was his great new friend, an outlandish and flamboyant charmer named Louis Martinz.

Louis's background is worthy of note: Louis Martinz was born in Panama in 1940. His parents, who owned the country's only cement factory, were members of the Panamanian oligarchy, and he grew up surrounded by power and privilege. He was educated in the United States (Georgetown, Wharton) and returned to Panama as a young man, initially to work in the family business. Once home, he became an active supporter of Dr. Arnulfo Arias, Panama's three-term president, and by the time he was twenty-eight he was appointed as Arias's Chief of Protocol.

Arias was married to Dame Margot Fonteyn, the famous ballerina, and was overthrown on October 11, 1968, in a coup staged by General Omar Torijos and his strongman Manuel Noriega, who became the country's first dictator and chief of intelligence, respectively. Louis was exiled to the United States for the next ten years, and during that time, he became very involved in the New York arts community. Through Dame Margot Fonteyn, he met Rudolf Nureyev, and the two became friends. Louis had a beautiful duplex apartment in the Hotel des Artistes, and Nureyev would often stay there. Even in his political exile, Louis had a taste for the high lifestyle, and the considerable financial resources to satisfy that taste.

When he sought me out in 1972, he was one of the most decadent and ebullient party-givers in the city. He was about five-foot-six, and sharp-featured, and he wore his long dark hair swept back; he had a distinctive Roman nose, big bridged, but thin and elegant; he looked like a model in one of those Ralph Lauren Polo ads. What I remember most vividly about Louis is that he was always dancing, jumping, flitting about New York as if he didn't have a care in the world. He was colorful. He was so concerned about his stunning appearance that when he was arrested and thrown into exile after the 1968 coup, all he cared about, he told me later, was that the newspapers ran a good picture of him on the front page. That was the depth of his political involvement. Still, he had a sharp mind and a biting wit, and the two of us got along terrifically.

(Item: Louis Martinz, it should be noted, outlasted Torijos and Noriega; his party has since been returned to power, and he now serves as the spokesperson for the Panamanian government.)

Louis and Giorgio ran in the same circles in 1972, and as that circle grew to include me, Louis decided that we should meet. One day in late January, during the height of my initial Willowbrook involvement, he called me at the station and introduced himself. He was charming on the phone, like an old friend, and indeed we did have quite a few friends in common. He complimented me on the Willowbrook stories, and I could tell by his tone that he was sincerely moved by what he had seen.

There was a reason for his call, Louis said. He was throwing a birthday party for Marian Javits, the wife of the then senior senator from New York Jacob Javits, and he wondered if I might be able to attend. Marian Javits, at the time, was notorious for flaunting convention; unlike most senator's wives (or husbands), she never lived in Washington with Jack during his long tenure. She chose instead to remain in New York, and there made herself into one of the great dames of New York society. Dames, as in dame. The Pat Buckleys and Nan Kempners of that world blanched at anything less than the European-style grande dames, but not Marian. Marian was a full-blooded woman. She was the doyenne of the whole New York modernist-art explosion, and surrounded herself with a court of artist-admirers that included Andy Warhol, Jasper Johns, Robert Rauschenberg, Frank Stella, and the jewelry designer Kenneth Jay Lane.

I left Edie home for this party. Louis specifically asked that I not bring her along. Marian wanted to meet me, he said, alone. Of course, as Louis and I talked on the phone that first time, it became apparent that the evening promised a chance at a liaison with the wife of a United States senator. At the time, this wasn't as obvious as it seems in the retelling. For all my balls and chutzpah, I never imagined that a woman like Marian Javits, nearly twenty years older than I was and married to a powerful, influential man nearly twenty years older than she, would have designs on this local television reporter. I was pretty full of myself then, but not full enough to imagine this. Marian was part of the establishment, even if she made it her business to fly in the face of it. Plus, she was glamorous. She lived in a fabulous apartment on Upper Park Avenue—a kind of artists' salon decorated by original (and now priceless) paintings given to her by her many friends—where she regularly entertained the likes of Henry Kissinger and Frank Sinatra. What did she want with me?

I went to the party and rang the bell. Louis answered the door and gave me a big hug, and a loud hello. This was the first time we'd met, and the exchange reminded me of the exaggerated warmth I got back from Giorgio at that first meeting. There were more than a dozen people on the first floor of the duplex when I arrived. "Geraldo!" Louis enthused. "Geraldo! So good of you to come. Geraldo." We were standing in a narrow hallway that extended from the front door by about ten feet, and in this closed space his greeting came back at me louder than it had to. He was announcing my arrival to the rest of the room, and after a bit more of the same, he gave up on any pretense and simply hollered, "Marian, he's here!"

Marian hurried out to the hallway and embraced me, tight and warm. I was flattered and aroused. This forty-eight-year-old former actress and model had the dark hair, bright eyes, and full lips of a gypsy. I responded to her embrace with great enthusiasm. Sure, I was married, but so was she. To a senator. If she didn't care what the others at the party thought, then why should I? We went up to Louis's second-floor bedroom. By the time we came down, the party had broken up, or moved on. As it played out, Louis had staged the whole event simply so Marian and I could meet.

And so began one of the most enduring romances of my life, a sustaining passion. Despite the age difference, and despite the fact that we were always publicly committed to other people, we had an enormously fulfilling and adventurous affair. Marian was as attractive to me in 1985, when we parted for the last time, as she was in 1972. I was in love with her, without question, but there was more to it than that. I was also infatuated with her, and captivated by the heart-stopping drama of being with her.

It was an on-again, off-again relationship, but it had legs. When we were on, I would steal an hour from the newsroom and run over to her apartment. After filming my story for the day and tracking it, I would wait for the live studio portion of the broadcast at six o'clock at Marian's. I knew no one else would be there, and that she would be waiting. There was a tremendous sexual pull between us, and I couldn't be in the same room without wanting her.

Of course, the pulls of our separate lives prevented our being open about our relationship, so we found this way to be together. It satisfied us and caused the least amount of pain (and bad publicity) to the other people we cared about.

I remember our stolen moments fondly, and with great passion. One, in particular, stands out. I arrived at Marian's late one afternoon—she had since moved into a stunning duplex on Fifty-seventh Street, which made our frequent rendezvous that much more convenient to the Sixty-sixth Street newsroom—and the place was crawling with Secret Service agents. Henry Kissinger, secretary of state at the time and at the height of his power, was due for dinner that night. I saw what was going on and figured I'd leave and come back later.

"No," Marian said, "let's go inside." She wasn't the type to let a small thing like the Secret Service get in the way of romance.

So, as the Secret Service searched the rest of the house, and checked her phones and did whatever it was they were supposed to do, Marian and I moved into her mirrored bathroom (where we could lock the door). It was one of the most thrilling sexual experiences I've ever had, made magical by Marian, of course, and by the sheer illicitness of the moment. Marian, too, was charged by the danger. Though she was a product of the forties and fifties, she had a real sixties head; she was two steps ahead of everybody else. Her public life was set against the political and society establishment, and she found a special charge in tweaking that establishment, goosing it; I loved being her accomplice.

That night I returned to the apartment for the dinner and was given a place of honor at the table, to Marian's right. Henry Kissinger, who at the time was treated like an inspired world leader by the press and the public, and who was about to be awarded the Nobel Peace Prize, sat across from us, and it was all I could do to get through the evening with a straight face. I felt sure he knew what went on there that afternoon—the Secret Service was in the next room, combing the apartment, how could he not know?—and the thought of his knowing made the memory even more improperly delicious.

Marian and I were like two teenagers when we were together. She was an attractive woman, in great shape. I'd never been with a woman that age before (which is my age now), and the difference factored into the attraction, for both of us. We were separated by a generation, and yet we were drawn to each other. We gave each other tremendous pleasure, but there were other aspects to our long affair.

I don't know if I thought about our relationship at all, at the time, or was simply reacting to it, swept up by it. I was very much aware, of course, that this wonderful woman was married to the lion of eastern establishment liberal Republicanism. At times, this thought alone was enough to get me off. I was also aware that I had a relationship with Edie to maintain. I did a lot of rationalizing, trying to make peace with myself over what I was doing. But I didn't stop long enough to dissect the situation, to see what it meant.

There was a different ethic in place then, and I didn't feel as guilty about things as I would now. Edie had come from this hippie existence, where free love was the imagined ideal; in Marian's world, among her cultured artist-friends, monogamy was not the ethos. It was well known, in certain circles, that Marian and I were having an affair, and wherever I turned, I took away a sense of approval, not disapproval. The relationship was encouraged and nurtured by those around us. The senator and Marian had an understanding that predated my arrival. She had had other admirers, which was fine as long as there were no scenes and no scandals. There were none.

Of course, I never told Edie about Marian. Maybe I was a coward. Or maybe I liked the strange mix of guilt, excitement, and power that came with sustaining these two relationships.

SAN FRANCISCO

After Willowbrook, I found it very difficult to get started again at work. There was a kind of going-through-the-motions to my reporting in the ensuing weeks, and after a while of this, I began to realize I needed a kick in the butt. The routine stories had begun to bore me. Everything looked thin and unimportant. I wanted all of my stories to have the bite and urgency of Willowbrook, but of course, that wasn't possible.

I had trouble with balance. I had begun to be seen by the rest of the world as an in-house rebel, a jet-setting outlaw, a street-fighting muckraker; I liked these new images, indulged and encouraged them, but without a story to match them to, without a place to aim my righteous indignation, I was adrift.

MARTY BERMAN: As long as I've known Geraldo, it's never normal or boring for very long. There's always something. You never have to worry about being bored because something's going to happen.

You know, just wait another week or two and something's going to happen, and if nothing happens he'll make it happen. He will precipitate a crisis, because he likes it. It's not the crisis he wants, but the action.

If there was nothing to incite my activist yearnings within *Eyewitness News*, then I could at least go out and do some good on my own. The first of these efforts, naturally, was on behalf of the children still living in Willowbrook, and in institutions like it throughout the state. The stories, and their attendant images, had created a palpable buzz, but in the weeks after, the buzz began to die down. I wondered how to convert this new public awareness and outrage into action, before it completely dissipated.

Naively, at first, I expected the system to respond, but I soon saw that this wasn't going to happen. The state may have restored twenty million dollars to its Department of Mental Hygiene budget, but that was a surface move and I didn't see anybody looking to take things any deeper. Over time, I learned that you can't just ask people to be disgusted and outraged over a set of horrors and expect some good to come out of it; I learned that lobbyists draft bills and that unions determine agendas and that government is an incompetent monolith that responds only to its own self-interests. I also learned that, in order to effect sweeping change, you have to be specific, you have to target attainable goals and channel your energies toward achieving them.

All of this was a revelation to me. I began to look on television as a tool, not just to rake muck, but to establish programs and set agendas to alleviate the ugliness I had helped to unearth. Through Willowbrook, I became almost evangelical about taking these children out of these big institutions and putting them into small group homes. The successful, working models I'd visited in California convinced me not only that it could be done, but that it should be done, and it became my operating philosophy in the care of the mentally retarded. Of course, it wasn't exactly my philosophy; there had been a lot of research, conducted by a growing number of mental health professionals, to support this shift to smaller, more humane facilities. I merely saw this movement as the light to lead these children out of darkness, and I labeled it as such.

My motives were pure. At least I thought they were at the time, and that counts for something. To be hard on myself, I'm sure there was also a hidden agenda. It was like the old Disney cartoons, with a good Pluto angel and a bad Pluto devil; one had a halo and one had a pitchfork, and the real Pluto was torn between the competing advice. I think now, looking back, there were several things driving me, a halo and pitchfork, both. There were times when you could have attached me to a lie detector and administered sodium pentothol and asked me if my involvement in the Willowbrook story and in the charitable works that succeeded it were anything other than altruism on my part; I would have said no, and the test would have showed me being absolutely truthful. At other times, though, it would have been a lie and the test would have found me out.

I did stop to think, on occasion, this is great for my career. I did stop to think, on occasion, this could mean another raise. Yes, I knew the scathing reports and my off-camera efforts would ultimately help liberate those children, but there was a part of me that also knew I'd give myself a tremendous career-boost in the bargain. I recognized that Willowbrook accelerated my meteoric rise to celebrity, and I wanted to keep it going.

Whatever my motives then, I became a full-fledged activist, lobbyist, and amateur politician. I became an advocate, in every sense. At the urging of the Catholic Charities organization in Brooklyn, I launched a series of efforts that would eventually grow into the One-to-One Foundation, which became a kind of lobbying group and charity fund-raiser designed to fundamentally restructure the way the mentally retarded were cared for in the metropolitan area and throughout the state. Over the next ten years, One-to-One would raise more than five million dollars, open more than one hundred group homes for more than one thousand mentally retarded residents, and see the state's mental health budget nearly double as a direct result of our efforts.

One-to-One took its name from our firm belief that anything less than one-to-one care for our mentally retarded children was not enough. Don Farber was my attorney at the time (he was also Kurt Vonnegut's attorney), and Dan Pepper was my accountant (and Kurt's), and the two of them helped me to set it all up. Giorgio di Sant'Angelo and Louis Martinz became involved. Leo

Kayser became involved. The debutante Francine LeFrak, the daughter of billionaire New York real estate developer Samuel J. LeFrak, became involved. Eleanor Guggenheim, Mayor John Lindsay, Dick Cavett . . . almost everyone I knew during this time became involved in the elaborate effort. Even Marian and Jacob Javits checked in with their support.

The actress Geraldine Fitzgerald also became involved, in a big way; she and I would actually cofound One-to-One and serve as its cochairs in the first few years. A respected veteran of stage and screen, and of great and good works for many area charities, Geraldine opened doors to me that would have either remained shut, or been shut in my face. She brought in an entirely different set of deep pockets than I could have ever hoped to reach, and introduced whole new segments of New York society to the disturbing living conditions of the city's mentally retarded children. The One-to-One Foundation would not have happened without Geraldine's hands-on and heartfelt involvement. That she would later distance herself from the charity, and from me, doesn't diminish her lasting contribution, or her boundless dedication.

In our gestating stages, in early 1972, One-to-One was a skunkworks operation, at best. We didn't even have a name yet, or a Geraldine Fitzgerald, or a tangible objective; all we had was the passionate conviction that the state's mental institutions were outmoded, underfunded, understaffed, and ill-conceived. We were determined to shut them down, all of them, and to create in their place a network of small group homes in communities throughout the area.

We set up shop in the basement of 77 West 66th Street. There was plenty of room down there (the way I was going, it must have seemed to management I'd take over all of it before the year was out), and we filled it up pretty quickly. We had at least a half-dozen volunteers (local college students, for the most part) and we raised money, organized events, and managed to constantly keep the name of Willowbrook and the plight of the mentally retarded in front of the public. We lobbied community boards. We found reasons to shoot follow-up stories for *Eyewitness News* and other area stations. We fought endless zoning battles, in our efforts to secure and convert housing to our needs. We tapped into existing governmental programs, where we could find them. We wanted to keep the money we raised as seed money, because we knew we could never raise enough money to inaugurate these homes in any significant way. We were not the Kennedys or the Mellons or the Rockefellers. We were just a bunch of concerned, active, and, in some cases, high-profile people, collecting nickels and dimes from the working class.

PAUL DOLAN (director, One-to-One Foundation, 1974–1982): Our greatest decision was how to spend the money we took in. Most charities develop their assets and dole out a small portion of those assets to fund its programs, or research, or what have you. That was one way to go, but some of us felt very strongly that this was not the way to go for us. We wanted to spend the money. What was the point of investing five hundred thousand dollars and building one group home with the fifty thousand dollars earned in interest when we could build ten group homes right off the bat? Geraldo saw it the same way I saw it. We weren't the Ford Foundation. We weren't in the charity business. We were in the business of getting it done, and to get it done we had to spend the money.

In early spring 1972, we were casting about for a way to demonstrate the workability of our one-to-one concept and hit upon the idea of emptying out all area institutions into Central Park on one summer day, and matching each one of our mentally retarded children with a volunteer. I was learning, through my friendship with Bernard Carabello, that familiarity was the best way to overcome fear and ignorance regarding the handicapped. What better way, we all thought, to breed that familiarity than to stage a gigantic, feel-good event like this one?

It was a high-concept idea, one that would certainly move us a long way toward our stated goal of helping these children lead richer, more independent lives in their own communities. It was also a huge undertaking—there were, roughly, twenty-five thousand mentally retarded children living in metropolitan-area institutions—and it was going to cost a great deal of money to orchestrate. We needed to do something to raise some money and we needed to do something big. Eventually, we came up with the idea of a benefit concert. It was an easy, natural fit, but it wasn't such an obvious one. This was long before the days of Live Aid and Farm Aid and Band Aid; up until this time, there were a few small-scale efforts involving small-scale talent, but other than George Harrison's Concert for Bangladesh, there had been nothing quite so big as we envisioned.

We were still without a name, or an identity, at this early point, and so we dubbed the day in the park and the benefit concert "An Extraordinary Event," which is what we were hoping it would be. I seized on the name because I wanted to make it clear that my involvement was on a one-shot basis. I was not in the business of raising money or running a charity, I thought at the time; I was a reporter. Yet here I was planning a concert.

My thoughts moved immediately to John Lennon. Our friendship was still strong, although it had been back-burnered. John left the Village for San Francisco toward the end of 1971, and we hadn't been in touch for several weeks. I didn't know it at the time, but he apparently had a substantial heroin habit in those days and had gone to the Bay Area to get himself detoxed. The benefit concert was the impulse I needed to try and resurrect our friendship, and I flew out to California to enlist his enthusiasm, unaware of his drug problems.

The John Lennon I found in San Francisco was a different animal than the one I'd last seen in New York. He seemed especially jittery and nervous, and I learned later that it was partially due to the detox. It was also a function of the fact that there was a crew around us most of the time, which was a first for us and our relationship. I'd always made it a point never to let my job bump into our friendship, but I made an exception here because of our planned benefit concert. If John agreed to perform for us, I wanted to surround the occasion with as much footage as I could put together.

These were tough times for John. He was already under attack from Attorney General John Mitchell, who was seeking to deport him as an undesirable alien because of a previous conviction for marijuana possession. The breakup of the Beatles had by now been cemented by several years, and he had made a life for himself with a woman who was blamed for this breakup and who was then one of the most unpopular popular figures in recent memory; at the time, it was widely held that Yoko Ono had stolen John Lennon's mind and his free will.

But hard times or not, I went after him. I was relentless in my pursuit. I told John everything he wanted to hear, everything I thought would put the notion over the top for him. I got it in my head that the fate of the mentally retarded children hung on his decision. With John Lennon to headline our benefit concert, I thought, we'd surely get the attention and the money we needed to help the children back home. He was lukewarm about the idea at first. As I wore him down, we caught up on old times, partied a little, toured the Bay Area, hung out together. He kept the news about the detox program from me (he kept it from everybody), but he was forthcoming about everything else. He even picked up an acoustic guitar and serenaded me for hours with old Beatles tunes. He'd finish one song and then ask, "What'd'ya wanna hear next, Geraldo?" with that great lilting accent of his, and I'd toss out a request and he'd either say, "Aw, what'd'ya wanna hear that for?" or he'd play it. His guitar was plugged into one of those twenty-five-dollar baby amps, and he was just vamping. I still have the tapes from this "private concert," and they are among my most cherished and prized mementos.

Eventually, John and Yoko agreed to do the benefit concert, and their involvement marked the true beginnings of the One-to-One Foundation. It would also mark the end of our friendship.

The logistics of putting together the concert was our undoing. There were so many details, so many bits of business, that we became estranged over the ordeal. I remember we were all so enthusiastic about the concert that we added another show, and it was to present us with one of the event's near-disasters. Ticket sales for this second show—a weekday matinee, scheduled on short notice—were lagging well behind expectations, and at one point John became concerned that he would have to go on before a half-empty house. Yoko didn't want him to be embarrassed like that, and so Allen Klein wrote a check to the charity for fifty thousand dollars (the money came, indirectly, from John), and we gave the unsold tickets to the mentally retarded children and their

One-to-One volunteers. We reported it to the press as a grand gesture on John's part, but he was motivated as much by fear as charity.

Incredibly, that same fear nearly brought about the still-hoped-for Beatles reunion. John and Yoko called Paul and Linda McCartney in England and invited them to appear at the benefit, in a move sure to pack the house and make the appearance less nerve-wracking for John than it was promising to be. As the date neared, he grew more and more frantic at the thought of performing a full concert without his old mates. He'd performed before as a solo artist, but for some reason the thought of fifty thousand people in Madison Square Garden got to him. Paul refused, and history was left unmade.

I had advised the charity to sell the rights to simulcast the concert to a syndicated radio program called *The King Biscuit Flower Hour*. John and Yoko, meanwhile, had sold the television rights to ABC-TV. John was outraged that the radio rights had been sold, and he refused to sign the release validating the sale. The radio deal was for fifteen thousand dollars; even in 1972, it was a lot less than those rights were worth, but the deal was in place and we needed the money.

"John," I begged, "just sign the release, it doesn't mean anything."

"There's no such thing as me signing something and it doesn't mean anything," he answered me back, curtly. "My signature always means something. I don't want to sign this."

Regrettably, I threatened him with bad publicity—"How would you like it if everyone knew you were withholding money from this charity?"—and essentially strong-armed him into allowing the *King Biscuit* simulcast.

There were a lot of lesser disagreements, and the rock 'n' roll press was constantly after me to bad-mouth John. They were tipped off to our differences and wanted some dirt, but I wouldn't give it to them. The standard line we used was that I was in charge of the event, and John and Yoko were in charge of the music. But there was now a wedge in our friendship that would sink deeper before it began to disappear. They came back to New York, to their Bank Street apartment, for the weeks leading up to and following the concert, and our relationship continued to disintegrate. The concert itself was a smashing success, but the friendship it had been built on was left in pieces. By the time they finished editing the concert footage for network television, John and Yoko had cut me out of the entire special. This was their way of getting back at me. I was the emcee of the show, I was onstage all the time, between acts, filling the downtime between sets—indeed, the whole event stemmed from my convictions—but to judge from the ABC special, I was hardly involved at all. (The concert is now available on videotape.) I was a speck on the screen, dancing onstage with Bernard and a crowd of organizers at the concert's grand finale.

But our differences should not obscure the fact that John Lennon helped to put the mentally retarded on the map. Maybe he never intended that. Maybe he did the concert for his own reasons. Maybe he wanted to beat the immigration rap that was already bubbling up against him. Maybe he did it because he was fighting back from the early commercial failures of his solo career, and he needed something to remove the tarnish from his post-Beatles image. Maybe he did it because I forced him to do it. The reasons don't matter. He did it and he helped untold numbers of people. More, he participated in the process of positive social change, on an issue that didn't directly concern him.

The end result was historic, in so many ways—as rock history, as part of the movement toward progressive care for the mentally retarded. And it was historic, for me, because John Lennon had touched my life, and I—at that time, anyway—had touched his.

The One-to-One concert was the last John and I saw of each other for several years. The Nixon administration had drawn its last breath. John Mitchell was a bad memory, but the Justice Department had finally gotten John's deportation case before a judge in the Immigration and Naturalization Services courtroom in downtown Manhattan. I had been following the case in the papers, along with everybody else, when Yoko reached out to me on John's behalf. She wanted me to testify at his hearing, and I agreed. I offered to do even more; I covered the story for *Eyewitness News* and mustered righteous indignation for my old friend.

There were only four witnesses to testify on John's behalf. Sculptor Isamu Noguchi told Immigration Judge Ira Fieldsteel that the U.S. was the best place to bring up a child of mixed parentage like the Lennons' son Sean, then nine months old. Actress Gloria Swanson said she thought John was a good influence on the younger generation. Norman Mailer testified that Lennon was one of the greatest artists in the Western world. And I told the court about the Lennons' efforts on behalf of retarded children, and about the nearly three hundred thousand dollars raised as a direct result of their efforts. I opened our books to INS lawyers, and informed the judge of the opening of The John Lennon/One-to-One group home in Queens. (The home, now called Imagine, still houses ten mentally retarded young adults.) I said I could not imagine a country that wouldn't be better off with a citizen like John Lennon, and I meant it. But I had to do more than convince the court that John wasn't a doper, and that his character was sound. The immigration laws were very specific, and they held that the artistic creativity of a person, or the genius of a person only counted on his behalf if the talent was unique and not easily duplicated by a native citizen. It should have been no contest— this was John Lennon, for God's sake!—but still we sweated the decision.

John was very friendly to me in the courtroom, during and after my testimony. Yoko was still cool though. It was almost as if she saw my efforts here as a kind of payback for the concert. She flashed me looks from the witness dock all that afternoon, looks that seemed to say, "We deserve this much from you." John earned his green card on August 9, 1976, just over four years before he was killed. "It's great to be legal," he told a crowd outside the courthouse. "This is where the action is."

Even without Yoko's stamp of approval, John and I had a warming in our relationship, which lasted for about a year. We saw each other socially during this period, not as often as during our first wave of friendship, nor as comfortably, but it seemed like we were getting there.

Just as we were getting back the momentum we had lost, John separated from Yoko and retreated into his well-chronicled "lost period" on the West Coast, with May Pang and Harry Nilsson. By the time he returned to New York a few years later, we had grown apart. We were different people. I'd been divorced and remarried. He'd returned to Yoko, but he once again fell to drugs and drink; it would be some time before he picked himself up again.

John moved into the Dakota, the medieval-seeming apartment building featured in the movie *Rosemary's Baby* and located at Seventy-second Street and Central Park West, while I was living at Sixty-fourth Street and Central Park West, and we saw each other on the street every now and then. Things were always cordial between us, but that was where it ended. I ran into him and Yoko in November 1980, just three weeks before he was killed. *Double Fantasy* had just come out, and it looked like it was going to be a big hit; Sean was five years old and a beautiful little boy; John had dried out and was promising great things again. The three of us talked for about twenty minutes on the corner in front of my building, and we made what may or may not have been one of those forced social vows to see each other soon. I remember going back up to my apartment afterwards, thinking how nice it would be, and unexpected, to get our friendship going again.

Three weeks later, I heard the shots. I actually heard them. I was only eight blocks away, it wasn't even a half mile. It wasn't unusual to hear shots ringing out in New York City, and I didn't know what they were at the time, but I heard those shots as clearly as if I had been on the scene. About an hour later, I got a call to come in for a special *Nightline* segment on the assassination. That's how I heard. I thought it was a crank call at first. I didn't want to believe that John was gone, in such senseless, brutal fashion. My immediate reaction was similar to the way I processed the news of Michele Clark's plane crash; I wanted to undo my finding out; I wanted to hang up the phone and pretend it'd never rung.

I went on the air with Ted Koppel and reminisced about John, and our friendship, and the One-to-One concert. It was a Monday night, and there was a football game still going on, and so we had some time to pull footage from the concert, and from my trip to San Francisco. I was choked up on the air, and it was difficult to get through the show. There were so many memories of that brief, golden period in both of our lives, and they were all balled-up

together to where I was baffled by them. It didn't feel like I'd lost
a friend, though, and I remember being surprised by that. John
and I were friends once, but our friendship ended in the aftermath
of the One-to-One concert. What I did feel for John on that cold
December night was gratitude. I remain eternally grateful to him.
Whatever his motive's, or Yoko's, John did something for me that
he didn't do for anybody else. He gave the last fully rehearsed, full-
blown concert of his life, because I asked him to. Nobody can
minimize that, and there's nothing I can find out about John
Lennon, courtesy of Albert Goldman or any other schlock
biographer or hanger-on, that will in any way detract from his
supreme contribution.

Shelter Island

As 1972 hit its stride, the One-to-One effort began to take up a
good twenty to thirty percent of my waking moments. Work and
play filled the rest. Marian Javits and Louis Martinz became my
full-time social directors (and tour guides) during this time, and
through them I found myself getting deeper into the New York art
and social scenes. The city quickly becomes a very small town
when one confines it, as I did, to the hip social class. I started
seeing the same people, over and over. My nights were filled with
the likes of Andy Warhol and Rudolf Nureyev and Mick Jagger, and
all manner of models and socialites and counts and countesses. My
days were marked by work, and by my liaisons with Marian and, as
the year wore on, with an assortment of young women.

I had a unique seat to the strange goings-on in the city during
that time. I was both a part of the glimmering scene, and also at
some remove from it. I have a very vivid memory of standing in a
corner at a party and watching Andy Warhol watching everyone
else. Warhol was a kind of cult leader, and a voyeur. I was
fascinated by the way he saw the world, and the way the world let
itself be seen by him. He was always near the center of the best
parties, with Halston and Elizabeth Taylor and Liza Minnelli, and
he would just sit there and let the spectacle wash over him. He
often provided the drugs and sometimes the settings, and these

stars of the moment would perform. He was like a puppeteer, always two steps away from the main spotlight. It's always struck me as strange, in the years since, when people described Andy Warhol as being a part of that crowd, because he wasn't a part of it at all, at least not from where I sat. He was the ringmaster, never one of the circus clowns.

One party in particular, in early summer 1972 stands out. Louis was there, and so were Marian Javits, Giorgio di Sant'Angelo, Rudolf Nureyev, Mick Jagger, and a host of glitterati. At some point, as we were getting ready to close the joint, I suggested to Louis that we all go back to my place on Avenue C. There were about fifteen of us, all together. Louis, ever the proper party-giver, resisted the idea at first; he didn't think I had anything adequate to serve on such short notice. But I persisted. I had loud music. And booze. And a great apartment. And that was enough.

So we all tumbled out of the club, and I climbed into my Volkswagen, and led a caravan of three limousines down to the Lower East Side. What a picture we must have made, a brand-new "superbug" and three stretch limos, snaking along those dirt-poor, crime-infested streets while the rest of the city slept. It was as if we were traveling in some airtight and exclusive bubble, or maybe in a kind of glass-bottomed boat, able to look out at the unhappy wonders we'd pass and still not be touched by them, affected. We were a rich, happy, and famous band of untouchables.

Everyone began having a great time, and Edie and I were running around making sure everyone had something to drink. The music was blasting. Louis was flitting from one room to the next, and I remember Nureyev marveling about the apartment and the neighborhood. There was a lot of dancing and merrymaking and a swirl of marijuana smoke about the place. Even Nureyev was out there dancing, having a grand time. I was nearly two years into this celebrity crowd by this point, and I should have been used to these people, this behavior, by now; but Mick Jagger? Rudolf Nureyev? in my Lower East Side living room? dancing?

The party was moving along at full steam and I disappeared into the kitchen to mix some drinks. I was pretty much oblivious to everything but the task at hand, but then, suddenly, someone snuggled up behind me. I felt an arm around my waist, and I made a kind of half pivot to see who it was. It was Nureyev, and he was moving in time to the music, pressing himself against me from behind. He was being playfully suggestive, overtly sexual, and before I had a chance to even think how to respond, Jagger approached me from the front and started doing the same thing. They were kidding, and giddy, but there was also something seriously competitive going on between them. Nureyev said, over my shoulder, to Jagger, "He's a virgin, you know." And then they laughed, and Jagger joked, "Oh, well, we can break him in." The two of them continued in this way for probably only a half minute, at most. Nureyev made a joke out of running his fingers through my long hair.

I squirmed out from between this odd sandwich and laughed the whole thing off. But the incident lingered. Underneath their silliness, they were making a play, and underneath my initial shock and discomfort, there was a spark of attraction. This was 1972, and there was a kind of androgyny in the air; the dominant sexual philosophy, at the time, was to try everything, at least once, as long as you didn't hurt yourself or someone else. I was a part of that crowd, and let a part of me buy into that philosophy. I was nothing if not open-minded. And here were Mick Jagger, the bad boy of rock 'n' roll, and Rudolf Nureyev, the most renowned dancer in the world, recently defected and at the height of his career and celebrity, conspiring in an impromptu and playful battle for my affections.

I hate to disappoint, but nothing happened beyond the playful exchange in my kitchen. But if I were ever going to have a homosexual experience, it would have been that night, with Rudolf Nureyev and Mick Jagger.

During that same time, Random House paid me fifteen thousand dollars to write a quick-hit instant book about Willowbrook, which they published that June. It was basically a blow-by-blow account of the entire developing story, along with a history of the institution and of the care and treatment of the mentally retarded in New York State. The book was illustrated with still photos pulled from Bob Alis's filmed footage. It was a worthwhile project, one that dovetailed nicely with my goal to keep the horrors of Willowbrook out there before the public until we were able to erase them; it also fit in nicely with my pitchfork agenda to expand my professional horizons.

And, what's a book without a publication party? Mine was given to me by Marian Javits, at the Watergate apartment she occasionally shared with her husband in Washington, D.C. It was a gorgeous apartment, and a terrific party. Marian and Jacob Javits were there, of course, and Edie, and a stunning guest list that included Kurt Vonnegut, Henry Kissinger, Frank Sinatra, Secretary of Defense Robert McNamara, influential senators Edward Brooke of Massachusetts, and William Fulbright of Arkansas, and CBS News star Eric Sevareid. If some disaster had befallen that apartment on that day, the tragedy would have made the front page of every newspaper in the world.

The party was also in honor of Jack's recent birthday, and he and I were tandem guests of honor. It was a relatively intimate affair, with no more than thirty or forty people. Most of the guests were friends of Marian and Jack's, with some media and publishing types thrown into the mix. Copies of the Willowbrook book were set up about the place, and Kurt's steady Jill Krementz snapped pictures for me. It was a grand and attention-getting gathering.

The Javits's apartment opened up onto a lovely patio, and because it was summer, much of the party was centered there. Marian wore a sleeveless summer dress with a provocatively plunging neckline. Edie, befitting her ephemeral nature, had on a long, soft gown of the sort worn by princesses in Arthurian legend. I wore a tightly tailored white suit, which in retrospect seems a horrible fashion failure.

After the meal was served, buffet-style, Marian took me aside and told me there was something she wanted to show me. I didn't think anything of it. The patio was abuzz, and nobody noticed us slip away. We disappeared inside for a short while.

The only things that kept Marian and me apart were our diverging (and conflicting) lifestyles. I stated earlier that my fidelity to my young and beautiful wife disappeared with Marian. To be truthful, it didn't just disappear; it went into hiding.

During that same summer of 1972, Edie and I rented a house on Shelter Island, with Kurt and Jill. Shelter Island is an idyllic East End retreat, located roughly between Long Island's north and south forks. It's connected to the mainland by ferry, and dotted by great old houses on wooded properties with sweeping lawns leading down to the bay. Kurt and Jill used the place only once or twice the entire summer; the rest of the time it was left for Edie and me. It was my first summer home, and my first taste of the Hamptons. I grew up on Long Island and barely even knew the Hamptons existed. It was a whole other world. It was all about money and power and excess; it was an extension of the privileged life I'd been exposed to through Marian in Manhattan, and I adored it. Yes, the house was a rental, and yes, half the rent was fronted by my father-in-law, but those things didn't stop me from playing the part that came with the trappings.

That house was the setting for some uninhibited escapades that summer. There was one night (and day, and another night) that characterizes that whole period. A bunch of us piled into a motorcade of cars and headed out to Shelter Island. It was well after midnight when we left the city. Edie was with me, and some of the One-to-One volunteers, and some of my new jet-setting friends.

ILENE BERG (coordinating producer, *Good Night America*): What proceeded to take place was the 1972 version of a mild orgy. Lots of grass, and lots of Quaaludes, and a lot of bed-hopping. Edie had an old chum named Sunshine, who had come from the West Coast. This was the tail end of the flower-child era, and we were all still hippies to one extent or another. So Sunshine, a very beautiful woman with long, flowing black hair, came out to Shelter Island with us. It was a real bizarre group of people. Mostly women. I remember Geraldo being in bed with several girls. Then I remember them moving to the bathtub. And then a magazine reporter came out with her photographer. And I, being the very, very dutiful little advance woman that I was, and not participating in this sexual group grope, decided I had to head them off at the pass and take care of the journalists and protect Geraldo and be a good little P.R. lady. But the reporter managed not only to make it past the bedroom door, she actually got into the bathroom and, as I recall, said, "Oh, this looks like fun," and took off her clothes and jumped into the bathtub with the other six people who were there. At some point during the proceedings, Geraldo was making it with Edie's friend Sunshine. And at some later point, I saw Geraldo come screaming out of the bedroom saying, "I'll kill him, I'll kill him." He was talking about the photographer, who had gone off into the fields with Edie. The way I heard the story was that Edie was getting back at Geraldo because she saw him making it with Sunshine. She was devastated, and crying hysterically, because Geraldo was making sounds with Sunshine that he didn't make with her. Geraldo's double-standard reared its ugly head at that moment. It was okay for him to be in the bathtub with several women, and to make it with Edie's friend, but it was not okay for Edie to go off and make it with the photographer.

I had a fierce case of the double-standards back then, and even Edie's one-time flirtation wasn't enough to keep me in line. There were times there I was so far out of line, I wasn't even on the right page. In my defense, in 1972, the sixties mind-set was still lingering. And, after Marian, I could no longer resist the various temptations. With great practice, I became expert at juggling several relationships at a time—with Edie, with Marian, and with any one of a dozen or so of my new-found admirers. This juggling required that I develop a whole network of trysting places in close proximity to the newsroom. I used to use Sly Stone's apartment in the Century on Central Park West. Sly and the Family Stone were a hot group that year ("I'm Gonna Take You Higher!") and he had become a friend. Other friends, with apartments in the neighborhood, let me make copies of their keys.

One of my favorite romantic playgrounds became the boiler room in the newsroom basement. I discovered the boiler room not too long after I moved my headquarters down there; it was convenient, private, and warm. I discovered the room on an impulse born of necessity. I had two cute and smart young women working for me at the time, college coeds from out of town who were infatuated with the television news business and their proximity to the local star of the day. They were attractive and dedicated, and after a (short) time the infatuation became mutual.

On one unusually slow news day, things heated up to where all indications suggested an urgent need for privacy. We found it, in the boiler room, and from that day forward the three of us would regularly disappear there. All we had in the way of furniture was a chair, which made our entanglements daunting and creative, but we were always up to the challenge. This particular relationship, begun as one of my many dalliances, blossomed into one of my great romances. (Two of my great romances?) We were together often, over a period of years, but I was never intimate with either individually. When one moved back to California, years later, the relationship with the other also came to an end.

No one said no to me in those days. They should have, but they didn't. I had everything I ever wanted, and things I never even knew I wanted but didn't mind having. It was common for women working for me in those days to wind up in my bed. It was almost like a part of the job description. Edie must have known, but we never confronted each other. Other than that one time out in Shelter Island, it never came up.

When it did, finally, we had to separate and move on.

CENTRAL PARK

I was distracted from the slow breakdown of my marriage to Edie by the gradual buildup of One-to-One. As we were careening toward the Madison Square Garden concerts, and the gathering in the park, it became quickly apparent that the foundation would outgrow and outlast our wildest expectations. It also became clear that any ongoing effort would be too much for me to handle.

My involvement was a distraction not only from my personal life, but from my professional life as well.

DOUG JOHNSON: I have one distinct memory of that period and I've recounted it many times. Imagine, if you can, the circumstances we had in that newsroom over there, as Rivera went from Willowbrook and sprung from that, and created One-to-One. This is a newsroom, for Christ's sake, and in the basement we had Yoko and John and all these stars traipsing around ordering coffee. This is a newsroom. That memory depicts Rivera's hot image, it depicts the madness of those early years of the 1970s, the society, and it depicts *Eyewitness News* and what it was becoming and how it would change the business forever. All those people, all over the newsroom. It was hysterical. It was madness. It was great. It was a lot of fun. It was Camelot.

*   *   *

Our inaugural events were resounding successes. Stevie Wonder, Roberta Flack, Sha-Na-Na, and a host of other acts joined John Lennon and his band Elephant's Memory, for two (barely) sold-out shows at the Garden. The artists really put their hearts into it, from John on down the lineup.

The afternoon's events in Central Park required the most attention. We literally moved twenty-five thousand mentally retarded children, from area institutions as far away as upstate Rockland County, and matched each child with a volunteer. Everybody in city government was involved—the mayor's office, the police and fire departments, the sanitation workers. We had volunteers from every local college, and from every uniformed service. We were New York's "in" charity that summer, and we all got in our buses and vans and cars and descended on Central Park like a loving swarm.

I ran around the city like a madman, between the park, the Garden, and the newsroom. I had a concert to emcee, a festival to preside over, and a story to shoot for the six o'clock news. For the broadcast piece, we filmed the children in the park and set it against John's song "Imagine," which at the time was merely a hit single and not yet the anthem it has become. Still, the song gave us the ideal message, the custom-made background music for what turned out to be a perfect day in the park.

We continued with our high-profile fund-raisers, which included another concert the following summer (with Judy Collins, Bill Withers, John Denver, Peter, Paul and Mary, and the dueling banjo players from the movie *Deliverance*), and what would turn out to be an annual telethon on WOR-TV, Channel 9 (which I cohosted that first year with Geraldine Fitzgerald), and assorted one-shot events: celebrity softball games, boxing matches, picnics. We also became a kind of media clearinghouse, providing research materials and documentary footage to print and broadcast reporters in other markets who were working to help deinstitutionalize care for the mentally retarded in their home states. We didn't want to limit our efforts to New York, and the most directed and cost-effective way we thought to expand our base was to make our information available to anyone else who wanted it, to encourage other journalists to seek out and expose Willowbrooks in their own states.

Within our first year, we opened two group homes in New York City and began to see a hopeful end to generations of mistreatment and neglect. We now had working models in our own backyard, and across the country, of small group homes providing one-to-one care at a cost per child below the cost of institutional care. We continued to expose the deplorable conditions; more, when my own station became saturated, we would feed additional leads and story ideas to reporters at the other local stations. We became the mouthpiece for parent and church groups whose goals coincided with ours. We successfully lobbied legislators in Albany; the state budget for the Department of Mental Hygiene increased dramatically in that first year, as it would for the next ten years.

Still, the One-to-One Foundation was not without its critics. Some of the blasts came from within the organization itself. After losing a struggle for the contol of the board of directors, a woman named Karla Munger, our first executive director, resigned from the group, taking four staff members with her. Karla then charged that the organization was letting more than five hundred thousand dollars in donations sit idle in the bank, when we should have been using the money to fund research, or programs, or to open group homes. Her allegations sparked an inquiry by State Attorney General Louis J. Lefkowitz, who found no evidence of mismanagement or wrongdoing. Technically, the allegations were not entirely unfounded, I'll admit, but they were misdirected; yes, we were sitting on a lot of money, but that was because our concerts and telethons had raised far more than we expected. From the beginning, our operating philosophy held that it was better to spend money on the right projects than to rush to spend the money simply because we had it. Before Paul Dolan signed on, One-to-One really didn't have a clear system of getting and spending; our hearts were in the right place, but most of us had never raised or disbursed charitable funds before.

The worst thing about the charges was not the attorney general's investigation. I was confident we would be cleared as soon as investigators could examine our books. The real damage was done by *The New York Times,* which had been contacted by Karla, and which ran a short story citing her allegations. The reporter never even called me to get our side. I called the paper's metropolitan editor the Friday morning the story appeared and complained bitterly. He acknowledged the lack of fair play and ordered a follow-up story. It ran the next day, essentially putting the charges of a single disgruntled employee into context. Of course, far fewer people read *The New York Times* on Saturday than on Friday, and the allegations haunted us long after the investigation was completed. Although I make a habit of forgiving my enemies, I never forgave Karla. She had not only attacked me, she had attacked the charity, and the charity was above reproach.

We lost Geraldine Fitzgerald in the fallout of negative publicity surrounding the investigation; we never spoke about it, but my read is that she felt she could better lend her name and her enthusiasms to other, better-organized causes, and so she quietly distanced herself.

Once the investigation was over and Paul Dolan was installed, we rebounded handsomely. Our most critical moment at One-to-One—and, indeed, our crowning success—came early in 1975. I had just produced my second Willowbrook documentary in December 1974; "A Case Against New York" tracked the dismantling of that institution in the nearly three years since I first reported on conditions there; we also reported on the efforts of various groups to spur a shift in mental health treatment throughout the state. The special broadcast captured a great many national awards and, more importantly, captured again the public attention that had first been juiced in January 1972.

PAUL DOLAN: Nobody remembers that Geraldo stayed on that story for years and years and years. Nobody remembers that second documentary that he did, which to my mind was the more substantial and the more dramatic piece of reporting. And I think you can make the case that it was that second special that directly led to the closing of Willowbrook. You can also make the case that, without Geraldo Rivera, Willowbrook might still be open today, that our mentally retarded children would still be receiving inadequate, inhumane care.

Shortly after we aired "The Case Against New York," Governor Hugh Carey signed into law the Willowbrook Consent Decree, which required that the state close the facility over the next several years. (Carey, as a Brooklyn Congressman, had been active with the early efforts of Catholic Charities to seek alternative housing and care for the mentally retarded.) It was the culmination of three years of hard work, and the first substantive indication that my reports, and our One-to-One efforts were going to succeed.

CHAPTER EIGHT

THE NEW YORK PANHANDLE

My marriage to Edie survived Willowbrook in name only. We were still together, but there was a wedge between us now that we would ultimately never get past. We moved to the Village, in part because I had been spending more and more time away from home, and Edie was afraid to be alone in our old neighborhood. I think we also felt that a change of scenery would help us.

I needed a change of scenery at work, too. Or, at least, a shifting of gears. I hadn't had a breakthrough story since Willowbrook; indeed, all of my talked-about pieces had been Willowbrook-related since the story first broke. Most of my colleagues in this business will tell you they experience a kind of death after any big story, a letdown, and I think one of the reasons I got so caught up in the fund-raising efforts was that I wanted to distract myself from the newsroom. When the adrenaline rush of a great story leaves you, you are left empty. I held onto that Willowbrook adrenaline as long as possible, because it is the toughest thing in the world to get it up and going again, to start from scratch on what may or may not be the next great story. I was like a writer staring at a blank page—intimidated, daunted—and I was trying to do everything I could to avoid the confrontation.

I found the seeds to my next effort at summer's end, in the grape boycott that was fast catching hold across the country, particularly among Northeast liberals like myself. For a long time, I had been wanting to do a piece on Cesar Chavez, whom I considered the Hispanic equivalent of Martin Luther King, Jr. I had met him years earlier, as a young attorney, when Chavez was struggling with his fledgling United Farm Workers union against local growers allied with the powerful Teamsters Union. I was hugely impressed by that first encounter. Chavez was determined to improve the plight of migrant farm workers and his strength was evident in the deep lines and gaunt features of his Mexican-Indian face. Here was a man who would starve himself, or endure any conceivable abuse in order to make more humane and equitable the way American agriculture had always done business. Cesar Chavez struck me as the most important Hispanic in modern American history. That first impression stayed with me and deepened; after my career change, every time I saw Chavez in the news, I wanted to do a story on him, but I was a local reporter in New York, a country removed from his activities out west.

Also, as a kind of parallel, I should note here that I had been greatly influenced by Edward R. Murrow's "Harvest of Shame" reports. I saw myself as the logical successor to Murrow—if not Murrow reincarnated, at least Murrow reinvented—and I invoked the comparison at every chance. I had long been searching for a way to carry Murrow's flame to Chavez's infant agricultural labor movement; the grape boycott gave me the opening I was looking for.

Of course, my world at that time was contained within a fifty-mile radius of the Empire State Building, and all of my stories had to be rooted in that universe. In local news, you need a local spin, no matter how compelling the story. A trip to California, for an essentially California story, was out of the question, and so I set out with my crew for the farming communities in the shadow of the Empire State Building. In the shade tobacco fields of Connecticut, the vegetable fields of New Jersey, and the apple orchards of upstate New York, we found extensions of the very same abuses, the same human exploitation, highlighted years earlier by Murrow. We filmed eight-year-olds working as stoop labor in the fields; we reported on the shamefully low wages and horrendous working conditions of the transitory migrant workers; we showed the shanties, without sewage or toilets, where these workers were forced to live; and we highlighted the efforts of various legal services attorneys and activists who were working for positive change.

We came back with miles of explosive footage, yet there was something missing. At the end of it, I realized, the piece had no drama, no adventure, no compelling reason for our essentially urban audience to watch. The core of the piece, really, would have to be an understanding of how these conditions had been allowed to persist, but words alone could not explain the isolation of these migrants' lives, or the miseries and degradations they were made to suffer; words alone could not explain why they didn't just walk off the farms and into better-paying jobs, why they didn't seek education, or better living conditions, or government assistance. I needed pictures to help show how the farmers—through fear and intimidation—kept their workers in place and in line.

I went out looking for a fight. The same angry juices, the same righteous indignation that had fueled the Willowbrook stories, returned in full force. I was again the combative social activist, and I had a new target. I sought out the most regressive farmers, the ones most resentful of outside interference, and I was determined to make them show their true selves on camera. The migrant counselors directed us to a farm in the New York panhandle, north and west of Westchester and Rockland counties, to where the state line elbows west; they had had trouble here before—the counselors, seeking reforms, had been thrown off the farm and told never to come back—and we went expecting some of our own. We drove onto the property and started to interview some of the migrants in their outlying shanties.

It was only a matter of time, I knew, before the farmers were alerted to our presence. Within minutes, the farmers surrounded our car. There were maybe a half dozen of them, maybe more. They were big, and they were pissed, and the issues of right and wrong did not appear to weigh too heavily on their minds. They had clubs. One of them had a shotgun. One of them tried to grab the camera from Bob Alis, and I came running forward to take the brunt of the assault. That has always been my rule—never let the crew take the hit—and this was one of the earliest applications of that rule. I took the blows meant for Bob and his camera and returned what I could.

We backed ourselves into the car, cameras still rolling. I was the last one in, and as I tried to start up the car these farmers reached in through the windows, still trying to grab the camera, the microphone, and whatever else they could reach. I peeled out and we drove across the rutted field, the car bouncing wildly, the farmers still running after us. (On the audio track of our escape, you can hear Davey Weingold, my sound man, shouting, "Geraldo, slow down, man, you're going to kill us, Geraldo, watch it, watch it, we're going to be killed.") Finally, I hit the dirt county-road, and we dusted off into the sunset.

BOB ALIS: Talk about your hairy moments. And this was just on some onion farm in Pine Brook, New York, up in Orange County, but it was still pretty exciting. I've been in dangerous situations with Geraldo in all parts of the world, and I never thought anything bad would ever happen to us. I just believed that Geraldo would get us out, or we would get out. It was a belief that we were bigger than the danger, that we had to get the film back to the office to get it processed, get it on the air. It was like a driving force. If you will it, so shall it be. I always felt we'd make it, and I'm not an optimist by nature. But Geraldo had good vibes with me. I trusted him.

Bob Alis captured the whole struggle, my first filmed street-fight, as all-out as you could get. I took some and gave some. The scuffle was the last piece of the puzzle. The series, which we would call "Migrants: Dirt Cheap," was now whole—the club-wielding farmers told us all we needed to know about the migrants' oppressive isolation—and it sparked quite a controversy when it aired. News management took the panhandle fighting sequence and used it to promote the series; it became the hook. The feeling at the station was we had to do something to get people to watch, because the subject matter alone was too remote and depressing to sustain viewer interest over several nights. There is a self-defensive tendency among television viewers, who are bombarded on a daily basis with bad news, to tune out when they see something on the air that leaves them feeling powerless and frustrated. The condition of these migrant workers would have been a classic example of this—as the plight of the homeless is now—and we fought against it by promising a chance to see me, in action, doing battle with a band of oppressors in the city's backyard.

The fight wasn't staged, or stunted, although it was hoped for and anticipated. I recognize there are those who would criticize my approach here, but my objectives, to me, were beyond reproach. I wanted to get people to watch and to care about what they saw, and if it took the tease of a brief, heated confrontation to accomplish this, if it took a bit of real-life theater, then it was worth the risk.

The series was a huge success. It won awards and it got ratings. State inspectors in that part of the country were alerted to conditions in the field; child-labor investigators became more diligent in their search for violations; the farmers were shamed into accepting and even accelerating positive change. What "Migrants: Dirt Cheap" did for me at the station was establish a kind of commercial track-record. I became bankable and promotable. My stories drew viewers, and viewer response (an important barometer of success in local news), and from that point on I simply told the news manager what my next project would be. Management would actually refer to whatever it was as "Geraldo's next project."

"Geraldo's next project," then, after "Migrants," was another multipart series, called "The Littlest Junkie." Actually, there were several, lesser stories in-between, but this was the next breakthrough piece. This one started on one of the back pages of *The New York Times,* in a tiny wire service item out of Washington, D.C., about children being born addicted to heroin because their mothers had been addicted during pregnancy. The story wasn't more than a paragraph, but its description of these infants, going through withdrawal, moved me to action.

My first call was to Harlem Hospital, where I learned that, indeed, as heroin use grew to epidemic proportions, this was becoming a real and desperate problem. Calls to other city hospitals confirmed that there had been increasing incidents of addicted children being born in our poorest, most drug-infested communities. I put the word out in the newsroom that I had begun work on my next special—I actually had the title, "The Littlest Junkie," before I went out with a camera crew—and I set out for Harlem Hospital to see what else I could learn. I spoke to some of the doctors there, and the administrators, and began to get a sense that my outrage was shared. The entire hospital staff was pained by the reality of prenatal addiction.

As my investigation evolved, it became clear that the way to bring the story home for the viewer was to bring it down to size, to tell the large, sweeping story with small, delicate strokes. I made hasty arrangements to actually film, for the first time, an impending delivery which, due to the condition of the mother, doctors thought might produce an addicted infant.

It was easy enough to plan a story like this one, to intellectualize it, but it was another thing to go out and do it. In many ways, the scene I saw in that Harlem Hospital delivery room was more disturbing than any I'd seen in Willowbrook. I had to look away when this frail child was born, her hands trembling, her limbs shaking, her entire body convulsing. She was New York City's littlest junkie and I ached for her. I knew my viewers would, too. I just wanted to beat the shit out of the parents. That was my first and most abiding emotion as our cameras recorded that scene. How dare they? I wondered, how could they? I didn't understand addiction; in those days, nobody used words like codependency and denial. The very idea of a brand-new baby being brought into this world convulsing like a junkie was anathema, and I could not muster any sympathy for a mother who would do this to her unborn child.

I interviewed the parents after the birth and came back with some pretty vivid stuff. I was combative with them, at first, but then I let up when I saw the impact this little child had had on them. The parents, and that desperate little girl, helped me to bring a broad, dehumanizing story down to human terms. She made an unthinkable story somewhat thinkable; the specific was made more understandable than the general, more relatable. Her tragedy, and her parents', had an impact in a way that the mere listing of a thousand similar cases could not. Of course, we rounded out the series with the requisite statistical add-ins, and expert interviews, but it was that newborn child—struggling, convulsing—that people remembered.

At the parents' request, I became her godfather. Her story doesn't have the happiest aftermath. I maintained a relationship with the family for several years after her birth—I brought gifts and helped out, whatever I could do—but then they fell out of touch. They disappeared. I tried for a long time to reestablish contact, but I couldn't track them down. As often happens in the ghetto, among welfare families and drug addicts, the little girl's parents moved so many times, they covered their tracks. I always told myself that they knew where and how to find me, if they needed me.

It was my goddaughter who needed me, this past Christmas, 1990. Her parents had since split and, now eighteen, she had her own problems; she still suffers from the circumstances of her birth. She called me from a halfway house in Westchester County, and I went up to visit her. She had been telling everyone, for years, that Geraldo Rivera was her godfather, and nobody believed her. Her mother finally convinced her to call, and I'm grateful that she did.

My renewed relationship with my goddaughter, the one-time subject of a local news piece filmed minutes after her birth, invites a personal comment: I can't help but feel guilty sometimes at how my life has changed so dramatically over the years, and at how the people I have met along the way who have helped spark those changes have often stayed in the same place, or taken two steps back. It is a curious and difficult thing to deal with when your job is to report a real story, about real people; the telling of the story impacts on your career, but it also impacts on the lives of the people involved. Our work depends on other people's problems and failures and tragedies. Most of my colleagues tend to forget that in this business and try to stay uninvolved. Whether for reasons of ego, Puerto Rican compassion, or Jewish guilt, I tend to become a kind of Pied Piper to the struggling souls I come into contact with through my work. They become related to me, in a way, connected.

"The Littlest Junkie" earned my second Columbia Du Pont Award, and scored big in the ratings. (It was the highest-rated locally produced documentary in television history; as far as I know, it still holds that distinction.) I was back on top of the world. The series was such a runaway success that its impact was felt clear across the country. Our sister-owned and -operated station, KABC-TV in Los Angeles, asked me to reedit and repackage the piece for airing in that market. I flew out and did some additional local reporting on prenatal addiction in Southern California. Other than my talk-show appearance with Dick Cavett, it was the first time I was on the air outside New York. It was unexpected and unprecedented play for a local news story, and an indication of how far my gut and my heart would take me.

In fact, KABC management asked me to stay on at the station, and I gave their offer serious consideration. For all my bluster about New York being the center of my universe, I was starting to think about moving on. I wasn't tired of New York so much as I was worried New Yorkers would soon grow tired of me. There were, at every turn, constant and nagging reminders that the city had a way of gobbling up its celebrities, and spitting them back out at an alarming rate.

I declined the KABC offer and returned home, but my sights were set on bigger things. I had charmed New York, to borrow a line from the *Life* magazine profile of a year earlier, and I was ready to take my act on the road.

PALACE THEATER

Life bumped into television again that same fall; the one almost knocked over the other, and for a while it looked like a career-threatening collision.

For several months, I had been mining the local lecture circuit—at a speaking fee of seven hundred and fifty to twelve hundred and fifty dollars per appearance—and after Willowbrook and the rush of the One-to-One events had subsided, I began to expand these talks to include topics of interest other than mental retardation. The natural extension, that fall, was the 1972 presidential election. The campaign between Richard Nixon and George McGovern, as I saw it, left voters with the clearest ideological choice possible; at least it left this particular voter with the clearest ideological choice possible. Like so many others of my generation, I looked on George McGovern as our opportunity for change; he struck me as noble, honorable, quixotic, refreshing, and untraditional. The campaign seemed almost a holy crusade.

New York City was the only island of pro-McGovern sentiment in the nation, except for Massachusetts and the District of Columbia, and I realized later that my notions of shared perception were somewhat clouded. Still, I was going to vote for McGovern, and I wanted to talk about why.

And so I did, repeatedly and without incident, until one night when I gave a speech at Queens College. In attendance were members of a right-wing student group called the Young Americans for Freedom, and they complained to news management at WABC-TV. The complaint wasn't over something I'd said, it was over the fact that I'd said anything at all. I was a newsman, the students maintained, and had no business taking a stand on a political election. I tried to diffuse the situation by donating my speaking fee—nine hundred dollars—to the school's Hispanic Student Association, a move that accomplished nothing; what was at issue was my on-air objectivity.

I was not actively campaigning for McGovern at this point; I was merely expressing my admiration for him and his candidacy in a very fiery way. My talks were not in any way connected to the McGovern campaign, at least not yet. Since I never covered politics on television, I didn't see any conflict; when one arose, it looked, at first, as if I'd walk away from it with one of my pro forma wrist-slaps. But the incident still had some unraveling to do. I had previously agreed to speak at a celebrity benefit for McGovern at the Palace Theater, to be held in mid-October, and my name had already appeared on ads and fliers announcing the event. (This was to be my first active campaign appearance.) A local print reporter noticed my name on the Palace Theater roster and connected my appearance there with the earlier complaint at Queens College. Al Primo, with his eyes set on a promotion from local news to network, was backed into a corner. There I was, his star reporter—his ratings-grabber—and I had been caught where newsroom ethics and tradition said I didn't belong.

Primo was under incredible pressure. He did not want any embarrassments on his watch, and he needed to show his bosses at the network that he could control his stars, and so he gave me an ultimatum: Withdraw from the Palace Theater event, or face a suspension, without pay, until after the election. He issued the same ultimatum to sportscaster Jim Bouton, who had just written the controversial and best-selling *Ball Four,* and who was also scheduled to appear at the benefit.

The election was nearly a month away, and, with my recent raise, the loss in salary would have approached ten thousand dollars. It was a great deal of money (and my new lifestyle was forever requiring great deals of money to keep itself going), but I wasn't about to let ten thousand dollars stand in the way of my principles. I've always had a "let's go!" mentality, or trigger-point, and, having made a "let's go!" decision, having gone forward, there was no question that I would follow through, even if it meant being fired.

The incident became an industry-wide cause célèbre; personally, it also became a question of honor. I don't know what Jim Bouton's feelings were on the subject (as a sportscaster, he was spared much of the second-guessing directed at me), but I wasn't going to recant on the commitment I'd made to the event's organizers; more, I wasn't about to let the tired ethics of my profession dictate the way I lived my life on my own time. I refused to back down, and so did Bouton.

Our resulting suspensions divided the community. The sense I got from the streets, and from my mail, was that most people admired my convictions, regardless of their own political orientations; they liked that I was a principled person—a wild card, but a principled wild card—and they liked that I was willing to risk my job to stand up for something I believed in. Also, almost all of the young people I heard from during this time agreed with my actions; it was more a young-old division than a right-left division.

The broadcast community itself was not divided at all. There was a general consensus that I had stepped over the line of journalistic integrity. My estimable colleagues in the television news business, almost all of them from the old-line, establishment school of broadcast journalism, took numbers and waited in line for their chance to condemn me and my actions. It was like a public flogging.

Daily News television columnist Kay Gardella interviewed some of my more prominent critics and reported their views in a roundup piece that carried the following gems:

MIKE WALLACE (correspondent, *60 Minutes*, CBS News): I think it's dead wrong. We're all Caesar's wives and, particularly in this climate, we have to be viewed as impartial. Privileges and responsibilities go with any job. So we are not discussing just the fact of impartiality, but the appearance of impartiality as well. If Rivera or any other newsman goes on television and voters know him as a McGovern man this taints *Eyewitness News'* coverage.

HOWARD K. SMITH (then coanchor, *ABC Evening News*): As private citizens, we should all vote and contribute to the party of our choice, but as newsmen not make a public display of it. In television, we enjoy a special privilege of being allowed to talk to a lot of people and this should not be abused.

JOHN CHANCELLOR (then anchor, *NBC Nightly News*): I'm from an old-fashioned school. People involved in news should not endorse. We have public and private roles to play. To be a journalist, one must suspend the private part. However, in the case of Rivera, who is a local reporter, I don't think I'd have taken income away from him. I would have simply taken him off any political coverage for the duration of the election.

WALTER CRONKITE (then anchor, *CBS Evening News*): Basically, I'm on the company's side in that they have the right to ask newsmen to refrain from campaigning, since people are not sophisticated enough to accept that a man can wear two hats.

SAM DONALDSON (then correspondent, ABC News): I think it's just awful. Candidates, movements, and causes are the things we cover. As newsmen we cannot put ourselves into a position to be criticized. You can't have a boot in both camps and jump back and forth. I think it's difficult to go off on a leave of absence and become identified with one group and then return and be impartial. There are basic tenets of journalism over which you do not cross. You learn them as you grow in this business. If Rivera did not know them, someone should have told him. I don't think you can campaign for any candidate without coloring your work. We should report political activities objectively, not as advocates.

The debate extended outside the industry and was soon joined by people like Ira Glasser, the executive director of the Civil Liberties Union, who wrote a public letter to Al Primo in which he called the suspension "an unconstitutional violation of Geraldo Rivera's right to free speech and association." To my knowledge, the only other journalist to support my stand was the writer Nat Hentoff, who referred to me as a "maverick" in one of his columns, and wrote, "It would be a severe loss both to journalism and to the already-much-battered spiritual state of the nation if there were to be no place in the straight media for the Geraldo Riveras of the profession. Rivera has had so great an impact on television because he is passionate, and he will not, nor should he be forced to, constrict that passion as a private citizen."

The incident reached its head when I argued my case on public television with ABC News President Elmer Lower, the first of two news division presidents to stand between me and my first network news job, who said, "Without credibility, a reporter, in my view, is nothing."

Indeed, all three networks (and most major newspapers) had long-standing policies in place prohibiting their reporters from taking sides on behalf of any political candidate or party. Those policies, I know now, made sense. They still do. But I was blind to the industry's standards and practices in 1972. Or, maybe I did recognize them and thought they simply didn't apply to me. I was bigger than the establishment, I thought. I was operating on some other, higher plane.

MARTY BERMAN: Professionally, I always thought there was a danger that Geraldo had become too big a celebrity, that his celebrity would become so big it would be very difficult to, you know, be out Sunday night in a tuxedo at the opening of the Met, or whatever, and then on Monday have to cover some drug story in East Harlem. I thought it would become a real problem as things progressed and I think that's what happened. I thought it would and I think it did. I think maybe part of the reason that there was this Geraldo backlash, at some point, was that somehow he didn't wear his celebrity correctly at the beginning. He didn't pull it off. Whether he flaunted it or it was just flaunted by the media, all that superstar stuff just hurt the other image, the journalist image.

Back then, I was so convinced of my invincibility, and my total independence, and my ability to flout convention and make my own rules, that I made a stand over what should never have been an issue. I didn't belong on that Palace Theater stage, but I was bullheaded about my right to be there. I justified my behavior by arguing that I wasn't a standard reporter; I was more of a commentator, and therefore not subject to standard rules of thumb. I also argued that I had never reported on politics, or government, and was therefore professionally removed from the issues of the presidential campaign. And I held fast to the misplaced notion that I had the same right to the same freedoms of speech as any other citizen, as long as I didn't abuse my on-air time.

Al Primo, to his credit, carried out the suspensions. But, to my surprise (and delight), he also eventually found a way to pay me during my downtime. He did this quietly; I don't think anyone else in the newsroom knew about it. It was a shrewd move on his part, and a grand gesture. He wanted to discipline me, thereby muting the mounting criticism, but he didn't want to hurt me or piss me off.

I was off the air for about three weeks, and I used the time to campaign for George McGovern. (I was paying for it, I thought, so I might as well keep at it.) There was a time there, just after the convention that summer, when it seemed as though McGovern had a legitimate shot at the Oval Office. But then, by the end of September, when Senator Thomas Eagleton dropped off the ticket after it was revealed that he had been treated with electroshock therapy, that shining moment was lost. I remember Pete Hamill, the newspaper columnist, taking me aside at one of the campaign events and joking that if McGovern had been elected with Eagleton as his vice president, the country would have been bankrupted by the electric bills.

The entire McGovern incident, for me, stung far longer than a slap on the wrist. I was not punished for my actions, not really— hell, I got a three-week paid vacation out of the deal—but I suffered because of them. The controversy began what later became my institutional estrangement from the network news division. I had set things up to where there was an us-versus-them mentality in place; I defined myself as different from them, and they wanted nothing to do with me. Up until this time, I had been on a path that would have eventually taken me to network news, but suddenly there was a wall I could not get past. There was no way Elmer Lower would pluck me from the local ranks after this.

OKLAHOMA

Jerry Weintraub, the entertainment mogul and former president of United Artists, was a would-be talent agent at the end of 1972. He was married at the time to Jane Morgan, the singer, and she was his first client. His brother was a dentist. His father was a very prosperous jeweler. His mother was one of my biggest fans.

He was running a company called Management III—they had a small second-story office in a dusty brownstone in the fifties, between Third and Lexington avenues, and he was looking to expand his client-base beyond his marriage. His mother knew Jerry was looking for media and entertainment clients and she urged him to give me a call. That was our introduction.

I still did not have an agent, and my recent working trip to Los Angeles had started me to thinking about the directions my career was taking, and not taking, and so I agreed to meet with him. I found Jerry to be a very engaging, tough, funny, and often brilliant man. He was a big guy, powerfully built, who could shift easily from backslapping bonhomie to biting analysis. In our first meeting, he laid out what I should be doing, and what he could do for me. It may have been a standard agent pitch, but I was taken by his gumption and his demeanor.

We went into business together on a handshake. Or, on a contract drawn up on a restaurant napkin. (Neither one of us can remember.) Almost immediately, he renegotiated my *Eyewitness News* contract, bringing my salary up to around three hundred fifty thousand dollars. It was an incredible amount of money, and I once again upset the entire salary structure of the newsroom and the anchor desk.

What impressed me about Jerry was that he also entered into immediate negotiations with ABC News, exploring the possibilities of a network news position for his new client. He was determined to nationalize what he called "this New York phenomenon." I was reluctant to cut loose the umbilical chord of New York and *Eyewitness News*, but I sat back and watched Jerry do his stuff.

JERRY WEINTRAUB (former talent and booking agent; former president, United Artists; president, Weintraub Entertainment Group): I felt Geraldo had a lot to offer. He was doing a lot of in-depth reporting that nobody else was doing. He was up in Harlem, he was in the streets, he was banging down doors in drug centers before it was popular. He was doing a lot of things that were very different, number one. And number two, he had long hair and a moustache and he was good looking and he was young and he was three hundred and sixty degrees from everybody that was in the news business. There was nobody like him. And I thought that he had a chance to really break through, to become a very, very important television star.

Jerry arranged a meeting with ABC News President Bill Sheehan, who had since replaced Elmer Lower (and preceded Roone Arledge) and made his pitch. "Your news is a piece of shit," he told Sheehan. I don't know if this is a direct quote, but it was how Jerry related the exchange to me: Here's Geraldo. He's the hottest thing. How about it?

Sheehan let on that the network was somewhat interested in my talents, but only if I agreed to accept the starting correspondent's salary of fifty thousand dollars. He knew what I was making at Channel 7, and yet he expected me to take a three hundred thousand dollars pay cut just for the honor of a network position. The offer was Sheehan's way of saying, "Thanks, but no thanks."

There was, I surmised, a feeling within the news division that my success was somehow fabricated, and fleeting, that I no more belonged in the guise of a television newsman than did an ex-jock, or a former beauty-pageant queen. My style was aggressive, brash, personal, and clearly at odds with established practice. I was different, and nobody knew what to make of me.

Jerry Weintraub responded to Sheehan's lowball offer by creating the blueprint for all of my subsequent moves. He explained it to me later by saying, "Look, Geraldo, if you can't make it in the news division, fuck the news division. Keep your job at *Eyewitness News*, take their money, and I'll get something going with the entertainment division."

Plan B was an end-around move that, if successful, would produce the same results as Plan A. Viewers have never made a distinction between programming supplied by a network's news division and that originating in the entertainment division. Indeed, in the head-to-head morning news competition, NBC's *Today Show*, and CBS's *News This Morning* are news division productions, while ABC's *Good Morning America* is produced by that network's entertainment division, and nobody cares. The content and format of these three programs are interchangeable; without Katie Courie, Paula Zahn, and Joan Lunden, there'd be no telling them apart.

In 1973, the typical television viewer did not draw a line between news and entertainment; it was a corporate distinction—esoteric and arbitrary—based on budgets and the perceived purity of broadcast journalism. Jerry decided—logically, brazenly—that if he could not turn Geraldo Rivera into a network newsman, he would simply sell me as a network personality. His strategy seems sound now, even inspired, but at the time it was farfetched and out-there. Nobody had ever defied a network news division in just this way, and I worried that the move might find a way to backfire.

But we'd made a "let's go!" decision and went forward. Meanwhile, as Jerry tried to muscle me onto network television, I beefed up my local celebrity reporting. I suppose I did this on the theory that we were now pursuing an entertainment division position, and I therefore needed to showcase my glamorous and glitzy work.

A look back through some of my reporter's notebooks from that period, and through the tapes of stories filed, turned up some interesting anecdotes:

Muhammad Ali was the most important sports figure I ever met, and a personal hero. He was a great fighter and, more important, a great and principled man. He was exotic, intelligent, and self-made. In his prime, Ali had the remarkable ability to focus, to make you feel at the center of his attention; he could pick you out in a Madison Square Garden crowd and communicate that focus with mere eye contact. I interviewed him in conjunction with those epic Ali-Frazier fights of the early seventies. In 1973, he was training somewhere in the mountains of Pennsylvania, a couple hours' drive from Manhattan, and I went out to do a piece at his camp. It was to be one of my most memorable personality profiles, with a capper that at the time I could not relate on the air, but which I can tell now, years later, in print. I climbed in the ring with Ali, and we filmed it. We were just fooling around, although I had started to box again and prided myself on my fitness and nerve. But I was like a toy to Ali in the ring, a foil for one of his jokes; in a true fight, I would have lasted as long as it would have taken him to find me. He was a good sport about it, and the exchange gave unique spin to a man who was one of the most written-about and talked-about personalities of his day. The capper to the piece was this: Ali, a Muslim, had a couple of "wives" at the time, but there was a beautiful woman with him at the training camp who was not a part of his regular entourage. She wasn't one of his wives. After we finished our interview, and our sparring, he pulled me aside and asked me to drive this woman home. She lived in New York, and one of his wives was due at camp momentarily; he was worried that her presence in camp would bring him heat at home. We laughed about being fellow travelers, and I agreed to help him out. His attitude was, look, I gave you a good interview, I boxed with you, I made you look good. Now, help me get rid of my girlfriend before I'm found out.

Bette Midler, in those days, had not yet reached the heights of her celebrity, but she was a pretty big deal in New York. She had a cult-following among New York's gay population through her wild, vamping shows at the Baths, and her outrageous antics (and great voice) were beginning to attract national attention. I went to

interview her at her home in the Village and was surprised at how
small she was. She had great tits, and a personality to match. The
rest of her was tiny. We were in the bathroom, preparing for the
interview, and at some point I put my hands on her breasts. She
loved it, and we fell into a passionate embrace, which segued
immediately into a brief and torrid affair. Bette had an enormous
sexual appetite in those days. She went on tour a week or so later
and asked me to join her. Of course, I was still married to Edie but
I cooked up some lie and joined Bette backstage in Oklahoma City.
We made love right after the show, and then she took a bath, and
then she wanted to make love again. She was insatiable. The next
morning, her band flew out to Tulsa and we decided to drive, and
I remember stopping at least once, in the middle of the Oklahoma
desert, in a compact rental car, and making love on the road.
Later, I tried to show off my navigator's knowledge of the
constellations. But she was less interested in stars than sex. After
the Tulsa show, I finally said, "You're exhausting me, honey." And
so she ended the relationship. Because I couldn't keep up with her.
Bette is now a happily married parent, and a socially conservative
person, but back then she was wild, and hungry, and one of the
few women who were just too much for me to handle.

John Denver became a good friend during this time, when he
agreed to appear at the second One-to-One concert. "Rocky
Mountain High" was just out, and he was on top of the world in
the summer of 1973. He was a true star, with a string of hits and
the promise of more to come. He had actually signed on with Jerry
Weintraub and Management III shortly after I did, and Jerry
convinced him to do the show. I interviewed John when he came
to New York, and in a classic case of hyperbole I referred to him
on the air as "the next generation's Bob Dylan." Of course, the last
eighteen years have rendered that remark embarrassing, but I had
enormous professional respect for John at the time.

Judy Collins also appeared on the second One-to-One bill, and
on *Eyewitness News*, and became a friend. People forget that Judy
was pretty wild in the late sixties, early seventies; she used to hang
around with Janis Joplin, and the two of them would drink each
other to sleep. Judy told me she had suffered from the Irish Virus,
a reference to her fondness for Irish whiskey. Her career has had a
lot of peaks and valleys to it, and at the time we met, she was on a

kind of plateau. Our friendship fell somewhere between her long-term affairs with Stephen Stills and Stacy Keach, and what stayed with me most was a long ride in Central Park, in a horse-drawn carriage, during which we talked about our lives and our entanglements, our hopes and our failures. We were like two ships passing in the night, but when we passed, for that moment in the park, we connected and opened up to each other in a way that was unusual for me, and memorable.

I also met Richard "Cheech" Marin that summer, and he and I would go on to forge a close and enduring friendship. I interviewed Cheech and his comedy partner Tommy Chong, after a concert in the Sheep Meadow in Central Park, and they subsequently appeared on my One-to-One telethon. Their second Cheech and Chong album was out and making a big splash on the charts. One of their doper shticks on the album was a spoof of my work; they invented a broad caricature of me—Horrendo Revolver—which was funny and on-target as hell. I was flattered by the (somewhat twisted) attention and took it as an indication that my work (or at least my name and my style) was being noticed outside of New York. Now the Geraldo Rivera spoofs have gotten to where you can't listen to a late-night monologue, or sit through a prime-time sitcom, without hearing some joke at my expense. But Horrendo Revolver was the first (and still one of the funniest), and I loved it.

My celebrity profile pieces became a staple on the newscast, and with each one I helped to reshape the genre. Whether I was boxing with Ali, or shooting hoops with Johnny Mathis, or tending goal against soccer legend Pele, the pieces all tended toward the participatory and the familiar. In fact, one of my first negative notices from the *Times,* which came during this period, charged that my profiles were all *en famille,* that I sought to establish too much of a relationship with my subjects. They were right; I did. But that was my style, and it worked. It made the celebrities more relaxed, and it made the interviews looser, more informal. I became a kind of surrogate for the audience; they saw me having fun with their heroes, so they had fun. We established a three-way partnership—the star, the journalist, and the viewer.

These star turns became the backdrop to Jerry Weintraub's network push. His strategy was to build a show around me, a second-generation television news magazine, a hip *60 Minutes* for the rock 'n' roll generation. He saw an opening in the network's late-night time periods, and he went after it. The *Dick Cavett Show*, which for three years had been a nightly fixture at the network, was cancelled in January 1973 when network programmers finally realized Cavett would never mount a serious challenge to NBC's King of the Night, Johnny Carson. Actually, Cavett wasn't cancelled; he was pared down. He was given one week of shows each month, to fill out his contract; Jack Paar was lured out of retirement and given another week each month, in a talk-show offering called *Jack Paar Tonight*. The open late-nights were usually filled with made-for-television movies, variety shows, and a Friday-night concert program, *In Concert*, produced by Dick Clark. The entire hodgepodge was bundled together and presented under the umbrella title of *ABC's Wide World of Entertainment*.

The network's top management at that time was a dream-team: Michael Eisner, now head of Disney; Barry Diller, now head of Fox; Marty Pompadour, now a well-connected owner of television stations; the late Elton Rule; and Leonard Goldenson, the godfather of ABC, and its chairman. This group would later be seen as one of the most creative and successful ever assembled to run a television network. They made the news division look very much like a network stepchild. Jerry sold these guys on our idea for a hip, late-night magazine show, and they gave us sixty-five thousand dollars to do a pilot.

The great thing about the entertainment division deal, as Jerry Weintraub explained to me, was that it put me in business for myself, and so I formed my production company—Maravilla, Spanish for miracle. At Channel 7, I was a hired-gun; my work was owned by WABC-TV. The same situation would occur when I joined the network news division. With my own production company, though, I would now own the program, and the network merely purchased the rights to air the show two or three times, depending on the deal. After that, the rights to the material reverted back to Maravilla, and if I could find a way to market it— in syndication, or overseas—then I could make money from the project all over again.

I decided to call the show *Good Night America*, which was a lyric from the Steve Goodman song "City of New Orleans," made popular by Arlo Guthrie. It seemed like the perfect title, and a cool reference, and when I pitched it to the ABC dream-team they all agreed. I trademarked the title, we built a cheap set—in Dick Clark's *$25,000 Pyramid* studio on Fifty-eighth Street—and we were in business.

Sixty-five thousand dollars, in television, does not go very far, and so we did that first show on the cheap. (I didn't even draw a salary, the budget was so thin.) I recycled two previous efforts—"Migrants: Dirt Cheap" and "The Littlest Junkie"—and made them over for a national audience. I put together packaged pieces on The Beatles and Carole King. For a format, I borrowed a little bit from *Ed Sullivan*, a little bit from *60 Minutes*, and a little bit from thin air. For a wardrobe, I donned a turtleneck and bell-bottoms. I opened with a monologue, and then I introduced my parents (a nice touch, the *Times* said in its review) and some famous members of our studio audience (George Plimpton, for that first show). Next, we threw to a packaged piece on one of the monitors, and then we came out of that for an onstage discussion of what we'd just seen. Cesar Chavez was in the studio to talk about the exploitation of our migrant farm workers; a doctor from Cornell was on-hand to talk about prenatal addiction. I held my goddaughter in my arms; the original littlest junkie was now about six months old and recovering from her traumatic birth. Looking back, it was not that different than the format I use for my talk show today, except we covered several topics in our ninety minutes, and we often featured musical guests.

The *Good Night America* pilot had its first airing on Monday night, July 30, 1973, up against *The Tonight Show* (with substitute host Jerry Lewis) and a movie on CBS. I wouldn't exactly call our debut a runaway success. Reviews were mixed and our ratings were only marginally better than programming usually occupying our time slot; we finished ahead of Jerry Lewis in the New York and Los Angeles overnight ratings, but fell to third place in the national tally.

But, even if we didn't take the country by storm, our showing was enough to secure a thirteen-week commitment from the network for more of the same.

SANTIAGO, CHILE

ABC News President Bill Sheehan may not have wanted to hire me as a correspondent, but he wasn't above borrowing me when it served his purposes. In late September of 1973, after we'd produced the *Good Night America* pilot for the entertainment division, Sheehan asked me to travel to Chile, on loan from Channel 7 to the news division. The Chilean army had just rebelled against President Salvador Allende, and fighting was still going on in and around the capital city of Santiago. This was the coup that started with a truck driver's strike, pitting the independent truck drivers against Allende's socialist government. We would later learn that the strike was fomented and funded by the CIA, in association with the Chilean military, which wanted to bring down the first freely elected socialist government in modern Latin America.

I was surprised and delighted by the assignment. I was tabbed, I felt sure, because I spoke Spanish and could assist Charles Murphy, a veteran network newsman and the main ABC correspondent on the scene. But I didn't care why they looked to me, only that they did. This was my shot, I thought. This was my chance to show the network news brass what I could do. Too, it was a way to erase some of the long list of negatives attached to me by management since the McGovern campaign incident a year earlier.

The assignment did not get off to the smoothest start. I had to get a passport, quickly, and a press pass, and whatever other documents I needed to make the trip. By this time the Jerry Rivers rumors had begun to heat up, and I must have taken a dozen calls from news management asking me what my real name was. "No," they'd say, "we know Geraldo Rivera is the name you go by, but we need your real name for these documents." They also didn't believe I really spoke Spanish. "Are you sure you can speak Spanish?" They did everything but ask me to take a quiz. It seemed for a while there that I would not even get to my proving ground in Chile without first proving myself yet again to the corporate types who ran the show. There was also a small debate over how I would be credited if any of my reports found their way to air. I argued that I should sign off my pieces like any other network correspondent: "Geraldo Rivera, ABC News." Management countered that I should be billed as a contributor: "Geraldo Rivera, for ABC News."

Again, it was a subtle distinction, noticeable only to a handful of industry watchers and journalism students, but I fought against it just the same. I won the argument, but it left me wondering whether these guys really wanted me to work for them, or what. I departed New York with a combination of emotions. I was tremendously excited at the looming adventure. I had never held any aspirations to be a world-roving correspondent, but there I was, jetting off to parts unknown to cover a brutal military coup. I was filled with adrenaline and anxious to get started. I was proud of what I had accomplished in winning the assignment, but I was also overly sensitive and suspicious of news management and its motives. I felt like I was being watched over, scrutinized, second-guessed, as if I had been given the assignment reluctantly and the slightest slipup would put an end to my network news career before it had even gotten started.

In Chile, Allende had just been killed in the presidential palace. The coup had been successful, but the city was still under siege, still in turmoil. The palace was still smoldering. There were bodies and rubble all over the streets, and there were bodies floating in the river. Thousands of Allende loyalists had been corralled into the large stadium. The city's infrastructure was dotted with shell holes from RPGs (rocket-propelled grenades) and bazookas; even my hotel room had been hit before my arrival. I had never seen such fear, devastation, and confusion.

And on top of everything else, the city was struck by a massive earthquake during my first night there. The quake registered a 7.3 on the Richter scale. Buildings swayed and people screamed. No one was seriously hurt in the quake, that I recall, but our high-rise hotel felt like an amusement-park ride and several buildings and roads were damaged. I stood right beside Charlie Murphy when he filed his ABC radio report, and I could feel the rumble of the aftershocks as he spoke.

Despite the earthquake, Charlie and I landed the first interview with the victorious General Augusto Pinochet Ugarte. It was to be one of the most aggressive interviews I'd ever conducted and, ultimately, one of the least noticed. I jumped all over Pinochet, and Charlie just backed off and watched. Charlie was a good old boy from Texas, and a terrific reporter; none of the resentments or uncertainties directed at me from the news division had filtered down to him, and he was helpful and encouraging throughout our time together. He let me take the lead in the Pinochet interview, thinking we would conduct the interview in Spanish, but I quickly reverted to English and the help of a translator when I realized my Spanish could not adequately express my heat and indignation at Pinochet's coup. I treated him as if he were the director of Willowbrook, or a landlord who refused to provide heat for his tenants. "How could you tear down a freely elected government?" I demanded. "How could you declare this a victory?"

The terror and violence of Pinochet's anarchy was too much for me, and I let my anger pour forth. I was not at all polite or deferential—I crawled all over him—and I could tell that he was somewhat startled and unsettled by my demeanor. Charlie, too, was shocked at the direction the interview was taking, but I think he was also impressed at my bullying passion. The Chilean army officers were Prussian-proper and very somber. They felt their coup was righteous and motivated. Other reporters looked at the blood spilled by Pinochet and still managed to conduct their interviews with respect and decorum for the new Chilean leader.

It was, I thought, an excellent interview. It was brave and telling and different. Pinochet's steadfast defiance spoke more about the man and his methods than any polite question-and-answer session. His cool, entitled manner in the face of my high and mighty accusations lent new insights into this man who had forced his way onto the world stage. I was thoroughly satisfied with my performance and thought to myself, now my move to network is undeniable, inevitable, unstoppable. I thought it was only a matter of time before my colleagues and bosses sent word of praise and congratulations.

Things didn't exactly happen the way I envisioned. Charlie and I went over to the office of the Associated Press, in what was left of the heart of the city. I was still flush with the victory of my Pinochet interview, and we were talking vaguely about whether or not the new government would allow us to get the film out of the country. We weren't really worried about it, we were just talking. All of a sudden, the alarms went off on all the A.P. ticker-tape machines. The room, which had just been bustling with important activity, fell silent. The wires started reporting that the Egyptians had just crossed the Suez Canal, into Israel. The Yom Kippur War had begun.

You could physically feel the focus of world attention leaving Chile for the Middle East. I was holding a scoop that was old news before it even made it to air. The footage would make it out of the country, but there was still a chance that no one would see it.

I was back in New York the next day, in time to watch my debut as a network correspondent. I wasn't needed on the set for the taped piece, but I stayed in the newsroom until the story aired. The interview ran on a Sunday afternoon discussion program. I watched it come up on the monitors and I heard my "Geraldo Rivera, ABC News" sign-off, and I thought to myself, okay, I'm a network correspondent. Yes, it was a Sunday afternoon, and nobody else was watching, but still, I had arrived.

TEL AVIV, ISRAEL

Israel was reeling from the initial Yom Kippur assault. Egyptian President Anwar Sadat concentrated an unbelievable amount of firepower on the Suez Canal, and the Israelis were overwhelmed by it. The Israeli army at that time was suspect; it was unkempt, undisciplined, and arrogant over its successes in the Six Day War of 1967. The Israelis had thought the Suez Canal was an impenetrable line, that no one could ever cross it, and they were stormed by surprise.

Syria also invaded as Sadat and Assad deployed their SAM missiles in unprecedented numbers. The Associated Press had begun to transmit pictures from the region, but in the first days of the conflict there was no real information system in place. The foreign bureaus for the three networks were as surprised by the attack as the Israelis, and they were forced to rely on wire-service accounts, or freelance reports from the Israeli press. News accounts of the invasion, in those first days, were scattered and unreliable.

The American Jewish community was in panic. There was widespread concern that the Arabs would be victorious, and Jewish

organizations throughout the country were rallying to send money
and lobby for other American support for Israel. The New York
society crowd, of which I was still a sideline member, did its bit
for the cause. Marian Javits hosted a lavish fund-raiser and briefing
in her beautiful Fifty-seventh Street apartment, to which she
invited all of the society swells, Jewish and otherwise. She asked
me to give a pitch to these ladies, and I went out and did my
homework and reported back that there were seventeen hundred
Israeli dead in the first three days of fighting, that Arab advances
were mounting, and that Syria, too, was gaining in the area around
Mount Hermon in the Golan Heights. I brought wire-service
photos with me to illustrate my talk. The gathering was like an
exclusive, private newscast, and I was its anchor.

I spoke passionately on behalf of the Israeli effort, so passionately,
in fact, that I moved myself to action. The next day, the Tuesday
after I'd returned from Chile and the fourth day of the Middle East
war, I managed to get seats for Bob Alis and myself on an El Al
flight to Tel Aviv. The flight was a special charter, returning home
with Israeli reservists. I booked the seats first, and then I went to
Al Ittleson for approval. Al had been promoted to news director
when Al Primo was kicked upstairs, and I needed him to approve
the trip. It is highly unusual to send a local newsman a half a
world away, without the resources of a foreign bureau and without
any real experience in overseas reporting, but I made what turned
out to be a convincing argument that New York's Jewish
community was large enough, and vocal enough, to suggest that
the conflict was in many ways a local story.

Al Ittleson signed off on the trip, and I was dispatched to Israel
as a local reporter for *Eyewitness News*, with the understanding
that I was also available to the network if it turned out they needed
me. Almost immediately, I encountered tremendous resistance
from the network newsmen already stationed there. My reputation
preceded me, and it told my sudden colleagues I was a hotshot.
They saw me as someone out to steal their thunder, or their
airtime. Beat reporters, I learned then and have been reminded
many times since, are a jealous and protective bunch. They are
like junkyard dogs, the way they piss on and guard their territory.

My ABC colleagues made themselves unavailable. In fact, the
ABC News London bureau chief, Bill Milldike, who was in charge

of the network's coverage in the region, seemed to go out of his way to hurt me, withholding technical help, postponing the satellite transmission of my stories, and even asking the Israelis to keep me off the one truck of journalists heading out for a specific theater. It was interoffice sabotage, and at one point I confronted him about it and said, "I don't care if you help me, you bastard, just stay out of my fucking way." The bitter encounter only added to the estrangement.

Bob Alis and I took up residence in the Sheraton Hotel, on the beach in Tel Aviv, and we set up our own minibureau, with long-distance help from influential New Yorkers. With assistance from Bob's Israeli wife, we successfully lobbied the Israeli defense forces for access to the various fronts. We were generally given access a day behind the network guys, which pissed me off a great deal but which Channel 7 didn't mind; even a day late, their own local accounts were far more personalized than anything their competition could put on the air.

BOB ALIS: We had this tiny little car, this Fiat, it was like eight feet long. And I remember Geraldo would sleep in the front, which was uncomfortable because of the transmission, and he would let me sleep in the back, where I was crunched up, but a little bit more comfortable than him. We were going fourteen, fifteen, sixteen hours a day, with no relief, and the network was giving him a hard time getting on the bird to transmit his stuff. There was one time, we were in the Sinai, in the Fiat, and we were coming back with the film and we got a flat tire. The air was out of the spare. Geraldo gets out of the car. He's been working hard, his ass is dragging. He lays down on the ground, arms outstretched, and he says, "God, we'll never get this footage on the air." I'm worried about how we're going to get out of there and he's worried about the footage. There were rumors of Egyptian commandos in the area. Along comes an Israeli bus, and I flag down the driver. I tell him, in Hebrew, the problem. Now, the Israeli buses all had these pneumatic doors on them, and the driver was able to make some kind of connection and inflate the spare with the pneumatic valve. We put the spare on and we get out of there and Geraldo says, "This is really the land of miracles."

*   *   *

We were there for three weeks, and everyday there was something new. I took up with a beautiful Yemenite-Israeli girl, who was working in the army's communications office, and she turned out to be my single best resource. (She also turned out to be my most memorable personal distraction for those three weeks.) She came to live with me in the Sheraton, and I remember having a tremendous fight with hotel management when they wouldn't let her upstairs because she was dark-skinned. I had my office back home call the hotel manager and blow some smoke about lawsuits, and eventually they backed down.

We worked all day and all night. We were seven hours ahead of New York, and the satellite-feed went out at five o'clock in the afternoon, New York time, so we weren't finished until after midnight. We were in bed by two, and up with first daylight, at five. For three weeks. To a reporter, war is heaven, Civil War general William Tecumseh Sherman's dictum notwithstanding. Assuming you don't get killed.

I operated as a lone wolf. Milldike had no control over me and the stories I covered, and I didn't feel constrained by the gentlemanly traditions of pool reporting and pack journalism. Screw those network guys, I thought. I went out on my own, to see what I could see, and if I established a contact that would take me into a new situation, that's where I went. I did not care if I stepped on anybody's toes, or got in any other reporter's way, or made anybody else look bad by comparison; I had a job to do.

One of these roving assignments sparked what has since mushroomed into two decades of harsh criticism of my work, and led directly to my permanent estrangement from the network's news division under Bill Sheehan.

BOB ALIS: We were in a shelling attack on that trip to Al-Kuneitra, and that was the first time we were really scared. There was an Israeli officer with us, all of the reporters were assigned to an officer, and he says, "You guys better take cover." And Geraldo says, "No, I'm going to do a stand-up." The guy says, "Look, this is my third war. You guys want to get killed, good luck to you." And he takes off. And we're on top of a two-story building, and Geraldo starts to talk and all of a sudden you hear "plink, plink, plink, plink," and he bends over and picks up a piece of metal and it's hot and he throws it out of his hand and says, "Oh, shit, man, this stuff can really hurt." And I say, "Let's get the fuck out of here. Do your thing and let's get the fuck out of here." And Geraldo finished his stand-up and we left.

We were in another shelling attack on our way back into Israel, more perilous than the first. We were returning from the Golan Heights when we started to hear the rapid-fire blasts. I could actually see, in my rearview mirror, the explosion of the artillery shells as they danced across the field toward our vehicle. They were gaining on us, and with each blast the dirt was being splayed in every direction, and we were right in the middle of it. We were bracketed by heavy Syrian artillery.

BOB ALIS: We were driving back, we were with another Israeli officer by this point, and he says, "Pull over, take cover." Geraldo's driving, I'm filming. Geraldo pulls over and the Israeli officer gets out and jumps into a ditch. And Geraldo says, "Keep shooting." And he does a stand-up while the shooting is going on. This is crazy. Nobody does a stand-up during an attack. You've got to visualize this. He gets down on one foot for some reason, and I'm standing up and shooting him and I'm panning from the shell explosions over to him. The Israeli officer says, "Hey, you guys got to take cover," and Geraldo tells him, "When I finish."

We sent the film out on the bird later that night—New York just loved it!—and Bob Alis and I went to sleep thinking we had just filed the most incredible combat-footage possible. We had, but it would be another week or so before I found out just how incredible the story appeared to my colleagues. It was, I would learn, too much to be believed.

Back in New York after the war ended, I was interviewed by a *TV Guide* reporter about my experiences, and he asked me to respond to charges that I had staged this dramatic artillery attack. I was taken completely by surprise and I got my back up.

"What charges?" I wanted to know.

"Well, maybe rumors is a better word," the reporter said.

Rumors? Who would spread that kind of rumor? My first thought was that my new foe Bill Milldike was out to pay me back for going my own way. Sabotage by disparagement. It seemed like just the sort of thing the newsies would do.

I shifted my attention back to the reporter. "That's a fucking lie," I said. "Who told you that?"

It turned out that Roger Grimsby was the source of the rumor, and not Milldike. The story Grimsby was spreading—to all who would listen—was that the artillery explosions in our air-piece did not seem authentic to him; he had fought in Korea and knew firsthand, he said, what real artillery looked and sounded like. My story, he claimed, grossly exaggerated the proximity and intensity of the barrage.

Given the evidence on the film, it was a patently ridiculous charge. Still, over the next two days, I heard from a dozen other news operations, seeking comment or corroboration of the dreaded charge of staging. The wide play told me I had even more enemies in this business than I'd thought. There was a receptiveness among my fellow journalists that told them the story might be true. It sounded good to them. People had always figured that my success had to be in some way synthesized, that it had been achieved by some artifice rather than ability, and now these same people had been handed an outrageous claim that seemed to confirm their preconceived notions.

I countered the charges by offering up the outtake footage for review. I argued that I would have to have had Walt Disney's optical laboratories and special-effects crews to superimpose the explosion of artillery shells. Even the air-piece, I thought, was eloquent testimony on my behalf; you could see the dirt kicking up at my feet, as the shells exploded around me. I could not see how anyone could view that footage and come away thinking it had been staged. Even Bob Alis spoke out to repair my reputation (and, by extension, his own). I had been in the business long enough to recognize how cutthroat and jealous other reporters can be, but I was still thrown by the very suggestion that I might have fabricated, or trumped-up a story. I took it personally, and I entered a kind of damage-control mode; I made sure that every person who approached me with suspicions walked away knowing how misplaced those suspicions were.

What to do about Grimsby? That first night, right after I spoke to the *TV Guide* reporter, I called him down to my basement at 77

West 66th Street. "Come on down," I told him. "I have to talk to you." It was dinnertime. The six o'clock news had come and gone, and the basement was empty.

I did not know what I would do when he got down there, and I was surprised at what happened next. Not as surprised as Roger, though. I jumped him. "You motherfucker," I said, "you sonofabitch, you're trying to destroy me."

I started to beat the shit out of him. I knocked him down. I got up on top of him and started to throttle him. I punched him in the face. Grimsby was no match for me. His attempts to fight back were feeble. He was about fifteen years older than I was, and he was out of shape and unprepared for my attack, but there was no way he was getting the better of me that night; I could have done anything I wanted to him, without resistance. I actually had my hands around his neck and I was squeezing him, and screaming, "I'm going to kill you. You tried to destroy me, I'm going to destroy you."

After about a minute of this, I snapped out of it, and I climbed off of him and walked out of the room. I just left him there. I went over to Marty Berman's apartment and told him what had happened. If I'd thought the charges that I had staged the Golan Heights artillery attack were enough to damage my career, then surely word of my assault on a major market anchorman would cost me my job, maybe even get me arrested. I was frantic; Marty was reassuring. We watched the eleven o'clock news and Grimsby came on and you could tell he'd been beaten up. His face was all puffed and swollen. He looked like hell, but he had a reputation as a barroom brawler, and no one gave a second thought to his appearance.

To his credit, Grimsby never ratted me out. Years later, he would tell John Johnson and some of the other reporters about the incident (he claimed I coldcocked him and surprised him and that's how I managed to defeat him), but he never called the cops and he never told management. He knew he was wrong, I'm sure, and he was a strangely proud man. In all the years I worked with him, he never once filed an expense voucher, because he had too much pride to ask for his money back.

Our on-set duels had now reached off-set, down into the basement, and in a curious way I think we both found a new respect for each other after the confrontation. Of course, I hated the man—completely, and with a hard vengeance—for what he had done to my reputation, and he never apologized for it, but he accepted the blame, shouldered my rage, and moved on. I admired him for that.

But even a humbled Roger Grimsby could not undo the damage he had already caused. I may have been able to shake the initial charges regarding the artillery footage, but the memory of those charges would linger.

NEW YORK UNIVERSITY

Good Night America made me the first of the late-night hipsters, a journalist/talk-show host for the pre-Letterman, pre-*Saturday Night Live*, pre-MTV generation. The evolution did not happen overnight; in fact, it would take about nine months, after the initial July 1973 airing of the pilot, before I started to see some encouraging signs of life in this new venture.

The pilot installment was aired a second time, in December, to better numbers and better reviews, and then we returned to the airwaves on April 3, 1974, beginning an every-other-Thursday-night run that would last for three years. We were hoping to tap into a new audience—young, college-aged or -educated, smart, politically and socially aware—viewers who were new to after-hours network television. The show was still being shot on the cheap; Dick Clark's studio alone cost us as much as the grand prize on his pyramid—twenty-five thousand dollars—which left us about forty thousand dollars, out of which we had to pay a staff, and produce the rest of the show. The money was dirt, and we wound up piggybacking on my *Eyewitness News* efforts to make ends meet. If Channel 7 sent me on location to do a story, then there was a good chance a nationalized version of that story would turn up on *Good Night America*. Conversely, if there was a location piece we could not afford for the late-night show, I'd finagle a local assignment to the same area to cover our costs.

We put the show on the air every two weeks with smoke and

mirrors, always looking for ways to cut corners and maximize our budget. Occasionally, we'd even accept a press junket (which included travel and accommodations for me and my crew), if we thought it would yield some interesting footage, at no cost to my production company. In our very first show, for example, I accepted the invitation of Baron Arnaud de Rosnay of Mauritius to attend the opening of a resort called Las Hadas in Mexico. The baron's plan was for two jet-loads of jet-setters—one from Paris, one from New York—to convene on the resort for a grand-opening celebration. The guest list included a king, four princesses, seven barons, designer Kenneth Jay Lane, actors George Hamilton and Michael York, and dozens of rich and famous freeloaders.

Also in that first show, we offered an in-depth look at what I called the victimless crime of prostitution, including field interviews from across the country with hookers and their clients, and an in-studio interview with a madam and a prostitute who had recently gone straight. It was a titillating, mildly lurid report that was typical of the kinds of stories we would go on to do, and the way we would do them.

Our second show was the turning point. It involved a behind-the-scenes battle that once again pitted me against the news division, and almost sent my career up in smoke. Literally. When the smoke cleared, *Good Night America* emerged with some unexpected attention, and a newfound momentum.

In an effort to bring to light the growing movement to legalize marijuana, I smoked a joint on the air. I was the first newsman to ever smoke dope on television, and as far as I know, I was also the last. Actually, footage of me lighting up never made it to the second *Good Night America* broadcast; it ran once as a promotional tease before the show, but was then censored by network brass before the full report ever aired.

Remember, back then, marijuana was considered to be less harmful than booze; several states had recently adopted or were actively considering legislation to legalize or decriminalize the drug for personal use. The "Just Say No" Reagan years were nearly a decade away, and the public attitude toward recreational drug use was as relaxed as it would ever be. Several prominent businessmen and political leaders, including Senator Javits, were members of the board of the National Organization for the Reform of Marijuana Laws. (I also served on the NORML board, until 1978.)

In this climate, then, I arranged with a New York University professor, who was conducting a federally sanctioned marijuana experiment in his laboratory, to "administer" the drug to me on-camera. I took a page from my object-lesson book of 1971, when I was suspended by WABC-TV for buying a bag of heroin, and this time made all the necessary disclaimers and modifiers; I told viewers that the marijuana I was about to smoke was supplied by the federal government for the NYU experiment and reminded them that in most parts of the country what I was about to do was against the law. I laid out all the urgent, don't-try-this-at-home! warnings that have now become common to the point of parody.

And then I lit up. I actually got stoned. It was the only time I would ever appear before a television camera under the influence of drugs or alcohol, and the effect was startling, although it did not impact on my performance as much as it did on my ABC bosses. I was extremely careful that the tone of the packaged piece surrounding this scene come across as clinical, and responsible. I demonstrated how the eye vessels turn red and the mouth dries and explained the mildly euphoric effect of the drug on the user. There were no black lights and strobes to our story; it was all straight, professional, and matter-of-fact. We even compared the physical reactions of a group of students smoking marijuana to another control-group smoking a placebo. All of this was shot on film in the week or so leading up to our broadcast.

The only sensational thing about that show was the promotional piece we prepared to go with it. We wanted to get people to watch, and so we teased the report with a shot of me smoking a joint. Within the context of the show, these pictures had a kind of sanitized integrity; out of context, it was merely a shot of Geraldo Rivera getting stoned. ABC News President Bill Sheehan happened to see the promo the first time it aired and he blew a fuse. He made a panicked phone call to our office and ordered us to edit the marijuana segment from the ninety minutes we were readying for broadcast. Keep in mind, Sheehan was in charge of the news division, and *Good Night America* was an entertainment division production, but he was still powerful enough at the network to make things difficult for us.

I refused to reedit the piece, and Sheehan wound up killing the promotional teases that had been scheduled but had not yet run. My job at *Eyewitness News* was threatened, and the future of *Good Night America* was thrown into question. Over time, I relented to network demands, at least in part. Sheehan, though not directly in charge of *Good Night America*, was indirectly in charge of me; *Eyewitness News*, the local newscast of the network's owned and operated New York affiliate, was an ABC News production, which made Sheehan my boss, by extension, and he exerted pressure down through that chain of command.

I complied with his demands by blacking out the footage of me lighting up, and in its place put a wide band with the message, "Censored!" across the screen. I also took out an ad in the *Times*, at my own expense, using the same "Censored!" band as a banner headline and explaining to readers what had happened; I also urged them to tune in and see what all the fuss was about.

Bill Sheehan had stung it to me, again, but this time I stung him right back.

As a direct result of Sheehan's suppression, our ratings increased substantially for that second broadcast. Late-night viewers, alerted by my cries of censorship, were drawn to our show. Critics, who had in large part been willing to let the show air unnoticed, suddenly started to pay attention. I had, it seemed, a hip, new following, and the beginnings of a new career.

CHAPTER NINE

VENICE

I fear that in many ways I peaked, professionally and personally, in 1973. I have only come to consider this in the process of writing this book, but I think there is ample evidence to support that statement. I had invented myself by then, as a journalist, as a television personality, and as a man. I had made myself over in an image that satisfied me. Like a has-been/still-is rock star, who has written the hit song, the melody, the only thing left for me to change was the lyrics.

In the same way, I worry that the whole rest of my life has been a kind of afterthought: P.S. Geraldo went on to become prosperous and world-famous, and he had a talk show, and he had a late-night show, and he was in the network news business, and he fell in love—a few times more and, finally, for the last time.

The new lyrics, then, after the quietly successful launch of *Good Night America,* were set against the melody of WABC-TV. *Eyewitness News* had been my anchor and my meal ticket for going on four years—the salary I was able to extract from the *Good Night America* budget was less than twenty percent of my Channel 7 draw—and while my status as an emerging national persona was still uncertain, I wanted to, at least, cement my position in the New York market. I needed to pay some attention to local reporting. Trouble was, after Willowbrook, the migrants, and the littlest junkie, I felt an incredible pressure to top myself every time out, to see that every story broke new ground, righted unthinkable wrongs, won awards, changed the world.

It was an impossible and intimidating challenge, and I answered it by rephrasing the question. For the first time in my career, I invented something solely for the sake of what television could do for the community, and not also about what it could do for my career. I created, along with former PBS producer Peter Lance, an innovative, interactive, ongoing consumer-action feature, designed to help the little guys in our audience do battle against corrupt landlords, sleazy businesses, neighborhood crime, and the cold, cruel city itself. Today, virtually every major-market local station has its version of these consumer-action reports, but nobody was doing it regularly at the time.

For the next two years, from the beginning of 1974 through the end of 1975, the Channel 7 Help Center became the main focus of my local reporting. I went out on other stories, here and there—an occasional multipart series, or celebrity profile—but for the most part I concentrated on helping our viewers help themselves. It was a shift in emphasis that brought about rich personal rewards and considerable civic good, and satisfied a leery station management that, despite my burgeoning national efforts, my heart and muscle still belonged to *Eyewitness News* and the people of New York. Also the Help Center's narrow, manageable focus allowed me to absorb the demands of my every-other-weekly network show. Despite my moonlighting job at *Good Night America,* I was on the air as often as I had ever been for *Eyewitness*

News, although an argument could be made that the quality, or at least the scope of my local reporting suffered.

I moved my office out of the basement at 77 West 66th Street, and into the ASCAP building on Broadway, between Sixty-third and Sixty-fourth streets, where the network had leased several floors. There, Help Center volunteers soon outnumbered ABC employees; at one point we had twenty Fordham University law students (all receiving course credit), and about thirty other volunteers, ranging from high school kids to senior citizens, following up on the hundred or so written requests for help we received each day. From this steady stream, we would pluck four or five stories each week to feature on the six o'clock broadcasts, and for these I would put on my supermuckraker's cape and descend on the scene with a camera crew to kick up some dust.

Generally, the Help Center stories that made it to air leaned toward the routine: a jeweler who misplaced a family heirloom, a plumber who charged a few thousand dollars to unsuccessfully repair a leaky faucet, a dry cleaner who damaged a wedding dress, a plastic surgeon who promised more than he delivered. But some of the stories had dangerous elements, like the time I went undercover as a rabbi to infiltrate a welfare hotel and the time a fraudulent faith healer attacked me for exposing his illegal practices. The stories we did not cover on camera were tracked to their resolution off camera. Every viewer who wrote to us with a legitimate problem received our assistance. We prepared several information booklets containing names and numbers of various government agencies and businesses who had shown an ability to solve problems and a willingness to cooperate; law students never gave legal advice over the phone, but were quick to refer viewers to Legal Aid, or other appropriate agencies. We became a clearinghouse for all kinds of problems and hardships. The center grew to be such an integral part of the station's success, and a pipeline into the community, that I came to be seen as part of management in a way. I had so many people working for me, under me, around me, I probably should have worn a tie to work. (Peter Lance usually did.)

The Help Center emerged from the notion that the tragedies that stuffed the nightly newscast—crime, poverty, drug use, child abuse—needed more than retelling. They needed remedies, and they needed our hard efforts toward encouraging those remedies. I had splashed on the New York scene by making news, and now I wanted to unmake it, to ease the frustrations and hardships of the system.

I first met Peter Lance in 1972, when the two of us worked on a public-television special, for WNET-TV, called "VD Blues," a live (and incredibly frank) discussion about venereal disease; Peter was the producer, and I was the host, and we sought to mix the public-service elements of the program with a dash of entertainment. PBS had actors dressed up to play condoms, and other bits of Woody Allen weirdness. We were pretty far-out, even for public television, even for 1972. Still, our positive experience with "VD Blues" encouraged Peter and me to rethink the boundaries of the medium, to consider again what it was that television could do, and what it was supposed to do. The following year, we teamed on a proposed public-television program called "Consumer Help," which never quite got off the ground but made enough of a dent to pave the way for the Help Center.

Peter was filled with nervous energy. Half Irish, half Italian, his father a retired navy man in Rhode Island, he seemed to effect the privileged manner of the prep-school WASP, but never quite managed to pull it off. He was abrasive, and when we reteamed a year or so later, we developed a kind of good cop/bad cop rapport. I was often making repairs on people Peter had pissed off, and sometimes, vice versa.

But he was an invaluable collaborator. At Channel 7, he became my eyes and ears. He selected the Help Center stories we would pursue for broadcast and produced those segments as well. He was also the first of the handful of people I trusted to write for me. Editorially, he became a more valued and substantive colleague than Marty Berman, who had by this time become executive producer of both *Good Night America* and the Help Center. Marty was the schmoozer of the team, the politician. He ran interference with local news management, or with the network. He dealt with Jerry Weintraub. (I don't think Jerry even knew who Peter Lance was.) Marty was the big-picture guy. Peter, as producer of the Help Center, was the grunt, the leader of the worker bees.

With Marty and Peter as buffers and support, I removed myself even further from the newsroom. My office wasn't even in the same building as my *Eyewitness News* colleagues', and I had as little to do with them as was professionally possible. I turned up on the set for my few minutes of airtime and didn't even stay in the studio long enough for Al Primo's patented chitchat at the end of the broadcast. I became totally oblivious to the bad vibes and resentments directed at me. They were discernible, but irrelevant.

Unfortunately, my marriage to Edie was not thriving along with my career. By 1974, when I started to travel extensively for *Good Night America,* we were hardly together. I was sleeping with everything in skirts, and we both saw there was nothing to keep the marriage intact. I moved back to Avenue C, which I had been renting to my kid brother Craig. There was no argument to spur the split, no outward dismantling of the relationship. We did not do anything legally to dissolve the marriage, we just separated. In fact, we would get back together from time to time over the next year, for a few weeks, or a month, but things would never be the same between Edie and me. We even tried two or three reconciliation vacations, usually accompanied by Giorgio di Sant'Angelo, and others of that crowd. I remember meeting her one summer in Rome, where she had gone ahead to be with Giorgio and Andy Warhol and his flamboyant cohorts in a *palazzo* overlooking the Eternal City. I arrived a week late, missing most of the party. The two of us then went north to Venice, but even the gondolas and a stay in Hemingway's room at the Gritti Palace (with the best view and most luxurious linens on the planet) were not enough to reforge the relationship.

MARTINIQUE

Edie and I were finally divorced.

At my urging, she signed divorce papers prepared by my attorneys. She didn't even think to ask for alimony, until Louis Martinz (who had started the dissolution of our marriage by introducing me to Marian, but who by now had become a friend of the Vonnegut family) told Edie she was a fool. I agreed to pay twenty-five hundred dollars a month, and did, for about six months. I later wrote Edie suggesting that since she had a famous and wealthy father she didn't need my money as much as I did. Edie wrote back, agreeing to waive future alimony payments. Like her paintings, this woman was innocent and beautiful, even in divorce.

As soon as I had the signed papers in hand, I jetted off for a quickie divorce in Port-au-Prince, Haiti. After a painless, rum-soaked, three-day stay at the Hotel Olaffson (a wonderful, wooden-framed, twenties-era building that looked like a setting in a Graham Greene novel), I was again single. For the first time in three years, I had no one to lie to. I celebrated by going directly to Club Med on Martinique.

I arrived at the door of an old friend—one of the veterans of the Shelter Island orgy who had been inspired by that sexual anarchy to leave her faithful but quiet and unadventurous schoolteacher husband, and go to work for the famous resort chain. She handled my unannounced visit gracefully, housing me that first night until a bungalow became available.

When one did, I was off and running. I fell in love my first day there, with a secretary from New Jersey. Judi Beck was a lovely, tall, rail-thin blond, on holiday with her airline-stewardess sister. She worked for a midlevel executive at Johnson & Johnson and lived with her mother, a divorced RCA factory worker, in a modest home in central Jersey. I put on an incredible full-court press for her attentions. She had no chance. I didn't come on as much as I rolled over her, promising an enduring, high-style relationship before sunrise.

The biggest news in the outside world at the time was the imminent approach of Comet Kahoutek. Already glowing brightly in the Caribbean night, the comet dominated all conversation not related to suntans or romantic entanglements. By the second day, I had become a kind of wise old guru to a happy band of younger guys, many of them also sparring for Judi, and one impressed follower christened me after the comet. I strutted around the resort, rum-drunk and answering to the nickname Kahoutek.

Judi knew who I was, through the *Eyewitness News* broadcasts back home, and our affair was soon in high-gear. You have to understand, the typical Club Med romances have a shelf life of about a week, and our week passed too quickly. She left the island not knowing if we would ever see each other again; I left knowing that we would.

Several weeks later, I reappeared in Judi's life, in grand style. I was in her neighborhood on assignment. The first Arab oil embargo was in effect, and it was sending the price of gasoline soaring. I had a tip from an oil company employee based in Elizabeth, New Jersey, who told me that New York Harbor and its approaches were jammed with fully-laden oil tankers. The vessels had obviously sailed well before the Arab OPEC members had turned off the spigots. If the tip panned out, and the oil companies were indeed hoarding a store of oil and ripping off consumers at the pump, then I would have another breakthrough story.

I convinced the news desk to rent me a helicopter, and Bob Alis and I went out to film the tanker parade. The tip was solid, and I had my scoop. After securing the story, I set out for the girl. I had the pilot fly me out to the Johnson & Johnson helipad in central Jersey, where I paid a noisy, dramatic, and unannounced call to Judi at her office. She ran into my arms, through the wind and noise of the chopper blades.

Judi Beck thought she would never see me again, and here I had swept her up like a knight in blue-jeaned armor. A few days later she left her job and came to work for me.

I was in love again, and life was good.

BEVERLY HILLS

Over time, *Good Night America* hit a stride. We began to see certain kinds of stories as *Good Night America*-appropriate, as something we could do better than any other talk show, magazine show, or news program on television. We developed a feel and a pace that were entirely our own; we didn't look like anything else on television. Our infrequent scheduling made it hard for viewers to make us a habit, and the late hour made it tough on people who had to go to work the next morning (there were no VCRs in those days), but we eventually overcame these obstacles to enjoy a long and notable run. And once viewers found us, and stayed up with us, they usually came back for more; our audience grew from one edition to the next.

The reviews, though often kind, were frequently harsh. Some were harsher than others. *The New York Times*'s John J. O'Connor, who had checked in nearly three years earlier with a more favorable assessment of my work than I could have written myself, screened the first batch of *Good Night America* shows and was not at all impressed. "Tonight's eleven-thirty edition," he wrote on June 6, 1974, "devoted to interviews with Hugh Hefner, publisher of *Playboy* magazine, and Jane Fonda, the actress, is nothing short of dreadful. As an interviewer of other 'celebrities,' Mr. Rivera keeps tripping over anxiety about his own celebrity. The result is, too often, embarrassing."

As if this last was not bad enough, he concluded, "Mr. Rivera has come a long way from his perceptive and sympathetic essays about the poor and hopeless on the streets of New York. Evidently, too long a way."

There was a heavy rock 'n' roll bent to those first *Good Night America* shows, and we leaned that way in part because of the younger viewers tuned in to the late-night time slot, and in part because we had inexpensive (and virtually unlimited) access to musicians. There was always someone passing through New York on a concert tour who was willing to come on our air for a number, or an interview, or both; an appearance on our show sold records and tickets, and the stars found in me someone they could relate to, someone they could trust to tell their stories in a relaxed, informal setting. We interviewed Grace Slick, B.J. Thomas, Bill Withers, Sha Na Na, Kris Kristofferson, Don McLean, John Denver, Carole King, and dozens more, and in almost every case the conversations were accompanied by a live or taped performance piece.

Our tight budget discouraged on-location interviews, but we struggled for ways to incorporate them into the show, usually on the cheap. It was easy enough to take a camera crew backstage at a local concert, particulary since I was still something of a local concert promoter myself; whenever possible, I would hype our One-to-One benefits, promoting them with backstage interviews for *Good Night America* and *Eyewitness News*.

*   *   *

RITA KATSOTIS (former One-to-One Foundation staff member): Greg Allman did a One-to-One at Nassau Coliseum. I think he was married to Cher at the time. He was a bit tipsy, to be polite. And we were all backstage, standing around, listening, and Geraldo would say, "Why would you do a concert like this? Why would you get involved with a charity?" And there would be twenty seconds of dead silence. And then Geraldo would say, "Because it makes you feel good?" And Greg Allman would say, "Yeah, it makes me feel real good." He had to spoon-feed him every answer. And fortunately, with the editing, we were able to cut it all together quite nicely when they were done.

I interviewed Paul and Linda McCartney in Seattle, Washington, where they were appearing with Wings in Paul's first full-blown North American tour since he'd split with his former mates. It was one of his first national television appearances in a long time, and people watched in what were for *Good Night America* record numbers. We conducted the interview in Paul and Linda's hotel suite, and in various locations in and around the Kingdome, where the band was scheduled to appear.

Paul was easily the most flip, glib, casual, grounded, and confident of all of the Beatles, and I didn't care for him nearly as much as I did Ringo Starr, George Harrison, or John Lennon. He was likable enough; what I didn't care for was what he represented in the unraveling puzzle of Beatles lore. Perhaps I had been predisposed in this way through John Lennon. I had spent long hours listening to John and Yoko moan on about Paul's intransigence and manipulation, and I had chosen sides against Paul before I ever met him. Through John, I saw him as the enemy.

But Paul was also affable, clever, and accommodating. If there was a celebrity charm-school, he would have graduated at the top of his class. Also, he seemed to be extremely practical, and mainstream; although he would later be busted for bringing pot into Japan, there was no trace of the hippie about Paul. He was, by 1976, very much the proper businessman, already buying up whole libraries for his expanding music publishing enterprise, and that propriety permeated his personality.

This meeting with Paul held nothing like the pinch-me awe I

On the frozen shores of the Arctic Ocean, with my Good Morning America *crew, 1976.*
(Courtesy Geraldo Rivera collection)

Sharing the spotlight with ABC News colleague Barbara Walters, 1977. (Courtesy Geraldo Rivera collection)

With third wife, Sheri, and Fidel Castro, Havana, Cuba, 1977. (Courtesy Geraldo Rivera collection)

With Willie, after learning Pop would need bypass surgery, 1978. (Courtesy Geraldo Rivera collection)

With buddy Cheech Marin, after the
birth of my son Gabriel, 1979.
(Courtesy Geraldo Rivera collection)

With guerilla troops behind Vietnamese lines in
Laos, on assignment for the ABC News magazine
20/20, May, 1979. *(Courtesy Geraldo Rivera collection)*

With sisters Irene (left) and Sharon. *(Courtesy Geraldo Rivera collection)*

With soccer great Pelé. *(Courtesy Geraldo Rivera collection)*

At the 1980 Puerto Rican Day Parade banquet, with my proud father.
(Courtesy Geraldo Rivera collection)

At sea with my new love, C.C. Dyer, and my forty-four foot sloop, the New Wave, *1981.*
(Courtesy Margaret Cabot)

Breakfast in bed with my beautiful boy, 1981.
(Courtesy Geraldo Rivera collection)

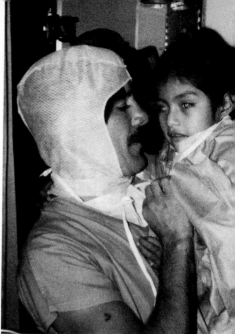

In Peru, to report on project Orbis for 20/20 in 1982. The on-camera moment when the child pictured here regained her sight after a cornea transplant stands as one of the most thrilling and gratifying of my career.
(Courtesy Geraldo Rivera collection)

With Craig, aboard the New Wave, *1982.*
(Courtesy Roger Mauser)

In the bush, Guatemala, 1982.
(Courtesy Geraldo Rivera collection)

Father and son, Central Park West, 1983. (Courtesy Geraldo Rivera collection)

With Barbra Streisand at one of her Malibu homes, 1983.
(Courtesy Geraldo Rivera collection)

Admiring the engagement ring, with my everlasting love, C.C. Dyer, 1986.
(Courtesy Geraldo Rivera collection)

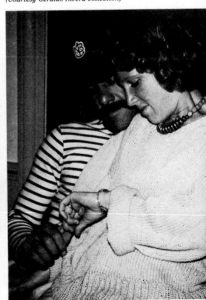

Basement theater: mining the depths of
Chicago's Lexington Hotel in search of
Al Capone's secret vault, April 27, 1986.
(Courtesy Geraldo Rivera collection)

With Bernard Carabello, at the 1987
closing ceremony on the pastoral
grounds of Willowbrook State School.
(Courtesy Geraldo Rivera collection)

Fallout from my November, 1988 run-in
with neo-Nazi hatemongers. *(Courtesy Geraldo
Rivera collection)*

The Reverend Ernie Cockrell, best man
Gabriel, and soon-to-be mother-in-law
Peggy Dyer surround C.C. and me at our
informal, impromptu wedding rehearsal on
Buzzard's Bay, July 11, 1987.
(Courtesy Timothy Dyer)

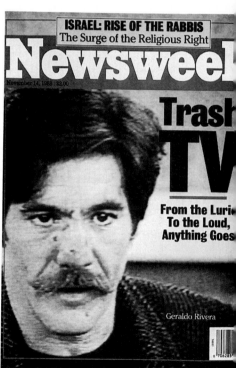

ISRAEL: RISE OF THE RABBIS
The Surge of the Religious Right

Newsweek

November 14, 1988 · $2.00

Trash TV

From the Lurid
To the Loud,
Anything Goes

Geraldo Rivera

With Charles Manson in
San Quentin, April, 1988.
(Courtesy Geraldo Rivera collection)

Family portrait (left to right): Irene, Craig, Mama,
Sharon, and Willie, 1989. *(Courtesy Geraldo Rivera collection)*

On a 1989 trip to New Jersey's Great Adventure
amusement park, with "my kids"——the inner-
city students the Maravilla Foundation has
promised to send to college upon high school
graduation. Flanking the group are personal
assistants David Rosado and Jo-Ann Torres
Conte, and teacher Carmen Ocasio.

(Courtesy Anthony Conte)

Caught by surprise having coffee at
Rough Point, 1990. *(Courtesy Tak Konstantinou)*

felt in meeting the others. Paul always seemed the most shallow of the group, the least profound. I thought of him as a kind of Barry Manilow, a polished tunesmith. John was the true rocker of the group; Paul was the crooner. Still, those interviews led to a kind of professional friendship between us; Paul would make himself available for my cameras whenever he was in the country, and he would do his best to make both of us look good. Eventually, I hired Linda McCartney's brother John Eastman, to be my personal lawyer, which meant that Paul and I would hear of each other's doings and whereabouts over the next several years. This link, through Paul to his brother-in-law, would serve as another reminder of my emerging celebrity stature. Their people had become my people.

Of course, our *Good Night America* segments were not devoted entirely to music. We touched on all aspects of popular culture. In March 1976, when Norman Lear's warped late-night soap-opera spoof, *Mary Hartman, Mary Hartman,* was a runaway hit in its first season, I flew out to Los Angeles to profile the show's star, Louise Lasser. Louise had been married to Woody Allen some years earlier, and she was, at that time, Hollywood's flavor of the month. She was even on the cover of *Time* magazine and joked during our interview that she was the only actress so honored who could not get her agent on the phone. She had a wonderful self-deprecating sense of humor. Her trademark in those days were the long redheaded braids she wore on the show, and she looked like a pixie housewife, with a personality twisted to match her hair.

She was delightful and charming. She was also flaky. I enjoyed her company, at least at first. There wasn't any sexual pull between us, but we each had a free evening to look forward to and so, after our interview, I took Louise out for dinner, and then to the Troubadour to see a show. We were photographed leaving the nightclub by the paparazzi, and over the next weeks every people page and gossip column in the country linked the two of us romantically.

They were off in their reporting. Louise and I did return to her house in the Hollywood Hills, where the lights were dimmed low and the music was playing soft and sweet. She mixed us some drinks. We started to get comfortable, and as our evening wore on, she took off her hair. It was a shock. I had no idea her trademark locks were a wig. Underneath the red braids was a short, gnarled, close-cropped head of hair. She looked more like Sinéad O'Connor than the times allowed.

I went through the motions of romance, but the hair had thrown me. I started making noises about someone waiting for me at home, and about having a previous commitment, but Louise had an argument to counter every lame excuse.

The next day, she sent me a telegram, marked personal delivery only, that esssentially thanked me for the night before and described me as "touching, warm, and gentle." Whatever else she may have been, Louise Lasser was not a shrewd judge of character.

The *Good Night America* format took me to all corners of the cultural scene. I conducted the first interview with author Clifford Irving upon his release from prison after publishing a book he claimed to be Howard Hughes's autobiography. The hoax was one of the biggest stories of 1974, and we got to its perpetrator before anyone else. Irving talked passionately about pitting his ambition against his scruples, about his wild and, ultimately, failed gambit; he had a sense of humor about the ordeal, and for the first time the American public saw a human side to what had been trumped-up as a hardhearted deception.

For another author-guest, I reached out to my now-estranged father-in-law. Kurt Vonnegut appeared on the show, to read from his new book and talk about his life and career. It was a gracious gesture on his part, considering how things were with Edie and me. In fact, Kurt and I would remain close for the next several years, despite the souring of my marriage. I was actually quoted as saying the thing I missed most about being married to Edie was my father-in-law. My relationship with Kurt lasted until the early 1980s, when I began to speak publicly about my infidelities. These days, I suspect, Kurt hates me with a fervor, not only for the way I mistreated his daughter, but for what he must see as the insensitive swagger in speaking openly about that period in my life.

Gradually, we shifted from celebrity-driven personality pieces to more substantive segments. At the end of our first season, for example, we devoted an entire edition to the various conspiracy theories surrounding the assassination of President Kennedy. Despite a threatened lawsuit from copyright holder Time-Life, we aired a brief film clip taken from an eight-millimeter home movie shot by a Fort Worth retail jeweler named Abraham Zapruder and presented it for the first time on national television. (The studio audience gasped audibly at the horrifying slow motion images.) The startling footage revealed the president's head recoiling backward with the impact of the final bullet. The motion suggested to me, and to the several conspiracy theorists assembled on our panel, that there was a second gunman in front of the presidential motorcade, in addition to Lee Harvey Oswald, who was positioned behind and above the president's limousine, in the book depository.

In a related later segment, I conducted the first (and only) network television interview with Oswald's mother, Marguerite Oswald, during which she claimed that an FBI agent had shown her a picture of Jack Ruby on the day before he killed her son, and asked her if she knew the man.

These shows created a stir, and for the first time we began to be seen as an outlet for controversial outsider opinion. It became our turf. Remember, in March 1975, when the first Kennedy conspiracy show aired, Nixon had been out of office for less than a year; for one of the few times in our history, the American people were willing to believe that their government was capable of murder, conspiracy, and lies.

Good Night America, in many ways, was the pathfinder for contemporary shows such as *A Current Affair, Inside Edition,* and *Hard Copy.* We examined tabloid topics—the Bermuda Triangle, UFOs, prostitution—and dressed them for mass consumption. It may have been "news-lite," but it was also a pioneering, counterculture, late-night broadcast that helped pave the way for *Saturday Night Live,* David Letterman, and Arsenio Hall.

One of our hardest-hitting and most explosive shows unfolded during our first season, and helped to set a combative tone that would take me over the rest of the *Good Night America* run and on into the rest of my career. In September 1974, I invited the entire New York chapter of the Hell's Angels into the studio to talk about their politics and their lifestyle. They came out with their motorcycles and their leathers, and occupied an entire section of bleachers we had set up on the stage. There were about fifty of them, and each looked more menacing than the next. We cleared the audience from the studio for this segment, and added extra security measures in anticipation of fireworks.

By 1974, the Hell's Angels had roared onto the national scene with a sinister vengeance. In 1969, during a free Rolling Stones concert at California's Altamount Speedway, local members, ostensibly hired to provide concert security, stabbed a young black man to death; in the early 1970s, in New York, a police officer and several Hell's Angeles were killed in a confrontation. I reported on the gang for *Eyewitness News*. During a time of particular tension, I went out to their New York headquarters on East Third Street and filmed the members loitering around their long row of chopped Harleys. After a few minutes, I was confronted by one of the group's leaders, wielding a .45 at my nose to get his point across. "You can't film here," this guy snarled. "This is a public street," I reacted. East Third Street is not far from my place on Avenue C, and I felt the same proprietary interest in the neighborhood that they did.

I later learned that this exchange pissed off my Channel 7 colleague Duke Wade, who blamed me for riling up the Angels. "Why did you make them so angry?" Wade challenged. "Now they're not letting anyone on their block. You fucked us." He called me a scooper—it sounded like a schoolyard taunt—because I was looking to scoop the other reporters and not play by the rules.

Eventually, this initial near-violent confrontation developed into an odd friendship with Sandy Alexander, the president of the New York chapter. The Angels were friendly with the guys in Elephant's Memory, John Lennon's band at the time, and they wanted to come to the One-to-One concert. The common ground helped eased the mutual mistrust. The Angels wanted to clean up their image, and I offered to help, with more balanced pieces for *Eyewitness News*. Sandy and I became dog and cat friends; we were two different species, and at any moment one of us would set the other off.

Sandy used to wear his long, black, greasy hair back in a ponytail, and he always wore dark shades with a heavy black frame. His arms were heavily tattooed, his denim jacket cut off at the shoulders, and his fingers laden with skeleton-head rings that doubled as brass knuckles. He had the whole Hell's Angels look, but was able to mitigate the menace, somewhat, with a fairly agile mind and sophisticated vocabulary. Sandy could rap. He could also bullshit. He had a whole line about how the Angels were really outlaws, and how they started as a group of disillusioned World War II veterans, and how the bikes were an expression of their desire for personal freedom. He could make their movement sound like a gathering of Young Republicans.

I used to spend time with them in their tenement headquarters on East Third, a six-floor walk-up. They lived communally. They hid their weapons in the walls. They brutalized their women. I don't remember noticing this last with any great sense of outrage; I was more perplexed than indignant. I could not figure why these women put up with this behavior; one gang member would typically have a legal wife, a favored old lady, and a teenaged mistress. Often the Angel involved had children by all three of his perpetually abused women, and yet they kept coming back for more.

It was outrageous, and perversely interesting. For Sandy, there was a parallel charge in going with me to a fancy restaurant, or some society party. He was a brutal, bullying man, but not all the time. During those periods of calm, one could see texture and intelligence.

Sandy was the perfect guest for *Good Night America.* In those days, before the Angels fell victim to their own violence and dope dealing, there was a strange public fascination with the entire lifestyle, and I invited Sandy on the show to run his bullshit. The idea snowballed to where we booked the entire New York chapter, with Sandy to serve as spokesman. It became an entirely different segment than the one I had originally envisioned, but it promised at good television. And it delivered. The tension in the studio that day was thick enough to hold up a spoon. I wanted to push these guys as far as they would let me, and then I wanted to push a little bit further. I was confrontational with Sandy, on-camera. I called him a violent, defiant, and fearful man. I talked tough. Everyone in that studio—and, remember, there was no studio audience for this segment—felt certain the situation would erupt into violence. Everyone at home, we learned later, felt the same way. I don't know that I was hoping for something like this to happen, but I was prepared for it. And I'm sure there was a part of me that would have welcomed it, that knew (as long as I wasn't killed) a one-against-fifty battle with the Hell's Angels would be a no-lose proposition. I might have been beaten, but I would not back down. If I were to get hurt, it would be in some superficial way (with all our security waiting in the wings), and I knew a black eye or a broken nose would only add to the legend.

As things played out, the tough talk only led to more tough talk. We didn't come to blows, although the entire segment had a rough edge to it, a tension. We toed the line, but didn't cross it. Still, it was a benchmark show for us—memorable and talked-about—and it helped to solidify my emerging national reputation as a tenacious and combative reporter, willing to step into potential physical danger without concern for personal safety. I could bring back stories that others were too chilled to go after in the first place.

For *Good Night America*'s soft, titillating side, I traveled to San Francisco in June 1975, for a hookers' convention. There was a lobbying group called Call Off Your Old Tired Ethics—COYOTE—set up for prostitutes, ex-prostitutes, and advocates of prostitution, and they held a national convention to discuss things like escort services, advertising, and decriminalization of the oldest profession. It was a convention like any other (if you could somehow forget the industry in question), and we thought a visit there would yield an interesting piece. We were right. Margot St. James, the group's founder and leader, came on our show to talk about her various concerns, and the freewheeling interview and the risqué footage taken from the convention floor combined to give us one of our sauciest air-pieces.

The segment satisfied the prurient interests of our late-night audience and provided fringe benefits for this enterprising reporter. After the hookers' convention, I traveled to Los Angeles, where I was expected the next day at the Beverly Hills bar mitzvah of Michael Weintraub, Jerry's kid. I was expecting to attend the affair without a date, but something happened. Actually, two things happened: a blonde and a redhead. Two of my most cooperative COYOTE sources accompanied me to Los Angeles after the convention ended on a Friday, and we holed up in the Beverly

Hills Hotel. These were two of the most uninhibited working girls I have ever met, and we scandalized the joint. The manager even checked on us and asked us to keep a lid on our enthusiasms. The topper was that it was on the house; the girls were so tickled by the national television exposure, and by my celebrity, that they turned off the meter. I paid for their round-trip airfare, kept them fed and unclothed, and that was it.

On Saturday morning, as I washed away the delightful sins of the night before, and started to dress for the bar mitzvah, the girls put on the longest faces I had ever seen. "You're ashamed of us," sulked the redhead. "We're not good enough for your Hollywood friends," sulked the blonde. They reminded me of their favors and hinted at more. I finally figured, what the hell.

And so I arrived at the Weintraub estate with a hooker on each arm, each wearing skintight black dresses. They hadn't packed for a bar mitzvah, and their fuck-me garments hugged so close to their bodies it was like the girls were wrapped in cellophane. Neither wore a bra or underwear, and the dresses were as sheer as nylon stockings.

We made quite an entrance. Jerry, by this time, was a huge Hollywood success; he lived in a beautiful mansion on Doheny, just off Sunset Boulevard. His client list had expanded to include George Burns, Milton Berle, Georgie Jessel; every old vaudevillian still working in the entertainment industry was represented by Jerry, it seemed, and every one of them was at that bar mitzvah.

The bar mitzvah featured a lifesize ice sculpture of the bar mitzvah boy, and a star-studded "A" list of guests, including Frank Sinatra, John Denver, Elvis's manager, Colonel Tom Parker, and many others. The band segued from rock to "Hava Negilah" without effort.

Jaws dropped when I walked in. Network executives, who a year earlier would not have acknowledged me in an empty restaurant, flashed me knowing, approving smiles; they would have given me the thumbs-up signal if they could have done so without alerting their horrified wives. Nobody knew what to make of me, or my actions, at that party. What right-minded, would-be national celebrity goes to a straight, high-powered Beverly Hills bar mitzvah with a couple of hookers on his arm?

WOUNDED KNEE, SOUTH DAKOTA

Good Night America may have launched my network television career, but it did so at a price. It took me off the streets of New York. It made me less relevant.

With the Help Center occupying almost all of my local attentions, and the talk show filling my downtime, there was no room for the radical, liberal, street-fighting populist that first brought me to attention.

In an effort to restore some of the bluster, and luster, I looked to radio. Conveniently, radio also looked to me. In those days, ABC had an extensive FM radio network that included many of the major, album-oriented rock 'n' roll stations in the country. When it looked like *Good Night America* was going to be around for a while, the network approached me with the idea of doing a daily radio commentary, examining and interpreting world events as they impacted on young people. They wanted to turn me into a Paul Harvey for the under-thirty crowd, talkin' 'bout my generation, to my generation. I seized the opportunity. What a tremendous outlet, I thought at the time. What a pipeline. For two or three minutes, everyday, I would have the ear of millions of kids and young adults, suctioned to their radios, listening to my views on the events of the day, or to my social or political commentary.

The idea worked better in theory than it did on the air. The effort was hobbled from the start. Our first, and biggest, obstacle was getting clearance on the network-owned New York station, WPLJ-FM. The New York City station would not carry us at first, and as a result, I never heard myself on the air, never got any true feedback. About the only validation I got, that there was indeed a Geraldo Rivera radio commentary being broadcast to this nation's heartland, was a promotional T-shirt with my picture on it. It was the first time I had ever been given that kind of attention by a network promotion department. Solo, I had never been on a billboard, or the side of a bus. This was new to me, and I loved it. The picture on the T-shirt made me look a little bit like Sonja Henie with a moustache, but there was no mistaking that it was me.

I took subjects off the front page, or from the back of my mind;

on balance, the topics were far-reaching and thought-provoking. Sometimes, they were simply time-killing, filling the airwaves until I could think of a more salient topic for the next day's broadcast. Also, these commentaries were often opinionated and outspoken; sometimes, they were merely informative, offering the story behind the story of the day. I spoke up for handgun control, and in favor of death with dignity. I discussed human rights violations in the Soviet Union, warned about the consequences of toxic waste, and favored forced busing. And I spoke out against the PLO, the IRA, and the Puerto Rican terrorist grup, the FALN. The FALN responded to my attack with the first serious death threat I'd ever received, and I was on-edge for several weeks afterwards. The New York City Police Department, in its wisdom, decided to use me as a bait, to try to lure the terrorists into an attack against me; they assigned me a full-time detective, who started my car each morning and checked the packages coming into my ASCAP office. Eventually, the threat dissipated, the detective disappeared, and I was left to piss off someone else.

STEVE NORTH (former writer/producer, Geraldo Rivera radio commentaries; currently, producer, *Geraldo*): We were in the radio studio one day, waiting to record, and Geraldo began flirting with a particularly cute desk-assistant. He was his typical playful self, and somehow he maneuvered this poor girl up onto a large table in the studio, and she was lying down, and she was just screaming with laughter as he tickled her mercilessly. This was normal behavior for him. The funny thing about it is that Howard K. Smith walked in the door, and Geraldo was facing away from the door and didn't see him, and Smith just kind of stood there, frozen by what he saw. Howard K. Smith has that odd look about him to begin with, with one eye slightly askew, and he just stood in the doorway, staring. He was not amused, and Geraldo just kept on tickling this girl. He was completely oblivious. It was a funny scene, but it was also indicative of how things were between Geraldo and the news establishment. They hated him, and he didn't care. Oh, I'm sure he cared, in a way, but he still went out and did things his way. He didn't act like he cared. He wasn't about to change for these people.

*   *   *

The radio show, once again, pitted me against my old network news adversary, Elmer Lower. Curiously (and hauntingly), Lower had stepped down from the presidency of ABC News to head the FM radio network, which, once again, made him my boss. (The broadcast news business is incestuous; if you screw somebody one year, he'll be back to screw you the next.) Lower didn't trust me, and his mistrust surfaced in a big way midway through my radio run.

I pride myself on never missing a deadline, and I had that same pride back then. I have had enormous deadline pressure on incredible, breaking stories. I have been up all night, sometimes several nights in a row, writing and editing to the very last minute, sprinting down West Sixty-sixth Street to get to the newsroom on time, or racing to make a satellite-feed in some distant country.

I tried to write and record each commentary as close to its airdate as possible, to keep things fresh and timely. I left the city one weekend without having a piece ready for the following Monday. I was out on the East End of Long Island, and I called in to inform the network that I would be in the studio on Monday morning with plenty of time before the feed. I left a specific message for Lower that I would be back in time. And, indeed, I did make it back, with a half hour or so to spare, only to find that Lower had already taken an old commentary and sent it out, as a rerun, to our subscribing stations.

I was furious. I stormed into Lower's office, ready to beat the shit out of him. How dare he undermine (and underestimate) me. I threatened to sue him and the network; I also threatened to abandon the radio commentaries altogether. That was the way I played things with ABC management in those days: Risk everything. The network always crumbled under the challenge. Of course, I would be fired ten years later, after backing the network into an entirely different corner, but at the time there was no denying me. I got what I wanted from ABC, an apology, but it was an empty victory. The radio commentaries did not last much longer, not because of Elmer Lower or any fallout from this incident, but because I never quite took to the medium. I'd grown up with television. Radio was no longer the galvanizing medium that it was, or that it would become again. The revolutions in talk radio were still several years away, and at the time I thought my opinions would receive fuller voice on the tube.

Looking back, I recognize that I squandered something here, that I missed a tremendous opportunity to plug in to a vast new audience. Radio, I realize now, allows for an intimacy not possible on television, not even in late night.

By the time the radio gig disappeared, there was a new sideline to take its place: morning television. For years, ABC had tried unsuccessfully to launch its own morning program to compete against NBC's dominant *Today Show*; the most recent failed-effort had been something called *A.M. America*, with Bill Beutel and Stephanie Edwards as hosts, and Peter Jennings as news anchor. The show featured semiregular contributions from columnist Jack Anderson, former senator Sam Ervin, former New York mayor John Lindsay, and future presidential candidate and then civil rights activist Jesse Jackson. *A.M. America* lasted for about ten months, barely registering a blip in the national ratings.

Finally, the time period was given over to the entertainment division, in the hopes that it would come up with a winning formula where the news division had failed; Bob Shanks, the executive in charge of late-night programming, was given the early-morning mantel, as well, probably under the sage network thinking that if he knew what worked for night-owl viewers he could also entertain the early risers.

Shanks, along with a frantic, creative-genius producer named Woody Fraser, borrowed from the proven *Today Show* formula to come up with a two-hour blend of news, interviews, and features. Their main innovations were using a living-room set instead of a news set, and hiring actors to serve as hosts instead of journalists, all designed to make the program more perky, chatty, and informal than a typical news broadcast. They decided to call their effort *Good Morning America*, which led to my first involvement with the program. Two years earlier, I had trademarked the name *Good Night America*, for Maravilla Productions, and ABC lawyers informed the entertainment division that it could not use the name *Good Morning America* without first obtaining my permission. My first thought was to hold these guys up for a great deal of money, but I was talked down from that position by a group of clear-thinking friends and advisors. The more practical strategy, Jerry Weintraub pointed out, was to gift the name to the network for a token fee, and tally up brownie points for future maneuverings.

At the same time, and unrelatedly, I started talking to Bob Shanks about contributing to the program. I was already an employee of the entertainment division through *Good Night America,* and Shanks had to assemble a supporting cast of not-ready-for-network-news stars to fill his two-hour soft-news hole. He knew he could rely on me to supply compelling and provocative reports on a variety of subjects, and I knew my national career needed some daylight exposure. It was a perfect fit, and I signed on as one of the inaugural reporters when the show debuted in November 1975.

The *Good Morning America* on-air positions were cast, more than they were filled. David Hartman, an ex-jock actor best known for a television series called *Lucas Tanner,* in which he played an ex-jock teacher, was brought in to serve as anchor. He had no experience, but he took to the role very naturally. Broadcast journalism is not rocket science, no matter what my colleagues pretend. David had a kind of Nebraska hominess, a keen and inquiring mind, and an ease on-camera that translated very well to the show's format. He was like a comforting cup of black coffee in the morning. As the years went by, someone should have decaffeinated him; David Hartman's image prospered along with the program's, and it wasn't long before he began to assume the airs of network news propriety. He came to resent, I think, the preconceived notions of the news division, about what our show was, and he worked against those preconceptions at every chance. He resented, for example, having to be teamed with a "real" reporter whenever he interviewed a "real" newsmaker.

Nancy Dussault, an actress who would later star in the Ted Knight sitcom *Too Close for Comfort,* was the show's cohost. She was intelligent, curious, and also without talk-show experience. Her role shrank as David Hartman's grew. She took on the more lightweight topics, while he tackled the serious issues. Nancy would leave the show after about eighteen months, when David and the rest of the GMA braintrust decided she appeared too flighty alongside the more serious image he was by then trying to project.

Erma Bombeck, a genuinely funny, able, and self-deprecating woman, was cast as the show's resident humorist; Rona Barrett became the house gossip, although she shied from the label. (She preferred being known as the show-business reporter, and for a time was the best-known and most powerful in Hollywood.) Steve Bell, a solid, skilled, generous newsman, read the news (in the only portion of the program produced by the news division) for five minutes at the top of each half-hour. And Bob Shanks cast me as GMA's roving people-reporter. The country would be my beat; its people, my stories.

Word of my hiring at GMA was met with great resistance at WABC, the local station still paying most of my salary. Already, I was juggling commitments to *Good Night America* and the FM radio network, while trying to deliver on my contract to *Eyewitness News*. My Help Center involvement had thinned to where Peter Lance was actually going out and conducting interviews for our air-pieces, and I was supplying the voice-overs later, in the editing. The prospect of another network position, further diluting my work for Channel 7, moved station management to issue an ultimatum: Remove myself from the GMA lineup, or risk my job at *Eyewitness News*.

My local news contract had another year or two to run—at this point I was up to about five hundred thousand dollars a year—but I was clearly in violation of the exclusive-services clause in the agreement. Still, I was unwilling to pass on the *Good Morning America* opportunity, or to relinquish the good thing I had going with *Good Night America*. (The radio commentaries only ate up an hour or so of my time each day, and did not really factor into the dilemma.) Besides, I thought I was too much of an asset to Channel 7 for the station to make good on its threat.

The station held fast. They cut me loose. I can see now that it was the right move for them, just as it was the right move for me. At the time, though, I felt like I'd been kicked in the nuts. The station had launched my television career, and even though my relationships with most on-camera colleagues, and most of management, were past the point of disinterest, I felt like I belonged there.

The most troubling aspect to this separation, I would learn, was that I was suddenly cutoff from the *Eyewitness News* archives. I could no longer reach into the Channel 7 vaults for a sound-bite from a story I'd reported on years earlier. A tremendous resource was effectively off-limits. So much of television news is cyclical and repetitive; everything news will be news again. My firing cut me off from five years of my professional history. My work was no longer my own; it belonged to WABC-TV.

I dealt with my dismissal by jumping into my new job. I was relentless in pursuit of a good story, and in the chance to blaze a new career path. In my first full year with *Good Morning America*, I was on the air as often as possible, sometimes reporting as many as three or four stories a week. If the airlines had had their frequent flyer programs in place back then, I would have put them out of business. I would fly into New York to introduce my pieces, when I could; for those times when I could not, I developed a signature sign-off from the field. "From Toledo, Ohio," I would say, "I'm Geraldo Rivera. Peace, and good morning, America."

I may not have been an official network newsman, but I had a signature sign-off, heard coast-to-coast, and it was the next best thing.

My deal with *Good Morning America*—I was hired as an independent contractor, through my company, Maravilla Productions—paid me over five hundred thousand dollars a year. I brought Marty Berman along with me, and my assistant, Marylou Pizzarello, and put them on Maravilla's payroll. I also hired Judi Beck, my love, to be my secretary, and she came to live with me during the week. (She went home to her mother's in New Jersey on the weekends.) I wanted to keep Judi close, and I needed Marylou to stitch together the various threads of my life, but I wasn't entirely sure where Marty fit in. He was a trusted friend, and I valued his opinion and news sense, but I no longer needed him as a producer. There was a team of GMA staffers at my disposal, at no cost to my production company. *Good Night America* alone did not justify his salary. But I kept Marty on, and he wound up serving as my principal administrator, still based in our old ASCAP offices on West Sixty-fourth Street. If there was a meeting to attend in New York, and I was on the road, he went on my behalf. If a piece needed to be shepherded through editing, he saw to that as well.

One of my earliest, and most representative stories for *Good Morning America* took place on the Rosebud Sioux reservation, in Wounded Knee, South Dakota. There, in 1976, the FBI had been called in to quell a modern-day Indian uprising. Several people were killed in the revolt, including an FBI agent. I was dispatched to the area and what I found was pathetic and depressing. The Native Americans of Wounded Knee, I learned, were made to live in horrible conditions, and to suffer unendurable hardships. The challenge, as it was years earlier with

Willowbrook, or with the migrant workers story, was to ask viewers to understand and sympathize with the plight of an exotic group that had no connection to their own small, safe world. The only Indians most of our viewers had ever seen were on *F Troop*; I had to sell the bleak images of Wounded Knee to a morning television audience more interested in the weather, or in an exciting new chicken Kiev recipe.

There was a built-in luxury in an ensemble show such as *Good Morning America* in that we could get away with five or six minutes of depressing footage, if we surrounded it with Erma Bombeck's humor, or Rona Barrett's gossip, and that is what we did here. We doled out the big picture in small doses—spread out over several days—and got our viewers to care about the oppression and hardships of these people.

What I remember most clearly about that trip, though, is a sidebar that never made it to air. It has stayed with me these years for the way it articulated the Indians' struggle. I went to the bathroom in one of the reservation's unheated outhouses, and I had the painful and humiliating experience of having my ass stick—frozen—to the rough wooden seat. Sitting there, unable to free myself from the frozen toilet, I could not help but realize how awful the living conditions truly were. The indignity of that moment spoke more eloquently to the struggles of the modern-day American Indian than any of the words or pictures that made it on my broadcasts.

At a different, later stage in my career, I would have talked about that moment on television, because it made its point in a personal way, but at the time I was still unsure enough of myself and my emerging national celebrity that I left it alone.

PROVIDENCE, RHODE ISLAND

In the spring of 1976, presidential politics threatened for a second time to push me off the air. This time trouble came looking for me, and I was ready.

Trouble came in the form of the clear-eyed and compassionate former governor from the state of Georgia. Jimmy Carter approached me about stumping for him in the 1976 campaign. The primary season was already underway, and Carter was making a surprisingly strong showing, but he needed to do a better job capturing the young vote in the northeast-corridor states if he wanted to win the nomination.

He came asking for my support, and for my help. After the harsh lesson of my McGovern involvement in 1972, I was reluctant to offer either.

MICHAEL HOROWICZ (former intern, *Good Night America*; now, news director, KCBS, Los Angeles): There was a man in the office, in Geraldo's office, and Geraldo came out and said, "Get this guy coffee, get this guy coffee." He said, "He's the governor of Georgia, he's gonna be the next president of the United States. Here's a dollar. Go downstairs and get this guy coffee." So I went downstairs to get the coffee, and I came back up and I just sat around and had about a fifteen-minute conversation with Jimmy Carter. And this was 1976. He was going around saying he was gonna be the next president of the United States. No one believed him. And it was him. It was him. It was an incredible thing.

Despite my reservations, Carter came to see me at my ASCAP offices, and we talked long and hard about his vision for the future of this country, about peace and economic stability, about honest small-town values. He seemed genuinely interested in my opinions, about his policies and my own, and I was struck by his sincerity and simplicity. I liked what he was saying, and the way he was saying it, and I wanted to hear more. He came back to my apartment on Central Park West, and we continued our talk.

I was greatly impressed by the man. Of course, I'm sure some of that first impression grew from flattery. No presidential candidate had ever pursued me before, and here he was, courting me, trying to earn my support. He was affable, with a kind of folksy charm that was easy to take. I wanted to throw my hat in his ring, and I would have, had I not already been burned by my McGovern endorsement in 1972.

Carter understood that I could not come out and campaign for him directly, but he had something else in mind. Would I consider emceeing a benefit concert in Providence, Rhode Island, in the weeks ahead? He planned to make a speech at the concert, which was to feature two rockabilly bands from his native Georgia, the Allman Brothers Band and the Charlie Daniels Band, and he needed someone to introduce him, and to fill the space between musical guests.

I agreed, with some hesitation. I saw no good reason why I should refrain from helping my candidate of choice—and Jimmy Carter very quickly made himself my candidate of choice—simply because of the constraints of my profession. But, I also wanted to avoid a repeat of the backlash of 1972. I told myself it was only a concert, and that I was not being asked to speak on the candidate's behalf. I also told myself that the concert was in Providence, far from the questioning eyes of my dubious colleagues; there was a good chance no one in news management would ever learn of my appearance, and if they did, I thought, I could dance my way out of any jam.

Once in Providence, I did away with my misgivings and gave the event my all. I was carried away by the excitement of the moment, and the heady thought that I was helping to chart our political future. I gave a real barn-burner of a speech. "There is a new wind blowing out of the state of Georgia," I declared, introducing the former governor, "that will change the face of American politics forever."

Thankfully, there were no repercussions to my appearance. Carter appreciated what I did for him, and he reciprocated the following year, inviting me to his first White House dinner, although as his term in office wore on he was not particularly helpful or forthcoming. I remember feeling cheated by that, duped; once he attained office I became just another journalist.

41 CENTRAL PARK WEST

The remarkable career-turn of *Good Morning America* was set against a tangled and tumultuous year personally. My love life was in tremendous flux. I had no idea what I was doing, or what was happening to me. My marriage to Edie Vonnegut was finally, and formally, over. In the months preceding our last breakup, Edie had taken an apartment at 41 Central Park West, through a new friend, the model China Machado. Actually, we took the apartment together, under my name (we wanted to give the marriage one last shot and Edie couldn't afford the apartment on her own). But I was back at Avenue C before my first week there was out.

The Lower East Side that I returned to when I left Edie looked different to me on this second pass. It was, of course, very much the same neighborhood I had departed less than two years earlier, but I no longer belonged there. The allure of living in this urban wasteland had subsided; I had lost my connection to the appealing aspects of this place.

The only good thing to come out of my return to Avenue C was my relationship with my new roommate—my baby brother Craig. He was just six years old when I'd left West Babylon at seventeen, and we had never been close. In fact, he was such a pudgy, unathletic little kid, I remember being embarrassed by him when I was in high school. I wanted nothing to do with him. But always, when I'd return home for a visit, he was loving, almost worshipful of his big brother, who was doing wonderful things in faraway places. By the time Craig reached high school, he started to come into his own; one year, he shot up from five-four to six-two. He had metamorphosed almost overnight. He became a ladies' man, and a jock. Unfortunately, he was never much of a student. After two dismal years at Kutztown State College, I encouraged him to drop out and come to work for me. He started out as a gofer— "Geraldo's kid brother"—and stayed for nearly fifteen years, eventually becoming one of the best investigative producers and reporters in the business. My new living arrangement jump-started what has turned out to be one of the most important and lasting friendships of my life. In those days—me suddenly single, Craig suddenly out from his parents' protective wings—the two of us were pretty crazy. We went out drinking, dancing, and whoring together. He traveled with me, whenever it was possible. He was my wingman, and I loved having him around.

Very early in 1976, Edie suddenly decided the new Central Park West apartment was too big for her, and she sublet it out to a friend of a friend. I was livid. The lease to the apartment was in my name, and I wanted it. I was tired of Avenue C, and longed for an address to signal my position as a network celebrity. The apartment was a beautiful, sixth-floor corner unit, with two bedrooms, overlooking Central Park and the Upper East Side skyline. At the time, the building was even rent-stabilized, which kept the rent at about four hundred dollars a month, less than half its real value.

I wasn't about to let this place go to some guy I didn't even know, and so I hired Leo Kayser to break Edie's tenant from his sublease. It cost me a couple hundred bucks, and a few pounds of aggravation, but we eventually got the tenant out and me in.

It was my first swell apartment—uptown and upscale—and it changed my life. I now lived in a building, and in a neighborhood, to match my lifestyle and stature. I no longer had to step over junkies and bag ladies on my way to and from work.

At the beginning of 1976, almost coinciding with this move, I made a New Year's resolution. I decided that I would never fall in love again, and that my next relationship would be a practical one. I wanted to marry again, soon, but I wanted to marry with my head and not my heart. I wanted a marriage to match my new apartment: convenient, prestigious, and maintenance-free. I had been in love before, and it hadn't worked; if love could indeed conquer all, I still would have been married to Edie. To my mind, then, all this crap about feelings and commitment, loyalty and monogamy, was just bullshit. And, because emotional relationships didn't work, I thought, I might as well cut myself the best deal possible.

I was out to marry for money, prestige, connections, and power. It was a decision that put an effective end to my relationship with Judi Beck.

Enter Francine LeFrak. Francine was one of three children of billionaire New York real estate developer Samuel LeFrak. Glamorous, blonde, she was an heiress in every way. She was elegant, superbly educated, and looked great in pearls. Her father was a self-made man, a short, fat, cigar-chomping man, given to loud and offensive behavior. (The family name had been Lefrak, with an accent on the first syllable, but Sam had it changed to LeFrak, accent on the second, in an apparent move to distance his fortune from his roots.) Her mother, like Sam, also Jewish, was his opposite; she was cultured, quiet, and thoughtful.

The family wore its wealth like a billboard. Sam had a huge

yacht, and he would pull into harbors uninvited, to clubs where he didn't belong and wasn't welcome. He was one part Donald Trump and one part Rodney Dangerfield. The LeFraks had a grand house on Long Island, and a lavish Fifth Avenue apartment. Their children went to the best schools, here and abroad. Francine attended L'Ecole Superieure de Neufchatel in Switzerland, and was presented at the Debutante Cotillion and Christmas Ball. These assimilated LeFraks were also major contributors to area Jewish philanthropies, and served on the boards of several prominent New York charities and organizations.

Francine, an art consultant and a former appraiser for Sotheby's, the auction house, was on the board of the One-to-One Foundation. That's how we'd met, and it was from that casual and respectful friendship that I decided to audition her to play the role of the next woman in my life. (A casting call also went out to Countess Diane Agostini, an Italian beauty and another member of the One-to-One board, but she didn't make the cut.)

In the first weeks of our courtship, it became very clear that both of us wanted to marry. Good, I thought. My resolution was proceeding on schedule. By summer we had come up with a statement of our resolve: "All the way." The phrase became our slogan, our rallying cry, and confirmed the direction our relationship was headed: all the way to the altar. I didn't love Francine and didn't pretend to. The relationship, for me, was about respect, affection, and pragmatics. Physically speaking, we were okay together. There was a comfortable, adequate passion between us. I never fantasized about Francine when we weren't together, and I often fantasized about other women when we were.

Francine, I thought, was in love with me. At least she said she was. Maybe we were both going along for the ride. We were headed for the altar—"All the way"—and I wasn't about to shift gears.

At the appropriate time, we went to her parents' Fifth Avenue apartment, seeking their blessings. Sam LeFrak was simply overjoyed by the news, although his welcome-to-the-family congratulations were tendered without the benefit of a key piece of information. I hadn't told Francine, or anyone else in her family, about my first marriage to Linda, taking the advice of my sometime-friend, Assemblyman Andrew Stein. The LeFraks all knew about second wife Edie—how could they not know?—but the fact of my first marriage had never been widely reported.

Stein, who at the time had been divorced and, subsequently, twice-engaged, once told me, "If you're married twice, everybody can relate to that. When you're married three times, they begin to think of you as a deviant, or a social misfit, or a person with a real problem." His thinking made sense to me, and I did not want to risk the good thing I had going with Francine's family by trying to prove him wrong, and so I kept quiet about Linda. More, I lied about it. I did not tell Francine about Linda until well after our engagement.

We broke the news to columnist Earl Wilson, who ran an item announcing our engagement in *The New York Post*. The whirlwind romance between a television personality and an heiress to a New York fortune was big doings, and the papers ate it up. "I'm as happy as a lark," Wilson quoted me as saying, and if it ran in the *Post* then it must be true. I also said, of Francine, "She's a beautiful, compassionate lady, and a good citizen." A good citizen! Jesus, how romantic.

The society page editors at *The New York Times*, I later learned, were steamed that Earl Wilson scooped them on our engagement, but they subsequently ran a large and proper article announcing our proposed union. In it, thanks to a little sanitizing and social-climbing poetic license, my dad was listed as the president of the Maravilla Production Corporation. I wanted the Riveras to look good, next to their son's new uppercrust in-laws.

Francine's Sotheby friends helped me to find an engagement ring suitable for my princess bride-to-be: a stunning Van Cleef and Arpel's diamond and sapphire ring in a precious setting. The thing set me back sixteen thousand dollars—at the time, the single biggest cash purchase of my life, leapfrogging the Avenue C apartment—but I looked on it as an investment in the future.

To celebrate this blessed union, Sam LeFrak threw Francine and me the engagement party of the decade, at Regine's on Park Avenue, at the time one of the hottest nightclubs in North America. It was a major event on the New York social scene. In addition to the jet-setting swells, New York Governor Hugh Carey was there, as was the governor of Puerto Rico, Rafael Hernandez

Colón, and members of Congress Herman Badillo and Bella Abzug. Anybody who had ever done business with Sam, or benefited from his charitable largess, turned out to wish us well. My personal guest list included the entire cast of *Good Morning America*, my family, feeling as out of place as the Beverly Hillbillies, and my old friend Frank DeCecco, who also felt alien and awkward in that glistening crowd.

Absurdly dressed (again!) in a mod white suit, I glad-handed my way through that party as if I were on some strange cloud. Being married, I thought, would be easy. Getting married was hard.

While my head was given over to my impending marriage, my heart was careening from Guatemala to Los Angeles. Two separate entanglements surfaced during my early courtship with Francine, and they would linger long enough to become more than just romantic distractions. The first of these was with a married newspaper reporter, based in Latin America; we were involved in a long and passionate affair, scheduled in and around my frequent Latin American assignments for *Good Morning America*. In my first few months with the morning show, I had been sent to the region on a half-dozen occasions—to Panama, for the canal treaty negotiations; to Guatemala, for the earthquake; to Nicaragua, for the flood—and I would always find the same reporters dispatched to the scene from their far-flung posts. It was almost like working the campaign trail, the way the same reporters would turn out to cover the same stories. The relationship got to where we would not even have to plan our trysts. I knew she would be there, and she knew I would be there, and we would seek each other out on arrival. It was an intimacy born of loneliness and convenience, but it grew more heated and intense with each trip.

The second of these extra-engagement affairs was with a woman named Sheri Braverman, part Sicilian, part Jewish ball of fire who happened to be married at the time to Chuck Braverman, who happened to be a friend of mine. (He directed the opening *Good Night America* credits, from Los Angeles, and produced some of our packaged pieces for the program.) Sheri was everything Francine was not, a thin brunette with no formal education and a wild heart. She was born to a blue-collar family from East Los Angeles. She was at the tail end of her second failed marriage. She was also dynamic and passionate, in a way that Francine could never be, at least not for me.

I was on a collision course—propelled by a sixteen-thousand dollar-ring and an engagement announcement in the society pages of *The New York Times*—to marry into one of the richest families in the country. My fate seemed inevitable; my head was screwed on tight and straight in New York, while the rest of my body was pointing south, to Latin America, and west, to California.

I would keep at least one end of my pragmatic New Year's resolution. I would be married again before the end of the year. But not to my fiancée.

CHAPTER TEN

HAMPTON BAYS

"I have been a compulsive traveler ever since leaving my mama's house, shortly after my eighteenth birthday," I reported on the air in a year-end summary for *Good Morning America* in December 1976. "But in my wildest imaginings, I never figured wanderlust could lead to this: one hundred and sixty-eight stories, filed from thirty-three different states and eight foreign countries. I traveled around two hundred thousand miles, crossed the Arctic Circle four times, the equator six times, and was made an honorary Cajun by the good-time folks of Lafayette, Louisiana."

It was a wild and crazy time, to borrow a phrase made popular on another new show that premiered that season—*Saturday Night Live*. My notebooks from that hectic first year as a *Good Morning*

America correspondent are filled with people, places, and stories that moved me, either to tears, passion, or wonder.

To chronicle my various adventures, I bought one of those mini, pocket-size atlases, filled with detailed maps from every corner of the globe. On the first page of the book, I wrote: "I pledge to see and feel every exotic place this small book and huge planet have to offer." The atlas listed, alphabetically, all the cities on this earth, and as I started to travel for GMA, I began to underline all the places I visited. Before long, my own markings began to obscure the rest of the book.

In Raleigh, North Carolina, for example, I reported from the North Carolina State Penitentiary, one of the most depressing places I've ever visited. The long-timers were kept four to a two-man cell; in some blocks, prisoners were made to sleep on mattresses on corridor floors. There was a literal reaching out— through the prison bars—as I toured death row, as if the inmates wanted to touch me, to make contact in some way, to feel for a fleeting moment, and in some strange way, that I would be their ticket out of there.

In Los Angeles, I flew in a Cessna with the former U-2 pilot Francis Gary Powers, as he filed local traffic updates for an L.A. radio station. Years earlier, Powers had played the central role in one of the Cold War's most embarrassing moments. In 1960, he was operating as a contract employee of the CIA when his plane was shot down over Russia, and he confessed to spying on the Soviets. President Eisenhower later compared Powers to Nathan Hale, the Revolutionary War spy who was executed by the British. I looked down at the snarled freeway traffic and listened to the once high-flying spy give his report, and thought to myself, oh, how the mighty have fallen.

In Louisiana, I interviewed David Duke in his Baton Rouge office, when he was still a robe-wearing member of the Ku Klux Klan, long before his grab for a Senate seat, and legitimacy. My crew and I taped several cross-burnings for *Good Morning America* and *Good Night America*. At a KKK planning meeting, to which we had been admitted by Grand Wizard Bill Wilkerson, a snaggletoothed, missing-link Klansman stared at me with his beady, hateful eyes. A mystery nagged at his racist conscience. Finally, he approached me and challenged, "Are you white?" in his heavy redneck drawl. I refused to answer and matched his stare with my own. "Are you white?" he said again, more closely examining the confusing pigmentation of my skin. Again, I ignored him. The truth of my bloodlines—Puerto Rican and Jewish— would have overloaded this guy's limited mental capacity.

In Brazil, I ventured about a thousand miles north of Rio, to the black city of Bahia, and there absorbed a carnival celebration, laced with the New World mysticism and homespun voodoo. The trip was made memorable by my traveling companion—the newspaper lady who captured my heart on nearly every Latin American trip. We rendezvoused in Rio, opposite the Hotel Triste on Ipanema Bay. I arrived early and waited. I had left behind my entanglements in the States, and I let the beauty of the moonlit beach wash over me. Then I saw her, crossing from the hotel to the beach. She was lit by the moon and the dim lights of the boulevard. She saw me, and we embraced. It was one of the most romantic moments of my life. We made love on Ipanema Beach and I remember feeling, for a moment, that there was no other place in the world.

In central Alaska, I covered the building of the pipeline, and I happened upon a valley, where the light struck the mountains in a way that left them looking purple, white, and blessed. And there were women working the pipeline—isolated, horny, *Good Night America* viewers—and I spent several long Alaskan nights surrounded by spectacular scenery and the damsels of the Great Northwest.

When I was moored in New York, which was not all that often, I would turn up at the studio to open and close my pieces on the *Good Morning America* set. Occasionally, I would pinch hit as substitute-host for a vacationing David Hartman. Morning shows run on killer hours and most on-camera staffers were in-studio by four-thirty for the seven o'clock live broadcast. I was no early riser. My apartment on Central Park West was only three blocks from the studio, so I took to arriving at the very last minute. The show was divided into seven- or eight-minute segments, as it is today, and I was able to get away with occasional oversleeping if my piece was not slated to air at the top of the show. The producers would chew me out for lack of professionalism, but I never missed a cue.

On one morning, when I was due to substitute-host, I rolled out of bed at 6:45, offered up the requisite "Holy shit!" when I looked at the clock, jumped in and out of the shower without shaving, and raced the three blocks to the studio. I made it, literally, with less than a minute to spare. I sat down on the set at precisely seven o'clock, my wet hair drying under the hot studio lights as I fudged my way through the first segment. I shaved during the first commercial break, and briefed myself, segment by segment, on the rest of the show. The resulting broadcast was not quite the disaster it could have been, and I still hadn't missed a cue, but this was too close even for me. Ever since, whenever I'm facing a morning deadline, I rely on redundant systems, setting two alarm clocks, or one clock plus a wake-up call.

When I was out on the road, I was grounded in New York by Marylou Pizzarello, a bright, big woman with a seductive voice; she could arrange better stories by telephone than producers can with unlimited travel budgets. She ran my professional life. That was easy; my personal life was hard, especially during Marylou's tenure. In the spring of 1976, Francine LeFrak was still wearing that lovely Van Cleef and Arpels sapphire-and-diamond setting on the ring finger of her left hand; Sheri Braverman was still encouraging passion to supplant pragmatism; Judi Beck had graciously stepped aside, but she had yet to relinquish her hold over me; and, my newspaper lady was still providing cosmopolitan heat and distraction from Latin America. There was a lot to keep track of, and Marylou did what she could to keep the spinning parts from colliding.

My head needed more straightening out than my schedule. As my *Good Morning America* responsibilities grew, and my national celebrity flourished, I started having second thoughts about the engagement to Francine. Those second thoughts were set against the splendid backdrop of Hampton Bays, on Long Island's East End. Francine and I rented a beautiful Victorian house there in the summer of 1976. It was the classiest place I had ever spent a night in. The digs were the signal of a new, good life. The house sat like a snapshot, on a bluff overlooking the Peconic Bay, where I anchored my engagement present from Francine: an old twenty-two-foot wooden sailboat, shallow draft, but sturdily built in Norway. She was my first sailboat, the culmination of a long-held dream, and I christened her the *Francina*. It was the perfect boat for the shoal waters of Peconic Bay, and the ideal symbol of my flooding unease. Francine could give me everything I had ever wanted, or would ever need. Well, almost everything. I could get everything else outside the marriage.

JUDI BECK: Francine was . . . incredible. I mean, she was like a caricature to me. She was like a bad dream. I mean, I could not understand that relationship at all, and I did ask Geraldo, years later, what on earth that was all about. And what I remember about that conversation, and Geraldo's memory may be different, but what I remember was that he had decided at that point in time he wanted to be mayor of New York. And Francine had the capability to make that happen.

There was, at that time, a whisper of speculation that I was considering a mayoral campaign. I suppose I started those whispers. Let me explain. I would often mention in interviews, as I have written earlier in this text, that my childhood ambition was to be mayor of New York City. That was the ideal to me, the pinnacle, the street kid's equivalent of wanting to live in the White House. At some point, after several such mentions, others picked up on the subtle suggestion. As the press geared up for the mayoral primaries, my verbalized fantasy was trotted out, analyzed, and handicapped by political oddsmakers. I sat and watched, willing to let a groundswell build around the idea, but I was not so filled with political whimsy as to stick my neck out and announce my candidacy.

Still, the talk continued. On June 28, 1976, the nationally syndicated columnist Liz Smith checked in with the following item in the *Daily News*, under the headline "Geraldo, the Running Man": "Are you ready for it? New York television personality Geraldo Rivera—that perfect ethnic mix for the bicentennial year, being half Puerto Rican and half Jewish—is seriously revving himself up to run for mayor in this City of Brotherly Shove. Geraldo, with his soon-to-be-wife, his new Adidas shoes, his flashing warmth, his big smile, his cute moustache, and his kinetic energy, would have a terrific ready-made constituency going for him, and maybe the Democratic establishment better think it over twice before they laugh."

When questions of my "candidacy" came back to me on the

rebound, I dodged them with the finesse of a true politician. I strung out the whispers and lent them secret fuel, because I wanted to see where they went. "With the doldrums of summer already pregnant with presidential politics," I told *The Soho Weekly News*, "any announcement by me concerning the mayoral campaign would be distracting and premature." Always, I kept all doors open in responding to queries about my intentions. If the idea of my running for mayor of New York didn't seem farfetched to opinion-leaders, I thought, then perhaps it was something I should pay attention to.

This protracted noncampaign for mayor became a kind of game to me, a tease, but I was also proud and flattered that people, some people anyway, were willing to take the idea seriously. Others, of course, laughed off the possibility as another reason to bash Geraldo Rivera. One easy joke was that my mixed heritage could only be a positive in a mongrel city like New York. Ultimately, I never explored the possibility of a mayoral run in any kind of substantive way, and no one from the political establishment ever approached me about considering a bid. Eventually, the talk fizzled and I never did anything to start it up again. A few years later, the Democrats offered me the congressional seat then held by discredited Congressman Fred Richmond in Williamsburg, Brooklyn, where my family had lived during the early years of my childhood. The district, I was reminded, was an ideal political fit, with its huge Puerto Rican and Jewish communities. But by then, I had no desire to pursue local office. I had become an American, rather than just a New Yorker.

Meanwhile, Francine's father began lobbying me to learn about his various businesses. Real estate did not hold much appeal to me as a line of work, but Sam LeFrak was thinking about branching out into music and television, and he thought these new interests would be perfect for his son-in-law-to-be. I agonized over his offers and seriously contemplated surrendering my hard-won independence. I only pulled back when I looked at Sam and saw the rest of my life, all laid out before me.

Sam reminded me of the guy on the Monopoly board—self-made, self-reliant, and selfish. He was a devourer who always got what he wanted, and he made it very difficult for me to turn him down. I knew that I could leave the television news business, sign on with Sam, and never have to worry about anything else for the rest of my life. I could suck up nutrients from the lap of luxury, forever. I also know that, by buying into the family business in just this way, I would sacrifice the lean and hungry nature that had allowed me to punch my way to some respectable successes of my own.

I feared that I would be consumed by Sam, incorporated by him to where I became little more than an aspect of his vast and frenetic enterprise, a subsidiary. If I married Francine, I married her father; my life, and my career, would be a spin-off.

Sheri did not come to me with the same kind of baggage. Of course, she was already married, to my friend Chuck Braverman, but that marriage was breathing its last before I even entered the picture. (The relationship with the married newspaper reporter was limited by geography and circumstance, and held no long-term promise, or threat.)

I had decisions to make, and the Hampton Bays house and the *Francina*, helped me with some of them. The house helped by eluding my grasp. It was a summer rental, but Francine and I sought to purchase it from the elegant French widow whose husband's Yankee family had owned it for generations. We loved that house, but the graceful old lady refused all reasonable offers, keeping it just out of reach. The real estate nondeal determined the next great decision of my life. Had we bought that house, perhaps I would still be with Francine. It would have fulfilled a boyhood dream and erased the mediocre memory of my childhood home. To own a magnificent piece of property on the water, with its grand Victorian house and sweeping views, my boat anchored in the backyard, and my heiress in the bedroom, would have been too powerful a lure. As we used to say in law school, to own a piece of ground, in fee simple absolute from the center of the earth to the infinite reaches of heaven ... it would have been an intoxicating enticement. The house, attained, would have sucked me in; it may have been impossible to give up. With the house out of reach, the idea of walking away from Francine and everything she represented was allowed to take hold.

The boat helped in this way: Francine and I invited Sheri and Chuck for a weekend visit; they were in from Los Angeles for some meetings in New York, and we convinced them to extend their stay to allow for some time at the beach. Sheri was anxious to get out of her marriage to Chuck, and she saw our affair as a means to her end.

As the weekend progressed, I wrestled with my own dilemmas. I was at a crossroad. I wanted to be with Sheri, and if I chose that path, life would be rough, exciting, and unpredictable. With Francine, it would be comfortable, paid-for, and predictable.

By Sunday night, Sheri had maneuvered the scene so that Chuck would go back to New York early on Monday morning, while she stayed on to enjoy another afternoon on the water. Francine, also, was encouraged to make an early exit to take care of city business, and accompany Chuck. Sheri and I, it was agreed, would stay out for the afternoon, close up the house, and meet Chuck and Francine back in New York, Monday evening for dinner.

With our mates safely out of the way, Sheri and I boarded the *Francina* and rocked the boat.

TRANCAS BEACH, CALIFORNIA

Sheri was a very different sort of woman than I was used to. She was competent, domineering, and intelligent. She was nothing at all like my first two wives, both ethereal, angelic WASPs, with long, flowing blonde hair. Sheri wore her dark hair short, in a style almost severe. She was more handsome than beautiful, a scrappy street-fighter from East Los Angeles. She had no education beyond high school, but she was the most formidable woman I had ever met.

After our idyllic afternoon on the boat, Sheri and Chuck returned to the Coast. I lingered for the next couple weeks in New York, plotting my escape while allowing the charade of my engagement to Francine to continue. Finally the pretense began to come loose. Suddenly, I had had enough of the city, and the relationship, and I needed to get away from both.

I asked Woody Fraser, the executive producer of *Good Morning America*, to meet me at the outdoor cafe of Fiorello's restaurant on Broadway, and I articulated my decision for the first time. My declaration surprised me almost as much as it did him.

"I'm getting out of here," I announced. "I'm not going through with my wedding."

"You're what?" Woody said. He couldn't believe it. He had been to our lavish engagement party just a few months earlier; our marriage was the talk of the town.

"Woody, I've got to leave New York," I said. "I can't go through with it. I can't. You've got to give me some slack. Please. You've got to let me work from the West Coast for a while."

"Okay," Woody said.

I was on a plane for Los Angeles the next day. I had not told Francine of my change of plans; I did not have the courage. Besides, it was not at all unusual for me to skip town on short notice, so it was possible she would just assume I was called away on a breaking story. She had no idea I was never coming back to her.

It was not like me to run away from confrontation, but I ran away from this one. This was more than a choice between two women; in my overstimulated introspection, it was a choice between two ethics, between a hard life and an easy one, between right and wrong. As I moved away from Francine, I realized that I needed to struggle in order to be all that I was capable of becoming. Sam LeFrak would have stopped my natural evolution. Under his suffocating largesse, I would have been like a wild thing raised in captivity, eventually losing my survival instinct.

I rented a car at LAX and headed straight for Sheri. She had used her few weeks to leave Chuck and was living in an apartment with a girlfriend who had also just left her husband. I scooped her up and made for the Pacific Coast Highway, with the intention of driving to the Big Sur for a long, romantic weekend. Along the way, I was distracted by the rental signs on the beach houses of Malibu. I pulled into a real estate office and asked to look at houses on the water.

On impulse, I was ready to remake my life. I suddenly longed to be bicoastal, to put down roots on the West Coast. L.A. was where the action was. New York was old and tired and part of my past. The red-eye, between the two cities, was a more glamorous commute than the crosstown bus. Plus, I wanted to put as much distance between myself and Francine (and the rest of the LeFrak family) as possible.

One of the first houses the real estate agent showed us was located at 31900 Pacific Coast Highway, on Trancas Beach, about midway between Malibu and the Ventura County line. Owned by a Beverly Hills dentist, the modern house was furnished tastefully and comfortably. There was more living space than I had any idea what to do with, but what sold me was the landscaping: The glass back-wall opened on the Pacific Ocean.

"When is it available?" I asked the broker.

"Right now."

"I'll take it," I said. I didn't ask about the rental price, and I didn't wait for Sheri's nod of approval. I was operating on impulse here; I had no time to think things through. I pulled our suitcases out of the rental car and into our rented home. We stayed for nearly two years. I kept the apartment on Central Park West during this time, but I made Los Angeles my base of operations. New York was for meetings, for my occasional *Good Night America* tapings, and for my in-studio morning show appearances; Los Angeles was for everything else.

A few days after I signed the lease, I finally mustered up the courage to make the dreaded phone call to Francine. "It's not going to happen," I told her, at last. I was tentative, and embarrassed. "I can't get married right now." I did not mention anything about Sheri; I did not have the courage to hurt Francine any more than I had to; I tried to sever things as cleanly and painlessly as possible.

For her part, Francine took the news like she'd expected it. She was not at all bitter on the phone. She made the conversation much easier than I had any right to expect. I told her to keep the ring, in part to ease my guilt, but also because I could not imagine Sheri, or anyone else I might take up with, being comfortable with such an elaborate (and previously owned) setting. (She mailed it back to me a couple years later.) I assured Francine that I would not say anything publicly about the breakup, which allowed Sam to leak the sad news in Earl Wilson's column in *The New York Post*. "Geraldo's in the air more than he's on the ground," he told Earl, blaming the split more on my hectic schedule than anything else. Despite Earl Wilson, the news of our breakup did not make anywhere near the same splash as our engagement. In fact, our split was handled so quietly that for years afterward people would ask me how it felt to be married to an heiress.

With Francine (and Sam) out of the picture, I settled into the L.A. scene pretty effortlessly. It was a smooth transition, made easy by time and place. Malibu is the prettiest spot in America within an hour's drive of a major international airport. It was the middle of nowhere and the center of everything, the ideal place for me to stop and refuel between my *Good Morning America* jaunts.

Trancas Beach is located several miles north of the famous Malibu Beach Colony, past Point Dume, Zuma, and Broad Beach. Our stretch was known as Outlaw Beach, christened for all the ex-bohemian dope-smokers who settled and grew old there. It was, in many ways, the L.A. equivalent of my apartment on the Lower East Side—hip, gritty, and downscale—and it seemed a world removed from the million-dollar homes and mindsets a few miles down the coast. The real estate abutting the beach was owned (or rented) by people like myself: young, blue-jeaned, antiestablishment, and suddenly successful. I was surrounded by an eclectic batch of neighbors, including Herb Alpert, Carole King, and Beach Boy Dennis Wilson.

My closest neighbor became my closest friend: Cheech Marin. We had maintained a kind of celebrity friendship since we'd first met in 1973, but we never saw each other outside of a working environment. When I found out he lived right next door, I immediately sought him out on the beach. "Hey," I said, "let's be friends."

Cheech and I had a world in common: We were both Hispanic and both starting out in new phases of established careers. (He was moving from albums to movies; I was still working into my role as a globe-trotting international newsman.) We spent happy hours fishing and talking about our lives. We were together all the time. We tooled around town in our antique convertibles, either in his '55 Chevy or my '54 Jaguar. We founded what we called The Lowrider Yacht Club, and the two of us—the charter (and only) members—would take a couple of kayaks through the surf, drop our lines through the kelp, and see what was biting. We cooked what we caught, and what we couldn't cook, we didn't keep. At night, we would sit around drinking tequila and occasionally smoking dope, although not nearly as often as one might expect, after listening to those routines from the Cheech and Chong albums. He was funny, and smart, and we seemed to operate on the same frequency.

My relationship with Sheri roared along. She filed for a divorce from Chuck Braverman. He was as outraged as Francine was outwardly calm. I was the villain of the piece, in his eyes, even though his marriage had been crumbling without any help from me. He was the cuckold and I was the interloper, and I probably would have reacted the same way if the roles had been reversed.

I ran into Chuck on a plane, years later, and I almost didn't recognize him. He had lost a lot of weight. He was happily remarried. He had a kid. We were both cordial, pretending at genuine interest in what the other was up to, but the meeting was weird and strained. We didn't spend a whole lot of time talking, even though we were sitting near each other. What an odd flight that was, separated by a few seatbacks from a man with whom I shared such an intimate and painful history. His life had changed, and so had mine, but too much had passed between us to be able to talk about it or get past it.

California was a joint-property state, and Sheri waved everything to expedite the divorce—if not a first, at least a rare occurrence in the Golden State. Chuck had a considerable estate at the time (far more substantial than mine), but Sheri wanted to make a clean, fast break. I flew with her to Miami, where Chuck was passing through on a film-shoot; she met him in the airport lounge, to sign the divorce papers. I waited in the terminal lobby, wanting to avoid a scene, but wanting also to be close by in case Sheri needed me.

After Miami, we continued onto Haiti, for another quickie divorce. Ironically, Sheri and I stayed in the same hotel, The Olaffson, where I'd celebrated (and mourned) the end of my marriage to Edie two years earlier.

Sheri's signing away her share of Chuck's assets and throwing her financial lot in with me, cemented our affair in a way I did not recognize at the time. It gave the relationship a kind of "us against them" spin; we had something to struggle for, and against; it became the two of us against the world. We were united, our fates and fortunes intertwined. There was nothing for us to do but get married.

The wedding was set for New Year's Eve, 1976, in the Trancas

Beach house. The celebration began that morning, on *Good Morning America*, when David Hartman, Nancy Dussault, and the rest of the team saluted us on the air with a champagne toast.

We had put the word out for the families to assemble—Sheri's from nearby Montebello, on the east side of town; mine from far-off Long Island, three thousand miles away. Although I had given up the LeFrak fortune, my parents were relieved. Sheri's folks were their kind of people—plainspoken, mixed blood, and blue collar. My mother was particularly pleased at the idea of a Jewish ceremony, my only one. We recruited the rabbi from University Synagogue on Sunset Boulevard in Brentwood. He performed the outdoor ceremony during a technicolor sunset, on our expansive brick patio overlooking a tranquil Pacific Ocean. By the time the golden hour had yielded to nightfall, the quiet sea-breeze was blowing a full gale. I don't remember thinking the violent change in weather a portent of our future together.

Our reception was as loose as my engagement party at Regine's had been uptight. Lots of booze and brotherhood. Craig was the only sibling who could make it, but my parents were there, and a sprinkling of celebrities, including Cheech and his wife Rikki, and Kris Kristofferson and his then wife Rita Coolidge. To my folks, and to Sheri's, the biggest star there was Rona Barrett. They never missed her morning gossip reports. That she would grace their kids' wedding meant it must be special, an event.

Almost immediately, Sheri began running my life. She had worked for ten years at Capitol Records, and she knew the entertainment business and office politics. Her instincts were solid; her business sense, sound. She quickly became my closest advisor. She traveled with me on stories. She ran the ASCAP office back in New York, and watchdogged the *Good Night America* staffers and volunteers. She scheduled my meetings and often accompanied me to them. With Jerry Weintraub, she negotiated a new contract with ABC, and she ran interference with the network when needed. She became a kind of frontperson for Maravilla Productions, a managing partner. I let her be my female Svengali; she told me what to wear, what stories to cover, what image to project.

In many ways, she began to take on the role long-filled by Marty Berman, and in fact, she launched a protracted campaign to phase Marty out of my life and off my payroll; ultimately, she succeeded.

From the start, the people close to me at work—Marty, Marylou, the GNA and GMA staffs—were resentful of Sheri's sudden power over me, and them. They did not know what to make of it, or what to do about it. The confusion was best illustrated on a trip to Panama, six months after we were married. Sheri and I were accompanied in the first-class section of the plane by Justin Friedland, a veteran ABC News field producer. When the in-flight meal was served, he noticed Sheri leaning over to my tray-table to cut the meat on my plate.

The producer thought he finally had our relationship figured out. "Oh," he said, "that's why she comes with you on these trips, to cut your meat."

The remark was clearly meant as a joke, but it pissed me off because a woman has never been more underestimated than Sheri was by that man at that time. She had one of the sharpest, most insightful minds I had ever encountered, and I let her call the shots because I knew her judgments would be unclouded by her own agenda. She traveled with me because we were partners and enjoyed each other's company. What was best for me was best for her.

Also, she watched my back when we traveled together. On that very trip to Panama, I would be arrested and roughed-up by goons working for the infamous head of Panama's secret police, the future dictator and alleged drug criminal Manuel Noriega. His boys came after me when I insisted on filming the brutal suppression of an antigovernment demonstration. When they grabbed me, Sheri protested loudly, and then she wisely split off when my arrest seemed inevitable. Her prompt and passionate protests to the American Embassy stopped the beatings in midstream.

Cheating on this formidable women was a challenge. Regrettably, and predictably, I was up to it. I was like a junkie when it came to other women, an alcoholic, and even my best intentions were not enough to keep me faithful for too long. I think Sheri understood this and guarded against it at every turn.

Sheri was circumspect, almost to a fault; she combed over every credit card receipt, and every long distance phone call, ostensibly to get back every spent penny from ABC, but also, I suspected, to uncover my tracks. She caught me before the ink was dry on our marriage license. I had not been with another woman since I'd run off to L.A. five months earlier, to be with Sheri. That changed in January 1977 when I was in New York to do some studio segments for *Good Morning America.* The flight back to Los Angeles was diverted to Las Vegas because of fog. Getting off the plane, I stepped in behind a stunning creature with tight jeans and long brunette hair. We struck up a conversation as we made for a bus, arranged for by the airline, to take us to a hotel where we were to holdover until our rescheduled flight out the next morning. It was a fleabag hotel, on the outskirts of town. I turned to my companion and said, "I'm not staying here. Why don't we go someplace else?"

We slipped away to the MGM Grand Hotel, which had just opened. I booked a suite and passed a delightful evening with the lovely young lady. As bad luck would have it, she knew Chuck Braverman and practically everybody else in our Los Angeles circle. Word of our "layover" reached home before I did, and when I got there Sheri was waiting.

It was only three weeks after our wedding, and Sheri wanted a divorce. I did not mean to stray, but I was intoxicated by chance and circumstance. Of course, trying to explain this to Sheri was like trying to convince a jury you didn't mean to rob a bank after you've been caught, in the act, on videotape. I was contrite, but she was outraged, and humiliated. She feared a lifetime of more of the same and was determined to cut her losses. It was hairdresser-turned-producer Jon Peters who encouraged me to make repairs with Sheri. I had interviewed Jon and Barbra Streisand for *Good Night America* in connection with the release of their *A Star Is Born* remake, and we had remained friends. "If you get divorced now," he counseled, "people will think you're mentally ill. They'll think you're crazy, unbalanced. You've only been married for three weeks."

I crawled to Sheri and begged her to take me back. She ultimately acceded, but knew I was not to be trusted. From that moment on, she honed her vigilance to an art form.

POINT-OF-THE-MOUNTAIN, UTAH

Most of my *Good Morning America* pieces were given over to popular culture. I continued to redefine the participatory celebrity profile—I played tennis with Billie Jean King (and lost), and rode the rails with Johnny Cash on his way home to Arkansas for his fiftieth birthday—and in almost every instance, the viewer came away with something fresh, or unexpected, about the featured personality. Occasionally, these soft stories would explode into something more than we anticipated. The best example of this, sadly, was Freddie Prinze, the part-Puerto Rican, part-Hungarian, New York-born stand-up comic (a "Hungarican"), who soared to fame on national television, and committed suicide at the age of twenty-two.

I interviewed Freddie on three occasions—once for *Good Night America* and twice for *Good Morning America*—and there was an immediate rapport between us, a bond forged by our backgrounds and our futures.

At the time of his death, in January 1977, there were only three prominent Hispanics on television—Freddie, myself, and the singer Tony Orlando. The three of us were often thrown together at various Latin banquets, festivals, or media events. We were friends, and family. (Of course, we weren't really family, although it was widely rumored that Tony and I—both Hispanic, both long-haired and moustachioed—were brothers, a ridiculous falsehood that proved almost as resilient and nagging as the charges that my real name was Jerry Rivers.)

Despite this public closeness, the nature of our very different and demanding careers meant that the three of us were rarely in the same place at the same time. Whenever we came together, it was for all the world to see. Our relationships, though genuinely close, were like grand, family-reunion photo opportunities. Our ties were fast, and yet they never matched public perception.

Beyond the small screen, our extended Hispanic celebrity family included Jose Feliciano, Rita Moreno, and Cheech, but in the 1970s the list began to thin after that. There were so few to go around we all felt a disproportionate burden as famous pillars of our community.

Freddie Prinze felt this most of all. For a brief time, he shone brighter than any star in Hollywood. He packed concert halls and nightclubs with his stand-up routines. His television sitcom, *Chico and the Man* finished its first season as the third-highest-rated show on the air, behind *All in the Family* and *Sanford and Son*. He guest-hosted on *The Tonight Show*. He dated Raquel Welch and was pursued by every other starlet in town. He entertained at a presidential inaugural. His famous tag line, "Ees not my job, man," had seeped into the American lexicon. He was a huge, crossover star.

He was also on the edge, his thinking clouded by sudden fame, unlimited drugs, and a morbid preoccupation with guns and Lenny Bruce. I was too distracted by the separate pulls of my own career to notice. I didn't see Freddie for the several weeks leading up to his death, and so had no idea how far he'd fallen. I'd seen evidence of his excesses before—he used to finish off baseball-size lumps of cocaine as if they were hors d'oevres, and chew Quaaludes like candy—but I chose to look away, or to identify them simply as a sign of the times.

I was shocked by his death. I felt cheated and guilty. But what cut most of all was the way people began to forget Freddie, to bury him, almost before his star-studded, paparazzi-packed Forest Lawn memorial service was over.

The public is fickle, and Hollywood most of all, but it struck me that we were all forgetting Freddie at an accelerated pace. He hadn't been around long enough to create a legacy, to become a legend; he had a brief, sensational career that was about to fade into oblivion. The worst indication of this was the news that James Komack, the executive producer of *Chico and the Man*, planned to continue the show without Freddie. They were going to bring in a younger Hispanic kid to take his place.

This last struck me as a final humiliation. I thought, in ten minutes, no one is going to know Freddie Prinze ever existed. And so I wrote about him. I went back and interviewed everyone who might have seen or spoken to him in his final days: his mother, his manager, his producer, his estranged wife, his girlfriend, his secretary, his psychiatrist. From their accounts, I pieced together the puzzle of his last hours on this earth, up until the moment he put a .32 automatic to his temple and pulled the trigger.

"Freddie started dying almost as soon as he got to Hollywood," I wrote in the resulting article entitled, "Nobody Ever Said 'No' to Freddie Prinze," published in *New York* magazine on February 28, 1977. "Freddie Prinze had a death wish, and he'd share it with almost anyone who would listen. He was going to make it big and fast, retire by the time he was twenty-five, and be dead before he was thirty."

I covered another famous shooting for *Good Morning America* around this time, also foreshadowed and self-inflicted. It was one of my many morning-show stories to cross from soft news to hard, but it was the only GMA sortee that damaged my reputation with my grudging news colleagues.

In 1976, an itinerate attorney named Dennis Boaz appeared before the Utah State Supreme Court and argued that his client, a convicted murderer sentenced to death, be allowed to die "like a man." For the first time in recent memory, a convicted murderer waived his rights to appeal his death sentence along the labyrinthine paths of our criminal justice system, and actually lobbied for his own execution.

The death of Gary Gilmore, by firing squad, on January 17, 1977, marked the first American execution in ten years. In the months leading up to that watershed moment, it was the biggest story in the country. I was dispatched to Salt Lake City and Provo to put together a couple backgrounder pieces for *Good Morning America*, and to be on-site, live, at the Utah State Prison in Point-of-the-Mountain for the execution. Like most everyone else in the country, I had been captivated by the twists and turns of the Gilmore story. Here was a cold-blooded killer, whom we had come to know intimately, who had somehow turned on our lurid impulses to become a twisted and tormented folk hero. I was vehemently opposed to the death penalty at the time, and yet I could not look away from the inherent drama of Gilmore's story.

On my first trip to Utah, on November 16, 1976, I found a media circus. Gilmore and his girlfriend Nicole Barret had just attempted a double suicide, on the eve of the Utah State Board of Pardons' hearing to determine whether Gilmore's execution would be allowed. Every news organization in the country, it seemed, had a representative on the scene, and the principals in the case were besieged by requests for interviews. We all scrambled for our own angle. I immediately sought out Dennis Boaz, a hulking, unkempt hippie lawyer whose job it was to facilitate his client's demise. I saw Boaz as the key to the story, and as my key to Gilmore, and I pursued him aggressively. I also tried to influence his actions. We wound up getting stoned, and the Thai stick we passed between us whittled away at my objectivity and news-sense. It also incited my passionate opposition to the death penalty. As the night wore on, I stressed to Boaz that his conduct was morally reprehensible. Eventually, I browbeat him into admitting that he could no longer support Gilmore's wish to die.

"Will you say that on television?" I asked.

"Yeah," he said. "Sure. I guess."

I put him on the air the next morning, live, and Boaz's emotions cascaded all over the screen. He was torn by indecision and guilt.

"After the discussion we had yesterday, and we talked for a long time, you don't even strike me as a man who believes in capital punishment," I started in. "I want to know why you've gone through this dreadful charade?"

"Well," Boaz said, "I got into the case not because I was an advocate of capital punishment, but because . . . he needed support, and I did support his own wish to, in a sense, take more responsibility for his own life and death at that time. And he was attempting to take responsibility by accepting judgment."

In the on-air interview, and in our private conversation the day before, Boaz allowed himself to be shaken from one position (his and Gilmore's) and into another (mine); set against the startling news of his client's suicide pact with his girlfriend, Boaz came across as a man of putty.

Gilmore heard about the *Good Morning America* piece in his hospital bed, where he was recuperating from his failed suicide attempt. He fired Boaz the next day. His wish to die would never be granted, Gilmore figured, if he retained an attorney who publicly opposed that wish.

Boaz was a spineless weakling who changed his position a second time, in order to win back Gilmore. He wrote a letter to his client the following morning, November 19, portions of which were later reprinted in a December 20, 1976 article in *New West* magazine. "On Wednesday morning, on *Good Morning America*, I stated that I could no longer participate in the process of execution," Boaz wrote. "That was a selfish, emotional, foolish, unprofessional act and unfair to you as my client. It was Soap Opera News . . . I hope that you can forgive my hyperemotionalism. It was definitely not a cool thing to do."

These about-faces cost me my inside track with Boaz, and any possibility of gaining access to Gilmore himself, and I was left to out-hustle the competition in some other way.

I returned to Utah when Gilmore's execution, just a few days away, seemed a certainty. The man's imminent death, by firing squad, loomed like a black cloud over the area. The spectre of a last-minute stay was also in the air. As the calendar turned into a clock, the mood among the journalists, protestors, and curiosity-hounds gathered on the prison grounds was tense and uncertain. I was up at about three o'clock on the morning of January 17, doing what last minute reporting I could, and preparing for the feed to New York. With the two-hour time difference, our show was broadcast live at 5 A.M., local time. Live remotes, in those days, were relatively uncommon, and I was somewhat distracted by the technology. As our broadcast neared, I could not move about as freely as other reporters. I staked out a piece of ground outside the prison walls for my stand-up. At 5:30, I went on the air and told David Hartman that from where we stood we would probably hear the volley of gunfire.

I remained on the air until it was over.

ROBERT SAM ANSON (taken from the journalist's notebooks, as quoted in Norman Mailer's *The Executioner's Song*): With the appearance of Gilmore, the reporters become a mob, a herd spooked into stampede. Camera lights tilt crazily up into the air as their bearers struggle to shift them into position. Producers are shouting orders. Directly in front of the prison building, Geraldo Rivera, attired in black leather jacket and jeans and looking cool, the way only Geraldo Rivera can look cool, is shouting into his mike. "Kill the Rona segment. Get rid of it. Give me air. You'll be able to hear the shots. I promise. You'll be able to hear the shots."

It was like the plug had been pulled on the entire scene, the volume turned down. We did not hear the shots. I started vamping about why capital punishment was such a horrible idea. I became emotional and overwrought. To a casual viewer, my performance might have seemed charged, passionate, and angry; to the insiders I came across as a loose cannon.

When the ABC News insert rolled around at the top of the hour, Steve Skinner, the ABC News location producer, had a decision to make: Do they report on the execution from the studio in New York or, do they go live to me on the scene? Keep in mind, I was an employee of ABC Entertainment, and the *Good Morning America* news inserts were a production of the news division. Steve, a former assignment editor and producer at *Eyewitness News* in New York, and an old friend, decided to put me on the air. I had a hot mike, he reasoned, the truck was all set up to go live. In me, he had an on-camera personality who was well known to his viewers, who was articulate, who knew the story, and who could ad-lib his way through a live update. It would have been a tremendous missed opportunity to cut away from the scene and back to the studio.

I was even more emotional on this second pass. I delivered the news of Gilmore's execution and all the attendant details, but I also railed against capital punishment. Perhaps my personal comments had no place in a news report, particularly in a story of such magnitude, but at the time I was caught up in the frenzy of the moment.

Steve Skinner was roundly criticized for his decision to put me on the air. Some of that criticism naturally extended down to me. After all, it was my editorializing that had thrown his judgment into doubt. The incident, as it was processed and interpreted by my peers (and enemies), was a final nail in the coffin, all but burying my hopes of ever becoming a member of the network news team. ABC News President Bill Sheehan, soon to be replaced by Roone Arledge, later allowed that such displays of emotion might be acceptable for a journalist covering the Hindenburg disaster, but not for a reporter assigned to an execution.

To the viewing public, I think I once again came across as a caring reporter who surrounded his story with bold personal commentary. To the news establishment, I came away with another black eye. My chances of ever becoming a network newsman seemed more remote than ever.

1330 AVENUE OF THE AMERICAS

Good Night America breathed its last on June 9, 1977, with a show on laetrile and UFOs. Production on the once-revolutionary late-night show had been slowed to once a month, we had no firm airdate for our next broadcast, and it seemed clear we were about to be cancelled, but I was still surprised by the ax. I took it personally. The show was like a child to me—my baby—and it had proven to be my ticket to national prominence. I had named and nurtured it from concept to franchise, and I protested its demise so loudly that I was also fired from my far more vital gig on *Good Morning America*.

Bob Shanks, the ABC executive in charge of late-night and early-morning programming, called me to his office one afternoon that June to break the bad news about *Good Night America*. He was a contemporary and a friend, but he was also like every other network executive I've ever met: a cover-your-ass survivalist. He was bright, and intense about his work, but he was more concerned with saving his butt than in putting it on the line for a good show. The numbers for the entire late night *Wide World of Entertainment* rotation had dropped off substantially, he said, and he could no longer justify what he continued to champion as a breakthrough second-generation news-magazine.

I was furious. I stormed into Shanks's office in the ABC tower at 1330 Avenue of the Americas and launched a tirade of accusations, intended for the entire network. You don't understand me! I fumed. You don't appreciate the asset you have in me. You're not making the best use of my abilities. My ego was all tied up in the late-night program in a way that it could never have been on the morning show, or with the local newscasts. On *Good Morning America* and *Eyewitness News*, I was part of an ensemble; on *Good Night America*, I sat at the center desk; I was the star.

"I can't believe it," I told Bob Shanks. "I can't believe you're pulling the plug."

"I'm sorry," he said. "We have to try something else."

I sulked and continued with my various laments. I even let on that I was thinking of leaving the network entirely. I mentioned this as an aside, not as a threat; I wanted to show Shanks and, through him, the rest of the network brass, that I felt unappreciated and underutilized. I wanted them to worry that one of their star correspondents was unhappy.

My public despairing backfired in a way I could not have anticipated. Shanks called me back to his office the next day. It was a beautiful late-spring morning, and I walked along Central

Park's perimeter to Sixth Avenue, and then down the few blocks to the network's executive office building on the corner of Fifty-fourth Street. I had no clue what to expect. Maybe they wanted to discuss a new time slot. Better, maybe they wanted a nightly version of the show. Better still, maybe they wanted me to star in another news-magazine vehicle, in prime time.

Whatever it was, I was ready to listen. I sat down across from Bob Shanks's desk and braced myself for good news.

"We've decided to accept your resignation," he said bluntly.

What? This was not at all what I was expecting to hear. "What the hell are you talking about?" I demanded.

"I've spoken with Fred Silverman"—the progamming genius brought in to do for ABC Entertainment what he had done for CBS, and Shanks's boss—"and he and I are in complete agreement."

"Complete agreement about what?" I had no idea what he was talking about.

"About our conversation yesterday. About how we don't love you or understand you. About all these other things you wanted to do with your career. About how you were going to resign."

Resign? So, that was what this was all about. My mind raced, trying to make sense of this unfathomable, unforeseeable turn. Probably Silverman and Shanks felt disenchanted with my performance, I surmised, or strapped by my six-hundred-thousand-dollar salary, or polluted by the steady backlash directed at me from the news division. This wasn't just about *Good Night America*, I knew. This was about something else, something bigger. Clearly, they must have wanted me out long before the misunderstandings of the day before.

Now, suddenly, they saw an opening in my contractual agreement and wanted to drive a truck through it.

"But, Bob," I tried, "I wasn't offering to resign, I was just . . ."

He cut me off. "We accept your resignation," he said again, more firmly this time, and he pushed some papers across the desk and asked me to sign them.

"I'm not signing anything," I said.

"You said you were resigning," Shanks insisted, "and now you have to resign."

I informed Shanks that I would not sign anything without first consulting Jerry Weintraub. I had a valid and binding contract with ABC, paying me a king's ransom, or at least a prince's; I was not about to void it simply because they asked me to.

Shanks was flustered. I was panicked. The meeting had not gone as planned.

I returned to my office in an absolute daze. I felt as if I had just been whacked over the head with a bat. I called Jerry Weintraub out in Los Angeles. It was still early on the West Coast, but that didn't matter to Jerry. He never slept. He had clients in London and New York, and he worked around the clock. He picked up the phone and I had no idea where to begin. Everything was running together, and I wanted to tell it all at once. What had happened was too much to be believed or understood. Somehow, I managed to deliver a coherent version of the morning's events.

"Calm down," Jerry said, after hearing me out. "I'll take care of it."

"When?"

"Right now," he promised. "I'll call you back. Don't talk to anybody."

Jerry Weintraub, I should mention, had become a major player in the entertainment business by 1977. In addition to John Denver and George Burns and the other great vaudevillians who turned out at his son's bar mitzvah two years earlier, he now represented heavyweights such as Frank Sinatra, Bob Dylan, and Elvis Presley, for their concert appearances. He had upscale offices on Wilshire Boulevard, two blocks west of the Beverly-Wilshire Hotel. He was one of the half dozen most powerful players in all of Hollywood, and an emerging heavyweight in the Republican party. I hung up the phone knowing that if there was anyone who could undo the career carnage of the past twenty-four hours, it was Jerry.

He called back about a half hour later. "I just talked to Roone," he said. "He wants to see you. Today."

Roone, of course, was Roone Arledge, the new president of ABC News. That spring, the network decided to demote Bill Sheehan to vice president and to replace him at the top with Arledge, the father of the successful *Wide World of Sports* format, the president of ABC Sports, and the pioneer of modern live sports television coverage. Sheehan was made to take the fall for the million-dollar wresting of *Evening News* coanchor Barbara Walters from NBC; her pairing with Harry Reasoner on the anchor desk was seen in the industry as a debacle. The call went out to Arledge, a man with no news background, to dig the network's perennially third-rated newscast out from this latest embarrassment.

"I want to put you on the *Evening News*," Arledge announced, taking my hand as I stepped into his office. "I'm a big fan of your work."

Jerry had prepared me for this possibility, but hearing those words—from this man, at this time—nearly knocked me over. Just like that, this short, carrot-topped, heavyset man erased years of blackballing and backstabbing by his predecessors. At last, the doors to the network newsroom were swung open wide. I was overjoyed and breathless at this sudden and wonderful turn. For years afterward, Roone Arledge could do no wrong in my eyes. After all, he'd had the good sense to rescue me from oblivion, and into the sacrosanct ranks of the network news division.

My career was made-over, in one roller-coaster day. I woke up as a roving correspondent for a fluffy morning show, and I went to bed a network newsman. I felt vindicated and proud. Through Roone, I now had the news division's stamp of approval. It was almost as if the new king had decided to knight the outcast. I thought to myself, I'll show these guys. I'll be the gutsiest, bravest, hardest-working, most respected and respectable journalist this business has ever seen. I vowed to honor Roone for hiring me, to validate him, because I knew he would take some heat for the move. I knew that it was only his naïveté that allowed him to hire me. If he had grown up in the news division, absorbing all those negatives against me, he never would have had the stones to go against the stream.

He called me Tiger at that first meeting. When we parted, with another handshake, he said, "Go get 'em, Tiger. I'll put on anything you do."

Word of my new assignment spread through ABC like a gas leak. By the time I returned to my office, there was a message waiting from Bob Shanks. The entertainment division wanted me back, he said. It was all a big misunderstanding. Ha, ha, ha. How could we let you go, Geraldo? You're a part of the family. Ha, ha, ha. Just come on back and let's pretend this never happened.

What bullshit! The man had essentially fired me that morning, and now, because a higher-profile network executive had publicly reversed that decision, he wanted me back, under his authority. The tug-of-war that ensued over my services represented network corporate politics at its worst.

Shanks and Silverman offered to share me with the news division, but Roone held fast. "Just go to work," he told me. "We'll sort this all out later."

Indeed, it would be three months before the mess of my contract was cleaned up by Jerry and the dueling network executives.

LA FINCA VIGIA, CUBA

My first coup at ABC News came during that summer of 1977, when I landed an exclusive interview with Cuban President Fidel Castro. Curiously, my show-business connections made the interview possible.

A friend at MGM helped arrange then hard-to-get Cuban visas for me and my crew, in order to accompany Ernest Hemingway's widow Mary on her return to the country in which she had spent most of her married life, from 1946 until her husband's death in 1961. The studio had purchased the film rights to her autobiography, *How it Was,* and was sending a high-profile production team to Cuba to scout possible movie locations. We tailed along and taped as director Sidney Pollack and company toured picturesque spots such as La Finca Vigia (the lighthouse farm), the Hemingways' country home just outside Havana, and La Floridita, the dark, wood-paneled bar in the capital's ancient downtown section, one of Hemingway's favorite haunts. I tried the Mojito, Papa's favorite rum drink and a specialty of the house.

Still following the advice of my old Columbia professor John Parsons and taking full advantage of every opportunity, Sheri and I, and our crew, eventually broke from the MGM team and took what was then a rare chance to record life in this workers' paradise. To my untrained eye, Cuba seemed to have fared well under Communism. Despite the trade embargo still rigorously enforced by the United States and its allies, the people seemed content, the neighborhoods clean. The harbor of Havana revealed why: row upon row of Soviet ships supplying the island nation with grain and other subsidies. I conducted spot interviews, in English and Spanish, and learned that the average Cuban citizen was essentially satisfied with his lot, although many young people yearned for the freedom of Florida, just ninety miles, and ninety light-years, away across the straits.

The highlight of the trip came on the night before our scheduled departure when Castro made an unexpected visit to a cocktail party in Mary Hemingway's honor. The party was peopled by Cuban film-makers, and dignitaries from the Cuban arts community. We were the only news crew on the scene. And in walked Castro. I was determined to make the chance encounter more than an exclusive photo opportunity. I listened in as he paid his respects to Mrs. Hemingway. Through a translator, the charming demagogue told her how much he admired *For Whom the Bell Tolls* and *The Old Man and the Sea,* which he claimed to have read three times.

I found a break in their small talk and, to Castro's surprise, began asking questions in Spanish. He stopped me to ask if Spanish was my native language. I told him it wasn't, but joked that with hundreds of Puerto Rican relatives I had to speak it in self-defense. He laughed, and I had the opening I needed. I asked America's new-world nemesis if he thought this Hemingway film project could aid in speeding the glacial pace of improving relations between his country and ours. He answered that the key to peace lay in imperialist Washington, and I knew I had a sound bite for the evening news.

Sheri and I chartered a Lear jet to Florida and edited the Castro interview at the ABC News Miami bureau. My plan was to edit the remaining Cuban footage at my leisure in New York; there was enough material for a multipart series for *Good Morning America*. (In this transitional period, between the news and entertainment divisions, I continued to file stories for the morning show.)

We sent the Castro piece to New York, via satellite, to good reviews, in time to make that evening's newscast. Later that night, on the phone to New York to receive muted accolades from the overnight assignment editor, I was told to cancel my plans for a minivacation in Miami and get home to New York as soon as possible. It was 9:34 P.M., and in New York, the lights had just gone out.

Sheri and I spent most of the night trying to get a flight, with no success. We were on the first plane to New York the next morning. By the time we left, news of the city's blackout had reached us as far more than a story of mass inconvenience. Power was still out, and sections of the city had erupted into violence, chaos, and anarchy. Despite the layover, I still had not missed the story.

On a busy news day, and this was a very busy news day, the sixth-floor nerve center of ABC News headquarters buzzed with producers, reporters, and editors running in and out looking for guidance, ripping wire copy, shouting instructions, or reporting the status of the pieces they were working for that day's broadcast. I presented myself to Av Westin, the veteran show producer, like a commando reporting for duty. Like me, Av had been a network news outcast during Bill Sheehan's regime, but had been rehabilitated by Roone Arledge. He told me to get my ass out on the streets, where I could team with any of several camera crews that had been filming the arson, looting, and rioting that had spread through the poorer sections of the city since the blackout had disarmed burglar alarms and vanquished inhibition.

I ran out to Central Park West and commandeered a Checker cab, offering the Dominican driver twenty bucks an hour to stay with me for the duration; he told me he could not risk his cab for that little, but confessed to being a big fan of mine, and so we settled at thirty. Next, I swung past my apartment a couple blocks south and asked my pal Cheech if he wanted in on an urban adventure. He and his wife Rikki happened to be staying at our place during a New York visit to promote his latest movie. They had been in a midtown movie theater when the lights went out the night before. They were sent out into a darkened city enveloped by a festive atmosphere, but that was the scene only in the nice neighborhoods. In Harlem, central Brooklyn, and the South Bronx chaos reigned.

I asked Cheech along because I thought he was brave enough, and interested enough to get a charge out of the deal. I could also use his help. All the Bronx Puerto Ricans knew who he was, and I figured the familiarity might come in handy. Cheech could watch my back. We raced up to Washington Heights to rendezvous with Anton Wilson, a freelance film cameraman who had been reporting the story since early morning. Anton was an eccentric intellectual, an accomplished inventor, and an honors graduate in engineering from Cornell University, who also happened to be one of the few cameramen willing to work with me. Cheech and I found him filming looters leaving a Thom McAn shoe store on upper Broadway.

After a passing patrol car alerted us to the more intense action up in the Bronx, we hurried north in a two-car convoy, the Checker leading. The scene uptown was apocalyptic. The steel rolling doors and metal grates had been ripped off the storefronts of almost every shop and supermarket. Most retail establishments had been stripped and then burned. Looters of all ages carted off everything they could carry with impunity. We found one group lugging a washing machine up to a third-floor tenement apartment.

ANTON WILSON (former ABC News cameraman): We followed these guys up to the apartment, and I remember being struck, the first of many times I would feel this way about Geraldo, that this guy could get us killed. There were twenty of them, and three of us. Clearly, we were in a hostile environment. These guys were showing us cases of liquor and appliances that they had stolen, and a motor scooter, and the camera's rolling. Any other reporter would have been totally intimidated by the situation, but Geraldo just turned to this one guy and he said, really pissed off, he said, "What the hell gives you the right to take this stuff?" And the guy says, "Well, man, I've been underprivileged, and I figure the blackout is God's way of giving me a chance." Geraldo said, "Forget about God. This is your local store! This is your neighbor!" He was really indignant. And, to me, what made this a great piece of journalism was that he was asking exactly what would be going through the minds of the people who would be watching the piece.

The rooms of the apartment were crowded with television sets, radios, refrigerators, and other high-ticket items. I was wild with the idea that smug white America was about to see a herd of Puerto Rican and black jungle bunnies drowning in ill-gotten excess. I stormed out of the apartment and led the team to the row of shops along 161st Street, between the Bronx Courthouse and Yankee Stadium. A fire truck was sitting in the middle of the street, but the firemen were only watching as a series of stores burned.

"What's happening?" I asked one firefighter.

"They won't let us work," he said, indicating the crowd of looters still scavenging through the smoldering ruins.

I got up on the truck and started shouting: "*Compañeros,* what the hell are you doing? How can you people do this? Don't you have any shame? Do you want the whole world to think we're just a bunch of animals?" I was lecturing these people, scolding them, and to the shock and surprise of everyone—the firemen, Cheech, Anton, and even me—the crowd listened and started slowly to disperse. They did not return the stolen goods, but they called it a day and went home.

The resulting piece was featured prominently on that evening's newscast, and resulted in my one and only compliment from my colleague Peter Jennings. (At the time, I described our opposing, favorite-son relationships with Roone and the rest of the news division to a print reporter by referring to Jennings as Christ and myself as the anti-Christ.) Jennings was then the network's chief foreign correspondent, and a second-generation emblem of the broadcast news establishment.

"Good piece tonight," he remarked casually at the end of the broadcast. "And right after Fidel. Not bad."

I thanked him in the same cool way his congratulations were offered, but with hidden joy of acceptance.

The joy was short-lived. As I left the building to return to my office down the block, I confronted a picket line set up by striking members of the National Association of Broadcast and Electronic Technicians (NABET). Like all my news colleagues, I had crossed the picket line with the approval of my own union, AFTRA, which had decided not to strike. I had been up for about forty-eight hours, charged by the Castro coup and the blackout reporting, and I was starting to fade along with the exhilaration of those stories. I was tired and dirty, and not at all in the mood for what happened next.

"Scab," one of the pickets shouted at me as I walked past their line.

"What did you call me?" I challenged. I knew these guys, and was not expecting any trouble. The taunt echoed, an intolerable insult. Fighting words.

"Scab," the striker said again. "Isn't that what you are, Mr. Jerry Rivers?"

That was it. I hit that bastard with a right-hand that sent him to the pavement. His NABET buddies rushed to his aid, but no one came at me to defend this guy. The cops from the Twentieth precinct were summoned, but they declined to arrest me. Later, the union would complain bitterly to Roone, alleging unfair labor practices and thuggery, but he replied coolly that I did not seem to him the sort of person who would assault anybody. Thankfully, the strike was soon settled, and the bad feelings eventually dissipated, but not until some valuable tapes of mine, which were stored in the network library, had been mysteriously erased.

YONKERS

I filed several reports that summer about the "Son of Sam" killer, who was wanted in connection with six murders and seven brutal assaults committed in New York City over the past year, most of them involving young women. The entire nation was gripped by the violent spree, as police tracked the elusive .44-caliber serial killer, who warned that he would strike again on the anniversary of the first slaying. On July 31, 1977, a year to the weekend after a teenage girl was shot and killed in her double-parked car in the Bronx, he did just that: A young Brooklyn woman, Stacy Moskowitz of Flatbush, was shot in the head while parked in a lovers' lane area near Dyker Beach Park; she died the next day. Her companion, Robert Violante of Bensonhurst, was blinded in the shooting.

Just before midnight on August 10, a 24-year-old postal employee named David Berkowitz was apprehended outside his Yonkers apartment building. Police had reportedly traced him there through a series of unpaid parking tickets, written to a car matching the description of the one used in his previous attacks.

When he was arrested without a struggle and advised of his rights, Berkowitz reportedly said, "Well, you've got me."

The following day, Roone sent me out to do an investigative piece on the arrest. Roone's theory, which I corroborated over the next hours, was that the cops had caught Berkowitz sheerly by accident, although all the news accounts to that moment had been extremely laudatory of police efforts. What actually happened, I discovered in my reporting, was that the New York City Police Department was merely responding to a tip from an auxiliary sheriff's deputy when they went to Berkowitz's apartment building with a search warrant. There was no great police work here, just serendipity, and that was the story I set out to tell.

Roone devoted a full nineteen minutes of our broadcast that evening to the Son of Sam case. To his untrained nose for news, this thing smelled like the biggest story that'd ever happened. The rest of the news division fumed at his judgment, but it was Roone's sandbox and we were his toys. Barbara Walters anchored the newscast from New York, introducing the various Son of Sam segments from her correspondents. There were five separate stories, linked by her scripted lead-in. I joined Barbara on the set for the intro to my own piece, during which I described Berkowitz as a beast and a monster. I tripped over the word alleged, which we were required by our legal department to use in all criminal matters pending trial; I said it with sarcasm, because I wanted to remind our viewers that this butcher had essentially confessed to his crimes. I was excited and angry; there was a venom to my voice as I spoke of this killer, a disdain that told viewers what I thought of this man and what he had done.

After the Son of Sam reports, Barbara threw to Howard K. Smith in Washington, for the rest of the day's news. Smith, very snidely, began his portion of the broadcast by remarking, "There *were* some other things that happened today."

The broadcast, in the minds of news purists, was a fiasco. It confirmed the fears of broadcast journalists already leery of entrusting a network news division to Roone, a man who had spent his entire career in the frivolous world of sports. My brand-new colleagues singled me out as the symbol of Roone's excess, and erratic news sense. The controversy quickly swelled to where the entire ABC News Washington bureau signed a petition, condemning both my emotional hyperbole and Roone's poor judgment, and spread word of that petition to top management and competing news organizations.

I was crushed. For years I had struggled for credibility and thought I had finally attained it. Once again, it had eluded me, and my reputation seemed shattered. Indeed, the fallout lasted longer than the document itself. The infamous petition was never found after that first day, but its impact can still be felt. Broadcasting historians have tried to locate the petition for nearly fifteen years, to no avail. In ABC News bureaus nationwide, the petition has vanished into legend, representing the mood of the newsroom at the front end of the Roone Arledge regime. Roone later admitted to me that he had placed too much emphasis on the Son of Sam story after Berkowitz's arrest, that he had run two or three stories too many before cutting away to other news. But these were not my decisions; these were not my stories. My story was a valid sidebar looking at the circumstances of the arrest, delivered perhaps with a shade more enthusiasm than what was comfortably allowed by journalistic convention. Still, I got the blame for the entire broadcast, and I carried the Son of Sam rap for years afterward.

The petition was a terrible blow, coming on the heels of victory. Roone did not have to defend himself against his critics—he was already invulnerable within ABC—but he defended me. He praised my reporting, my instincts, and even my occasional emotionalism. These were the things, he said, that brought me to his attention in the first place. In fact, he even sent me out the next day, on a follow-up to the same story. "Break stories," he told me when he gave me the assignment, "that's the way you'll tell them all to go fuck themselves."

I redeemed myself the following week, to a degree, following the death of Elvis Presley on August 16, 1977. The battle over my services was still being waged between the network's news and entertainment divisions. When Elvis died, both sides saw me as the logical person to cover the story. With my rock 'n' roll background, music industry contacts, and appeal to young viewers, no one else came close. Bob Shanks wanted to send me to Graceland, to work the story for *Good Morning America*; Roone wanted me on the case for *Evening News*.

I met them in Roone's office and watched the volleys. I felt like I was seated at centre court at Wimbledon.

Shanks, who was getting nowhere with Roone, finally turned to me and said, "Geraldo, I need you to go down there. Will you go down there?"

He was asking the wrong person. He had just fired me and now he wanted me to bail him out.

Roone answered for me. "Bullshit," he said, "he's not going anywhere. I need him to anchor the Elvis obit tonight at eleven-thirty."

Shanks lost.

And so I was given my first network anchor assignment, following the late local news with a half-hour special on the life and death of Elvis Presley. (August, 1977 was still pre-*Nightline*, or Ted Koppel would have handled the duties.) My excitement over the opportunity was tempered by the death of one of the true heroes of my growing up, but there was enough left over to get me pumped. I would tell the Elvis story; his legend was in good hands. For the first time in my career, I had the vast resources of an entire network news division at my disposal, with satellite hookups to Los Angeles, Las Vegas, and Memphis, and virtually limitless archives. We put together a compelling package of clips and sound-bites, topped by live interviews with key members of Presley's entourage and field reports from Graceland and Las Vegas.

NBC ran with its own late-night Elvis obit, but we blew them out of the water. The subject, format, and time slot all played to my strengths. Naturally, the young audience looking for an Elvis Presley tribute at that late hour looked to me, over David Brinkley at NBC, and the ratings reflected that in a big way.

The broadcast, coming so soon after the disaster of the previous week, was a big plus. Years later, when my *20/20* investigative team revealed the cover-up surrounding Elvis's death and life, it became easy to dismiss this earlier story as sugarcoated gloss, but at the time my Elvis obit demonstrated that there was indeed a place for a flamboyant, antiestablishment presence on the team. After the strong showing in the ratings, Roone even floated the trial balloon of teaming me with Barbara Walters on the news anchor desk, but the idea was drowned by the chorus of derisive laughter. Elvis may have solidified a place for me within the news division, but I would never be on the anchor-track after Son of Sam.

The ABC News team, at the time, was mostly made up of faceless reporters, with a few exceptions. Sam Donaldson was already a fixture as White House correspondent; Howard K. Smith, having been demoted from the anchor desk, provided commentary from Washington; Peter Jennings was the standout overseas reporter. For the most part, though, the anchors were the stars, and they were not shining too brightly upon my arrival. Barbara Walters, who had been brought in from NBC at great expense and with great fanfare, was floundering in her new position; despite her many gifts, she was not the panacea her widely and unfairly publicized million-dollar salary suggested. There was absolutely no chemistry between her and coanchor, Harry Reasoner. Reasoner was so disgruntled at the pairing, and so humiliated over the fact that Barbara was making more than twice his salary and stealing his spotlight, that he seemed to shrink and prematurely age. He hated having to work with Barbara, and it showed.

(A footnote: Roone Arledge finally got around to his anticipated revamping of the evening newscast in July 1978, when he introduced *ABC World News Tonight*, with the four-headed anchor team of Barbara Walters in New York, Frank Reynolds in Washington, Max Robinson in Chicago, and Peter Jennings in London. Harry Reasoner was lost in the reshuffling and returned to CBS; Barbara Walters soon left the newscast to concentrate on her celebrity and newsmaker interviews, and to eventually join the staff of the network's newsmagazine *20/20* as co-host.)

Av Westin, the *Evening News* producer when I signed on, became another of my supporters. Av had his own dreams of someday becoming the president of the news division (he was in line for the job after the firing of Elmer Lower), and he made himself expert at the corporate politics that probably cost him his job under Sheehan. Under Roone, he became a kind of bridge between the old-line news hands and their new boss. He played both sides of the fence. At one point, very early on in my tenure, he took me aside and said, "I'll take anything you produce. Roone wants you on every night. I want you on every night."

Indeed, my pieces made it to air far more frequently than any other reporter not assigned to a regular beat. Sometimes three or four stories a week, found their way on to the evening newscast. I think this was both a good thing, and bad. My new situation gradually revealed itself as an extension of my early days at *Eyewitness News*: distrust, suspicion, animosity, and hostility from the other correspondents; adoration and appreciation from management; and, a free hand from the assignment desk.

The studio itself was on the mezzanine of a narrow office building at 7 West 66th Street. The correspondents worked out of a bullpen on another floor, in a traditional newsroom setting. The wait for the elevator in that building was interminable, as I recall, and the staff took to the stairs whenever deadline loomed. (The building was only seven stories, but that was enough to keep everyone in shape.) I maintained my offices a few blocks away, in the ASCAP building, which exaggerated the distance between me and my colleagues, and reinforced the courtesy and special treatment from management. I had staked out my territory there and was reluctant to give it up, even though I probably should have if I paid any attention in those days to things like fitting in. Over time, my claim on those offices shrank along with my staff. With the passing of *Good Night America* and the Help Center, and with the relocation of the One-to-One offices, my little fiefdom had been whittled away to where the suite of offices no longer felt like "Geraldo headquarters." Still, I remained there, with Sheri, Marylou Pizzarello, and Marty Berman, because it was a way of distancing myself from the cold shoulders, and it was a subtle reminder to management that I was operating on a different playing field than everyone else.

Sheri continued to run my professional affairs (and to monitor my personal ones), and consistently sought to trim my Maravilla expenses. With the move to network news, she stepped up her campaign to shed Marty from my payroll. She no longer saw a place for him, after *Good Night America*. Everything he could do she could do better, she kept reminding me, and she could do it for free. She saw Marty as a financial drain and thought I was keeping him around solely out of friendship. She had a point— there was not much for him to do, and his salary did come out of my pocket—but I liked having him around. He was my friend, and I trusted him. Marty and I had been through a lot together, and I valued his judgment and his instincts.

Sheri didn't. Eventually, she convinced me to act. I took Marty aside one day and told him I didn't think there was a place for him anymore. It was one of the most difficult things I have ever had to do, but he made it easy for me. He had seen it coming, he said. He took the news with grace. In retrospect, I think the firing was just what he needed to give his career a kick in the pants. He had been stagnating with me for the past year or so, and suddenly he was forced to get out and do something, to get his creative juices flowing. He cashed in his pension money and took his family out west, and within a year he put together a syndicated daytime talk show called *Hour Magazine*, which was eventually hosted by Gary Collins. Marty put that show on the air, and it stayed there for eight years.

Sheri and I maintained the Trancas Beach house during this *Evening News* period, but I began spending most of my time in New York, when I wasn't traveling on assignment. I liked being in the city for the access it gave me to Roone. He would invite his favorites into his office on the third floor, to watch the newscast, and to share a drink afterwards. In those days, we did the first broadcast feed at six-thirty, when it was carried live in some parts of the country; if we needed to make any repairs or updates—if someone flubbed a line, or if a breaking story presented new information—we did it again at seven, when the show was fed to most major market affiliates on the East Coast.

Whenever possible, then, Roone's inner circle would go down to his office to watch the seven o'clock feed. Typically, the group consisted of Irwin Weiner, the vice president for business affairs, Jeff Gralnick or Justin Friedland, two of Roone's most trusted producers, and David Burke, Roone's aide-de-camp, who would play a major role in my demise several years later. Harry Reasoner and Barbara Walters were never in on these postmortems. None of the other correspondents were among the regulars. In fact, I was one of the few correspondents who had a direct pipeline to Roone. His door was always open; his secretary did not even announce me when I turned up in his outer office. Over time, Roone developed a reputation of being a hermit, of isolating himself from his staff.

He became famous for not taking anyone's calls, no matter who was on the line; that was the way he learned to deal with people, by avoiding them until the problem went away. But in those days, with me, he was open, generous, and giving, and he was free and constructive with his comments about my work: You're speaking too loudly, you're coming across too hard, ease off, step back. He was part motivator, part mentor, and part sponsor. He was my friend.

PANAMA CANAL ZONE

The summer of 1977 was also when I began covering the Panama Canal controversy, in a series of reports spread over several months.

Jimmy Carter, the best U.S. president that ever happened to Latin America, had begun negotiations with Panamanian dictator General Omar Torrijos, to relinquish U.S. control of the Panama Canal at the conclusion of its ninety-nine-year lease in 1999. World attention was focused on the region. I had begun working on a series of reports on the Canal Zone for *Good Morning America*, soon after reading the best-selling history of the fabled waterway by David McCullough, *The Path Between the Seas,* but I redirected my efforts for *Evening News.*

I spent great chunks of time in Panama, much of it with Sheri and my cameraman Anton Wilson. I interviewed Panamanians of every ilk, including General Omar Torrijos, who told me that American imperialism could no longer sustain itself in the region, that his people wanted self-determination, that the Canal belonged to Panama. I interviewed the Zonians—Americans living in the Canal Zone—and they talked about how we had paid for the Canal in American lives, and treasure. The Panamanians, they intimated, were just a bunch of woolly-headed Third Worlders. The Canal rightfully belonged to the United States. Anton used a time-lapse camera, uncommonly creative for news at the time, to show how the water levels changed when a ship traversed the Canal locks.

We covered the story from every angle, shedding light on a region and a people very much in the news. When we came back from our first trip to the region, I worked hard to convince the crusty newsmen in New York that we had enough material for a series. They were skeptical, because of my reputation and because multipart stories were not common on network newscasts back then. I actually had to sit down with them and screen the extensive footage. It was a hard sell, but we got the series on the air.

Roone thought the reports were great. He sent me one of his famed Roone-A-Grams, a handwritten note of congratulations that was seen as a big deal in the newsroom. If you got a Roone-A-Gram, you were doing okay.

Word of Roone's enthusiasm seeped down among his staff, and I began to notice a gradual warming. It took a while to spread, and it wasn't much, but it was something. At least I was tolerated.

I returned to Panama some months later, when Carter and Torrijos were about to sign the historic Panama Canal Treaties, and this follow-up trip was memorable for a more personal reason. I was sent to cover the hard news angle, and after a time the network also dispatched Barbara Walters to do one of her celebrity newsmaker interviews with General Torrijos. I had been chasing the elusive dictator all over Panama during this visit—literally chasing him, chartering a plane and following him to an island resort, then to his country retreat, and even slogging after him as he toured rain-soaked villages in Panama's interior.

ANTON WILSON: We knew we had to get to Torrijos for our story, but it was like a wild-goose chase. We followed him through a monsoon, in an open Jeep, and in a rickety airplane we had to land in the middle of this ridiculously bumpy field, it was like a rice paddy. At every stop, the general would say something like, Señor Rivera, you have come this far, I will give you the interview, but my advisors say I look like crap. I don't want to give the interview here. And we would follow him to the next village. He traveled by helicopter, and we were in a Jeep, driving through the jungle on these horrendous roads, in horrible weather. Finally, after this went on for an entire day, Torrijos says to Geraldo, Señor Rivera, I am truly sorry, but I cannot give you the interview. The politics are more important. I don't want to say anything to jeopardize the treaty. The end of the story is he let us use his plane to fly us back to Panama City, to make up for what he put us through, and Geraldo and I get on the plane and he is really dejected. We had been through hell, not to get the story. Sheri and my sound man sat in front, and Geraldo and I sat in back. Finally, Geraldo looked over to me and said, "It's still a good story." And I said, "Yeah, we got great shit in the can." And we both loosened up a little, and then he slapped me on the back and we just started to crack up. We were hysterical. Absolutely hysterical. Rolling on the floor, kicking and punching each other, slaphappy. And Torrijos's soldiers are looking back, and Sheri's looking back, like we're out of our minds. What we were kicking ourselves over, and laughing over, was the adventure. The adventure was the same, whether we got to Torrijos or not. If, after the fact, after you've done everything you could, if it doesn't work out, then fuck it, you know. At least we had the adventure.

When Barbara showed up, Torrijos was suddenly accessible. In Panama, as everywhere else, Barbara was more queen than commoner journalist.

I liked Barbara a great deal. In our small talk over the months we had worked together at ABC News, it had become clear that she harbored none of the hostility directed at me by our colleagues. She had her own newsroom resentments to deal with. In that way, we had much in common. We were also linked by my former flame Judi Beck, who had gone on to become Barbara's executive assistant. Barbara used to tell me that people like us would always carry the double-edged sword of celebrity: greater access to sources, but resentment from rivals and colleagues. Don't let it affect your work, she counseled. On some stories, especially in remote places, we will often cause a bigger fuss than the story itself. Don't worry about it. Just concentrate on doing better than anyone else.

I took her advice to heart and did not begrudge her her easy access to Torrijos. Instead, I sat back and watched as Panamanian politicians and the resident press corps deferred to her and stared at her. For some reason, she never overwhelmed me the way she did most other. I had a way of seeing her through unintimidated eyes. I would imagine her naked. I once told Tom Shales of *The Washington Post* that I thought she had great tits.

As Barbara went to work on Torrijos, I went to work on her. I met up with her the night she arrived, in the hastily assembled ABC News office in a Panama City hotel suite packed with editing, camera, and satellite equipment. As the network's resident Panama expert, I took it on myself to explain the lay of the land. She listened, until it became obvious that I was flirting. After what I had taken to be signs of encouragement, she put her hand on my face, gently, and said, "Now I know what Judi was talking about." Obviously, Judi Beck had done some talking about my aggressive charms. She continued: "Now I know why these ladies are all so crazy about you. I'm flattered, I'm really flattered, but I'm busy tonight. Sorry."

As it turned out, she was having dinner with Omar Torrijos. I was beaten by the general, and the moment was forever lost.

I was all over the map after Panama, covering everything from a raging forest fire in Southern California, where more than seventy-five homes were destroyed, to the aging of southern Iowa, where an exodus of young people threatened the lifeblood of the region. (I called this last piece "Old, Cold, and Poor," and received another Roone-A-Gram for my efforts.) And, increasingly, I covered Latin America like it was my backyard. I covered the Nicaraguan civil war and tore apart the greedy dictator Anastasio Samoza in an exclusve interview, months before Dan Rather got to him. I covered a devastating earthquake in Guatemala. I was also big-footed out of a story by Sam Donaldson, during President Carter's trip to Brazil. This last was a rude awakening. I went down early to do an advance piece, and then Sam came down with the entire White House press corps and muscled me out of the story. It was my first close look at the strange dance of beat reporting on the president's trail, and the perspective was both enlightening and disillusioning. One day, I spotted an A.P. photographer running through the halls of the hotel, announcing, "Amy Carter's the story today, Amy Carter's the story today." Sure enough, the next day, everyone ran with a photo opportunity story featuring Amy Carter. The pack decided what the lead would be, and everyone fell into line. It was an eye-opening lesson about how the media pack sometimes covers events of national significance, and a sorry display to a reporter long known for his maverick independence.

I learned a great deal during my short tenure on the *Evening News*. I tightened my reporting, because I knew it would be closely scrutinized by my enemies—in-house, and in the press—and my work benefited from the extra effort. Mostly, I learned about the kind of reporter I wanted to be, through the process of elimination. I did not want to be a party-line toady. In fact, I did not want to be like any other correspondent on the ABC News payroll. I was hired because I was different—involved, emotional, passionate—and I knew Roone did not want me to change that.

Still, there was not much room to grow at *Evening News*. Increasingly, I was being focused on the travails of Latin America. It was becoming my beat, in the way it has become the beat of virtually every Hispanic network reporter who has come after me. They don't assign Russians to cover the Soviet Union, Poles to cover Poland, or blacks to cover Africa. But for reasons ranging from language proficiency to racial stereotyping, it is where we are sent. I was out to broaden my horizons.

CHAPTER ELEVEN

RAMIREZ CANYON

I bought my first house (not counting Avenue C) in late 1977, a small, single-story ranch deep in Ramirez Canyon, in the foothills of the Santa Monica Mountains. The modest house—a steal, I thought, at two hundred fifty thousand dollars—was set on three and a half acres near the top of a short, steep residential road called Via Acero, overlooking the canyon and the Pacific Ocean, a mile away.

With my rent-stabilized New York City apartment on Central Park West (which I would soon purchase when the building was converted into cooperative apartments), I now had roots on both coasts. I divided my time among the swells of New York City and the decidedly different denizens of Malibu, priding myself on my ability to dash between the two.

The day Sheri and I moved in on Via Acero, a Saturday, we were visited by our new neighbor and the area's chief "wild thing" Jon Peters, who shared a palacial compound with Barbra Streisand, down the hill from our little house on the canyon wall. Actually, to say that we were neighbors doesn't account for the fact that there were thirty other homes around the perimeter of Jon and Barbra's spread. Barbra had accumulated seven adjacent properties over the years, with Jon acting as steward, and at the time of our arrival, she owned a couple dozen acres abutting hundreds of acres of state land at the back of the canyon.

Jon, with his Viking beard and long mane of hair, pulled up in a Jeep Wagoneer all-terrain vehicle and reintroduced himself. I had interviewed him the year before (when he convinced me to crawl back to my newlywed bride), and he wanted to stop by to welcome us to the neighborhood. Basically, he did what I had done with Cheech a year or so earlier. He pulled in, screeched to a stop, extended his hand, and announced that we were going to be friends. He was right, as he was about most things.

At about five-nine, one hundred and eighty pounds, Jon was built like a barroom bouncer, dressed like a gentleman rancher, and coiffed like a Hollywood hairdresser. He had Popeye-like forearms, bulging from a worn, but stylish Pendleton shirt, and he wore work boots, jeans, and a meticulously shag-cut head of hair. (Jon, the inspiration for Warren Beatty's movie *Shampoo,* was only two or three years removed from his previous incarnation as hairdresser to the stars; he still owned two or three salons at the time of this meeting.)

Even with the pretty-boy locks, Jon came off as rough and tumble, my kind of guy. He struck immediately as one of the most energetic and intense human beings I had ever met. At the time, he was taking his first, tentative steps as an independent producer, working on the movie *The Eyes of Laura Mars,* which starred Faye Dunaway. It was his first project sans Barbra, although he was still her Svengali, personal manager, counselor, and live-in love. They would later split, professionally and personally, and Jon would team with Peter Guber to produce the megahits *Flashdance* and

Batman, and, briefly to head Columbia Studios. Back then, Jon had a tremendous ability to focus on other people, to zero in on what was important to them, and to make whatever it was also important to him. It was almost as if he had no personal agenda, the way he let himself be enveloped by everyone else's. On that first Saturday, he was all over me about my work, my credibility, my representation, my personal life, and I never once got the impression that his interests where anything but genuine. He asked about Jerry Weintraub, about what he was doing for me, about the kind of attention he was paying to my career, about the contracts he'd negotiated for me.

It soon dawned on me that Jon was recruiting me as a client. He was flattering and persistent, and eventually his effort evolved into an all-out campaign. Barbra was his only other client in those days, and like Jerry Weintraub five years earlier, he was looking to expand his base. Unlike Jerry, Jon was impetuous, and I don't know if he'd planned to win me over before he set out in his four-wheel drive welcome wagon, or if it had just occurred to him when he pulled up the drive.

Jon was a spontaneous, restless, and generous creature. He was notorious in the neighborhood for doing things his way. The most flagrant example of this was his rechanneling of Ramirez Creek to suit the aesthetics of his property. To accomplish this, he launched the most expensive private construction job I had ever seen. He put in huge stone walls, and actually redirected the creek, which ran through the center of Barbra's properties. Ostensibly, he did this to protect their main house during the rainy season, but he also did it because he didn't like where the creek was and wanted to put it someplace else.

It was the most lavish movement of stone and earth this side of a public works project, and the source of great controversy in the canyon. According to his downstream neighbors, Jon's efforts caused the creek to run harder and faster during the rainy season. Cars were washed away. Some people were forced to evacuate their homes, temporarily, or to remain in them until the raging Ramirez Creek subsided. Once, I was stranded on top of Via Acero for eleven days, the longest single stretch of time I ever spent in Malibu, marooned by the floodwaters cascading from Barbra's property.

The extensive landscaping job seemed to crystallize the way Jon

Peters saw the world, and the way the world smiled back. He did what he wanted, whatever Barbra's money enabled him to do, and he always got away with it. He seldom sought permits or variances for the work on Barbra's property, he just had it done. He seldom let anyone in authority on the premises. When town inspectors responded to neighbors' complaints, Jon bullied (or schmoozed) them off his land. He threatened officials with lawsuits or wowed them with Barbra's celebrity. As long as I knew him, he always had a tribe of illegal Mexicans working as groundskeepers or construction workers. They lived, en masse, in one of the otherwise unused great houses on the land.

Everyday, the canyon echoed with orchestrated activity. Jon was moving mountains. As a result of his constant resculpting, Barbra's valley was overgrown with eucalyptus and evergreens. Much of Malibu was a desert—dry and brown—but Jon and Barbra lived in a tropical paradise. He took Sheri and I on a tour that first day, and we were thrilled by the surroundings, and by Jon and Barbra. The several houses from the once-separate parcels of land dotted their property like a Monopoly board. Every home was impeccably designed around a different theme. The main house was a rambling ranch, surrounded by lush gardens. Next to it stood a grand pink stucco home, which was used principally as a screening room. Barbra's favorite structure was farther up the sunny canyon wall, an exquisite art-deco chateau, impeccably restored in original pink and black tile. It was like an Erte museum, with 1920s furniture and fixtures. It was used as a pool house and opened out onto a period pool reminiscent of Hollywood's golden era.

Barbra and Sheri took to each other immediately and began a friendship that exists to this day. I was always uneasy around Barbra, partly because of her celebrity, but also because she always seemed more comfortable around women. The four of us spent a lot of time together—eating, playing, traveling. I remember a 1978 trip to Acapulco, which had just been hit hours before our arrival by a substantial earthquake. Despite the force of the quake, damage was contained; the locals were shook up more by the thought of what might have happened than by what actually did. We were not about to let a small thing like an earthquake spoil our vacation plans. That night, as we sat looking out at the bay through the Greek columns of an open-air restaurant designed to

look like the Parthenon, we were hit by an aftershock. Barbra went
ballistic. We made our way to one of the doorways, between two
columns, but she was still frantic. It was almost touching, to see
someone so formidable become unglued. Barbra was on-edge long
after the tremors subsided. She wanted to go home, but Jon
calmed her into staying.

Always, though, there was a coolness between me and Barbra, a
distance. For all the time we spent together, it would seem we
would have eventually gotten past that, but we never did. I think
there was the same kind of wedge between Sheri and Jon. What we
had, really, were two great and separate friendships, joined by
marriage.

This was just fine with Jon and me. Over the first weeks of our
friendship, he persisted in his interest in my career. He would turn
every conversation around to where I was made to defend Jerry
Weintraub, or my current salary, or the various professional paths
I had chosen.

"He's out of touch with you," Jon would say of Jerry. "He can't
pay attention to you. He has too many other clients. You're too
small for him."

Again, Jon was right, or I let him convince me he was right. He
convinced Sheri, first, and the two of them brought me around. I
may have been Jerry's first client, outside his marriage, but there
was no denying I was now also one of the smallest. Over the past
couple years, Jerry had started to move away from the management
business and into movie producing and concert promotion,
handling tours for Frank Sinatra, Bob Dylan, and, until his death,
Elvis Presley. He was making millions from these other clients; his
ten percent cut of my six-hundred-thousand-dollar ABC News
contract barely merited a line in his company's books. In fact,
Jerry and I had had little to do with each other since the day he'd
miraculously maneuvered me to network news. Of course, there is
not that much for an agent to do between contracts. In the agency
business, you oil the wheel that squeeks, and mine wasn't making
much noise.

"Six hundred thousand is nothing," Jon would challenge. "You
should be making a million."

A million sounded good to me. "You sure?"

"Definitely," he said. "A million. For starters."

Ultimately, I folded. At his urging, and Sheri's, I agreed to let Jon represent me, which left me with the unpleasant task of breaking the news to Jerry. I went to see him at his office on Wilshire Boulevard. Sheri came, to lend emotional support (and, probably, to give me the courage to go through with it); she waited in Jerry's outer office, while I went in to do what I now felt I had to do.

The words, at first, didn't come. I looked around Jerry's office and fumbled for an opening. As I searched for something to say, my eyes drifted to a memento-strewn shelf by a window overlooking Wilshire Boulevard, and focused on a picture of Jerry, John Denver, and myself, embracing in triumph after one of our most successful One-to-One telethons. I remember thinking, in the split second before I delivered the parting shot, Jesus, first Marty, and now Jerry. What the hell am I doing?

"Jerry," I finally said, "I hate to have to say this but I'm leaving you. I've hired another agent."

"Who?" he demanded.

"Jon Peters."

Jerry was incredulous and hurt. He hated Jon and everything he stood for. "I can't believe you're leaving me for him," Jerry bellowed. "He's nothing but a hustler. You're making a big mistake."

"You're too busy for me," I tried.

"What, too busy? I'm never too busy. I always have time for you."

He was right. He did always make time for me. Maybe this wasn't such a good idea. I tried a new tact. "You've got so much on your plate," I said. "I can't possibly be a priority to you anymore."

"You're the only news client I have," he countered. "There is nothing else on my plate in television news. There is no conflict."

On the surface, Jerry took the firing pretty well, but he did not let me off easily. He saw me squirming and made me work for it. Our relationship wasn't just about business. I was Jerry's first client. We were friends. He didn't even collect his commission during the first lean years. We had a history together, during which we had each prospered beyond our wildest imaginings.

I later learned, through Roone, that immediately after this

meeting, Jerry made frantic phone calls to several ABC News executives, warning them that I was unhappy with my contract and insisting that they not renegotiate. Jerry was hurt by the firing and he went out of his way to make sure I did not benefit from it. We didn't speak to each other for years afterwards.

JERRY WEINTRAUB: Yes, I was hurt by Geraldo's leaving. At the time. I didn't blame anybody. These things happen all the time. I don't know why it happened. I don't even remember. You have to understand where my life is now. I'm a very happy man. I'm fifty-three years old. I'm very, very wealthy. I have a lot of wonderful memories and I have a lot of things I want to do in the future. Geraldo and I were very good friends. We had a wonderful relationship. As far as I'm concerned, we still do. I hope he feels the same way.

I hired Jon Peters on a handshake. That was one of his big come-ons: "Just a handshake deal, Geraldo," he'd say. "Nothing's on paper. You can fire me any time you want."

We started spending all our free time together. We'd hang out, either in New York or Los Angeles. We'd work out, talk about women, and get drunk together. We were each involved with very dominant ladies, and we commiserated, and compared notes. We dreamt of our younger days, when we were free to roam and plunder and raise hell. We were like two old cowboys, swapping past glories and current woes.

Jon was wild in those days. His constant companion was an old Doberman named Big Red, the scariest dog in captivity. This Doberman was always pissed off. Once, he tried to rip the fender off my 1954 Jaguar. He actually scraped the paint and put a dent in the fender before Jon called him off. Jon was the same way with people who pissed him off. He had a hair-trigger temper. I watched him deck a crazed fan who was stalking Barbra on the ranch. Jon wasted him with a rising left-hook. I bailed him out of that one when I told sheriff's deputies that he had merely acted in self-defense. (Jon told me afterwards it was like having the pope testify on his behalf.) Years later, I came to Jon's defense again, this time in Aspen, where he was facing possible felony charges for sticking his antique Colt revolver in the ear of his gardener, who had become abusive over an unpaid bill.

Our friendship, in many ways, was built on macho one-upsmanship. When I bought a 900-cc Kawasaki motorcycle, Jon came home the next day with a 1000-cc bike. We drove those machines everywhere, up the breathtaking Pacific Coast Highway to Oxnard, and down around snaking Mulholland Drive. Even riding became competitive. One of us would get it going up to a hundred miles an hour and dare the other one to keep up. One day, during the summer of 1978, we came roaring up Winding Way, a well-named serpentine back road leading into Ramirez Canyon. Jon juiced his bike a little bit, and I juiced mine. We took turns kissing the lead. We roared past the actor Stacy Keach's house, leaning into a sharp turn. The road took a left in front of his house, then another right, and then there was a sudden drop-off, sheer, fifty feet straight down. We both knew these roads, but we were too caught up in the rush to know where we were, or what we were doing. I finally slammed on the brakes. Jon spun out, on the inside. I didn't quite spin, but I had to sort of lay the bike down to keep it from going over. My bike finally came to a stop at the edge of the cliff. The front wheel was hanging over the edge, and spinning wildly. Jon missed going over by about half a foot.

We were both scratched up, but not seriously hurt. We got up and brushed ourselves off, without exchanging a word. Jon climbed on his bike and rode off, slowly, back to his ranch. I drove back to my house. We never rode those bikes again.

We talked about it later, but not for weeks. I remember marveling with Jon, at how close we'd come, at how fine was the line between anecdote and tragedy.

Jon and I both boxed in those days, and we often sparred together. He was in my corner for the biggest athletic triumph of my life: a grueling One-to-One charity bout in Madison Square Garden's Felt Forum, which *The New York Post* later described as the best three-round amateur middleweight fight ever seen.

The annual One-to-One boxing matches began in 1973, as one of our rowdiest and most successful fund-raising efforts. We catered to the cash-rich, beer-guzzling Wall Street crowd, and featured some pretty good amateur fighters. I entered the competition that first year. I was in terrific shape and had always been a good street fighter, but my successes there did not translate into the ring. My instinct was to lead with my chin, to throw wild punches that a more disciplined fighter could dodge or deflect without effort.

I never got near my first opponent, although I lasted the full three rounds.

After that initial disappointment, I went into serious training. I had an image to maintain and a score to settle. I started going to the Sixty-third Street YMCA, across from my apartment on Central Park West, and hired a former Olympic boxing coach named Bob Chiocher to help me train. Whenever my hectic schedule returned me to New York, I was at the "Y." There, for the first time, I learned to box. I had fought before, but it was not the same. Bob taught me that boxing is a science, that grit and strength are no match against a sound technical fighter. A good boxer, I learned, is disciplined in his attack, controlled. An amateur is predictable, impulsive, and beatable.

Under Bob's tutelage, I became more formidable. He was a wonderful old man, and a sage in the gym. With his help, I won my next three annual One-to-One bouts, until the 1977 event, when I lost a controversial split decision to a stockbroker/club fighter named John McLaughlin. I bloodied his nose, but he scored more blows. The call could have gone either way, or been declared a draw, but it went to him. I smarted over that defeat for the whole year, until event organizers arranged a rematch; then, I was pumped at the thought of revenge.

Jon was one of my cornermen on that night in 1978, along with my brother Craig, and coach Chiocher. A boisterous crowd filled the Felt Forum for the charity card, including my pals Cheech, *Eyewitness* newsman John Johnson, former heavyweight champion Floyd Patterson, and former light heavyweight champ Jose Torres. We raised close to two hundred thousand dollars that night, making it one of our most successful events. The fights were refereed by Arthur Mercante, the third man in the ring for most of Ali's great fights.

I was the only celebrity to enter the ring that night, so the rematch was billed as the main event. The fight lived up to its billing. For two rounds, it was a bruising battle, with McLaughlin doing most of the damage. His jabs were snapping my head back to a staccato beat. Cheech had to prevent John Johnson from running to ringside to stop the fight. Sheri, sitting between them, had to turn her head from the blows. I remember slouching on the stool in my corner after the second round, my body limned with sweat and spent from the beating. Most of the packed crowd of five thousand beer-drunk Wall Street brokers were howling in delight. They wanted to see me get my ass kicked. Coach Chiocher gave me some technical advice about going to the body. Craig was almost teary-eyed in his concern. Finally, I looked to Jon, who challenged, "What? You gonna let this piece of shit beat you up in front of all these creeps? In front of your wife? Go out and kill this motherfucker!"

CRAIG RIVERA: It was the first time I had ever seen Geraldo scared. I always had this image of him as a fearless competitor, someone who would go out and do anything. But here, he was scared. Definitely. I don't think he'd ever admit it, but I could see it in his eyes. But after Jon yelled, his eyes went from cold to hot.

I was off my stool early, provoked to fury. At the bell, I charged into center ring, threw two sharp jabs, then unloaded an overhand right that caught McLaughlin just above his left eye. He fell to the canvas, and the crowd was stunned. I turned away from my fallen opponent and searched the audience for Sheri, shaking my right fist in triumph. My celebration was premature. McLaughlin was down, but not out. Mercante's yell focused me back on the fight. McLaughlin was up. I charged, unleashing a two-fisted barrage on my now helpless opponent. Mercante stopped the fight, and I had won a TKO.

Afterwards, I made a speech about throwing a lucky punch, praising my opponent, and maintaining that the retarded were the real winners of the fight because of the cash we had raised. The One-to-One matches continued for another year, but I hung up my gloves after the 1978 fight. I did not think I could top myself in that particular arena.

I have pictures from that fight, and film, but I don't need to look at them to remember. It is burned onto some permanent internal highlight reel. There's a funny thing about great moments in sports for someone like me, someone who always held out a dream of leading the underdog team to victory. I had always been a strong athlete, but never the star, never more than a part of the team. On this night, though, I was the standout.

Between escapades, Jon Peters paid close attention to my career. He watched every time I was on the air, usually encouraging. His criticisms, when offered, where sharp and incisive. I listened, but his eyes were focused on celebrity, not on journalism. He didn't care about the reporting, at least initially. What he paid attention to more were the visuals, what I looked like, how I came across, what kinds of stories best suited me.

"That old leather jacket," he'd say. "I love that."

Once, after an on-air confrontation with some Ku Klux Klansmen, he told me, "You've got bigger balls than any ten of those assholes."

One of Jon's first official tasks as my agent was to renegotiate my ABC News contract, and to secure a slot for me on the staff of the still-unnamed magazine show being readied by the news division for a 1978 summer tryout. I was still in the middle of a multiyear deal negotiated by Jerry Weintraub a year earlier, but Jon promised that he could get Roone Arledge to tear up my existing contract, cut a new deal, and get me reassigned to the new show.

Jon arranged for a lunch meeting for us with Roone and Irwin Weiner, in Alfredo's on Central Park South, Roone's favorite Italian restaurant at the time. The meeting started off pleasantly enough, with typical business lunch small talk. At this point in time, my relationship with Roone was still open and candid, and we talked about our common goals for ourselves and the network. Jon was quiet, but polite. He was out of this particular loop and did not have much to contribute.

By coffee, the conversation had shifted to the development of Roone's newsmagazine, which was going to be called *20/20*, and which was going to debut in June, for a trial summer-run. I had always told Roone that what I really wanted to do in life was to be the reporter who got the call at two o'clock in the morning, when the earthquake hits, when the war breaks out. I wanted to be his number-one fireman. He had given me that, at the network level, and I was grateful. Now, I wanted something else. I wanted to be the tough, investigative reporter called in to give a story substance and depth. One of Roone's maxims was that a story was always bigger on its second day, and I wanted to take that theory one step further. I wanted to insert myself into the story after the pack had devoured the initial details, to digest it, and then tell the viewers what was really going on. I no longer needed the first word; I wanted the last.

Roone and I spent a good deal of that lunch going back and forth about the long-form reporting possibilities in his new *20/20* magazine format. I was excited at the opportunity, and wanted in on the launch. I saw *20/20* as a chance to stretch, and to move forward with my career. I was well aware that networks had considerable difficulty launching prime-time news magazines in years past, and that the chances for a long-running success at *20/20* were no better than fifty-fifty. Still, I was enough of a gambler that I wanted to make the move. My career at *Evening News* (soon to be reinvented as *ABC World News Tonight*) had been tense and occasionally unpleasant, and I was eager for something new.

Jon let us chatter away about television news and the future of the network, and waited for the conversation to turn to the business at hand. Finally, just before the check arrived, Jon slammed his hand down on the table. He silenced the busy restaurant with the thud. It was like he was an E.F. Hutton broker, the way everyone in the place turned to see what it was he had to say.

"I can't stand this fucking small talk," he announced. "We came to negotiate. Let's negotiate." He was like a pitbull, waiting for his chance to pounce, and when he saw he wasn't going to get it, he pounced anyway.

Jon didn't come away from the table with the million dollars he had promised, but he upped my yearly take to seven hundred fifty thousand dollars, a twenty-five percent increase. He had also secured me the chief reporter slot on the *20/20* staff. Sheri would later step in and assist Jon with the fine print, but the basic deal was done in the last two minutes of that lunch.

I was heading to prime time.

ODESSA, TEXAS

The ABC newsmagazine *20/20* premiered on Tuesday, June 6, 1978. We were not an overnight success. In fact, the program was so severely criticized in the industry and in the press that we were for a time uncertain whether we would even be allowed to complete our trial summer-run.

The debacle was presided over by Bob Shanks, who had graduated from late night and early morning entertainment programming to become the news show's executive producer. For some strange reason, he hired Harold Hayes, a former *Esquire* editor, and Robert Hughes, an Australian journalist, as cohosts; one had no television experience, and the other spoke with an Aussie accent thick enough to scare a koala; neither was recognizable to American television viewers or particularly comfortable in front of a television camera. Shanks had them refer to themselves, and each other, as Hayes and Hughes, which was probably meant to eliminate viewer confusion but surely enhanced it.

Contributors to that first show, in addition to myself, included the former CBS correspondents Dave Marash and Sylvia Chase, ABC veteran Sander Vanocur, art expert Thomas Hoving, and science writer Carl Sagan.

The first *20/20* set was designed like an ersatz library, and the format called for the correspondents, one by one, to join the hosts around a large desk and present their air-pieces in a kind of staged show-and-tell. The pieces were bracketed by political cartoons, or occasional packaged films from outside producers. The premiere show, for example, featured a Claymation likeness of Jimmy Carter, lip-syncing to Ray Charles's version of "Georgia on My Mind." Oddly, Shanks brought the show in and out of commercial with definitions of ten-dollar words such as "arcane" and "exegesis" flashing across the screen.

As conceived, *20/20* was a hodgepodge, a dash of serious, investigative newsgathering, slick-packaged for mass and easy consumption. The format lacked definition, polish, and scope. We didn't know whether to pander, entertain, or inform.

The move to *20/20* was a major shifting of gears for me. I was off the air for all of April and May, preparing a bank of stories before our June launch and adjusting to the slower, more exacting pace of a television newsmagazine. I worried constantly about not being on the air for such a long period of time. Would people wonder where I had disappeared? Would they care? Dave Marash, my new colleague and, up until then, a hardworking anchor at New York's WCBS-TV, was actually approached on the New York City subway during this time by a guy who asked, "Hey, didn't you used to be Dave Marash?"

Dave and I used to talk about our need for a television fix. I had been on the air several times a week, sometimes several times a day, for eight years, and I was horrified at the sudden vacuum. The downtime was like a withdrawal for me, partly because I needed to feed this animal of a public image I had created, but more because I missed the adrenaline rush of seeing a piece through to deadline. I needed the charge of reporting a story in the afternoon, delivering it on the air that evening, and starting in again on the next thing the morning after. I missed the feedback, the heat, and even the controversy.

One of the investigative pieces I was working on during this downtime turned out to be *20/20*'s first lead story. Charles C. Thompson II, one of the producers assigned to the show's newly formed "Geraldo unit," had been contacted by the Humane Society about the continued use of jack rabbits as live bait to train the thoroughbred greyhounds raced at dog tracks around the country. Before the public, of course, the dogs chased mechanical rabbits around the track; on farms throughout the Middle West, though, the dogs were schooled on the real thing. Charlie started chasing this story down before I signed on at *20/20*, and when I joined the staff I inherited his legwork and enthusiasm. Together, we spent several weeks more tracking the coursing operation, from the dirt farmers of Odessa, Texas, who trapped and supplied the rabbits, to the dog tracks of Kansas and Oklahoma. We came back with riveting, grisly footage of the greyhounds mangling their kills, and we buffeted the disturbing visuals with numbers that contributed to the stomach-turning.

Charlie was an unusual character. A former naval officer, and a combat veteran of two tours in Vietnam, he was a triple type A personality. The only gear he ever used was overdrive, the only direction he moved was forward. He was an ace reporter, a former producer for CBS News. (He has since returned to CBS, producing for Mike Wallace at *60 Minutes*.) He was an investigative journalist from the old school, constantly on the phone, digging, probing, looking for some new angle he might have missed. The trouble with Charlie was his temper. When he got going, he could be extremely combative and intimidating, and he got going all the time. We worked together on dozens of stories over the years, and I was constantly apologizing to people for the way he would work himself up to where he was out of control. I used to tell people he was suffering from post-Vietnam stress syndrome. Charlie also had a thing for guns. People would listen to my explanation about his background, imagine what kind of piece Charlie was toting, and back off. We stared down a lot of bad guys in this way, and opened a lot of doors.

So, me and my wild-man producer put together a twelve-minute packaged story, which we called "Rabbit Kill." In it, I railed against the villains of the piece—the dirt farmers, the dog-track owners, the gambling syndicates—and called for legislation to put an end to these systemic horrors. (Indeed, our report helped to put more restrictive laws on the books.) It was, I thought, a solid story, exposing an operation that was not only bloody but illegal. Unfortunately, I was in the minority here. We took a lot of heat for that premiere show, and a good deal of it was aimed at our story.

The ratings were not bad (we finished second in our time slot, pulling a respectable twenty-five percent share of the audience), but the reviews just about killed us. The premiere edition of *20/20* was compared (unfavorably, I might add) to shows like *Rowan and Martin's Laugh-In*, *Monty Python's Flying Circus*, and a forgettable CBS sitcom called *Me and the Chimp*.

Washington Post television critic Tom Shales, in a review printed under the telling headline, *20/20*: Myopic Misfit," echoed the sentiments of most of his colleagues, delivered with his trenchant prose. "Watching *20/20*," he wrote, "the ABC newsmagazine, which premiered on the network Tuesday night, was like being trapped for an hour at the supermarket checkout counter, and having to read the front pages of blabby tabloids over and over again.

"*20/20* is the Top 40 radio of TV news, an animated smudge on the great lens of television and probably the trashiest stab at candy-cane journalism yet made by a TV network . . . *20/20* managed to take a gross leap backward and a garish leap forward at the same time, and if at first it gave us the giggles, it may on second thought justifiably give us the creeps."

Then it was my turn. "First to show up desk side was the redoubtable and self-parodistic Geraldo Rivera," Shales continued, "whose foray into investigative journalism on the first show was an endless and dubiously important exposé on how jack rabbits are killed during the training of greyhounds. 'The rabbits don't stand a chance,' said Rivera, who spoke, as usual, in tones of sepulchral indignation and allied himself with all the enemies of evil who have ever existed, Batman and Robin included."

Even my wardrobe offended Shales: "Rivera's on-the-job outfits are as flamboyant as his self-glorifying reportorial style. With a red bandanna around his neck and an open Western-style shirt, he looked like someone who should be accompanying Ratso Rizzo down Forty-second Street."

(Shales, I should mention, has the hairless face and chubby body of a palace eunuch.)

Betsy Carter, writing in *Newsweek*, was also unimpressed by my initial effort: "Warning parents that 'it's kind of gruesome' for children, reporter Geraldo Rivera went on to show endless footage of drooling dogs mauling the rabbits, with the cameras zooming in for the kill. With all the seriousness accorded an undercover Mafia investigation, Rivera surreptitiously tracked the export of jack rabbits from Texas with the use of reporter decoys and hidden cameras, and he ended the segment with the pious exhortation that Congress stamp out these 'petty barbarisms.'"

She also called my report "heavy-handed," "lurid," and "bloodthirsty."

I still stand by that piece, no matter what the critics said about it. The only poor judgment we showed in airing it, I think, was putting it on our first show. Fortunately, most of the viewers loved it. It seemed to establish a blueprint for our entire run; it told viewers that we were going to look long and hard into corners where no other news organization would even think to look. It told them that even the "petty barbarisms" we uncovered would be accorded the same full-blown treatment given to more common atrocities. Regrettably, without a more compelling human tragedy to measure it against on that first broadcast, it also signaled that our stories would fall on the soft side of hard news.

The "Rabbit Kill" backlash was dwarfed by the lambasting of the show itself. In-house criticism was even more scathing than what appeared in print. Overnight, we had become the laughingstock of our own newsroom and the entire television news business. Roone did a quick damage check on his new prime-time vehicle. He was not prepared to scrap the project, despite the easy temptation to do so. The launch represented a multimillion dollar investment, affiliate stations were committed to a thirteen-week summer-run, and he could not afford for his first prime-time news effort to fail. He moved decisively.

For starters, Roone fired Hughes and Hayes, who in addition to confusing audiences with their bland patter and twinned monikers had dropped the ball in a live interview with California Governor Jerry Brown. (The premiere show aired on the evening of the California primaries, and our cohosts neglected to ask the governor about Proposition 13, which came to symbolize a national taxpayer revolt, and was easily the most hotly debated measure on the ballot.) Bob Shanks was demoted, after only one show at the helm, and Al Ittleson, my old assignment editor from *Eyewitness News*, was brought in as a kind of coexecutive producer. And, in a startling reach for credibility and durability, Roone hired Hugh Downs, an unspectacular but reliable veteran of the *Today Show*, and PBS's magazine for senior citizens, *Over Easy*.

AL ITTLESON: Our setup, once we got going, was similar to the *60 Minutes* setup. There was Hugh Downs, and then there were our three major players. There was Sylvia Chase, there was Dave Marash, and there was Geraldo Rivera, and they each had their own unit, their own territory. Once again, Geraldo gathered his own group around him. He peopled it with a lot more people than we were paying for at the time. Interns, volunteers, whatever. I think he was probably covering some of the cost. Plus, his wife at the time, Sheri, was not an employee, but she would function in that unit in a supervisory role. And, in fact, we used to have meetings for senior producers, to which Geraldo was invited, and if he couldn't make the meeting he would send Sheri. It was a very unusual situation.

The changes were dramatic and immediate. By the time we returned for our second show the following week, we resembled our debut in name only. Gone were the arcane on-screen definitions and the fast-paced nonnews touches that had cluttered our first broadcast. In their place was a quieter, more orderly program.

"Roone Arledge didn't become the Toscanini of TV sports technology without learning when to hit the stop-action button," *Newsweek*'s Harry F. Waters hedged after our sudden revamping. "In went Hugh Downs and a journalistic sobriety that, while not as slick as CBS's *60 Minutes*, at least tapped the program's potential."

My second air-piece was critic-proof, although not by design. "Feral People" profiled the bums and beggars of our inner cities. The term accurately described the circumstances befalling our growing population of homeless people. I had been working on the story for some weeks. With my camera crew, I followed a woman who lived on the RR subway train, which ran from the Lower East Side to deep Brooklyn. Through her, I sought to give our street people a measure of dignity and hope, by explaining this poor woman's circumstance, and finding her a home and new start.

The resulting air-piece was emotional, solid, and above reproach. It was also one of the most talked-about segments of that second show. In retrospect, we probably would have been spared a good deal of front-end criticism if we had led our debut broadcast with the "Feral People" story, and come back to the coursing piece at a later date. Both stories were ready in time for the launch, but management deemed "Rabbit Kill" the hotter, more visceral of the two.

With the move to *20/20*, I finally relinquished my offices in the ASCAP building. Marty Berman and Judi Beck were no longer on the payroll, and sweet, solid Marylou Pizzarello was preparing to accompany her heart-doctor husband to an Italian clinic. The extra office-space seemed suddenly redundant, and so I joined the newsmagazine's team in a white, twenty-story building on the corner of Sixtieth Street and Broadway. (The offices, ironically, were located above the Capezio shoe store where Edie once worked sketching shoe designs.) It was the first time in nearly six years that I had worked as part of a team, and I was glad to come in from the cold. Sylvia Chase and Dave Marash were respected and admired colleagues, and in the first weeks of our shared tenure they had also shown themselves to be friends. What a relief it was to finally work with people I cared about and who cared for me.

SYLVIA CHASE: What's the first thing I remember about meeting Geraldo? Well, he's got the best buns in the business. I know that sounds terrible, but it's really one of the things I noticed about him. He has an absolutely marvelous physique. And I thought, gosh, what a good-looking guy. I'll confess it unabashedly. I was not prepared for what a great body he had. More important, he was always very accessible, very friendly, never held himself apart or acted in any way lordly. And I've seen people who have far less ability, and much less notoriety, who put on all kinds of airs. But Geraldo? Never. There was nothing about him I did not like, personally. There were, though, some things he did on-camera, some of the approaches he took to stories, that I found not to my taste at all. I remember watching him chase some hapless criminal in Akron down the street and down to a parking ramp and thinking that that was unattractive and that I didn't want him to sacrifice his dignity in that way.

My new office was relatively small, compared to the ASCAP space. I shared it with Sheri and decorated it with mock antiques and cheap artwork. It was my first "adult" office, and it was free of the sixties muck and clutter of my abandoned digs.

Marylou's penultimate act was to find her own replacement, and for this she reached into the ranks of young interns crowding our new office space and pulled out C.C. Dyer, a senior at New York University majoring in broadcast journalism, who had been working in the office as a novice researcher in exchange for course credit. Marylou took her final duties upon herself: She decided to warn the beautiful young redhead, who was about to step in as my personal assistant, against her new boss's romantic predilections.

*   *   *

C.C. DYER: Marylou didn't like Sheri. She said that was the main reason she wasn't staying on. But she loved Geraldo. She would tell me, "Oh, he's the greatest boss, you're going to love him." And then she got serious and said, "You should know, though, he's a real womanizer. Be careful." And I said, "Womanizer! He's married!" It was like the two things were mutually exclusive. Marylou looked at me like I was some hick and then she said something, I can't remember it verbatim, but it was something like, "I wouldn't be surprised if you were his next conquest." And I looked at her and said, "Me?" I thought she was crazy.

I never noticed C.C. in the ASCAP office before she came to interview for the job as my personal assistant, which says more about my elaborate distractions than it does about C.C. Of course, she was hard not to notice. She had a bountiful head of carrot-colored hair, and a bodacious body and personality to match. She was young, bright, and innocent; she bounded about the room as if all was right with the world.

I hired C.C. almost as soon as she sat down for her interview. The only question I remember asking her is, "How soon can you start?" I was immediately attracted to her, but not necessarily in a sexual way. She was so flawlessly WASPy, athletic, and practically smelling of Cape Cod pine and sea. An affair was out of the question. I was a happily married man, or so I thought.

C.C. immediately established the tone for our office. Her desk was out front, guarding the entryway to our new, downsized, and efficient headquarters, and her ebullient personality bubbled over the entire *20/20* staff. At one point, early on, I asked her to start dressing like Diane Keaton in the Woody Allen movie *Annie Hall,* because I thought the floppy hats, the loose clothes and the tweeds would help to set a relaxed and stylish mood for the entire team.

The *20/20* reporting units soon became rigidly compartmentalized. The core correspondents—Sylvia, Dave, and myself—were each assigned three or four producers, and assorted support staff. There was no pooling of effort. Sylvia's producers, for example, were not available to me, just as my producers were not at her disposal.

Sheri ran the unit as if it was an independent production

company. In many ways, her competent direction was merely an extension of her days helming Maravilla Productions, during the *Good Night* and *Good Morning America* days. The basic difference was also a tremendous relief: Our employees were now on the ABC payroll, not our own.

It became very clear that Sheri spoke for me at *20/20*. She relished the role. Management applauded her efforts, although she would frequently piss some people off. Many of our colleagues could not understand why they had to answer to this aggressive woman who was not even an employee of ABC News; she had zero news experience, just a high school degree. She had no formal authority over these people, yet at the same time, she had every authority over them. I was blind back then to the tensions that surrounded Sheri's presence there, but I can see them now. All I knew was that she was my partner in life; I trusted her. She made my business life more streamlined and allowed me to concentrate on stories rather than administration.

Sheri missed nothing. She handled all of the unit finances, and all of our personal finances. She filed my expense vouchers with network accountants. (I didn't even carry a checkbook at that time.) She attended meetings for me, helped to schedule my stories for broadcast, accompanied me on the more exotic working-trips, and evaluated unit personnel.

C.C. DYER: He asked me to dress like Annie Hall. He really did. I just looked at him. I didn't know what to say. He wanted me to look more New York, I guess. So I went out and spent money on clothes. I don't know if I looked like Annie Hall or not. I tried to look hip. He must have liked it, because he never said anything after that. I was wearing a lot of jeans and stuff. Meanwhile, I'm trying to dress like Annie Hall, and Sheri starts telling me to wear a dress, no pants. She wanted the office to have a highbrow look. She wanted me to answer the phone, "Mr. Rivera's office," and for years everyone had just been picking up the phone and saying, "Geraldo."

I didn't know it at the time, but the foundation for the rest of my life was laid that summer. I would go on to spend eight of the richest, most productive years of my career as a reporter for *20/20*.

And I would prove Marylou Pizzarello prophetic and emerge in the arms of another woman.

Studio 54

The background music for my move into prime time pulsed from the room-size speakers in a cavernous television studio-turned-dance club in New York's theater district. Studio 54, opened by impressarios Steve Rubell and Ian Schrager in April 1977, reigned for over two years as the hottest, most happening night spot in all the world. On any given night, beautiful people like Elizabeth Taylor, Bianca Jagger, Cher, and Margaux Hemingway could be found cooking up a sweat on the dance floor, while the likes of Andy Warhol, Halston, Truman Capote and photographer Francesco Scavullo worked the room as if it were their own. Outside, and in, the paparazzi camped to snap the comings and goings of the merrymakers.

Rubell was a promotional genius, and he surrounded his club with an air of exclusivity. He made a special point of courting the hottest celebrities of the moment—from the world of art, fashion, music, movies, television, publishing, and politics—and denying entry to second-tier swells and run-of-the-mills who didn't quite possess the "heat" he was looking for. The lines at the door usually snaked around the block, as would-be patrons waited to be plucked from their ordinary lives and invited in to see how the other half partied. Studio 54 was a playground for the ruling class, and a carrot for the working class; gaining admission was the cultural equivalent of natural selection.

Recreational drug-use was at its peak in those days, and drugs were as much a part of the Studio 54 phenomenon as the music and the celebrities. Back then, marijuana was seen as benign a vice as it would ever be; Quaaludes were the uninhibiting aphrodisiac of choice; and cocaine, for those who could afford it, was the hip status drug of the moment. The coke spoon supplanted the peace symbol as the sign of the times. In this brief and curious window, toward the end of the 1970s, cocaine was the big unkept secret in society circles. With so much to lose, I never touched the stuff, but in a place like Studio 54, it flowed like beer.

For some reason, Rubell welcomed me into his strange and wonderful world. I was there on opening night, and every few weeks thereafter. Whenever I was in town, and Sheri was safely out of the way in Malibu, I would invariably wind up back at Rubell's place. I strayed from Sheri in those days, on something more than occasion, but I had established my own ground rules for my transgressions. My marriage was important to me, and so I made sure my outside encounters never became more than one-night stands. Sheri was such a vigilant roommate that I would have been found out by anything more. It was my sincere intention never to enter into another marriage-threatening relationship, never to hurt Sheri in any way. Sideline entertainments were okay, only as long as they were contained and spontaneous.

One visit to Studio 54 yielded an outrageous surprise, and almost shook me from my strict extramarital operating procedures. Margaret Trudeau, the estranged wife of Canadian Prime Minister Pierre Trudeau, was one of the notable celebrants on the dance floor. I watched her as she left the floor and flitted among the VIP booths, and I couldn't help but notice what this gorgeous creature was wearing. Or, more accurately, what she was not wearing. She had no underwear on beneath her short dress.

Back then, Margaret was in all the papers, all the time. In the space of a few months, she had gone from being the proper, young Anglo wife of an older, French Canadian politician, and a caring mother to his children, to being the wildest woman in all of New York. She left her husband, to great scandal back home and in the international press, and tried on an assortment of lovers and lifestyles to shake the cobwebs from her establishment past. She was living what for her was an aberration, a kind of carnal awakening. It would pass, and she would attempt a reconcilliation with the prime minister, but at the time it seemed that her walk on the wild side was a one-way trip. I wanted to meet her.

And so I walked up to Margaret and struck up a conversation. She had seen me on television. I had seen her on television. We had something to talk about. We started dancing. I found her delightful and desirable. Her reputation had preceded her, but there was nothing sexual between us on that first night. We talked and laughed, but she saved the last dance for the guy who had brought her there. When we parted, we made plans to meet each other the next day.

The following afternoon, we rendezvoused at the apartment she was borrowing from a friend and walked to Central Park. We held hands. It was an Indian summer day, and the city seemed to spill into the park, in a reprieve. We kissed. I didn't care who saw us. We rented a boat, and I rowed us to a remote corner of the reservoir. The sun baked down hot. I took off my shirt, and we embraced. Right there, the estranged first lady of Canada leant new meaning to the term head of state.

We returned to my apartment on Central Park West, for a wild weekend. It was incredible, being with Margaret. It was like she had never been made love to before. It seemed as if she were unleashing years of pent-up frustrations, freeing herself from the pressures of her world, catching up on everything she had missed. When we came up for air and spoke, Margaret didn't talk at all about the life she'd left behind. Canada was a world away for her. She didn't volunteer anything, and I was reluctant to probe. The journalist in me wanted to know everything, but the lover in me kept my mouth shut. She was like a housewife who had run off with the gypsies.

Our two days passed in a beat. My best intentions, to keep romantic entanglements away from my marriage, were left bobbing up and down on a rowboat somewhere in Central Park. Sheri's return to New York coincided with Margaret's leave-taking. She was off to London, to escape the harsh spotlight that had followed her to New York. I gave serious thought to joining her—surely, I thought, I could find a European story for *20/20* to justify the trip—but I let the opportunity pass. What we had was a moment together. What Sheri and I shared was a lifetime.

I told Margaret to call me at the office when she got back to town. Instead, she called me at home the following Tuesday night. Sheri answered the phone. Her piercing gaze searched my lying eyes as she handed me the receiver. "Margaret Trudeau," she announced coolly. "Calling from London."

I danced my way out of the situation by telling Sheri I was pursuing Margaret for an interview. She let the suspicious call pass, but tightened her watch and cut down on the days she spent at our home in Malibu. I was not to be trusted. The affair with Margaret Trudeau ended as quickly as it began. There were a few more phone calls, despite Sheri's watch, but we never saw each other again.

Only one other night at the disco stands out, for the way a second beautiful lady snuck up on my cheating heart, and for what it reveals about the curious nature of celebrity relationships. It was a weeknight, late. I stayed home until midnight so I could call Sheri out on the West Coast and tell her I was going to bed. (Nobody went out before midnight anyway, so the night was still young.) The Studio 54 crowd, on this night, was typical. I made my way down to the basement, the most exclusive gathering place in this most exclusive of clubs. The basement was essentially bare and unfinished, left looking pretty much like the storage area it was when Rubell and Schrager had found it. They installed their trademark theatrical lights down there, and a sound system to match the one upstairs, but the surroundings were rough and basic. The sweet smells of marijuana lifted the atmosphere from drab to euphoric. Warhol was there, sitting against a wall, taking it all in. Halston was also there (often, according to Warhol's diary, dispensing cocaine and Quaaludes to the faithful). The music was the same as it was upstairs but the room moved to a beat all its own.

Liza Minnelli was also there on this night, but her presence was not remarkable. Her absence would have been more noticeable. She was a Studio fixture, dancing, partying, raising hell. She has since spoken candidly about her excesses, and she was never more excessive as she was during the disco's heyday. I had seen her there several times before, but aside from public person politeness, we had never spoken. On this night, though, our eyes met, and we worked our way toward each other across the sea of people.

We were both married at the time, and Liza's husband, Jack Haley, Jr., was probably in the building, but she didn't seem to care. She was going about a million miles an hour, energized by the frenzy of the place and numbed by whatever she had spent the evening ingesting. We briefly embraced, and then she grabbed my hand and pulled me through the crowd to the ladies' room. I was enormously attracted to Liza. She was a vivacious beauty, wide-eyed and seductive, but I also wanted her because of who she was and what she represented. I felt about her exactly the way I have read people felt about her mother Judy Garland. She had lived a life tarred by tragedy and overkill. She was reckless, wild, and out of control. And fragile. She didn't have to say a word to communicate these things. Indeed, we had yet to say much of anything, but I started to think of her as a wounded bird. I had an inexplicable urge to protect her, take care of her.

The Studio basement bathrooms were the site of their own private parties, which is what Liza apparently had in mind. She pulled me into a stall, and we enjoyed a hot grope and grind that was made all the more exciting by time and place. Rowdy laughter and loud, stoned voices careened off the thin metal half-walls of the stall. We still hadn't spoken much to each other, beyond our hellos and our body language; the moment grew spontaneously, from the midst of this bacchanalia.

After a while of this bathroom passion, Liza pulled away. She was reckless, but not reckless enough to make love to a virtual stranger (a newsman, no less) in such a public (and uncomfortable) setting. She doused our passion as abruptly as she had kindled it, and left me leaning against the stall's wall, trying to figure out if what just happened had really just happened.

That first nearly silent and unconsummated encounter began a years-long series of romantic near-misses between us that I would come to think of, alternately, as wonderful and frustrating. The next time I saw Liza was some months later, at a party in her honor at Calvin Klein's stunning penthouse apartment overlooking the 59th Street Bridge. Sheri was back home in Malibu, and I was out on the prowl. Since our initial close encounter, Liza had left Jack Haley, Jr., and taken up with artist and producer Mark Gero, who would become her third husband. When Liza saw me at the party, she beckoned me to join her on the couch, shooing away her previous companion. She clung to me for the rest of the evening. She didn't care what anyone else thought, Mark Gero included. Every few minutes, she'd lean into my ear and whisper, "I've got to get out of here." Or, "Take me away from all this. This sucks."

Whenever I responded and suggested we disappear, she found some excuse to stay. She was all over me, in an overt way, but when I showed signs of taking our physical relationship to the next level, she would pull back. I don't know what it was with her. Maybe she was frightened and confused. Maybe she was just torn between losing herself and holding onto what control she still had. Maybe she was just a tease.

The situation repeated itself every time we met. The eternal optimist, I was drawn in every time. The next time I saw her, in January 1980, I had a *20/20* camera crew with me. Liza had very graciously agreed to an extensive on-camera interview—her first in long while—and I flew out to the Beverly Hills Hotel to meet her. While the crew set up in my suite, I paid a visit to hers, and our going-nowhere passion started up all over again. Finally, I thought, I was going to make love to this great lady. There was no way she was backing out of this opportunity. We were alone. The door was locked. I was certain.

But, again, my best efforts were dashed. Liza took me to the short side of the point of no return, only to pull away. There was a camera crew next door, she said. They would know what we were doing. Not now. Later. After the interview. After the interview would be better. It'll be better then, Geraldo, after the interview. You'll see.

The subsequent interview surprised me. It was a tremendous success. Liza was exceptionally soulful and giving. She spoke openly about her relationship with her mother, about her hopes for her own career, about where her life was going. As we talked, it occurred to me that we had never really opened up to each other before. Granted, Liza was doing almost all of the talking, but I was still thrown by her honesty. It is ironic, and somewhat disturbing, that it took a microphone and a camera crew to get us talking. What a peculiar moment that was for me, sharing these intimacies in such a public way. It was the first time Liza had talked to me about who she was and what she was feeling, and the fact that the rest of the world was listening in seemed to make it easier for her. It was a performance and a personal moment, both.

After the interview, she invited me back to her father's house. Vincente Minnelli, the great director, lived in the flats in Beverly Hills, just across Sunset Boulevard. He was elegant and polite, but I could tell he didn't like my being there. His instinct must have told him I was lusting after his married daughter, and he flashed me sad, disapproving looks all evening. He loved Liza too much to say anything, but the visit was memorable for its tension and uncertainty. He looked at his daughter and saw the same wounded bird I had seen.

Liza and I had a few more slow teases before it was over. The last was in Chicago, in early 1986. I had been fired from ABC News some months earlier and was in town for some meetings with my new partners, the Tribune Broadcasting Company. Liza was in town to record a rock 'n' roll album, a departure for her and a comeback effort of sorts. I had been through hell, and she had been through rehab, and we found ourselves, for the first private time, with a lot to talk about. She invited me back to her hotel. She was staying in the Mayfair Regent, a beautiful old hotel on Lake Shore Drive, overlooking the water. On the way up to her room, the hotel concierge tossed me the same disapproving glance I got from Liza's father. Everyone was very protective of her. Upstairs, we talked about how our lives had changed in the years since our first meeting. She talked about how she was trying to make a go of her life, how she had sobered up and become a much more responsible person.

It was a sweet, tender moment, but I wasn't willing to let it go at that. I thought, now that she had regained some control over her life, things might be different between us. But it was not meant to be. After a sweet embrace, Liza made some excuse ("It's not a good time for me, Geraldo"), and I made to leave. I felt sheepish for making this last attempt, ashamed, frustrated. I wanted to say something about it, to apologize for it or explain it away, but I didn't know where to begin.

As I reached the door, I turned to give her a final look.

"I love you," she said.

I had no idea what she meant by that. I still don't. Did she mean she loved that I listened to her and offered her a shoulder? Did she love that I didn't force myself on her? Did she love that I was also someone who had risen from the dumps to some kind of phoenix? Did she love me in the Hollywood sense, the way Don Rickles loves Bob Newhart?

I had no idea how to respond, and so I just let her words hang there. They were the last words to ever pass between us.

VERONNA, MISSOURI

As I settled in at *20/20*, I made a concerted effort to do the best possible job. I loved my work and secretly longed to capture the respect of my colleagues. I had been haunted by the David Berkowitzes, Gary Gilmores, and George McGoverns of my career for too long. I set out to lower my high profile, decelebrate my image, and concentrate on solid reporting. The slightly slower pace of the weekly newsmagazine allowed me to be more selective in my stories, and more meticulous in my reporting.

The extra efforts paid off. Generally speaking, the critics tended to ignore me after the maligned "Rabbit Kill" story, and I read their silence as a grudging compliment. Of course, most of our pieces were not ready for review before air-time, but I took my grudging compliments wherever I could find them. Still, my public persona did shift—subtly, gradually—to where I was no longer seen as the rock 'n' roll newsman. I could gauge the shift on the street, in airports, through the mails, and I welcomed the change. There is no longevity for daring, hot-tempered objects of teeny-bopper affections. I wanted to be taken seriously, and for a long time.

Several factors contributed to the slow turn. The most important was the flight to quality on the show itself. The hiring of Hugh Downs was a symbol of this, although the move was initially met with some cynicism. Hugh was one of the most underestimated men in television news at the time. And, I admit, I shared in the underestimation. Hugh seemed able, but not swift. The word on him was he could deliver his lines, but not read between them.

We were all wrong. Very quickly, Hugh showed himself to be supremely intelligent. He was, and remains, one of the best-informed generalists I have ever met. Mention a topic, and he'll tell you something about it you didn't already know. He was a constant source of surprise to me in those early days. He knew about the various species of fish off Florida's Gulf Stream. He knew about astronomy. He knew the geological history of the Southwest. He was a diver, a pilot, and an accomplished adventurer. I look at the three anchormen at the major networks and can't help but think Hugh Downs is a match for any of them. He is one of the most formidable and facile broadcasters working today, and his hiring at *20/20* erased the fresh memory of our first show fiasco and set us on the right course.

Colleagues Sylvia Chase and Dave Marash also contributed mightily to our new credibility. Sylvia is a great reporter. Even then, she was widely acknowledged as among the best and the brightest in the network's pool of young correspondents. Unlike me, she brought no activist agenda to her work, and her objectivity was embraced by the television news establishment. She flew in to town, got the story with evenhanded thoroughness, and put it on the air. The very objectivity championed by her news colleagues kept Sylvia from becoming a household name, but her superior reporting and stellar reputation within the industry helped to pull our show from the opening night dungheap.

Dave Marash, a veteran local anchorman at the time of his hiring, was a more unorthodox broadcaster. A grizzly bear of a man, with a stentorian voice, Dave had a way of commanding the camera's attention. His only failing was his perceived liberal ideology. He was always quick to take on big business and big government, and was seen by many in the me generation as anachronistic.

Of course, my own air-pieces did more to restore my personal credibility than anything or anyone else. On my first international assignment for the show, I traveled with Charlie Thompson to Germany to investigate a report that members of the Berlin Brigade, the principal American military unit assigned to defend West Berlin, were using (and, shockingly, a few even trafficking in) Turkish heroin. We corroborated the claim, and the antimilitary revelations in our story set up an adversarial relationship with the Pentagon that existed throughout my *20/20* tenure.

We pissed off the Defense Department again with our very next story, when Charlie and I brought the Agent Orange controversy its first real national television attention. From 1962 to 1970, the American military routinely sprayed the Southeast Asian countryside with a chemical compound, Agent Orange, designed to kill the trees and vegetation used as cover by the enemy. Our government dismissed the outraged North Vietnamese claims of resultant heart disease, birth defects, respiratory problems, spontaneous abortions, and cancer as Communist propaganda, and declared the defoliant spray harmless to human beings and animals.

By 1978, however, a number of subsequent developments placed those initial U.S. assertions into doubt. Agent Orange, it was revealed, produced an unwanted, inevitable by-product known as dioxin, the most poisonous manmade substance known to researchers, even more toxic than the mustard gas we feared Saddam Hussein might deploy in the Persian Gulf. In 1976, several years after the military suspended use of the defoliant, an accidental explosion in a chemical plant in northern Italy released lethal quantities of dioxin into the area, killing cats, rabbits, and wild birds flying overhead, and causing respiratory problems, liver problems, miscarriages, birth defects, and increased incidences of cancer among the evacuated population. Several hundred residents had still not been allowed to return to their contaminated homes two years later. A follow-up investigation, conducted by some of the world's leading scientists, confirmed, just prior to our report, that the dioxin contributed to the animal deaths and to the various human ailments.

Charlie and I began looking into the story after I was contacted by Paul Reutershan, a twenty-eight-year-old Vietnam vet from Connecticut who was dying of a colon cancer he claimed was the result of almost daily exposure to Agent Orange during his two-year tour as an army helicopter pilot. Paul, a brave young man who looked on his role in the defoliation, known as "Operation Ranch Hand," as a strategic necessity to help allied forces in the war effort, beat the drums in an effort to call attention to the devastating side-effects of the spray.

"I died in Vietnam and I didn't even know it," he told our cameras, and, indeed, he would succumb to the cancer by the end of the year.

With that first spark from Paul Reutershan, we launched the most thorough and extensive investigation of my network news career, following a trail that took us all over the country, and even on to Italy. We went to Chicago, to interview a VA counselor named Maude DeVictor, who was the first health official to link the lingering physical problems of area veterans to the defoliant spray. I spoke to Dr. Paul Haber, a VA medical investigator, who made the disturbing claim that the mere presence of cancer in Vietnam veterans who had worked with the defoliant was "coincident fact." I met with Dr. James Allen, a researcher at the University of Wisconsin, who supported the theory of ailing veterans that their cancers could have stemmed from exposure to dioxin. And we went overseas, to Seveso, Italy, a small town north of Milan, to examine the aftermath of the chemical explosion there.

What we put on the air that first week was frightening testimony to government inefficiency and denial, set against the deep personal tragedies of the afflicted veterans. But the story did not end there. We were back on the air the following week to look at the domestic harms posed by dioxin. The poison, inherent in the chemical compound known as 2,4,5-T, was found in commercially marketed herbicides regularly used to control rice crops and cattle ranges, and to clear highway rights-of-way.

We found the most graphic evidence of dioxin's dangers in Pittsville, Wisconsin, on a small family farm that had been accidentally sprayed with the 2,4,5-T herbicides. There, farmer Harold Freedlund offered graphic descriptions of pigs being born dead, or with two heads, or with no anal openings. He showed us horrifying pictures of deformed cattle, which we recorded on camera. Worse, we viewed the actual frozen carcasses of three-legged and two-legged cows, and the mangled forms of his existing livestock. His wife Nettie told us of her repeated miscarriages, and the persistent ill health of her children.

I also visited the picturesque town of Coast Range, Oregon, where an epidemic of unexplained miscarriages caused a group of concerned citizens to band together to limit the use of the herbicides by the lumber companies in that area. The tragedies of these people removed the dioxin fear from the jungles of Southeast Asia and brought it home.

We confronted spokesmen for Dow Chemical, one of the leading manufacturers of the 2,4,5-T sprays, at the company's headquarters in Midland, Michigan. There, in that company town where Dow was God, I listened to a doctor named Perry Gehring tell me his products were "absolutely safe." He insisted that the dioxins present in commercially marketed Dow sprays, when used on a daily basis and at high concentrations, would still present a risk "less than one-one-thousandth of eating peanut butter."

Up against the visuals of freak animals and dying Vietnam veterans, Gehring's assurances seemed flip and hollow.

The weird sidebar to the two-part Agent Orange story took place in Veronna, Missouri, where I went, without Charlie Thompson, to film an abandoned steel tank containing forty-six hundred gallons of dioxin-contaminated waste—enough poison, officials estimated, to kill every person living in St. Louis—and to talk to local officials about the various dioxin leakages in the area. While there, I visited a nearby horse farm that had been victimized by an accidental dioxin spill some years earlier. The current owners (the farm had changed hands since the incident) were annoyed at the sudden media attention focused on their property, and didn't take too kindly to our presence.

My brother Craig was with me on that leg of the story. After leaving college back in 1974, he had worked his way up from gofer to production assistant and was then one of the best associate producers on my 20/20 team. Lou Kidd, a lumbering Texan who weighed in at about 250 pounds, was my cameraman; Larry Smith, a part-time pharmacist who stood five-seven and weighed 140 pounds, was sound man.

The cowboys who now owned this horse farm were notorious in the area for the way they had recently assaulted and ejected an Italian television crew from their property. The local environmentalists were appalled at their conduct, not only because of the cowboys' violent, bullying behavior, but because they were also suppressing access to valuable evidence that could potentially lead to the suspension of 2,4,5-T production in this country.

With my crew, I descended on that horse farm on Tuesday, July 30, hoping for cooperation but expecting fireworks. We were met at the gates by a an unruly cowboy, who we took to be the owner of the place. He was big, about six-two, and rangy, dressed like a cliché in dirty Levis, cowboy boots, and hat. With him were three buddies, looking pretty much the same.

This dusted-over cowboy walked right up to Lou Kidd and punched his camera. The guy actually knocked the lens off, rendering it inoperable. We were taken completely by surprise. We expected that the confrontation could lead to some pushing and shoving, but we figured they would at least come out talking. I jumped on the guy, wrestling him to the ground. We rolled around—pulling, tugging, clawing—before Craig stepped in with some of the cowboys to separate us.

"Let's go," I said, taunting my adversary, shaking myself loose from Craig. We were on the shoulder of a two-lane county road. "We're on public property," I kept on. "Let's go. Right here."

The cowboy took a swing, a huge roundhouse right, which I parried. I stepped in on him and started working him over, surgically, like a boxer. It was like the third round of that Garden fight all over again, with bare knuckles. At thirty-five, I was in the best shape of my life. My opponent was overmatched. The guy was bigger and stronger but he was a brawler; without surprise, or a weapon, a brawler will never beat a boxer. After a couple minutes, he just dropped to his knees. His face was pulverized. I stopped jabbing. The guy had not landed one effective punch.

The crew and I cleared out quickly. The piece had to be ready for air by that Thursday night, and we still had interviews to do; more immediately, we feared being detained by the local sheriff. During the fast drive to the next county, I noticed that the knuckles on my left hand were chewed up and throbbing. I washed out the wounds at first chance, and went on to do a few more local interviews late that afternoon.

By evening, my left hand had started to swell. It was obviously infected—by what, I was not sure. By the time I flew back to New York the next morning, my hand was the size of a softball. Dr. Walter Taub, my longtime personal physician, was unable to treat the wound and sent me to a hand specialist at Lenox Hill Hospital.

The second doctor made his diagnosis immediately. He told me the infection was caused by frequent, violent contact with human teeth. "It's the most dangerous kind of infection," he cautioned.

My mind raced. What if the cowboy was eating the crops from his field? What if he was infected with dioxin? Could he pass it on to me, through his saliva?

The doctor admitted me to the hospital. He was afraid the infection would spread and I might lose the hand. They hooked me up to an IV, and started pumping me with antibiotics. Medically, the situation was soon under control. Trouble was, I still had a piece to edit, for broadcast the following night. The only thing to do was to bring the editing equipment to my hospital room. Tony Pagano, the editor came and set up shop, bedside. I voice-tracked the piece from my bed, and edited it, leaning up on one shoulder.

As far as I know, it was the only time a network newscast was edited from a hospital bed.

LAOS

At the end of our initial summer run, *20/20* slowed to a monthly schedule, and I was left runing at half speed. I had been on the air virtually every week during our tryout, and now, suddenly, I had to pull back.

Two notable things happened during this slower-paced monthly run. One of them was personal: Sheri became pregnant, late in 1978. The news changed my life, forever. We had been talking about having children for quite some time. I had wanted kids for as long as I could remember, but I always held back because the last thing I wanted to do was raise a child in divorce. But Sheri and I had been married for over a year and a half, and I thought we were set for life. Despite my transgressions, I felt secure enough in the marriage to start a family.

The time seemed suddenly right. The baby was due in August, which gave us plenty of time to find a place for him/her in our hectic, bicoastal lifestyle.

The other notable development was professional: I was reteamed with my old Help Center colleague Peter Lance, who joined the Geraldo unit as a producer. Peter had gone off to law school after *Eyewitness News* pulled the plug on the Help Center, and now that he'd graduated he decided he never wanted to be a lawyer. What he wanted to be was a reporter, on-camera, and he thought a stint with me at *20/20* might bring him closer to that goal. Whatever our personal differences, and there were many, Peter was an excellent producer, and a great writer, and so I took him on without hesitation.

We would work on several pivotal stories together for *20/20*. His first producing effort aired November 30, 1978, and called to mind some of the consumer advocacy reporting of our previous collaboration. We examined the not-yet-brewing generic drug controversy, which pitted the major drug companies against the Food and Drug Administration, Medicaid, and various consumer groups. What we found, alarmingly, was that the pharmaceutical industry was a big business, like any other, and that consumers were being duped into spending grossly inflated prices for brand-name drugs where chemically exact generic equivalents were available at a fraction of the cost. Valium, for example, is no longer protected by patent, and is widely (and cheaply) available under its generic name diazepam. We interviewed detail-men for the pharmaceutical companies, who maintained that brand-name medications had as much merit as brand-name appliances, even though the FDA requirements governing the manufacture of those drugs were precise, and applied both to brand and generic.

In many states, New York among them, pharmacists were required to post notices alerting customers that generic equivalents to many medications were often available, but our investigation of city drugstores revealed that these regulations were being honored only in the breach. During the filming, several Broadway drugstore owners attempted to eject us physically from their premises. Peter stepped between one enraged druggist and the crew, intercepting an assault that was no doubt directed at me. I applauded Peter for his spunk, but cautioned that, as point man, it was my job to take the on-camera blows.

The resulting air-piece sparked a growing awareness of the generic drug industry, and helped redirect millions of dollars away from the big drug companies and back into the pockets of the American consumer.

My next turning-point story came as *20/20* returned to its weekly schedule. Working through an international Quaker organization, Peter had obtained visas to allow our crew into Laos, in Indochina, ostensibly to film the reconstruction of that impoverished and embattled country in the wake of the Vietnam War. Once there, however, we discovered a second, more compelling agenda. The American military, without consent of Congress or the knowledge of the American people, had bombed Laos massively during the war. From 1965 to 1973, we dropped what amounted to two tons of bombs for every man, woman, and child living in the northern part of that country, at a cost to American taxpayers of over three million dollars per day. One historic region of that country, the Plain of Jars, became the most heavily bombed piece of earth in the history of warfare, and villagers there were still under attack from detonated bombs, which had left the jungle countryside a virtual minefield.

The Laos I found on arrival was a country under siege and without hope. Long, sad lines of refugees waited to cross the Mekong River into Thailand, seeking relief from the oppressive Pathet Lao and Vietnamese regimes now ruling their war-ravaged country. We visited the Thai refugee camp near Nong Khav, on the Mekong, across from the once-proud Laotian capital of Vientiane, and tried to capture on tape the heartache and struggle of a displaced people.

The Vietnamese presence in Vientiane and in the smaller, outlying villages, was everywhere apparent. Officially, Laos was no longer an occupied country in that summer of 1979, but the Vietnamese troops had not yet withdrawn. Lou Kidd and Larry Smith were able secretly to record the omnipresent Vietnamese soldiers, as we trekked through the country under government escort.

After our first foray into Laos, we retreated back to Thailand, to plan our next move and recharge our batteries. The good works of American missionaries seeking to rebuild the area was a strong story, but it was not the giant we had seen, despite government efforts to sanitize our tour of the country. The story we wanted to tell, the story we had to tell, was about the guerilla resistance movement of the Laotian rebels seeking to reclaim their country from Communist outside rule.

Bangkok was rife with the western flotsam of the Vietnam War. American GIs—attracted by the cheap drugs, cheaper hookers, and the exotic intrigue of life at the edge of the free world—still littered the city. The discharged and the deserters were like hungover conventioneers who had missed the bus home. The city was an exotic and intoxicating mixture of East and West, and we set out to soak up its various and unseemly pleasures. One evening with Peter, I discovered a rowdy strip-joint called the Cowboy Bar. We were excited by the idea of heading back into Laos illegally and were burning off some excess energy in anticipation of our adventure.

I was pulled from the revelry by a tap on the shoulder, and I spun around to find a beautiful American woman.

"Hi, Geraldo," she said.

"Hey." I figured her for one of the hookers working the room—why else would a beautiful woman be in a seedy place like this?—and I started to come on to her the way I would have come on to a hooker: "Hi, sweetheart, what's a nice girl like you doing in a place like this?"

She stopped me and said, "I'm not working here."

"Oh," I said. "Sorry."

As it turned out, this lovely expatriate was fleeing an arranged marriage set up by her wealthy Connecticut WASP family. She told me she was never going back to her fiancé and was planning instead to marry the next man she met who would leave his job and get a sailboat and take her around the world. That was her dream. I told her I was in no position to make her dream come true, but saw no harm in our keeping each other company.

I invited her to stay with me at the Oriental, the city's most opulent hotel—twenty employees for every guest, the guide books boasted—and she agreed. And so we started an urgent, but finite affair. The relationship was notable for its lack of bullshit. I was open and honest about my marriage to Sheri, and about my intentions to stay married. Sheri was about seven months pregnant at the time, and I made it very clear to my unexpected lover that my life was half a world away.

Over the next several days in Bangkok, plans for our return into Laos took shape. Peter Lance unearthed an ex-CIA operative named Robert Schwab, a short, tough former Marine who looked like a page out of Soldier of Fortune. Schwab, and an ice-water-brave Thai army officer, agreed to take us back across the river into Laos, and behind the Vietnamese lines to meet with the guerilla rebels. He also held out the promise of proving, definitively, whether or not there were still American prisoners of war being held in that country.

What an exhilirating adventure this was turning out to be. I did not serve in Vietnam and, as I mentioned, always felt quietly guilty about that. Here, I thought, would be my chance at enemy territory, and my opportunity to serve my country by locating (and liberating?) America POWs. In my head, I made myself over as Rambo, years before the character was ever invented.

The self-assumed mission was filled with danger. For one of the few times in my broadcasting career, I was afraid—for myself, and for my crew. It was a fear of the unknown, compounded by specific fear of this particular enemy. In 1979, there was still an aura of invincibility about the Vietnamese. They had defeated the French, and then the Americans, and they were resourceful and ruthless. We had no idea what awaited our late foray into this once and forever war, but I was certain that if our efforts were found out— an American television crew, behind the lines!—we would be treated harshly.

Despite fear and uncertainty, we made preparations for the trip. We were too far along to turn back. Before we left Bangkok, I returned to my lady friend at the Oriental. I swore her to secrecy and told her of the plan to go behind the lines. I wanted that edge on our romance. I wanted her to know that I could die the next day. The illicit danger lent special fuel to our passion, and I carried that energy with me into the field as night fell.

It was pitch-black when we arrived back at the border with Schwab and the adventurous Thai army officer. We were scheduled to meet four Lao freedom fighters who would take us back across the river into their occupied country. It was raining relentlessly. We waited on the outskirts of a tiny village, in a shack near the muddy bank of the Mekong, the hard rain beating on the corrugated aluminum roof. We waited for three hours. I slept off and on and wondered if our guides were really coming. Maybe they'd been attacked on their way across. Maybe it was a setup. Maybe this wasn't such a good idea.

Three of the four freedom fighters finally arrived on our shores. The fourth had been killed by a land mine. His chewed remains were in one of the boats, pulled from the field in the Southeast Asian tradition of denying the enemy knowledge of its battle successes.

Finally, our crew had to make a decision. The dark, the jungle rain, the dead body . . . all of it mixed together to leave us feeling uncertain. We were exhausted, scared and soaked to the bone. It was crunch time. In the glow of our flashlights, we made our next moves. For me, it was a no-brainer.

"I'm going," I announced, stating the obvious. I don't think anyone there thought I would back down. No guts, no glory. No power on earth could have kept me on the Thai side of the river. The crossing, and the adventure awaiting on the other side, loomed as the last great story. It was courageous and noble, and the moment had all the earmarks of martyrdom. In some ways, strangely, the substance of the story was not as important to me as the test of courage. This was my chance to exorcise the ghost of Vietnam. "How 'bout you, Lou?" I said. "You coming?"

Big Lou Kidd, veteran cameraman of Cambodia and Vietnam, was the only indispensable crew member. The odyssey had turned far more perilous than the offical trip he had signed on to film, and I was not entirely sure that this quiet, overweight, and self-effacing pro had the balls to continue.

"I'm coming," he said.

I turned to Peter Lance. "What about you, Peter?" I said. "You in?"

"You're talking about a life here," Peter said, vaguely.

"That's right," I acknowledged. "We are. We also need someone here."

"Then I'll stay."

"That's cool," I said. "Larry, why don't you stay back with Peter and work this end?"

"Great," he said, relieved at having the decision taken away from him.

Schwab and the Lao-speaking Thai officer stepped into their wooden canoe, as Lou and I loaded into ours and made our good-byes. With our rebel escorts, we set out in the predawn darkness in four boats. The rain thinned to a slow trickle. Our boat started to take on water as soon as we started to cross, and we bailed as we paddled to the other side.

We made it across in anxious silence and were met, thankfully, by about forty Laotian rebels, armed by the residue of the region's past wars and supplied by the supportive villagers who met up with them at various jungle checkpoints. Introductions were hastily made, and then we quickly set out on a thirty-mile inland trek, heading for our first encampment. As dawn broke, I remember thinking how ironic it was that the Vietnamese had long used the jungle and the night as allies against American military forces, and here we were, setting out with a rebel army using the same jungle and darkness as shields against them.

We walked for nearly eight hours, through mud and streams and heavy brush, until, finally, we came to a creek and a small clearing. There, we were met by neighboring villagers supporting the resistance effort, who as much as the freedom fighters were the lifeblood of the movement. Without force and firepower, the effort would flounder; without food and intelligence, it would die.

As we ate our evening meal, I interviewed some of the rebels and learned for the first time what it was, really, that they were fighting for. These people had no political ideology, and no fixed plan for the retaking and rebuilding of their country. All they knew, they said, was that Laos was their country, and they would not be made to live in abject poverty, under an oppressive outside regime. Theirs was a hopelessly unwinnable war, but to them it was also unavoidable. They were fighting for their freedom and for their country. They had no hope of victory, but they had no choice but to fight.

During these interviews, our Thai translator told me the guerillas were wondering if I wanted to see an ambush. Jesus, I thought, yes, but not if they were stunting for the benefit of our cameras. I had been extremely sensitive to the charges of staging ever since the Roger-Grimsby–inspired rumors had followed me back from Israel in 1973. Here, Lou and I would have gladly tailed along, cameras rolling, if the guerillas showed any kind of momentum of their own for the attack. But they were looking to me for their cue, and I wasn't giving one.

There was no ambush.

On the morning of our second day we were met with two terrifying developments. First, a heavy, Russian-built helicopter flew over our encampment, just a couple hundred yards away. Apparently, its crew never saw us. As it flew, almost directly overhead, I remember experiencing an almost drunken feeling of utter lack of control. The second piece of bad news was that the Vietnamese were in the area. We broke camp and retreated farther into the jungle. Lou and I were faced with a dilemma: Do we accompany the freedom fighters to an unknown destination and for an indefinite period of time? Or, do we wrap the piece here, thirty miles inland, after having tasted the resistance movement and recorded it for our viewers? We had not seen the evidence of American POWs promised by the quixotic Mr. Schwab, but we still had a tremendous scoop, and riveting behind-the-lines footage.

(A footnote: Schwab later made headlines, in August 1986, when he was freed from Vietnamese captivity, after trying to slip into Vietnam to rescue a girlfriend. He built a seventeen-foot plywood boat, stocked it with fifty plastic jugs of water, a plastic sextant and three small radio transmitters, and attempted to sail the South China Sea to "capture the imagination" of the Vietnamese and return with his long-lost lady love. Instead, the only thing that got captured was himself; the Vietnamese threatened him with a slow and painful execution unless he confessed to being an American spy. Schwab was so terrifed that his interrogators would carry out their graphic threats that he struggled to slice his handcuffed wrists with a piece of mirror. He was held in solitary confinement for more than a year and ultimately released.)

We chose to return to the Mekong, although that decision was not without its own peril. Unless we could successfully rendezvous with a second group waiting to guide us across the river, Lou and I, with Schwab and the Thai officer, would have to leave our bags behind, and proceed on our own. We did not know these jungles, and had only a rough idea of where we were headed. Also, we had no way of knowing if we could relocate the canoes that had taken us across the river two days earlier. We worried we would have to swim back across to Thailand and safety.

Happily, we were met halfway by other freedom fighters, who escorted us the rest of the way to the river, where our canoes were stashed. As we waited for darkness, we could hear the Vietnamese patrolling the area. They were actually close enough that we heard their voices. We waited in silence as they passed, hoping that they would not discover our dugouts. Then, cloaked by nightfall, we crossed the Mekong. As we left that hostile shore, it occurred to me that while we were home free, the rebels still faced the impossible prospect of fighting their unwinnable war.

I found Peter Lance holed up in the small Thai village of

Kemmarat, in the hotel nearest to our crossing. He had been in cryptic communication with ABC News in New York, trying to inform them that the crew was running behind schedule without alerting the Vietnamese army of the American television crew in its midst.

We had a triumphant, beer-swilling reunion. Then we drove back to Bangkok, collected our supplies, and headed directly for the airport. I did not seek out my American lady-friend. The premise of our relationship had passed; our being together had only made sense within the confines of that moment. Ironically, I did meet her again, several years later at a New York disco. She had returned to Connecticut, in despair of ever finding her Captain Courageous to sail her around the world. Sheri and I had separated by then, and I was at least theoretically available. I had even purchased a big sailboat—the *New Wave,* a forty-four-footer capable of girding the globe. But our changed circumstance did not encourage romance so much as it turned it off.

I was on the next flight, with my crew, to Los Angeles. After a stop at the L.A. bureau to put together a series on the Laos journey for network radio, I went on *World News Tonight* and broke the story of defiant anti-Vietnamese rebels seeking to win back their country. I ran a clip of our adventure and teased the material for our *20/20* broadcast later that week. We wound up running the story in two parts. And, truthfully, there was enough material for a third segment. The story was a coup, for the newsmagazine and for me. I had proven, once again, that I was unwilling to back down, no matter what. This was well before Gunga Dan Rather went behind the lines in Afghanistan, to much greater fanfare (and, ultimately, derision). What we had done was bring back exclusive footage of a small band lashing back valiantly at Vietnamese oppressors who had already proven too wily and formidable for the whole of the American military, or at least its commanders in Washington.

"The final irony," I told Hugh Downs on the air, as we came out of the story's second segment, on Thursday, June 7, 1979, "is that more than fifty thousand Americans died during the war in Indochina. They died fighting to prop up one corrupt regime after another. They died without ever finding the good guys."

BETH ISRAEL MEDICAL CENTER

My son Gabriel was born on July 2, 1979. He came five weeks early, and caught us completely by surprise. Sheri and I still had three Lamaze classes left to take, and I still had some thinking to do about how to fit a child into my life. Of course, even if Sheri had carried Gabriel to term, I would not have had everything figured out. In fact, it would take me years before I got a handle on being a husband and father.

Sheri's water broke just before midnight on July 1. We were lying in bed, at 41 Central Park West, when she leaned over and said, "Geraldo, it's time."

"Jesus," I said. "It can't be. The baby's not due for another five weeks."

"It's time," she insisted.

Like legions of men before and since, I panicked inside, but tried to maintain composure. "What do we do?" I said. "Let's call the doctor. What's his name?"—I could not remember his name—"Do you have his number?"

We eventually reached the doctor at home, and he told us to wait until morning before leaving for the hospital. I don't think either of us slept. I paced and worried. Sheri, as in control as ever, packed, joked, and assured me that all was well. With first light we were in a cab heading downtown to Beth Israel Medical Center, the hospital where I was born, thirty-six years earlier.

I was a bundle of emotions as we proceeded to the maternity ward. Of course, Sheri was a much bigger bundle, with a lot more on her mind, but I was in my own head. I thought about being back where I had begun my life thirty-six years earlier. A firm believer in hybrid vigor, I thought about the wonderful hodgepodge of ethnic traditions we were passing on to this child. I flashed back to the abortions from my younger days and felt a profound sense of unease. I thought about the kind of father I wanted to be.

Ironically, I had been putting polish to a story for *20/20* about the effects of alcohol on unborn children, and delivery rooms were on my mind at work and at home. The piece started as a kind of follow-up to "The Littlest Junkie," but we shifted our focus when we realized that the alcohol angle would have a greater impact on a larger segment of our audience. The story, which we called "In Utero," was scheduled to air in three days, and after getting Sheri settled in the delivery room, and hooked to a fetal monitor, I was back and forth to the pay phone. I spoke often to David Meyers, the producer of the piece, checking on late-breaking developments and making editing cuts over the telephone.

I needed to get the piece done, but more than that, I needed the distraction. I was scared to death about this baby, about what Sheri was going through. I couldn't help her. I made the trip between that pay phone and the delivery room at least two dozen times. I was on a deadline and a lifeline, both.

I desperately wanted a boy—for all the usual macho reasons—but I had spent the past weeks telling everyone who asked that I was hoping for a girl. I even managed to convince myself. I did not want to be publicly disappointed, and I did not want to be disappointed in my own heart. I needn't have worried. There was an intern, from India, who was in the delivery room with us, and when Sheri gave her final push and this doctor told me it was a boy, I let loose with a triumphant shout. I was overjoyed. I raced over to Gabriel and counted all his little fingers and toes, and when I saw that they were all there, I shouted out again.

Gabriel was a sickly baby. He was just over six pounds, which is a healthy weight for a baby born five weeks premature, but he was jaundiced. Sheri and I had to make a decision, immediately, whether to change the baby's blood to reverse the condition, or to put him under special lights to accomplish the same result. We were barely parents, and here we were being asked to make a significant decision on our child's behalf. Responsibility (and a feeling of frustrated ignorance) washed over me. What was the best way to go? The safest?

Our doctor was one of the most prominent hematologists in the city, and the idea of the alternative therapy, placing our infant son under harsh lights, seemed high tech and futuristic. We decided on the blood route. These days, my inclination would be to avoid such a transfusion if at all possible, but back then nobody worried about an infected blood supply. Gabriel rebounded quickly, and within five days he was home.

His birth encouraged me to turn over a new leaf in my

relationship with Sheri, but not before I raked over an old one. I celebrated Gabriel's birthday (and my own, two days later), while he and his mother were still in the hospital. I called up the twins—my two coeds from the basement boiler room at *Eyewitness News*—and we spent a final night in the tangle of each other's arms. The encounter seems heartless to me now, in the retelling, but our lovemaking was a personal celebration for me, and the way they chose to share in my happiness.

With that despicable deed behind me, the year after Gabriel's birth marked the golden period of my marriage to Sheri. I was a good and faithful husband, and a stay-at-home father. When I wasn't out on the road on a story, I was home with my wife and child. It wasn't as though I consciously set out to be on my best behavior; there was just no place I would have rather been than with wife and baby. I belonged with them.

Gabriel gave my life meaning and purpose. I had an heir. He was a yardstick to measure my life by, an affirmation of my existence, a reason for living.

What Gabriel's birth did not change, it tempered. I would still go out on assignment with little regard for my own safety; I would still think, it's okay if I get shot, as long as I get the story. The difference now was the afterthought: Yes, it's okay to go down with the ship, but it would be nice not to. It would be nice to be around to watch Gabriel grow up. I never had a death wish so much as a heroic fatalism. Gabriel didn't change that, but he was always on my mind. Each night when we were apart, I would (and still do) search the heavens for the first visible star. I pretend it is him. I tell him I love him, God bless, sleep safely my son, I'll see you soon.

CHAPTER TWELVE

MEMPHIS

From a commercial point of view, my finest hour at *20/20* came on Thursday, September 13, 1979, at 10 P.M., eastern daylight time. It was, arguably, the program's finest hour as well. It could not have come at a better time.

The entire hour of *20/20*'s first regular season weekly broadcast was devoted to the Geraldo unit's special report on the cover-up surrounding the facts and circumstances of Elvis Presley's death. The news-making, attention-getting segment, based on months' long investigation conducted by Charlie Thompson, Danny Goldfarb, my brother Craig, and me cemented the program's reputation as a hard-hitting, serious newsmagazine, and signaled the entire network news community that our team of producers and reporters was out to change the face of broadcast journalism.

Our investigation was actually inspired by Howard Hughes. In February 1979, in a report that proved extremely popular with viewers, we took a startling look back at the bizarre last years in the life of the reclusive billionaire. The resulting segment was one of the most talked-about pieces we had ever done for *20/20*, and it started me thinking of possible variations on the theme. If it worked with Howard Hughes, it would work again. I remember brainstorming with Charlie Thompson, casting about for another larger-than-life celebrity who had lived and died under mysterious, or at least unexplained circumstances. John Kennedy? I had done that already for *Good Night America*. James Dean? Too obscure. Elvis? Yes. The King.

Elvis seemed a natural fit, and we set out to produce a standard fifteen-minute piece to run on the second anniversary of Elvis's death on August 16, 1977—a *20/20* Thursday.

My relationship with Elvis Presley dated back to West Babylon High, when I took my place alongside millions of American high school students as a die-hard fan. His music was the soundtrack for my growing up; more, I saw his bold rebellion and confident swagger as aspects of character to be admired and emulated. I styled my teenage persona after his. Later on, when the Beatles stormed the airwaves, Elvis was supplanted as the exemplar of taste (and sight and sound), but his influence on me, and on many in my generation, never diminished.

I had the great fortune of meeting Elvis Presley, finally, in June 1972, just prior to his first concert appearance on a New York stage. Jerry Weintraub had recently reached agreement with Colonel Tom Parker to manage Elvis's concert tours. Jerry arranged a private audience with the King, backstage at Madison Square Garden, and the moment was like seeing Mount Rushmore. Elvis was dressed in the Vegas-type garb that characterized his later career: a powder-blue jumpsuit, with a plunging neckline and cape. He was all sequins, rings, and medallions, but I looked past the costume and saw only the blue jeans and black leather of his earlier years.

The meeting lasted only ten minutes, Jerry and I were the only outsiders in the crowded, cinder-block Garden dressing room. Colonel Parker was there, along with Joe Esposito, Charlie Hodge, and assorted members of Elvis's entourage. Elvis was preparing for a press conference, which I was planning to cover for *Eyewitness News,* but I arrived in his dressing room without camera or pencil. There was a swirl of activity around Elvis; he was the center of everyone's attentions. Someone was putting the finishing touches on his jet-black hair; someone else was sorting through his considerable jewelry. I remember Elvis from that brief first meeting as being extremely polite, almost to the point of awkwardness. He kept calling me "Sir," and it sounded oddly natural coming from his lips. I told Elvis about the time in junior high school my father took me to Robert Hall, to buy my first suit, and the salesman asked who my favorite star was. "Elmwood Prescott," I answered, the point of the story being that, at least to that thirteen-year-old kid, Elvis's image, and music, burned brighter than his unusual name. I asked him why he had waited so long to make his New York debut (not counting, of course, his various television appearances, including the famed Ed Sullivan broadcasts), and he told me he was never really sure that New Yorkers cared for him the way the people in the rest of the country did. He thought we were too citified to appreciate a country boy like him. He was down-home and overly cordial, a royal bumpkin calming a star-struck city slicker.

I made my good-byes (at Jerry's subtle signal, indicating my welcome was worn) and joined the bustle of reporters assembled for the backstage press conference. I managed to muscle my way to the front row, where my crew waited. Throughout the press conference, Elvis kept nodding to me to ask him questions. After our brief dressing room meeting, I was a familiar face to him, and he let me dominate the proceedings. I asked the first six questions, and the exchange started to look more like an interview than a press conference. It was a thrill and a scoop.

Five years later, on the night of his death, I scored another professional coup when I was asked to anchor ABC's late-night obituary broadcast for ABC News, a ratings triumph tainted by the tragedy of Elvis's death and by the faint rumblings of his drug use. On *Good Morning America* the morning after his death, I crawled all over Red West and Sonny West, Elvis's former bodyguards, and journalist Steve Dunleavy, authors of the just-published book, *Elvis: What Happened?*, which chronicled Presley's alleged drug addiction and dangerously erratic behavior. The initial reports coming from the Shelby County Medical Examiner's Office in Memphis indicated that Elvis Presley had died of heart failure, and I refused to believe anything else contributed to the death of the King of Rock 'n' Roll.

I was blind, but I wasn't deaf. Over the next two years I heard enough evidence to suggest that Elvis had a significant drug problem, and that his estate, with the help of various high-ranking Shelby County officials, sought to keep this fact from Elvis's still-adoring public. And so, with the exhilirating prospect of unearthing a scandalous medical-legal controversy surrounding the death of one of the most popular entertainers of all time, I dispatched Charlie Thompson to his native Tennessee to see what he could see.

Charlie, a former reporter for the *Memphis Commercial Appeal*, immediately teamed with his brother-in-law Jim Cole, another local newspaper veteran then working as a free-lance writer, and the two men launched a full-scale investigation. The massive effort would stretch on for months and would prove to be a model for the more extensive, broad-based, investigative pieces we would tackle in *20/20*'s future. Charlie and Jim immediately descended on the Shelby County Courthouse, where they examined Elvis's probated will, which revealed several suspicious loans to Elvis's personal physician, Dr. George Nichopoulos ("Dr. Nick"), totaling approximately two hundred thousand dollars. Charlie returned to the Commercial Appeal morgue to examine the "shit files," and there found an envelope containing a lab report for an E.A. Presley, dated August 17, 1977, based on a chemical analysis done at the University of Tennessee Medical School. The report revealed a laundry list of substances found in Elvis's body at the time of his death. A second report, prepared by Bio-Science Laboratories in Van Nuys, California, compared the therapeutic and toxic levels for the identified drugs with the actual serum levels found.

The Bio-Science chart, though filed in the Commercial Appeal morgue, had never appeared in the newspaper. It was never made public, despite its startling revelations about the condition of Elvis Presley's body at the time of his death. The newspaper, it seemed, had joined in the conspiracy of silence. The document it never saw fit to publish reported levels in Presley's body of diazepam (Valium), diazepam metabolite (Valamid), methaqualone (Quaalude), phenobarbital, pentobarbital, butabarbital, ethchlorvynol (Nembutal), and ethinamate (Placidyl) either below or within therapeutic ranges; it also revealed that codeine was present at a level approximately ten times those concentrations found therapeutically; morphine was found in concentrations approaching the toxic level.

Charlie sent me the reports by overnight mail to the West Coast, and we knew we were onto something bigger than either of us had imagined. We immediately lobbied ABC News vice president Av Westin and *20/20* executive producer Al Ittleson for more airtime, and for more time in the field. We started to think of the piece as a two-part story, and now targeted the show not for the anniversary of Presley's death (which fell in the slow, summer viewing period), but instead for *20/20*'s fall season debut on September 13.

Meanwhile, in a move designed to shake more fruit from the tree, Charlie brought suit on behalf of ABC News against Shelby County medical examiner Dr. Jerry T. Francisco in an effort to force him to turn over Elvis's autopsy. Dr. Francisco, we learned, was one of eight doctors to assist on the autopsy, during which no evidence of heart disease was discovered, and yet he broke from his colleagues and announced at a press conference that Elvis had died of a heart attack.

Charlie and ex-gumshoe Danny Goldfarb eventually enlisted the aid of former Los Angeles police sergeant John O'Grady, who at one time headed the LAPD narcotics unit and was by then working as a private detective to the stars. O'Grady had been hired nearly three years earlier by Vernon Presley, Elvis's father, and E. Gregory Hookstratten, his attorney, ostensibly to cut the singer's drug supply off at the source, and he stood now as a valuable store of information. Jack Kelly, the former head of the Los Angeles office of the DEA, assisted O'Grady in his private investigation and also became a tremendous resource for the *20/20* team. I interviewed both detectives, who corroborated the claims of drug abuse and fingered Dr. Max Shapiro, a Beverly Hills dentist known throughout the Hollywood community as "Dr. Feelgood," as one of Elvis's principal drug suppliers during the last months of his life.

Danny set up a preinterview with Shapiro and found a befuddled, middle-age man who appeared to practice dentistry without benefit of dental equipment. His office seemed better suited to a two-bit attorney than to a licensed medical practicioner. Shapiro appeared to have no clue what he was up against, or that he might have anything to conceal. Danny was actually able to sift through a pile of prescription forms on Shapiro's desk, while the addled dentist looked on: Each called for substantial doses of Percodan or Demerol, both strong, highly addictive central nervous system depressants frequently prescribed to a rogues gallery of the rich and famous. Shapiro, perhaps the only dentist in the country known to make house calls, was even scattered enough to offer his interrogator two Quaaludes, after Danny set him up by complaining of being unable to sleep from jet lag.

I followed with an on-camera interview the next day, and found Shapiro even more out of sorts than Danny let on. "How do you feel about being called Dr. Feelgood?" I asked.

"Dr. Painless would be all right," he said. The poor man damned himself with every word.

Later, with cameras rolling, I confronted Shapiro on the street outside his office building and asked to examine the contents of the medical bag he was carrying. He refused, but admitted he was toting narcotics. He also admitted there were no dental tools inside the bag.

During the twists and turns of our investigation, we also interviewed several members of Elvis's entourage, including Marty Lacker, the one-time foreman of the so-called Memphis Mafia and best man at Elvis's wedding to Priscilla, who offered firsthand reminiscences of his and Elvis's shared drug addiction. I also interviewed Ginger Alden (Elvis's young and lovely fiancée, at the time of his death, and the person who discovered his body in the master bathroom on the morning he died), and David and Rick Stanley (Elvis's now born-again stepbrothers, and two-thirds of the trio administering his medications), who offered a detailed account of the singer's final hours.

In time, we began to piece together a picture of Elvis Presley as a cloistered, paranoid, and powerful man whose friends and family looked the other way from his mounting addiction to various prescription medications, and whose wealth and fame secured him the confidence of doctors willing to prescribe those medications on an indiscriminate basis. There also appeared to be those among Memphis's medical and legal communities who were scrambling to protect what was left of the reputation of the city's favorite son and principal tourist attraction.

One of our biggest scores in this early going was an interview with Dr. Noel Florendo, a Memphis pathologist who participated in the autopsy. It was also, nearly, one of our biggest misses. Charlie, Craig, and a free-lance camera crew accompanied me to the interview. Dr. Florendo confirmed that the participating doctors agreed to announce that Elvis had died of unknown causes, and said that he personally found "no gross evidence of heart attack" in his examination. He also told me, on-camera, that he was shocked that Dr. Francisco, the Shelby County medical examiner, publicly insisted that drugs did not contribute to the singer's death. The interview was a direct hit, yielding firsthand confirmation of the autopsy contradiction. The candid admission was yet another volley of artillery in our mounting case against Shelby County, and a validation of our exhaustive efforts.

Indeed, the videotaped interview was too valuable to entrust to the overnight mails, or to the trunk of Charlie's car, and so I instructed Craig, my hardworking and usually reliable kid brother, to hand-carry the tape back to the *20/20* offices back in New York.

The next morning, in one of those unsettling, we'll-look-back-on-this-later-and-laugh developments, Craig called me at home with some disturbing news.

CRAIG RIVERA: I got back to New York and I put the tapes away in what I thought was a safe place, only when I went to find them later, they were not where I thought I'd left them. I was frantic. I called Geraldo, and he was frantic. Charlie went crazy. He wanted to kill me. It was a key interview. The last place I remembered seeing the tapes was on the roof of my car. I thought, you know, maybe I drove away with them on the roof. And so we were going to offer a reward, whatever. Next thing I know, after all this, I opened my briefcase and there they were. That was the safe place I had found to keep them. I just forgot. I walked into Geraldo's office to tell him, and I said, "Never mind," you know, like the

Gilda Radner routine from *Saturday Night Live*. That was big at the time. "Never mind."

With the Florendo tapes back in hand (and safely duplicated), the only glaring hole in our puzzle was Dr. Nick. He had dodged repeated requests for an interview, and as the September airdate approached, it seemed likely our piece would have to stand without note or comment from Elvis's longtime physician, although we did have a definitive paper trail linking him to his patient's overmedication.

Conveniently, at half past the eleventh hour, the State of Tennessee served up Dr. Nichopoulos on a legal platter, charging him with "unprofessional conduct, gross incompetence, gross ignorance, gross negligence, and gross malpractice concerning his dispensing of narcotic substances." The document filed against him listed twelve patients Dr. Nick was accused of overmedicating, including Elvis and fellow rocker Jerry Lee Lewis. According to the charges, in the seven months leading up to the singer's death, Dr. Nick had written prescriptions to Elvis Presley for more than 5,300 Schedule Two narcotics—Amytal, Biphetamine, Carbrital, cocaine hydrochloride, Demerol, Dexedrine, Dilaudid, Percodan, Placidyl, Quaaludes—and large quantities of injectible medications. Worse, on the day before Elvis died, Dr. Nick had allegedly prescribed nearly seven hundred pills—Percodan, Dilaudid, Dexedrine, Quaaludes, Amytal. It was enough medication to keep a small-town pharmacy stocked for a year.

On September 6, with our broadcast just a week away, I traveled to his Memphis office, located in a small mall, to make a last pitch at Dr. Nick. I told him he basically had no choice but to deal with me, on-camera, and he could do it on his turf or mine. If he declined me an interview, I threatened, I would camp outside his office with my cameras rolling, stick a microphone in his face when he left the building, and force on him the indignity of brushing me aside.

Dr. Nick finally realized it was better to confront me in his own office, in a refined, gentlemanly manner, than to dodge me publicly, particularly in light of the charges just brought against him.

Roll tape.

"The records indicate that, especially in the last year of his life, you prescribed medications to Elvis Presley in quite extraordinary large amounts," I started in. "Why?"

Dr. Nick's white hair and ashen expression made it look like he had just seen a ghost. "I can't comment on that, and I don't believe it is true," he replied.

"Well," I challenged, "the records we have, Doctor, and I will say this as gently as I possibly can, indicate that from January 20, 1977, until August 16, 1977, the day he died, you prescribed to Elvis Presley, and the prescriptions are all signed by you, over five thousand Schedule Two narcotics and/or amphetamines. It comes out to something like twenty-five pills per day."

"I don't believe that."

"Well, is it something you would like to refresh your recollection of, or something that you deny?"

"I deny it."

Nichopoulos looked like a scared animal caught in headlights. He fidgeted in his chair and looked away. His body language was even more damaging than his lame denials. Finally, he unclasped the microphone from his lapel and announced that the interview was over.

The exchange had gone better than we could have hoped, and worse than Dr. Nick could have imagined.

Incredibly, the state charges against Nichopolous were not immediately reported by the wire services, and for a short time it looked as if we would break the news on our broadcast. Such a scoop was rare for a weekly newsmagazine, and we moved quickly to make sure the piece was ready by the following week. Eventually, we knew, some other news organization would pick up on the charges.

We started to press Av Westin to give over the entire hour to our investigation. We had enough material to fill a two-hour documentary; there was no question our efforts could sustain a blockbuster hour. After screening our footage, Av agreed, although it was clear he'd made the decision with considerable reservations. If the show bombed, *20/20*'s prospects for a long, regularly scheduled prime-time run were indeed bleak.

On the Tuesday before broadcast, word of the charges against Dr. Nick finally broke on the national wires. Our exclusive was gone. Of course, it was unreasonable to assume a story like that would go unreported for more than a week, and remarkable that it stayed under wraps as long as it did, but we were hoping to make every splash possible with our Thursday broadcast. Instead, I placed a damage-control call to Jeff Gralnick, who had succeeded Av as the *World News Tonight* producer, and offered him a three-minute version of the Nichopoulos story. We beat the other two networks to the punch, and scored some tie-in publicity for *20/20* in the bargain. (My detractors even figured we planted the Tuesday leak to hype Thursday's show.) And so we restitched our story to accommodate the late-breaking news on Dr. Nick and waited for opening night.

I fielded my introduction from Hugh Downs at 10:01 P.M. on September 13. I opened the story by describing Elvis Presley as a giant on the American cultural landscape. I talked about his profound influence in terms every viewer could understand: He had sold more than one record for each family on the face of this earth. We showed footage of Elvis at his peak, and at the sad, bloated end to an otherwise-tremendous career. I knew we were about to topple a legend, and I took great care to let his fans down as gently as possible.

The *20/20* air-piece made the following points, in the clipped litany that has since become a personal trademark:

"Item: No real police investigation was ever made. At nine in the evening, on the same day Elvis died, before it was medically or scientifically possible to know for sure why or how he died, the Memphis police declared the case closed.

"Item: Elvis's stomach contents were destroyed without ever having been analyzed.

"Item: Dan Warlick was the man in charge of the medical examiner's investigation. Dr. Jerry T. Francisco, his boss, claimed Warlick had made an extensive search for drugs at Elvis's home, Graceland. In fact, Warlick admitted to us that he had never searched the house trailer of Graceland's resident nurse, the house trailer where all the drugs were kept.

"Item: There has never been a coroner's inquest.

"Item: The Shelby County district attorney was never officially notified or asked to determine if there were any violations of criminal law.

"Item: No attempts were made, even after the toxicological reports were completed, to find out where Elvis had been getting all those drugs.

"Item: All the photographs taken of the death scene, all the notes of the medical examiner's investigation, and all of the toxicological reports allegedly prepared by the medical examiner are missing from official files.

"Item: Officials of the county government believe there has been a cover-up."

It was ironic that these revelations were delivered to a network television audience by a man who had fiercely guarded the Elvis legend against the interlopers as recently as two years earlier, when there was enough evidence to invite at least casual skepticism. But, in fact, the interlopers were right. Elvis's legend should have been tarnished. He was a weak, undisciplined, and addicted man. Like Howard Hughes, he lived in terrible isolation, surrounded by sycophants and hangers-on who were beholden to the central figure for their livelihood. He created a bizarre and artificial world for himself, a world that ultimately destroyed him.

People still ask me, twelve years later, if I did not feel a certain responsibility to protect the Elvis legend. Who was I protecting? Whatever my emotions, Elvis was dead. And, anyway, what is a legend? In Elvis's case, it was an estate, generating profits for survivors who had done nothing to earn the money in the first place. Nothing I said during our program could detract from the genius of Elvis Presley as a musician, as a pioneer, as the first white man to recognize and champion the synergy between rhythm and blues and rock 'n' roll.

Reporting this piece, I said at the close of the broadcast, was "a melancholy personal experience. I wanted it not to be true."

"The Elvis Cover-up" edition of *20/20* became the most-watched public affairs program of the 1979–80 television season. We tallied a twenty-three rating (representing twenty-one million households), and a forty-three percent share of the viewing audience. It was, and remains, the highest-rated *20/20* ever broadcast. We won our time slot by a wide margin and finished as the third-highest-rated show that week.

We had arrived. Av took me aside the next morning to tell me the numbers. I had called ahead—I always check my ratings—but pretended not to know. "Magnificent broadcast," he said, clapping me on the back. "Magnificent."

"The Elvis Cover-up" was the perfect blending of a popular, racy topic with the precise, classic techniques of investigative reporting. We abolished gossip and hearsay from an essentially tabloid story and replaced them with hard-hitting documentation.

I did not change the world, the way I had with Willowbrook, but I look on the Elvis piece, in many ways, as another milestone. The story here was about an institution of a different kind—the institution of celebrity. It was about one person, but it was also about all of us. Its shocking truths did not change the way we lived, but it changed the way we thought about our heroes.

The broadcast instantly established *20/20* as a major player, able to compete on the same field with *60 Minutes*. It established me as top gun among *20/20* correspondents. It established bulldog producer Charlie Thompson as one of the best investigative reporters in broadcast journalism. And it established my team as the ass-kicking class of the industry. Agent Orange, Laos, and, now, Elvis . . . there was no story too big for our net, no truth too hidden for our microscope. Even a completed air-piece would not erase a story from our dockets. Indeed, we would return to the Elvis story three times in the next eight months, from the temporary suspension of Dr. George Nichopoulos's medical license through the grand jury indictment against him on May 16, 1980. Ultimately, despite our efforts and what seemed to me the overwhelming evidence against him, Dr. Nick was acquitted on all criminal counts, a year and a half later.

LEBANON

In 1979, Lebanon was one of the most dangerous, unstable places on earth. It was only natural that I go there.

Curiously, the impulse for this first foray into that volatile arena—in December 1979—came from an American evangelical group, which had established a twenty-five-thousand–watt gospel/ country-western radio station in South Lebanon. The High Adventures Ministries, of Van Nuys, California, developed the "Voice of Hope" signal to pour out the word of God to "Free Lebanon," the thin stretch of land (roughly the size of Los Angeles) along the Israeli border occupied by Major Saad Haddad. Haddad was a modern-day crusader—zealous, courageous, and naive. He and his mostly Christian militia sought to establish the enclave under his nominal control as an independent nation, allied with Israel. His grand scheme: to liberate all of Lebanon from Syrian and Palestinian forces. The radio station stood as a unifying force in a divided land; Haddad used the Voice of Hope to communicate with his troops, and with his people.

I was attracted to the effort by the Zionist stance of the Christian militia movement. I had always looked on Israel as both a Jew and as a North American geopolitican; it was a fortress state, the only pro-Western democracy in the troubled region, but the fact that it was also a Jewish state made the situation there personal. I had a lot of reasons for wanting this Voice of Hope Christian radio station to succeed—for one thing, it was antiterrorist, which in this part of the world translated as anti-Palestinian—but I also saw in it an opening to a broad, substantive story on the region. I wanted to use the radio station as the hook to examine the good works of the evangelists (and to juxtapose the odd twang of country music against the war-torn wasteland of the Lebanese countryside); but also, and mostly, I wanted to look at the efforts of Major Haddad and his Israeli allies to forge a peaceful coexistence.

Craig was with me on this trip. And since the enclave was cutoff from Beirut's airport, we entered through Israel. It was Craig's first visit to the Holy Land, so we used the occasion to take care of some family business. We traveled to the Western Wall in the old city of Jerusalem, where rent-a-rabbis had set up an unusual concession, administering quickie bar mitzvahs to visitors from the diaspora. I sprang for the forty-dollar fee and Craig, who had yet to make this rite of passage, formally became a man. Despite the low fee, it was a priceless moment. For me, the makeshift ceremony stood as symbol and ritual, representing at least the trappings of my religion if not the true spirit. For Craig, it was the unexpected embrace of a heritage long ignored. And for my family, with two sisters already claimed by the Church, it was a last stand against creeping assimilation. Mama was overjoyed when we returned home with the news, but it would be sometime before we got there.

"The nation of Lebanon is not merely divided," I wrote in my notebook when we finally crossed the border, "it's completely shattered, torn to pieces by fighting that's pitted the political left against the right, the Moslems against the Christians, the native-born Lebanese against the Palestinians, Israel against the Palestinian Liberation Organization. And to complicate the situation even further, as if it needed further complication, the northern part of Lebanon is under the occupation of thirty thousand Syrian troops, Syrian troops who say they are there to keep the peace."

I later used those notes as the on-air introduction for the piece.

Haddad was one of the most interesting figures I have ever met. He was a small man, and somewhat out of shape, but he had big, well-formed ideas. He looked older, and more tired than his years, but he impressed me as a thoughtful, caring leader. He spoke in a broken, halting English, but his passions and convictions broke through our language barrier. Haddad, a Christian of noble spirit, ran the South Lebanese army with significant local Muslim support, giving him a rare, broad-based coaltion in that fractioned part of the world. Bolstered (and bankrolled) by the Israeli Defense Forces, he had staked a claim on that six-mile slice of land and hoped to one day expand his base north, throughout Lebanon. Trouble was, he was flanked by Syrians, Palestinians, and United Nations peace-keeping forces with opposing agendas.

The Palestinian stronghold, on the banks of the Litani River near the Lebanese town of Sidon, was Balfourt Castle, a thirteenth century fortification. The Crusader castle dominated the landscape; you could see it from twenty-five miles in any direction. It was situated on the highest promontory in South Lebanon, the southernmost area of Palestinian-Lebanese control.

Haddad's Christian militia would regularly fire shells over the castle's thick, ancient walls, while the PLO lobbed back mortars in a nighttime artillery duel. We were invited to film the fighting by the South Lebanese army, and I jumped at the chance. What a strange battle this was. The United Nations soldiers, in this case Gurkhas from Nepal, manned a guard post on the Litani River, while the Palestinian-Lebanese and Israeli-Lebanese forces squared off, hidden in bunkers on opposing banks. It was all very civilized, and surreal. Haddad kept an outpost on the southern banks of the Litani, and he would send an armored personnel carrier once a week, from the Israeli border city of Metullah, for a changing of the guard and supplies. Once his soldiers rode through the hail of fire to the Nepalese, there was an unnatural calm at the center of the deadly storm. And then, as they made their way back out of the valley, they were assaulted again by enemy fire. The SLA personnel carrier was bombed, shelled, and machine-gunned on the approach and retreat.

This ritualized changing of the guard appealed to my sense of journalistic theater.

ANTON WILSON: Haddad told us that every time he changed his men, all freaking hell broke loose. Geraldo's eyes lit up, and he turned to me and said, "Great, you and I will go down in the personnel carrier and we'll film that." I was game to do that, but I told him I thought it was a lousy shot. I mean, it's going to be pitch-black, it's ten guys huddled into a little vehicle, we could do it in a closet in New York City and no one would know the difference. So Geraldo said, "Fine, I'll go down in the tank and you film it from the outside." And then I reminded him that it was not really necessary for him to be in there, that no one was going to know. It's not like we were going to chiron the screen or anything. "Geraldo's in here." He said, "You're right, I don't have to be in there, but I'm going anyway." And so he went, and nobody ever knew. I don't think they ever used the footage anyway. But he went, and they were under fire the entire time. He was absolutely hoarse when he got back. He was talking into a tape recorder the entire time. He was yelling, "We just took a hit," or whatever, into the tape, and then when he came back he was like a kid who had just come off his first roller-coaster ride. He loved it. He was absolutely enthralled by the experience, and obviously high from the experience, and he was smiling. He clearly got off on it.

*   *   *

I returned to Lebanon a year later, again by way of Israel, to produce an hour-long special entitled "The Unholy War." This second, far more substantial piece was sparked by one of the newest members of the Geraldo unit, a scrappy, eccentric, and often brilliant producer from Washington, D.C., named Barbara Newman. A veteran of National Public Radio, Barbara had extensive contacts within the Mossad, the Israeli intelligence arm, and we had been kicking around a number of ideas for a story making use of those connections. At one point, during this back and forthing, the Israeli consulate offered to cooperate with us on an investigation into Israel's preparedness against terrorism, and we embarked on what was to have been a multisegment report. We were given tremendous access, inside the Mossad, inside top secret radar installations, and inside Israeli Defense Forces headquarters, both in Tel Aviv and up north, in Haifa. We were allowed into Israeli prisons, with our own interpreter, to talk to Arabs being held for various acts of terrorism.

After about a month of research, we had assembled a terrific story; we needed only a capper, another hook to tie our loose ends together. It came to us courtesy of a high-ranking Israeli intelligence official. I did not name him in the resulting air-piece, and I will not name him here, but he was the undisputed spy master. Ruthlessly, and with fatal efficiency, he ran the Mossad's counterterrorism efforts in Israel and overseas, and was plugged into every corner of the region. This hook was so strong it redirected the entire piece.

"The Arab world has found its savior," this source told us one afternoon, when we were searching for leads on the terrorism story. "Peace is at hand." We listened for the rest of it. "This man will bring peace to Lebanon," he added, "and will make a treaty with Israel."

"Who?" I wondered. "Major Haddad?"

"No," he said. "Haddad is a sideshow. The real story is in Beirut. His name is Bashir Gemayel"—the youngest son of Pierre Gemayel, the founding president of the Christian Phalangist Party that ran Lebanon following World War II—"and he runs one of the militias."

"He's a warlord?" I asked.

"In a sense, yes, he's a warlord," my source explained, "but he is not like other warlords. He has killed, but only to consolidate his power. He is not a murderer. He is a strong, firm man, one who is not afraid to kill a fellow Christian if it will bring about stability."

I had to meet this guy. Any man who could convince a hard-core pragmatist like my intelligence source that he was the savior of the Arab world was someone to be reckoned with.

Our contact arranged a rendezvous, but it was in East Beirut. It was impossible to travel directly to Lebanon from Israel, and so we journeyed first to Rome, to cover our tracks. Then it was on to the Hotel Alexander, the only hotel on the Christian side of Beirut. The city had been divided since 1975; the so-called "green line" bisected Beirut the way Fifth Avenue cuts Manhattan, separating the Muslims to the west from the Christians to the east. As far as I knew, no big league Western journalist had ever spent a night on the eastern side of that city; the Alexander was avoided like the plague by the beat reporters, who stayed, instead, in the more opulent and politically correct Commodore Hotel on the Muslim side of town. As a result, world coverage of the conflict in Lebanon was given a persistent anti-Israeli slant, seen as it was from the Palestinian-Arab point of view.

We were treated like dignitaries at the Alexander. The locals were practically "salaaming" to us as we entered the lobby of the functional, utilitarian hotel. We arrived at night, and before we even checked our bags we were advised that Bashir Gemayel was on a nearby rooftop, observing the nightly firefight between East and West Beirut.

ANTON WILSON: We went up to a bombed-out building right on the front line, literally across the street from a PLO-Syrian–held building. It was night and very dramatic. I had hooked up a night-scope, an image intensifier, it's like what the military uses, and I believe it was one of the first times it had ever been applied to a video camera. What it did for us was let us shoot when it was pitch-black. Geraldo decided to go up on the roof of the building, to interview Bashir, with the firing in the background. And Bashir said, "I'm not going out there." Keep in mind, Bashir was an absolute daredevil, he never thought about his own safety, but he said, "It's stupid. You're going right out in the line of their fire."

And Geraldo said, "Yeah, but it'll make a great shot." Two of Bashir's soldiers agreed to go out on the roof with Geraldo, and he looked to see if I was coming. I thought it was absurd, and I said so. I said, "Forget the fact that it's dangerous, forget the fact that we may get killed, it's a lousy shot." It was a boring shot. Three guys crawling around in debris. It was silly. But, you know, Geraldo was very, very adamant about it. So finally I just agreed to do it, but I would not allow my crew to come out on the roof with us, so we used what we call a DMC cable, where the recorders and everybody else stayed inside and I was on the outside. Ironically, I was the one that was in the most danger, because Geraldo and the two soldiers crawled out behind this partition or wall or something, and I was out there with this phosphor from the videoscreen lighting up my face. And we got the shot, and it was used in the piece, but it was a stupid shot. It looked like three rodents crawling around in a garbage bin.

Bashir had a magnetism about him that was extremely impressive. In many ways, he was cut from the same charismatic mold as General Torrijos of Panama, but there was more substance to him, more thoughtfulness to complement his personality. He was in his early thirties, about five-ten, slightly pudgy in the cheeks but otherwise fit. He wore his short, dark hair combed straight back. He was not swarthy, in the way of many Arabs; in fact, his skin was actually quite pale. He spoke perfect English, but with a thick French accent. And he commanded a room like no regional leader I have ever known, then or since.

Bashir's vision was to unite Lebanon, all of Lebanon, by making it clear to the Muslim and Christian factions that the country's true enemies were the foreigners, the Syrians who were occupying vast swatches of their country. Unlike the quixotic Major Haddad, Bashir had a plan. He had made secret alliances with the Iraqis and the Israelis, who fed his Lebanese Forces weapons and intelligence, respectively.

At one point during our stay, after we had videotaped everything there was to see on Bashir's Christian side, we crossed the green line to West Beirut. It was a dangerous crossing, and a bizarre and frightening undertaking. At the time, it was a free-fire zone. The fighting along that fractious, bloody border was often at close range, with snipers an ever-present danger. We made the trip because I wanted to film the Palestinian and Syrian army positions. I covered the Star of David tattooed on my left hand with makeup and a Band-Aid, and met first with PLO spokesman Mohammed Labadi. He had his American girlfriend with him—a stringy-haired sixties relic from Detroit—when I interviewed him in PLO headquarters. Their offices were done up like the Young Lords' headquarters in Spanish Harlem a decade earlier: posters of Nasser and other great Arab leaders shared space with images of Lenin and Ché Guevara.

"We know you've been to Israel," Labadi said to me finally. It was a chilling moment, during which I had an absurd flashback that almost made me laugh out loud. In Labadi's place, I saw the ruthless Japanese officer from all those World War II B-movies, the guy with the beady spectacles, grinning as he interrogated his American prisoner. "Don't try lying to me," I heard the B-movie Labadi say. "I know your ways. I have studied in your UCLA."

My hands got cold and clammy. This guy was hip and dangerous. He knew not only who I was, but what I was about. He recognized my slant instantly as one aiding and abetting his enemies. It would have meant nothing to this man to see me dead; I wanted to be someplace else. I started to finesse my way around the charge, but decided that the truth would be our only out. We had been burned—our tracks uncovered, no doubt, by another journalist—and I chose to diminish that act of treachery by confronting it. I had been to the enemy nation, the Star of David was burned into my skin, I had nothing to lose.

"Yes," I said, "we've been to Israel, but I want to get your side of the story."

The strategy worked. At least it got us out of that building. Labadi agreed to show us only the Palestinian hospitals in the south of Lebanon, where we could film children who had been maimed in Israeli air raids, and women who had been beaten by the Israeli military. We were denied access to the PLO training camps. What he offered us, basically, was the same civilian victimization spin Saddam Hussein offered to CNN during the war in the Persian Gulf. He offered us his bombed baby-milk factories.

I didn't take it, although I was not fool enough to refuse the offer to his face. I thanked him, told him to make the necessary arrangements, and retreated with my team to the Commodore, vowing never to set foot in the PLO headquarters building again. If I went back there I might never make it out. I knew I could get the Palestinian-Syrian side of the story some other way, without the approval of the PLO. The way I got it, basically, was with good old American money. I bribed my way into the Palestinian refugee camps, and behind the Syrian positions on at the green line. I gave a Syrian colonel five hundred dollars and he gave me and my cameras access to everything. For a thousand bucks, I am certain, this guy would have sold me Syrian secrets.

The story, when we finally got out of West Beirut (an adventure in itself) and put it on the air, hit with the power of an explosion. The Israeli-Jewish community absolutely loved the piece, but lots of others hated it. The Palestinians complained bitterly that we did not even identify them by name, and that we did not once mention their "legitimate" rights to a homeland. We only mentioned them, they said, in the context of terrorism. Even in the *20/20* newsroom, the story was seen as Israeli propaganda. Despite the adrenaline rush of reporting the piece, the thrill in seeing our butts safely out of West Beirut, and the contagious fervor of Bashir Gemayel, I was embarrassed into rethinking my position on the Palestinians.

There were at least two sides to that story, and I had been fair to only one of them.

BARBARA NEWMAN (former producer, *20/20*; currently, Washington bureau chief and senior producer, *Now It Can Be Told*): I was crucified for that piece. And that was because it was so effective. We didn't talk bullshit. The rest of the press, you have to understand, including Peter Jennings and all the other Western correspondents assigned to the region, grew up with the Commodore Hotel mentality. They developed a Third Worldism, an anti-U.S., pro-Palestinian slant, based on the fact that Israel in their eyes became an aggressor in 1967, a militant, imperialist power. These people hated Bashir Gemayel. Everything they believed in, Bashir foiled. They used to talk about the massacres of the Christians, but no one ever talked about the massacres done to the Christians. It was one-sided, and people today admit it was one-sided, but anyone doing research on Lebanon still pulls up this old, biased stuff.

*   *   *

I returned to the region several times over the next few years, propelled by the high-stakes, blood-and-guts drama, by my inborn affinity for the Israelis, and by a growing bond with Bashir Gemayel. By 1982, Bashir had completely thrown in his lot with the Israelis. I remember going with him to a high point just outside West Beirut and looking down on the city at the exact moment the Israeli Defense Forces opened up an incredible artillery barrage. The shelling was so intense it created a dense fog of dust and gunpowder that lay thick over the west side of Beirut. We were on high ground because Bashir had been tipped to the pending assault, but both of us were stunned by the ferocity and extent of the barrage.

I stood with Bashir and Fadi Hayek, his boyhood friend and closest advisor, and I searched Bashir's face for emotion. I expected to find pain, or bewilderment, but found instead a strange smile. It was Lebanon, his Lebanon, under attack, and yet he was witnessing the humiliation of a people who had tormented him since 1975. Finally, his look seemed to say, the enemy of my enemy is my friend.

The PLO fled West Beirut, and the IDF occupied the city. I walked with Bashir through the Muslim sections and watched as he received the accolades of his people. They called him "Sheik Bashir," and it seemed he would lead Lebanon into a new era of peace and prosperity. He walked alone, without security; at the time, with the safety of his people attained, there was no reason to be concerned for his own. His friends told him to be careful, but he would not listen.

The provisional Lebanese government set a date for the democratic elections a few weeks away. Bashir announced his candidacy and I returned home to work on other stories, having scooped reporters in the Middle East with my access to the Lebanese forces leader. Here was a man, a visionary, an Arab prince who was going to be the president for all people, and I had, in effect, brought him to the attention of the American audience.

The following month, after his overwhelming election, Bashir held off the international press until the newly elected president could give his first interview to this reporter. Our *20/20* camera crew was on hand in Beirut to record the proceedings, but I conducted the exclusive interview via ship-to-shore radio, from my sailboat, the *New Wave*, anchored in the Atlantic Ocean, several miles off Long Island's East End. The interview, which aired August 26, 1982, one day after Bashir's election, was a personal vindication, and professional triumph.

Days later, while visiting the party headquarters of the Phalangist coalition founded by his father, Bashir Gemayel was killed by a terrorist bomb. He was definitely the target, although in the ferocious explosion a hundred others were killed or wounded along with him. The bloody hand of Middle East politics had reached out to strangle all hope.

I collapsed against the wall when I heard the news. My knees buckled, and I felt weak. Again, as with Michele Clark and John Lennon, I wanted to erase what I'd heard. A good, dear friend was dead; and, I knew, his land and his people would soon be tortured for having loved him.

I went on *Nightline* that night to reflect on Bashir's life and death, and the appearance turned into a kind of debate with Peter Jennings, with Ted Koppel acting as moderator. I went on first and talked about the slain Arab prince and his ancient family, and predicted that his death would lead to disaster and anarchy throughout the region. Next, Jennings came on to contradict me, and claimed that Bashir's older brother Amin—a self-centered disco king—would simply step in and take his place. Koppel did not give me a chance to rebut and it seemed I was once again stiff-armed by the network news establishment.

Thankfully, a Middle East expert came on and corroborated my view that Amin would never be the leader his brother was. Bashir Gemayel was a crusading prince. I may have overromanticized him, but I could definitely tell a strong, honest man from a weak, dishonest one. Within a few days, the leaderless and enraged Christian forces marched into West Beirut and massacred hundreds of Palestinian civilians, including women and children. It would never have happened if Bashir was alive, and it spelled the doom of his dream for an independent Lebanon.

AKRON, OHIO

After Elvis, and Lebanon, and the stories in-between, I went to work with a confidence I had not felt since joining the network news division. My reports won awards, viewers, and even occasional critical recognition. There was no stopping me, or so I thought.

AL ITTLESON: Geraldo had a strong relationship with Roone Arledge and he used to take advantage of that. If I talked to him about cutting a piece down from twenty-three minutes to eighteen, and he disagreed, he would go directly to Roone, over my head. And, for the most part, Roone would take Geraldo's position. Maybe Geraldo was right and I was wrong. I'm not saying that. But certainly, Geraldo knew how to take his problems away from his immediate superiors and bring them to a higher court. I give him credit for having that power. I didn't particularly like it when it was happening to me, but I recognized it for what it was. He had a lot of power at that time.

I thought I could do no wrong at *20/20,* but it wasn't long before I was made to think again.

One of my first stories of 1980, in February, was an Emmy Award-winning piece called "Arson For Profit," produced by Peter Lance with the cooperation of the Better Government Association. The report alleged that a cadre of North Side Chicago businessmen was buying tenement properties, insuring them for huge sums, and burning them down, often with no regard for tenant safety. Outrageously, the slumlords were allegedly operating in collusion with several insurance brokers. We named names and provided documented evidence of the misdeeds.

The businessmen blindsided us with a lawsuit. Even then, I thought we had these guys nailed, but flaws began to appear in our case after a well-funded and stubborn counterattack by several of those named. One problem: We had used a hidden camera to obtain damning audio and video evidence against the businessmen. That is a fine tactic in most jurisdictions, but it is illegal in Illinois. We finally settled the lawsuits, but the hassle set the frustrating tone for the entire year.

Another story, the following month, resulted in charges of plagiarism that were in many ways harder to dispel than those of libel and slander. "Formula for Disaster" examined the nutritional deficiencies of a soy-based infant formula. The report had all the earmarks of some of my earliest crusades for *Eyewitness News.* It had a clear villain—Syntex, the manufacturer—and sympathetic victims—the long list of wounded children and angry parents. Trouble was, most of our piece was (unwittingly) based on the investigative reporting of local newswoman Lee Thompson, at WRC-TV, the NBC station in Washington, D.C. Free-lance producer John Fager did most of the research for this report, and he borrowed generously from the WRC piece. I had assumed, naturally, that his findings were original to our project and followed up his leads quite unaware of the mounting breach of journalistic ethics.

The story itself was airtight and charged with emotion—I held Gabriel in my arms for my stand-up and said, "Any parent of an infant child has to be appalled by what this company did." But the fallout was as damaging to me personally as it was to Syntex, the offending manufacturer. I was attacked in the *Washington Journalism Review, The Washington Post,* and by WRC officials for lifting Thompson's work and passing it off as my own. I had never seen her air-piece, and had no knowledge of it during our research, but I was made to shoulder the charges of non-attribution because of the sloppy efforts of a free-lance producer. It was one of the most humiliating moments of my career, and one of the most infuriating. What cut most was that I had always gone out of my way to credit sources for my stories; network news rips off local stations as a regular method of doing business, but I always made a point to credit the station, and the reporter, for even the smallest contribution to one of my stories.

The galling aspect to these charges was that people wanted to believe them. I firmly contend that my network news adversaries were predisposed to believing the worst about me. It was like they anticipated it. If it played out that I cribbed my air-piece from local news stories, my colleagues could not have been less surprised, or more delighted.

I fought back the only way I knew how. Instead of sending John Fager into exile, I insisted he work with me on a follow-up piece. It took us the better part of a year, during which my involvement was interrupted by many other stories, but we kept at it until Lee Thompson's preliminary investigation stood merely as a foundation for a far more substantive piece of reporting. For this second pass, Fager uncovered the startling information that the formula manufacturer was aware of the deficiencies in its product before bringing it to market. We interviewed leading medical authorities and government watchdogs. We examined medical journals and company records. We reported the hell out of the story, and were awarded with a national Emmy for our efforts.

The score was settled, the cries of outrage quelled. I never worked with Fager again. He was a nice guy, and an otherwise fine producer, but he had subjected me to a year of embarrassment. The nadir came at a White House ceremony honoring the parents of the affected children for their successful campaign against the company; in front of the assembled press corps, President Carter made a point of applauding Lee Thompson, while unmistakably snubbing me.

As it turned out, I simply weathered that crisis to make room for a few more. In April, I was hit with the threat of another big lawsuit, this one over a story about the faulty aluminum wiring used in more than two million homes built between 1965 and 1973. Aluminum wiring, once thought to be a safe, inexpensive alternative to the traditional copper wiring found in most homes, was proven to be the cause of hundreds of devastating electrical fires in communities throughout the country. The report, which we called "Hot Wire," contended that the Kaiser Aluminum & Chemical Company, one of the nation's largest manufacturers of aluminum wiring for residential electrical use, ignored findings by its own research scientists that the aluminum wires posed a significant risk when grounded by steel-plated support screws. Indeed, the broadcast reported that the risk of an electrical fire in an aluminum-wired home was fifty-five times greater than the risk in a copper-wired home, and Barbara Newman and myself uncovered various confidential documents that indicated Kaiser officials were aware of the risks associated with their product.

"It's like a time bomb built within your walls," cautioned Consumer Product Safety Commission spokesman Robert Kelly, of the faulty wiring.

Kaiser denied our allegations but declined our repeated requests for interviews with company officials, and chose to defend itself in another forum. The company sought five minutes of uninterrupted (and unedited) air-time on 20/20, to make its case and invalidate our report, but refused to make a spokesperson available for follow-up questions. ABC News rejected the proposal. Kaiser then took out full-page ads, in major newspapers across the country, denouncing *20/20*, the "Hot Wire" report, and me. The company claimed it was the victim of "trial by television," and pressed its demands for equal time to answer our charges.

Nearly one year later, and after the beginnings of a lawsuit, the network caved in and allowed Kaiser to broadcast its short, unedited rebuttal on the premiere edition of a talk-back program called *Viewpoint*, which, for a time, preempted *Nightline* about once every two or three months. In exchange for the privilege of airing its case against me and ABC News on the same airwaves used to challenge the company, Kaiser agreed to drop its case against us.

The Kaiser-produced response was preceded by a pared-down version of the original *20/20* broadcast; this last was included to bring viewers up to speed (and reinforce our case against the company). Next, Ted Koppel interviewed me and Kaiser spokesman Steve Hutchcraft. *The Washington Post* noted the next day that Koppel seemed tougher on me than he was on Hutchcraft; I noticed it at the time of the interview, and found myself wondering which one of us was supposed to be Koppel's colleague. Hutchcraft claimed that there were more than two million fires in the United States in the previous year, and that no court blamed even one of those fires on faulty aluminum wiring. I countered by pointing out that Kaiser had settled several cases out of court, some for hundreds of thousands of dollars, before they could be adjudicated.

Hutchcraft argued that, in television news, the reporter stands as judge, jury, and prosecutor. I pointed out that allowing Hutchcraft, or another Kaiser spokesman, to appear live and unedited on the original broadcast would have been anathema to responsible journalists everywhere.

"The only way that the defense can make its point," he asserted, "is through the voice of the accuser." I countered that the charges against Kaiser originated in several federal agencies, not at *20/20*.

We debated to a draw, which I saw as a victory for Kaiser. Clearly, the arm of big business slapping back at any other correspondent would have been deflected by the network news establishment; when the slap was aimed at me, though, it was allowed to sting. The message I saw in this: If Geraldo did this investigation, and this company is saying that he lied, then he lied. Aluminum wire has since been banned in residential use.

The controversy surrounding my work continued. Two weeks later, in a report entitled "Injustice For All," I looked at the perversion of the legal process in Akron, Ohio, where a confiscated-weapons scandal had been festering for over a year. The story started with two honest cops, who managed to trace a gun that should have been destroyed, or kept in the possession of the court, through a pawnshop and back to a probate judge named James Barbuto. The corrupt judge, our investigation revealed, had been selling, keeping, or giving away weapons that had been in the possession of his court. But this was just the tip of the iceberg with this guy. He allegedly offered reduced criminal charges to arrested prostitutes in return for sexual favors, ran an escort service from a government-subsidized office adjacent to his courtroom, and wore women's undergarments beneath his judicial robes. Several local businessmen, we learned, also received favors from Barbuto's hookers. Most disturbingly, the judge was one of Akron's most powerful and prominent citizens.

"I am innocent of any wrongdoing," Barbuto told our cameras at the front end of our investigation. "Period."

As the special prosecutor's investigation got underway, the judge's confidence unraveled under the force of overwhelming evidence against him. We reported that he had hired a hit man—a local thug who had previously served time for various charges—to intimidate the women assembled to testify against him. I learned of these threats before the special prosecutor, and I got to the alleged hit man, William "Bobee" Brooks, ahead of investigators working the case.

My plan was to get Bobee to give up the judge on camera. I invited him to lunch, to discuss the case we were building against Barbuto, and to win his confidence. Bobee Brooks was black, about five-five, well-built, with a prominent gold tooth. He dressed like a pimp. We had lunch at an Italian joint favored by local racketeers. On the way out of the restaurant, the owner came up to me and asked me to pose for a picture for the restaurant's celebrity wall. What the hell? I thought, and I grabbed Bobee and said, "Come on, let's take a picture." (My policy is to take a picture with anyone.)

Despite the chummy lunch, and my pleas that he give up the judge, Bobee wasn't talking, and so we continued with our investigation. We used hidden cameras to film interviews with the hookers, who were too scared to point the finger at Barbuto for the record. I worked with the special prosecutor assigned to the case, Orval Hoover, and with the two police officers who had launched the investigation. Eventually, it came time to confront Bobee Brooks on camera. I had given him his chance to answer charges against him like a gentleman, but he had turned me away, so I went after him with every trick. I met him behind a hotel. My camera crew hid across an alley, in a van. He knew something was up, and so I signaled to my crew to show themselves. Bobee started to walk away from the camera. I followed, hurling allegations at his back. Aren't you the hit man, Bobee? Isn't it true that Judge Barbuto hired you to intimidate these women? I tailed him like an avenging shadow, but he kept moving. He kicked up the pace. Soon, he was running away from me and my crew, and we ran after him. You threatened to kill those women, didn't you, Bobee? Vic Losick, my cameraman, tailed us down the streets of Akron at a full sprint, his CP-16 film camera held rock-steady on his shoulder.

I wore a wireless microphone during the exchange, and we captured the sights and sounds of a local thug, running scared before the righteous indignation of the people's reporter.

We had a major story, and it hit like front-page news. A businessman friend of Barbuto's identified in the piece sued me immediately, Bobee Brooks sued, too, and Barbuto threatened to do the same. The local papers charged that my dramatic chase footage with Bobee was staged, and pointed to the picture we had taken in the Italian restaurant as proof that he and I were friends.

This was my fourth scandal in ten weeks, and I was reeling. I was fighting for my life. I was surviving each attack, but just barely, and not without cost. Each lawsuit or charge, however unfounded, whittled away at me. I worried there would soon be nothing left.

I offered the outtakes from the Barbuto piece to a panel of Ohio journalists and challenged them to prove their lying charge of staging. The businessman accepted a modest settlement, offered by the network's now-leery insurance carrier, and he agreed to drop his suit. Bobee Brooks was subsequently convicted on other charges and is currently in prison. And Barbuto was convicted of gross sexual imposition and intimidation, validating the case we'd made against him. He resigned from the bench.

But then, just when I thought I had dodged yet another bullet, I was hit with a massive suit by one of the women interviewed in the piece who contended we called her a hooker. She charged me with libel, slander, violation of privacy, surreptitious use of a hidden camera, and wiretapping. I went on trial in federal court in Cleveland. The trial lasted twenty-six days.

I actually leapt for joy when I was ultimately vindicated. It was a relief for me, an unleashing. I had been waking up each morning during this entire period wondering what new piece of shit had hit the fan. I started having nightmares as I moved from one crisis to the next. I had the same dream, almost every night. The setting would change, but the situation would stay the same. I could be in the jungle, or the desert, or the city. I would be challenged, always by something or someone bigger, or more formidable. Each night, no matter what the matchup, I was overmatched. And then I would fight. I would never lose, but I would never win. Invariably, I would wake up before I lost, just at the point where exhaustion and fear were about to claim me.

SEATTLE

My world took two unexpected turns in the midst of these protracted legal hassles. One nearly changed my career; the other turned my life upside down. On the professional side, Ted Turner offered me an enormous amount of money to join his then fledgling twenty-four-hour cable news operation. On the personal, I fell in love—again, and for the last time.

The Cable News Network offer shocked and flattered me. My old friend and Lower East Side roommate Leo Kayser had resurfaced to engineer the deal. (Jon Peters and I had, amicably, parted professional company after he and Sheri negotiated my then current ABC contract, and after Sheri later convinced me she could do the job just as well on her own.) A good old boy from

Alabama, Leo was very aware of Ted Turner and CNN. By the spring of 1980, the all-news, all-the-time experiment already had a substantial presence in the Deep South. "This man is going to be huge," Leo predicted, with remarkable prescience. "CNN is going to rival the networks."

I thought Leo was crazy. CNN had only cleared about ten percent of the country by that time. It was not available in New York or in Washington, D.C., and therefore had yet to impact on the country's political, financial, and communications power centers. Its prospects for long-term success were anything but certain.

But, crazy or not, I let Leo take me through the motions with Ted Turner. I flew down to Atlanta. The actor Walter Matthau was in Turner's office when I arrived, and the three of us small-talked about politics, Hollywood, and television news. It seemed an odd way to go about what was supposed to have been a job interview, but I quickly learned not to be astonished by anything Ted Turner did. He was practicing his putting during the entire meeting. He had a big, sprawling office, with picture windows overlooking Atlanta, and I sat and watched as he worked on his golf game.

Finally, Matthau excused himself, and Turner made his pitch. He offered me a respectable salary—about five hundred thousand dollars—and spiced that offer with a substantial percentage of company stock. He kept on with his putting throughout our discussion. I sat down with Leo after the meeting and we computed that, with any luck, the value of the deal, after the first eighteen months, would have eclipsed Dan Rather's then celebrated two-million-dollar CBS contract. The deal would have made me the highest-paid talent in the television news business.

I was floored by the offer. Leo urged me to take it, but I held back. My ego got in the way. No one I knew received CNN. Hell, whole chunks of Manhattan had yet to be wired for cable. Indeed, even Daniel Schorr, the former CBS newsman brought in to front the CNN news operation, was so disgruntled at not being able to monitor his own network in Washington that the company installed a satellite dish so he could watch himself on television.

Nevertheless, the CNN offer was too rich to turn down without thinking twice. And yet, I knew I could not work for a skunkworks news operation that could not even be seen in our nation's capital, no matter how visionary the enterprise or potentially lucrative the opportunity. At the very least, though, I wanted to parlay Turner's offer into a hefty pay hike at ABC. And so I formally notified the network of my CNN negotiations, all the while hoping Roone Arledge and his vice president for finance, Irwin Weiner, would step up with a raise substantial enough to make it easy for me to turn down the cable deal.

The strategy worked, and ABC gave me a thirty-three percent increase to one million dollars per year. One million dollars! Ten years after Al Primo hired me, on a handshake, at three hundred dollars a week, I crossed into the rarefied air of the salaried millionaire. It was a meteoric rise, and an outrageous amount of money. True, my lifestyle did not change much, making the leap from seven hundred fifty thousand dollars to a million, but my thinking about money was transformed by the magic plateau. For the first time in my life, I did not care how much anything cost. That was the practical meaning for me.

The new contract offered financial security, but I did not see it as a victory. It was simply one less thing to worry about. After the pummeling I had taken in the first months of 1980, it was a validation, an affirmation that I still belonged in the big leagues.

As for the love affair, well, it is the understatement of a lifetime to admit that it, too, took me by surprise. I had been (relatively) faithful to Sheri in the year since Gabriel's birth. I was very happy being a father and happy to let Sheri run virtually all aspects of my life. She had negotiated the blockbuster new deal, and my finances were in the best shape they had ever been. Our home ran as efficiently as our office. Our relationship had gone beyond romance; she was my partner for life.

But I was never any good at leaving well enough alone. C.C. Dyer, my breath-of-fresh-air personal assistant, had been promoted to production associate during the CNN negotiations, when it appeared we might lose her to another unit of the *20/20* production team. Suddenly, she was liberated from her desk to travel on stories. She looked different in this new light, transformed. She was, for the first time, available, out from under Sheri's vigilant gaze. The prospect rocked me, causing exhiliration and confusion, both. I had watched C.C. blossom over the previous two years into a remarkable young woman—un-selfconsiously sexy, funny, and buoyantly optimistic. She was totally unaffected by office politics, or the petty bickerings of network news. In the office, she was a reliably positive force in my professionally hectic and personally predictable life.

A daughter of privilege, nothing bad had ever happened to C.C. She operated in her own, fun-filled sphere, and I wanted to bring her world into mine. I wanted her to rub off on me. I wanted a transfusion of her excitement and vitality.

C.C. DYER: We were in Seattle. It was June 1980. It was late at night, and we were in this dive of a restaurant, a Mexican restaurant, with Charlie Thompson, Danny Goldfarb, and the rest of the crew. We were drinking margaritas. And Geraldo asked me to dance. It was a real fast dance, and we were having a great time, and then the next song came on, and it was a slow dance and he said, "Come on, let's dance again." So I said, "Okay," but really, what I was thinking was, oh, God, I've got to slow dance with my boss! And then he started to hold me tightly. Very tightly. Like lovers hold each other. It wasn't like a boss and his employee. And I remember thinking, God, this feels great! And then, suddenly, right in the middle of this slow dance, he just gave me the most passionate kiss. It went on for at least a minute. I was just melting. I just couldn't believe it. And then, we were still kissing, still on the dance floor, and Les Solin, our cameraman, came over to tell us that our food was here, it was on the table, and then that was it. I was totally flustered. We went back to the table and I could barely eat. I could barely speak. My heart was pounding. Everything felt great. I mean, the kiss felt great, the dancing felt great, he felt great.

We did not make love that first night. It was C.C.'s call, not mine. She retreated to her hotel room following dinner. I fought the obsessive temptation to beat down her door, disappointed and yet also relieved that the moment of truth had been avoided. C.C., I knew, was an elixir that would destroy my carefully constructed world, but I was compelled to take her. There were a few days more of desperate kisses as we traveled to cities up and down the West Coast. I felt like my life hung in the balance with each dramatic embrace. I weighed the implications of our pending affair, even going so far as to list all the reasons not to consummate our relationship. Still, I pursued her.

C.C.'s resistance made it tough to concentrate on the work, but the work was important. One of the stories we were working on during this West Coast swing was a major exposé on the pop psychology, behavior modification phenomenon known as Lifespring. Based in San Rafael, California, Lifespring was conceived by a charismatic businessman named John Hanley and marketed as a competitive cousin to the est movement. The story we were pursuing placed Hanley and his program in a very negative light, calling public attention to the recent suicides of several Lifespring disciples and alleging that the group was brainwashing its followers and bilking its investors. As a result of our damning piece, which C.C. associate-produced, Lifespring was forced to close more than half of its regional offices, and Hanley brought suit against me and *20/20* for one point six billion dollars. One billion six hundred million dollars! It was an outrageous figure, the largest sum I ever heard attached to a claim. (It was more than the gross national product of most countries.)

Ultimately, even before both sides began taking depositions, Hanley reduced his demands to seven hundred million dollars, and then to one hundred million dollars, and on down to a hundred dollars. He actually asked us if we would settle for one hundred dollars. He knew he had no case. Our story was accurate. We refused to settle, and Lifespring walked away empty-handed.

The Lifespring story exclamation-pointed the most litigious period in my career, but I mention it here because it was the first major story during which C.C. worked at my side. Sheri had traveled with me before, on countless assignments, but she was never the profound diversion that C.C. was on that first trip. C.C. was all I thought about and all I wanted. Oh, I concentrated on my reporting, don't misunderstand me, but underneath the work there was C.C. The earlier cluster bombs, from Kaiser Aluminum to Akron, Ohio, had been devastating, but I was able to dismiss the Lifespring lawsuit like nothing at all. It was for more money than all the others combined, but it was without substance and I was passionately preoccupied.

Finally, in Vancouver, three days after our first caress on that Seattle dance floor, C.C. and I went to bed together. "We're about to destroy our lives," I whispered to her, overcome by lust and doom.

C.C. DYER: The next morning, we met in the lobby of the hotel, and he told me he loved me. And I said, "You love me? How could you love me?" Whether he meant it at the time, I don't know. He could have been doing what he did with all those other women beforehand. I don't know. I was thinking, God, what is it with this guy? How can he say this to me? But he said it all the time, and he said it with such conviction. And I was used to WASPy guys who don't let their feelings out. They give you a kiss when you get married, and they make love missionary style, and I was just not used to this kind of a man. I was so totally confused.

I have seduced, and have been seduced by, many women with premeditated agendas. C.C. was not one of them. Still, this innocent was in an impossible position. She never in her strangest dreams imagined she would wind up in bed with her boss, a three-time married man thirteen years her senior. What was happening between us was so foreign to her, and upsetting, that she was even moved to say, only days after we first made love, "I can't live this lie. I can't stand this. I can't pretend anymore."

I was thrown by her proclamation. Despite my initial feelings of dread, I had no intentions of leaving Sheri. The specific thought had not even occurred to me. C.C. was heat and youth and urgency, but Sheri represented home to me, family and stability. I did not want to give up one for the sake of the other and, typically, saw no reason not to have both. It would be difficult, and complicated, but I thought I could manage it. I was shocked, then, that C.C. looked on our nascent affair as a public, permanent thing. How could she assume I was going to throw away my whole life to embrace her? The thing of it is, once she planted the notion, I could not get it out of my head.

Characteristically, I stilled C.C.'s restlessness and convinced her to keep quiet about our affair until we had a chance to sort things out. Back in New York, we enjoyed our stolen moments wherever and whenever we could find them. I rediscovered the basement boiler room of 77 West 66th Street (*20/20* had since moved its offices back to the old *Eyewitness News* building) and claimed it for our own. We disappeared to C.C.'s apartment on the slightest pretense. We rendezvoused at the seedy Cadillac Motel at Newark Airport, or in the limo on the way to a shoot. We were like two young lovers, groping through first fits of infatuation.

Sheri was wise to us by August, despite our attempts at discretion. She whipped into my office during a reasonably benign exchange with C.C. and saw instantly that there was something passing between us other than moon eyes. C.C., flustered, scrambled for the door, and Sheri shut it behind her. "What's going on between you two?" she demanded. "Are you messing around with her?"

I had long made it a practice to deny everything where infidelity was concerned, and I stonewalled Sheri's charges like the old pro I was. C.C., though, was unpracticed, and less inclined to charade. Sheri ambushed her the next morning and said, "Geraldo told me everything." It was the oldest trick in the book, and C.C. fell for it. She crumbled and started crying, and told Sheri more than my wife, the mother of my child, could have possibly wanted to know.

Sheri and I had a horrible bout that night. But first, she had to keep up appearances. She went to a party, celebrating the success of *20/20*'s first full year on the weekly schedule. I stayed home with Gabriel. When Sheri came back she became hysterical. She jumped on my back and started pounding at me. "How could you do this?" she demanded. "How could you throw everything away?"

I just stood there and let her flail. She was in a rage, frantic. Finally, exhausted, she slumped to the floor and sobbed. I walked out on the balcony and looked out at Central Park, at the skyline of the sleeping city, and thought about jumping. I had blown it. Once again, I had let my dick lead away from a carefully constructed and contented life.

Things shook out over the next several days to where I was no longer in control. Sheri arranged for C.C. to be reassigned to another *20/20* unit and then she took Gabriel and left for the coast. I was whirling from the sudden upheaval and sought to bury myself in my work. I went overseas. I embarked on an incredible odyssey—to Mexico, Italy, Pakistan—to learn everything I possibly could on the manufacture and trafficking of heroin, and to get away from the mess I had made of my life. The resulting one-hour *20/20* special, "Chasing the Dragon," was a compelling, inside, and informative piece on the international drug trade; reporting it was a rousing professional thrill, and an elaborate distraction to my troubles back home. I had to convince Av Westin to let me make the trip—he was never keen on international stories unless there was a significant domestic angle—because I needed to put as much space between myself and Sheri (and C.C.) as possible. I had never felt more emotionally adrift. I inserted myself into the most remote, exotic, and dangerous situations I could find. I didn't care if I lived or died. I didn't give a shit about anything. I dragged Craig along to produce the piece, and cameraman Bill Philbin to shoot it; my recklessness rubbed off on them, and yielded the most exciting dope footage ever broadcast.

CRAIG RIVERA: I had made a contact with the DEA, in Karachi, Pakistan, and he hooked us up with an undercover operative who took us into the tribal territories along the Afghanistan border, on the far side of the Khyber Pass. The tribal chiefs were dealing tons of opium out of that region. We actually got into the enclave of one tribal chief. The place was set behind these high walls and huge gates, all beautifully decorated. The guy had a whole fleet of trucks. I had "Buster," our hidden camera, in my bag, and I was filming, and Geraldo sat down with this guy and started dealing. And the guy said, "How much do you want?" And Geraldo said, "Fifteen hundred kilos." And the guy laughed. "I can get you fifteen thousand kilos." He started quoting all these different prices, to transport it to Karachi, or to Europe, or New York. And Geraldo turned to me during these negotiations and whispered, in English, "You better go outside and check the tape." If the tape had run out, the camera would make a loud click, and a big rewinding sound, and we would have been dead. So I went outside to reload the tape. There's no question they would have killed us. When I rejoined Geraldo, they had all gone into the back, which was where they kept all the dope. There was opium, tons of raw opium, drying out in the sun. So I was filming the opium, panning around with my bag, and I panned up to Geraldo, and he said to me, still in English, but out loud this time, "Why don't you come around here, I think you're backlit." These guys were giving us this tour of their operation, and Geraldo was giving me camera instructions.

*   *   *

I returned home several weeks later and, at Sheri's urging, attempted a reconciliation. I also attempted to get things going again with C.C. I failed at the former because the air had gone out of our marriage; I failed at the latter because I was not yet ready to commit myself to another woman. Three marriages had gone sour, and I refused to start on a fourth.

Still, I allowed both relationships to resume an on-again, off-again course. I hopped from Sheri to C.C. all through the fall of 1980. I went through the motions with Sheri because of Gabriel; if there was any way to salvage our relationship for his sake, I was determined to discover it. I kept going back to C.C. because I could not stay away. But I knew I could not maintain both relationships. I knew it was not fair to either woman, or to Gabriel, or to me, to even try. I was no longer in charge.

I decided to buy a boat and sail away from my uncertainty. In our on-again moments, C.C. auditioned sailboats for me along the eastern seaboard. Whether or not she was to be a permanent part of my future, I was practical enough to recognize her knowledge of the sea. In December, she located a gorgeous forty-four-foot Gulf Star sloop in Miami, which I christened the *New Wave*, symbolic of my change of life. The boat cost me about one hundred fifty thousand dollars, and represented freedom.

C.C. joined me on the maiden voyage, across the stormy Gulf Stream, to the Bahamas. I was, at the time, a lousy sailor, but the boat was a long-held dream. I loved the image of myself at the helm—master of my own ship, controller of my destiny— but I had a lot to learn. The boat was twice the size of the twenty-two-foot *Francina*, my years-ago engagement gift from Francine LeFrak, and about five times as complicated. It was almost more than I could handle. My hands were blistered and bloody, and not much worked the way it was supposed to. It's a wonder that I didn't wreck the boat on some Bahamian reef in those first days.

Coming from a small coastal town in Massachusetts, C.C. knew about sailing, enough to keep the boat on a steady course. But she did not know how to navigate or read a chart. I knew that much from the years at Maritime College, but repairing a diesel engine, or properly setting the big sails were mysteries. So the two of us set off on our first deep-water journey.

After a long, rough-weather sail through the Bahamas, C.C. and I parted in Nassau. She returned to New York, and I left for Malibu, arriving on Christmas Eve in time for some dishonest celebration. This odd juggling became a pattern over the next several months. Aside from the enormous pull of Gabriel, the only things keeping our marriage together were Sheri's grit, and my desire for peace and professional continuity. Sheri continued to run my office during this time, although her influence was mitigated by our obvious estrangement. Also, she had laid the groundwork for a year-long project—a one-hour *20/20* special profiling her friend Barbra Streisand and the making of the movie *Yentl*—and neither one of us was anxious to see those efforts lost in our split.

Meanwhile, I was doing my best to stay away from C.C. I was terrified of another marriage and determined to avoid one at all costs. I was even moved to write her a "Dear C.C." letter, intent on ending our relationship. Tattered by a decade of folding and unfolding, the letter survives: " . . . Six months ago, my world seemed complete. Domestically, I was bored, true. But the power-ful anchors of family, job, partnership seemed firmly planted. Then I fell in love and since that time, the lives of three people directly, and many others indirectly, have been in turmoil. . . . You are too grand a lady to sully any further in this unwholesome triangle."

I sought romantic preoccupations everywhere, but C.C. haunted me. I would whore around with models and actresses, any pretty girl that would turn up, anything to distract me from my redheaded love. Craig fixed me up with a tall, sexy blonde model. For some reason I can no longer fathom, I gave this woman a fur coat and brought her to an office party to show it off. It was a heartless move that sent C.C. reeling in humiliation and sorrow.

Every week there was another woman in my life. Most were forgettable, but some were quite formidable. One evening, I found myself after-hours with Bianca Jagger, the model/actress/activist ex-wife of my celebrity acquaintance Mick Jagger. We left a club together and seemed to notice each other for the first time. Of course, our public paths had crossed many times, but this was a private moment. We were both single, or at least uncommitted, and we flashed each other "hey! why not?" looks, and hopped into my rented Lincoln Town car. It was summer, and I was staying at the Seventy-ninth Street Boat Basin, on board the *New Wave*.

Bianca Jagger has always been an interesting and, in some ways, enigmatic character. She is exotically beautiful; ten years ago, this was especially so. She is also a politically aware Nicaraguan expatriate who apparently cares deeply about her homeland. However, she still has work to do, and a party profile to lower, before she can alter her image as frivolous and self-indulgent.

The woman I took home with me that night was not as wild as I would have hoped, and not at all frivolous. We walked through the marina's spooky underground parking garage, and up to the Hudson River docks. Once on board the boat, I turned on the stereo. We talked and danced, our bodies moving to the rhythm of the tide. After a while, Bianca pushed away. There was something intelligently hard-to-get in her eyes; she looked at me as though I had some nerve, expecting her to be intimate with me on our first night together. She did not say as much, but I took her stiff-arming to mean I had to invest a lot more before I began to see any dividends.

"You can take me home now," Bianca announced.

I stood immediately, fumbled for the car keys in my pocket, and gallantly reached for Bianca's hand to lead her off the boat. In my distraction, I dropped the keys overboard, into the Hudson. It was four o'clock in the morning, I had dunked the only set of keys to my rented Lincoln, and a suddenly disinterested Bianca Jagger was waiting impatiently to be taken home. What a moment. It was like high school, with me wondering how the news of my misadventures would spread. I wanted to shout, "You should have seen me when I was younger. I used to be cool!"

I wound up calling a limousine, and the brief wait for the driver seemed interminable.

It was the last time I ever saw Bianca privately.

The lost evening was typical of my lifestyle during this time. At work, I was aggressive and energized, turning out solid, sometimes spectacular stories that soon erased the black marks of the previous months. At play, I was equally aggressive, even reckless. My marriage, in all but the legal sense, was over. My relationship with C.C. was preposterously inconsistent, the victim of my own sabotage. An informal separation agreement gave Sheri the house in Malibu, but she soon claimed the apartment on Central Park West as well. After the initial shock of losing the nicest home I ever had, I did not complain too loudly about being displaced, because, at least, with Sheri back on the East Coast, my son was also near. When the weather was too cold for life at the marina, I took my promiscuity indoors, to a hotel, and, finally, to a furnished sublet apartment near Lincoln Center. It must have looked for all the world like I was having the time of my life. I was miserable. Life was pointless. Beyond work and Gabriel, there was nothing.

Ironically, it was Sheri who turned me around. In spring 1983, we were in London, on the set of the movie *Yentl*, shooting the final scenes of our Barbra Streisand special. Sheri and I were no longer together as husband and wife, although neither one of us had taken the necessary steps to make our separation official. But after almost three years of this strange limbo, even this scrappy woman had accepted the fact that we would never resurrect our life together, or reclaim what we once had. She turned to me one day, during a break in shooting, and said, "You know, it's obvious that you care for C.C. Why don't you just admit it and be with her?" She said it in a disparaging tone, but I got the message.

I went jogging later in Hyde Park, and Sheri's words resonated. It was a Eureka! moment. As I ran, I saw the source of my dissatisfaction. I was keeping company with many women simply to avoid being with the one I really wanted. I raced back to the hotel and called C.C. in the States. I wanted to share my epiphany and to make it true. She was skeptical, at first, but agreed to meet me at La Guardia Airport. (She was out of town on another story.) From New York, we boarded a prop plane for a long weekend on Nantucket. We were all over each other on that plane, reunited after two long years of heartache and uncertainty. At that moment, I could have died happy.

We arrived during Cape Cod's daffodil festival. Nantucket was fresh, spring-green, and awash with yellow flowers. We took long bike rides and stopped on the beach to make love. We made love everywhere. C.C. was all I wanted, and she was mine. At last.

GUATEMALA

Guatemala City, in early 1982, was a curious mix of old and new, an uneasy blending of stark, functional modern architecture and centuries-old Spanish Colonial. The Mayan people were also a study in contrasts—they seemed almost incapable of violence, and yet the country was among the most violent in the world. The city was also the center of international attention, leading up to what were to have been Guatemala's first freely held democratic elections in a generation.

I was drawn to the region by the fighting in the bush and apparent turn to democracy in the cities, lured by adventure and a potentially good story. The presidential election was won by General Angel Anibal Guevara, the candidate of the ruling military-backed coalition, with a plurality of the vote. Three opposition candidates were arrested, following their charges of widespread electoral fraud. Peaceful demonstrations and protests were planned, to call for a recount or new elections. Tensions through-out the city and the surrounding countryside were percolating to a boil.

At the start of my sortie into the country, I attached myself to the government's second battalion, to record the military side of the story. It was an elite unit, and veteran cameraman Carl Hersh and I went with them deep into the Guatemalan jungle. The journey was planned as a quick hit, not much more than a photo opportunity, but it turned into much more. Instead of allowing us a couple of hours of aerial photography, our assigned helicopter pilot left us off and said, "We'll pick you up in a few days." We were ridiculously unprepared for a long stay on the wild side, but we had no choice. And so we tagged along with this rough and tumble group, up and down the jungle hills, looking out for rebel fighters. The soldiers in our group were Mestizos, a mixed-blood people eighty percent Mayan and twenty percent Spanish, and they were tough little sons-of-bitches. They could walk forever. There was some firing, as we patrolled, but it always came from our point man in the distance. We were in rebel territory and anticipated ambush at every turn.

The jungle days were hot and humid; the nights were cold as

ice. I had nothing to wear but the clothes on my back, and no bedroll to keep me warm at night. My shirt soaked through with sweat when the sun was high, and I shivered with damp chills when it went down. Carl and I were exhausted. Our unit made camp on the top of a defensible hill, and I tried to sleep. One image from that restless night has stayed with me ever since. Indeed, it is one of the most vivid images of my entire news career. I woke up, startled, to find a soldier standing guard over me. He was literally straddling my legs. It was a moonless night. There was no breeze, but it was bone-cold. And standing over me was this Indian soldier of the Second Battalion, his M-16 at the ready. The soldier grunted assurance at me, and I lay back down. I was precious cargo—an American television newsman and his crew— and the unit was not about to let any harm come to me. I stared at my protector, silhouetted against the starlit sky. I closed my eyes and slept.

The next morning I made the following entry in my reporter's notebook:

Eleven A.M., central standard time, 21 February, 1982. Even now, Cancer and Leo battle inside me, the compassionate and the warrior, the home-based succumbs to the adventurer. It is too seductive. Battle, disorder, chance increased, adrenaline called upon, capabilities challenged, the call, battle, war dog, the press, cheerleaders of death, piranha of misery, prophet, fool. She is the hypersensitive guardian of sanity (C.C.). Too often burned to believe (in me), yet forced by the overpowering will of the walker, warrior against peace, victor over family, despoiler of sanctuary, impatient moralizer, meat eater, self-destroyer, self-aggrandizer, success.

I also wrote this:

Evil hearts bane/Wild songs sustain/No pain, no gain/No guts, no glory.

Now, nearly ten years later, the entries seem bizarre, almost hallucinatory, but they suggest at the private battles I was waging in my own head, over the course my life was taking. That I had the notion to record these feelings, on a hilltop, surrounded by these vigilant Mayans, after a strange, other worldly night, suggests even further at my conflicted emotions.

When we returned to an embattled Guatemala City a few days later, Carl had to split due to a previous assignment. I was met by a new crew, free-lancers from Miami. These electronic reinforcements arrived prepared for battle, wearing old-style bulletproof vests. I scoffed at their overreaction. As it turned out, they were better dressed than I was. The peaceful protests had turned violent; there were riots throughout the city. The army moved to suppress the demonstrators, and I moved my Miami crew as close as I could to the action.

During the ensuing melee, we got too close. The military charged us. I stood my ground, identified myself as an American journalist, and expected to be told to retreat. I was not prepared for what happened next. I was hit by the butt of a rifle to the side of my head. The wire reports described the weapon as a pistol, and it could have been, but I remember a rifle. With those blows, you don't really see it coming. I was hit just above the left temple. I almost went down, but not quite. My knees sagged, but I did not fall. At the same time, the soldiers began pummeling my crew with kicks and blows. They all had their body armor on, so most of the blows rained down harmlessly. The cameraman recorded the attack, up until the point of first contact, when the cable to his recorder popped out.

We were corralled, arrested, and thrown into a van, in front of the entire international press corps. I was outraged, but beaten, by a man who could have been a brother to the soldier who stood guard over me as I'd slept back in the bush. I could feel the blood running down my face. My crew went to attend to me, but I stopped them. I wanted the dried blood as a badge, a weapon for the confrontation I knew would follow. I turned to the cameraman and urged him to get his camera rolling again. He did. He was scared to death, understandably, but he held the camera in his lap and videotaped during the ride in the van.

We were taken to intelligence headquarters, and I came out roaring. I railed, in English and Spanish, against the army action against us. I knew their commanding officers! This was an outrage! Apparently, something I said gave these guys pause; we were held for about an hour and then released.

The streets were deserted by the time we were released. A pall of tear gas hung over the town like an acrid fog. Broken glass littered the streets. Military patrols stood at every corner. Back at the hotel, I was besieged by reporters. The Associated Press had already run the flash that I had been beaten and arrested. I had become the focus of the story, at least for the moment, and at least among this group of mostly Latin journalists.

Meanwhile, my former love, the married newspaper reporter based in Latin America, heard of the beating and raced to the hotel. "What have you gotten yourself into now?" she asked as I was being stitched up by the hotel doctor. She looked as lovely as ever. I actually made a play for her, after the stitching, but she turned me down. (She predated C.C. and old habits die hard.) She said she felt old, and even a little ashamed of the wild, tender moments we had shared five years earlier.

Ironically, ABC would have been beaten on the story if I had not been beaten on the head. NBC had two crews on the scene to our one. They were better-positioned to record the riots than we were. Of course, once the wrath of the Guatemalan military was directed at me, our crew gained the advantage. I can handle an occasional beating, as long as the cameras are rolling.

Over the next eighteen months, my relationship with C.C. crystallized to become the love affair of a lifetime, as my marriage to Sheri hobbled toward divorce. (Our divorce did not become final until 1984, by which time she was beginning a three-year relationship with an up-and-coming young actor named Bruce Willis.) I was careful not to let my tumultuous love life infect my work, and one of the ways I kept them apart was to pump up the volume in my reporting.

This flurry of activity was also born of more immediate concerns. Our ratings were stagnant, even sagging, and Roone Arledge took me aside one afternoon and pep-talked me into working my ass off. He wanted me on the air virtually every week, and so I was.

BARBARA WALTERS (cohost, *20/20*): I remember little things about Geraldo. He used to come in to tape the show and he would be wonderfully dressed from the waist up, with gym shorts on. He sat behind a desk, of course, and he would wear shorts and running shoes, or whatever, and then from the waist up he would be wearing a good-looking jacket and a shirt and tie. That was Geraldo. He was always, to me, the kindest, most affectionate man. He was teasing with his affection. If somebody asked him what I was like, he would talk about how sexy I was. Anyone who's been called bright always wants to be thought of as sexy. I loved it. I thought it was dear of him, and he knew that I would think it was dear of him. He was one of the best investigative reporters I have ever worked with. He had great power on that program, that nobody else has had. I don't. He had his own staff, his own personal investigative unit.

I returned to Alaska, to chronicle the Iditarod dog race, and profile Susan Butcher, the first American woman to come close to winning that race. (She has since become a four-time champion.) While visiting her tiny hometown in the frozen Alaskan interior, I had a fight with the local thug, knocking him out in the snow; Susan, and the eighteen other town residents, all hated him and thanked me for my action.

I traveled with Carl Hersh to Peru, to record the good works of Project Orbis, a DC-8 aircraft outfitted as an eye clinic and serving the world's desperately poor; I observed a little girl's cornea transplant, and the moment when her sight was restored still stands as one of the most thrilling of my career.

I teamed with producer Dick Clark (not to be confused with the ageless Top-40 game-show host), a potbellied, chain-smoking veteran of CBS News, and he rivaled Charlie Thompson as my ace reporter during this period. We worked on a story about the spread of automatic weapons into the hands of civilians.

Dick also produced the first of my underwater adventures, which sought to tap into the huge ratings appeal of the National Geographic specials and Jacques Cousteau documentaries. I went diving with the sharks in the Bahamas, and in a shark tank off the coast of San Francisco. It was the ultimate macho experience.

HUGH DOWNS (anchor, *20/20*): He did that first sharks piece on his own, but we had an adventure with sharks sometime later. We were doing a story on seals, in Santa Monica, and we were down at a considerable depth, and we found some horn sharks at the bottom, they're sort of bottom-feeders. And both of us were taking these horn sharks by the tail, and they'd swim away and give us a good ride. They weren't very large. The longest was maybe five feet. And I didn't really realize how flexible these things were, and I had a hold of one by the tail, and he came around and got me in the wrist. Tore my suit. It was probably the most insignificant shark attack on record, and we were down there horsing around and Geraldo said, "You know, the ASPCA is going to get after us for bullying these things."

Some months later, Hugh and I dove for undersea treasure, off Mosquito Island, a tiny paradise in the British Virgin Islands. C.C. and Gabriel were with me on this trip. (I traveled with him whenever I could, particularly if the assignment promised excitement and adventure appropriate for a small boy.) The piece was made memorable by the sad news that reached me on the island's long dock: Dick Clark, my producer and fast friend, had died of a heart attack, at the age of forty-five, on the second day of the first vacation he'd ever taken. Dick's sudden death spoke volumes to me about the anxiety of our industry, about the internalized pressures of deadlines, ratings, and network politics.

With Charlie Thompson, I produced a series of reports on excess spending in the Pentagon that seemed to strike a nerve throughout the country. These reports, as much as the exotic adventure stories I was drawn to, stand as representative of my work during this period. Our repeated claims that the military's system of procurement for spare parts cost the American taxpayer in excess of one billion dollars per year set off a firestorm of controversy. Fifteen dollars and twenty-seven cents for a flat spring that costs less than a quarter in your local hardware store? A toilet seat for $642.32? Something was outrageously wrong, and we exposed the various abuses inherent in the open-ended proprietary rights granted in government contracts.

One of our principal sources and chief Defense Department whistleblowers for this story was A. Ernest Fitzgerald, a deputy Air Force secretary, who would later write a book chronicling our *20/20* reports on the waste, fraud, abuse, and hypocrisy of the Pentagon. Despite the extensive coverage of our investigation, his book, *The Pentagonists*, gave Charlie due credit, but failed to mention me by name. "Charlie's principal correspondent on camera dramatized the story with interviews, commentary, and examples," Fitzgerald wrote. "He even used the tried-and-true demonstration of holding up a series of rather ordinary-looking spare parts with quite extraordinary price tags on them."

I challenged Fitzgerald on the omission and was hit with one of the most flagrant examples of Geraldo-bashing I have yet encountered; his publishers were reluctant to print my name because they feared readers would not believe I had done this kind of reporting, and that my name would hurt the credibility of the book. The establishment simply refused to accept me, or my work, for what it was.

I also began a long association and everlasting friendship with producer Joe Lovett during this period. Our initial collaboration was on the first full-blown network treatment of the developing AIDS crisis. In May 1983, the major news organizations were still treating AIDS as a minor story. Our ignorant underestimation was apalling. *The New York Times* had not yet put the AIDS story on its front page; indeed, during the week of our broadcast, prominently displayed on page one was an item on the death of thirty Lippinzaner stallions. AIDS, and its malignantly speading terror, was buried on the back pages, even though New York was the epicenter of the epidemic. Even our story was two years late.

The piece, finally, was a sensitive portrayal of AIDS patients, and an informative look at as many aspects of the disease as we could fit into our alloted time. We interviewed Larry Kramer, of the Gay Men's Health Crisis, and several leading AIDS researchers, and offered a report that spoke to a nation's fears and validated the suffering of those claimed by the disease.

"We are at Ground Zero for this frightening medical mystery," I declared in the piece.

It was, objectively, a major story, and a breakthrough in the reporting of AIDS in the mainstream media. Joe and I would return to the subject many times over the next several years.

JOE LOVETT: There was one funny story, we were doing a piece on AIDS in the heartland, and Geraldo was out on another story, so I did the major interview of the piece, with a young woman in Lafayette, Indiana. So we came back, and I had put the story together, and Geraldo came in and I screened it for him, and he had a couple ideas to help the piece and that was it. Five minutes. Done. And he was off to work on another piece or something. So I turned to C.C. and I said, "He's so lucky to have a producer like me. All he has to do is put in five minutes on the story." And she became hysterical, and she said, "You won't believe what he just said. He just said, 'I'm so good that in five minutes I can make a story sing.'" And I think that's why we liked working together.

I did another drug story with Craig, in September 1983, taking our cameras to Heroin Alley, on the Lower East Side of Manhattan. This was one of the most amazing streets I had ever seen, a single city block with more than one hundred dope vendors. It was the illegal equivalent of the legitimate street markets that had sprung up on weekends throughout the city's ethnic neighborhoods.

CRAIG RIVERA: It was like Beirut down there, a real hellhole. We went into one of the shooting galleries, and I had my bag with the hidden camera in it. We were both dressed all grubby. Geraldo wanted to make a buy on camera. So we walked into this place, and there was a line twirling down the stairs, and we walked past the line. We went right up to the door. It was a peephole operation. You stick your money through, they stick the dope out. So we got to the top of the stairs and a guy goes, "Let me see your tracks." He wanted to make sure we weren't cops, right? "Show me your tracks." So Geraldo started arguing, "Fuck you. You want to see my money?" And he held out this big roll of bills, all fives and tens. "I don't want your money, man. Just roll up your sleeves." So they started getting all heated, and I thought, any minute, you know, they were going to break out their guns. Finally, another junkie on line bailed us out. He offered to cop for us if we got him a bag. It was a hairy situation, but Geraldo wasn't fazed. Nothing scared him.

I hit a smooth stride. Our ratings began to grow. The various lawsuits from 1980 had evaporated like bad dreams in the morning, and there were no new shadowss to take their place. No one criticized my work, in-house or elsewhere. The critics, interestingly, were silent about me, for the first time since the early days of *Eyewitness News*. Nobody damned me, but nobody praised me either. I liked the calm. I had found a groove, one that would allow me to exist in the high-stakes world of network news for as long as I wanted to, as long as I was careful. I was comfortable at work, confident and sure.

I should have known it wouldn't last.

PAMPLONA

The beginning of the end for me at ABC News took root on a follow-up trip to Lebanon, when I was reunited with Fadi Hayek, Bashir Gemayel's boyhood friend. The impulse for the piece was the United States lead intervention in Lebanon, and the subsequent bombing of marine headquarters in Beirut, which killed 241 American marines. I actually received the terrible news of that tragedy at the New Delhi airport, on my way home from a story in Nepal on the noble efforts of the Save the Children organization. Hearing how a single terrorist suicide bomber had wiped out so many marines, I changed travel plans and headed to Beirut, via Rome.

In Lebanon, the Muslims and Syrians were back in control. The bloodied American peacekeeping force was on its way out. I wanted to see how my Lebanese friends were faring during this most recent crisis, and in the wake of Bashir's death.

Fadi took me to visit Bashir's grave, in a tiny Christian village overlooking Beirut. The grave was marked by a picture of the slain leader, and surrounded by fresh-cut flowers. Mourners came and went as I stood there with Fadi. He put his arm around my shoulder and we wept. Silently, we looked down the hill, toward the devastation of Beirut, and once again saw the loss of all hope for Lebanon.

From there, I journeyed north to Tripoli, where I watched, on Wednesday, November 9, 1983, as a teenage Palestinian fighter had his right leg severely injured by a mortar shell. He was just a kid, and I moved instinctively to help him. It was clear the boy was not long for this war-torn world unless he was pulled out of the line of fire, and given medical attention. I grabbed him under the armpits as the firing continued on either side of us, and then turtle-walked with him back to the relative safety of the sidewalk. I fashioned a crude but functional tourniquet, and lifted the wounded boy, with the help of an ambulance driver who had just braved the crossing fire. Jane Hartney, the West's bravest camerawoman, and Milo Honein, her Lebanese sound technician, recorded the entire dramatic exchange.

Next, we went to the nearby hospital, on a tip that PLO leader Yasir Arafat was there. Indeed he was, and the resolute members of the international press waited by the front door. We went to the back door and intercepted him on the way out. Our cameras were rolling, and he started talking. He spoke freely, and openly, about the future of the PLO, and about his own future. Finally, with my last question—"Mr. Chairman, is the Palestinian revolution finished?"—the man looked up and seemed to notice me for the first time. Up until this moment I was a faceless American journalist, but now, suddenly, I was made. He did not say as much, but I knew in my heart he recognized me as the man who had done the "Unholy War" piece some years earlier—damning the Palestinian and Syrian presence in Lebanon, and praising the Israeli's—and as someone who had been marked for death by his organization in the wake of that piece. It was an incredibly dramatic moment when he made the connection. He did not say a thing, and I did not say a thing. Finally, he grunted, turned, and leaned into his waiting car. The interview was over. A few days later, Arafat left Lebanon, forever.

20/20 did not air until the following day, and so I made the Tripoli rescue, and the Arafat interview, available to *World News Tonight*. They loved our stuff, as I knew they would, and they wound up using our footage, and excerpts from the interview, in their report that Wednesday evening. Trouble was, they cut me out of both sequences. Obviously, I did not snatch the wounded kid out of the street just for the thrill of seeing myself do so on television, and I did not chase down Arafat simply to see myself manning the microphone shoved in his face. But, having done these things, it seemed reasonable to expect the company I worked for to air each story as it happened. No more. No less.

Instead, they treated me like an expendable free-lance bystander, and I was pissed. One of the reasons I was so incensed by the snub was because I was surprised by it. Things had been going so well at work that I was decoyed by the calm. What I failed to actively realize was that, despite my long list of recent (and past) successes, I was still perceived as an outsider in the network news business, a long-haired ethnic looking to kick up dust and rattle cages. If Peter Jennings, Ted Koppel, Sam Donaldson, or any of the lesser-known members of the on-air fraternity had had the guts to do what I had just done, the brass in New York would have shown the scene twice—once in slow motion.

Of course, I had too much pride to let anyone know I was hurt. Instead, I took the first opportunity to lash back. Av Westin, a brilliant editor in the wrong place at the wrong time, was caught in the crossfire, by telephone. At issue was a two-thousand-dollar plane ticket for C.C., who had come to Beirut to help edit our piece (and, admittedly, to relieve me of my war-fed loneliness). After editing me out of the *World News* footage, the network's subsequent refusal to pay C.C.'s airfare sent me over the top. After all, she was a *20/20* associate producer, and her trip was not exactly a Circle Line cruise. She was there to work, and she worked hard (and at considerable risk for her own safety). Indeed, as I waited to meet her plane, the Beirut airport came under fire from Druse militiamen positioned in the hills south of the landing strip; she was rerouted to Cyprus, and could not join the rest of the team until late the next day.

The fact that there were fringe benefits related to C.C.'s assignment did not liberate ABC from paying her expenses. I was crazed. I shouted at Av over the phone that I was going on strike, and vowed that the Beirut piece would be my last for the foreseeable future. Then I slammed down the receiver, and took C.C. on a trip to Egypt.

I held true to my word, without violating the letter of my contract. I went from being a weekly fixture on *20/20,* to an every-other-month contributor. I had produced thirty-one reports over the preceding ten months, but filed only two stories over the next three. I was making a point. Unfortunately, nobody seemed to notice, or to care. Roone Arledge would not even return my phone calls.

My relationship with Roone had soured since he first made a place for me on the network news team. His once-frequent Roone-A-Grams had dried up; our after-hours get-togethers were a memory. By 1983, with *20/20* established and the nightly newscast transformed, he had become the Howard Hughes of the news business, cloistering himself in his office, and making himself generally unavailable, even to his own staff and especially to me. He became notorious for not returning phone calls. He ran his operation on the odd assumption that confrontation avoidance was the best form of management. And, of late, he had been sending out silent signals that my work was not worth the million bucks he was paying for it.

Finally, one spring afternoon in New York, Barbara Walters, by now *20/20*'s cohost, cornered me in the hallway and pressed me on my inactivity. "So they hurt your feelings," she said bluntly. "They hurt everybody's feelings. What are you going to do, try and get a job at NBC?" Her implication—that no other network would hire anyone as volatile and controversial (and expensive) as me— hit home. More, she turned out to be right; my tentative inquiries at CBS and NBC yielded little more than indifference.

And so I ran scared. My contract was up the following year, and I had that big salary to protect. I did an immediate about-face, swallowed my lost pride over the buried Lebanon moments, and resumed work. With a vengeance. I did not announce my return to anyone but myself and, once I got going again, no one acknowledged the stoppage. I went on a tear, beginning in the summer of 1984. I swam with the whales, actually mounting one of the forty-five-ton giants in the middle of the Atlantic and riding the creature, on camera, until it swept me off. Guided by a great investigative reporter named Mike Masterson, my team helped indict two policemen in a twenty-year-old Arkansas civil rights murder. And, I scored an exclusive interview with the imprisoned Atlanta child killer, Wayne Williams.

The capper to this period of renewed activity was an exclusive interview with New York City subway vigilante Bernhard Goetz, in March 1985. *20/20* planned an hour-long, all-angles account of the controversial story that had gripped New York City for the past three months. I was assigned to re-create for our viewers the incident that had sparked the controversy: Four black youths allegedly harassed the gun-toting Goetz on a city subway, and were then systematically gunned down by their supposed victim, after what many claimed was only the imagined threat of violence. I

looked at the incident from every conceivable point of view—
Goetz's, the four youths', the other passengers' on the train—and
the result was a revolutionary approach to documentary journalism,
a kind of real-life *Ox-Bow Incident,* and a forerunner to the fact-
based "reality" programming of today.

Barbara Walters was assigned to interview Goetz, but he proved
to be an elusive subject. Everyone in the country was trying to get
to him. With my reenactment piece in the can, Av asked me if I
would help land the Goetz interview. I did not want to step on
Barbara's toes, but I did not mind stepping on the toes of her
producer Judith Moses, a typically uptight network news
establishmentarian. I had been working with Danny Goldfarb and
Eric Tate, the show's only black male producer, on the crime
sequence, and the three of us agreed to help out. We walked into
the control room and announced our decision: "Okay," I said, "the
Mod Squad is here. Let's go."

Our first coup was in securing Goetz's videotaped confession,
recorded when he was first taken into custody in New Hampshire
the week following the shootings. Next, we pursued Goetz's
attorneys—Barry Slotnik and Joseph Kelner—seeking an interview
with their client. Finally, the lawyers agreed to let me talk to
Goetz personally, off-camera, to try and persuade him to do the
interview. Once they did that, I knew I had him. There was no way
I would let Bernhard Goetz turn me down.

"Okay," he said, after hearing my impassioned pitch, "you can
ask me a couple of questions."

Trouble was, Goetz wanted to do the interview with me,
immediately, and not wait for Barbara, and I was not entirely
comfortable pulling the piece out from under my friend and
colleague. As my crew set up, I called uptown, to lay out the
situation for Barbara and Av. "I've got him," I said. "He wants to
do it now."

"Congratulations," Barbara said, proving herself once again to
be the classiest dame in the news business. "Go for it."

And so I did. Goetz's couple of questions turned into an
extensive, probing hour-and-a-half interview. As he spoke, he
seemed very agitated, self-righteous, and bitter. Occasionally, he
hunched over and clutched his belly. He chose his words carefully,
precisely, and yet revealed himself to be a racist vigilante who had

basically declared open season on bad young blacks. He was nervous, but extremely open. I don't think he realized the damage he did to his image with that interview, at least not as he was giving it. Later, I would describe him as being "nerdy."

As I understood the format, Barbara was to anchor the multisegment report, and so before I left Goetz, I convinced him to allow Barbara to meet with him. He would not have to go through the interview process again, I assured, but it was important that we get video of the two of them talking. In this way, Barbara could introduce the interview with authority and mention that she had had her own session with Goetz.

It seemed like a simple professional courtesy on my part, but it ricocheted. Judith Moses edited me out of the interview, and it was like Tripoli all over again. Barbara was totally blameless, and very gracious about the gaffe—indeed, she made a point of mentioning on the air that the interview was conducted by me—but Moses's skewed editing suggested that the scoop was Barbara's and not mine.

I kept silent at the time. I did not want to risk putting Barbara in a bad light. I mention it now, though, to put my position at ABC News into context. I was, on the one hand, an invaluable, tireless contributor, and yet some were still quick (and eager) to gloss over those contributions.

The personal highlight during this poststrike period helped to obscure the snubs: I ran with the bulls, in Pamplona. C.C., who was producing the piece, was with me for the glorious adventure. The attendant air-piece was a well-rounded feature on the history of the run, but the hook for me, obviously, was the chance to again risk everything. The thrill was exaggerated by a professional foul-up. I was schooled in the centuries-old sport by an American authority and colorful character named Joe Distler, a New York restauranteur who had been attending the event for years. I prepared for my initiation into Hemingway's rite of macho passage by downing as much sangria as my clear head could handle. The run originated in the corral on the edge of town, where the bulls were kept, and snaked from there through the ancient city of Pamplona, through a tunnel, and into the fabled bullring, the Corrida de Toros. The plan, hatched by Joe, was to join the stampede about a thousand meters before the dark and narrow tunnel, at a point when the bulls would be at full gallop and the thousands of *aficionados* and tourists long sidled from the chase.

I wore high-top sneakers, white pants and shirt, and a red sash, the traditional costume (at least down to the sneakers). I stood with Joe Distler, and dozens of other similarly dressed crazies, and waited for the stampede. The stakes were incredibly high in a race like this (in previous years, people had been trampled or gored to death), and I was acutely aware of everything as I waited for the bulls to make their final turn toward the homestretch. My heart thumped.

Tradition also allowed the toting of a rolled-up newspaper, the only weapon a real man could use against a bull to protect himself. The paper, of course, is worth zip, but I held it tight and it comforted me. Also, the metaphor—the long-arm of my profession reaching down to offer merely lip-service protection—was not lost on me, even in the heat of that anxious moment.

We felt the bulls before we saw them. The ground began to rumble and then, around the bend, we saw the flailing, white-clothed limbs of the front-runners. The bulls' horns bobbed and weaved behind them.

When the first of the crowd reached us, our group hopped out in front. The gravest danger here was that some frightened runner would trip you, and I was careful of other feet. I ran with everything I had. I was with the bulls. They were all around and alongside me. After about a hundred yards, I fell, tripped by man or bull. I panicked, but scrambled to my feet immediately and resumed the dash. I finished the run, triumphant, surrounded by bulls at the head of the crowd.

Sangre y arena. Blood and sand. I felt brave and alive. I came into that ring triumphant, as high as I had ever been in my life. The moment stood with my glory in the ring, several years earlier. Unfortunately, it soon appeared the moment would be lost, at least as far as posterity was concerned. Our cameraman had missed the shot. He could not see me in the crowd. There was a possibility that one of the Spanish crews had captured me at the finish, but we would be unable to view their video until the next day, after the second running of the bulls.

And so I had to do it all again. After all, what is a first-person participatory piece without some first-person participation? My pants had been ripped by the fall on the first day, my knees scraped and scarred. I was beaten up and not as agile as the day before. Gone were the passion of anticipation and the fear of the unknown. I have done this once, and now I know exactly what it is. Now I know that this is fucking crazy.

I was in even better position for this second pass, and finished the race with my arms raised in glory, in the midst of the herd. I was lost in the moment, but not so far gone that I did not recognize what a fantastic picture this would make: me, fists held high, surrounded by a herd of steaming, angry beasts, an arena full of bullfighting fans as a backdrop.

Again, my cameraman missed the shot. I was exasperated, and very disappointed. Again, there was no guarantee that the Spanish television crews had this second shot. And by this time, my new friends among the runners had started to rag on me. "Listen," they said, "even if you have the shot, you have to run with us again. The festival is four days. You are only half through."

And so, on the third day, I ran again. The courage here was not in the first run. That was accomplished with adrenaline and ignorance. But these subsequent runs took pieces out of me. This third time, thankfully, we got the shot, although I knew it was not quite the magnificent picture of the day before.

(As it turned out, the local television teams recorded every single one of my runs. And on three of the four days, my picture made the front page of the local papers.)

On the fourth day, as C.C. and I were about to leave, I was shamed by the runners into running again. I had come too far to leave with even this small cloud on my macho psyche and so, exhausted, bruised, and convinced that because I no longer needed to run I would be killed, I ran the fourth day. This time, I ran into the ring and kept going, right through the opposite tunnel.

I collected C.C. and left town before the exhiliration left me. We drove from Pamplona to the south of France, then on to Paris. I was on top of the world. There was no place to go but down.

CHAPTER THIRTEEN

49 EAST 96TH STREET

I should have seen the signs. In the summer of 1985, bad omens stacked up over the penthouse apartment I shared with C.C. at 49 East 96th Street like a fleet of jets waiting to land at La Guardia: After a respectable finish, Hugh Downs and I were disqualified from the prestigious Marion (Massachusetts) to Bermuda Yacht Race, over an inconsequential and blameless infraction at the start of the five-day ocean race; Sheri announced she would be moving permanently, with Gabriel, to the West Coast, over my loud (and legal) objections; and, ABC offered to renew my three-year contract without even a token raise, despite the surging popularity of *20/20* and its star correspondent. The foundation was laid for a precipitous slide.

412

The yacht race, and what I viewed as Sheri's stab in the back, were out of my control. (I fought like hell to keep Gabriel near, but feared no court would award custody to a globe-trotting dad over a stay-at-home mother.) The contract offer, though, was another matter. For the first time since the days of Al Primo, I had no one in place to negotiate on my behalf. The William Morris Agency, smelling ten percent, sought to win me as a client. The late Lee Stevens, then the agency's president, and Jim Griffin, his top TV agent, came calling in a Chrysler limousine and took me to dinner to sell me on their services. I was impressed by both men (and by the unpretentious limo), and flattered by the attention, but unable to see the need for representation at the time.

And so, ignoring the old adage (and perhaps proving it) that any man who represents himself has a fool for a lawyer, I entered into negotiations with Irwin Weiner for what I thought would be a simple renewal of my existing three-year deal. I started out asking for a significant raise and retreated to a symbolic one.

Irwin refused to concede even that. "Roone says there's no more money," he said finally, after one of our many telephone negotiations. "This is as far as we're going to go."

"This show is making all kinds of money," I countered, wondering if it was not too late to call in my William Morris suitors. "We're supporting the entire news division."

"Take it or leave it," Irwin replied.

Take it or leave it? A part of me knew Irwin was merely hardballing me into accepting his offer, but it had never occurred to me until just this moment that Roone was prepared to let me walk over a token percentage increase. "I'll have to think about it," I answered, telling him I would not begin work on my next story until we had a deal.

It was August 9. I was due to leave for two stories in the Philippines that evening. Irwin, too, was on his way out of town. "I'll call you from the airport," he said.

"I'll be here."

Actually, he called from his car phone. "Well?" he began.

"Okay," I backed down. "We have a deal."

"Three years?" he said, completing the terms.

"Three years."

I left the country that evening, openly disappointed at being renewed without a real raise, but privately relieved at being rehired. I was worried that my post-Lebanon strike a year earlier would be held against me.

My reporter's notebooks offer an easy clue to my frame of mind during the long flight:

August 9, 1985. En route Tokyo and Manila. Reenlisted with ABC for another three-year tour. I wanted more money, but not much more. Still got less than asked. No matter, it's still a whole lot. What now? Well, it's up in the air. The critics are impossible, but the fans are wonderful, and the adventures, and the planet, and my life. My plan? To try and avoid controversy while still being a swashbuckling taker of chances. To stay in shape, in love, happy. Happy is the key. No fun, not worth the struggle. The boat is a bother. The job's all right. Tired just now. Need sleep and excitement and a couple good stories.

The Philippines promised thrills and distraction. I was off to film an exotic investigative piece about the "Slave Ships of the Sulu Sea," and, unrelatedly, to chronicle the political unrest in that distant land. The former was a classic adventure. We sailed an old schooner to a remote part of the Philippines, where we found boys as young as ten employed as pearl divers. Working for between eight and ten dollars a day, the kids were required to free dive (without oxygen) to depths up to eighty feet. They made up to ten dives a day, often with severe consequences (burst eardrums, pneumonia, drownings). We boldly boarded the rickety, foul, and overcrowded slave ships, confronted the heartless captains and, later, the onshore owners. The piece was nominated for an Emmy for investigative journalism.

After a happy stop in Manila's red-light district (which C.C. busted me on after she found incriminating pictures), we reported the second piece, on the festering insurrection against Ferdinand and Imelda Marcos. Aside from an exciting counterinsurgency patrol with the Philippine army in the jungle, the story also included a palace interview with the glittering first lady.

But even the high drama of these two stories was not enough to shake me from my professional and personal funks. I was haunted by Roone and Sheri, two lapsed allies who had each turned against me in their own ways.

Two weeks later, on the return trip, I drafted the following letters in my notebook:

August 23, 1985. En route Manila to JFK. Dear Roone: So, we are to be contractually associated for three more years. I wonder if you'll have the guts to call me during that time. I doubt it. Tom Shales and Peter Jennings would not approve. Regards, Geraldo.

Dear Sheri: Do you still feel you are the victim? Can you, after your latest ploy, maintain the guise of hurt and anger? You are the supreme manipulater. Compared to you, I am an amateur. You are a cunning, premeditated, calculating machine. From separation until now, I have let you lead me. But my original sin has been exculpated by your treacherous behavior, and now I'm going to fight you. Only my love of my son protects you now. Best wishes, Geraldo. P.S. Still, in a stupid way, I care for you. We are once and future family. Pity us.

I never sent either letter. Indeed, reading them later during the same flight, I was surprised at my venom; now, six years later, I barely recognize my emotions. Why was I so filled with hate? What good did it do me? I resolved to overcome my geographical rift with Gabriel, and to work through my ideological differences with Roone and his underlings.

September 6, 1985. En route LAX to Nantucket. *New Wave.* Battered by the court decision regarding G.R. II's residence on the West Coast. And yet I am sure it will work out okay. My pending crises have passed. Thankfully. And I have emerged still holding the moral high ground ... What is the cold, hard assessment of this sixteenth year with ABC? Not great, not bad. I'm definitely not the golden boy. More than ever, I am the rebel. It takes tremendous energy and huge popularity to sustain this role. It is too visible, too controversial. Those who would attack/destroy are legion. Yet, I sustain. I am. Still, after it all, I am.

Undated entry, September 1985. Fuck Roone Arledge. His memory is too short to do him any good. Sixteen years and I'm still a contender."

The road ahead looked exactly like the one behind. Clearly, a stasis symbolized by my status-quo contract extension was beginning to take hold, and I was unable to get past it. I was tired of the lack of respect from news management and the critics who deigned to pass judgment, and secretly bored with the routine of network newsgathering.

I needed a jumpstart, and there was one waiting for me around the corner. Before I found it, though, C.C. and I spent a long Labor Day weekend with her family in glorious Marion, Massachusetts, on Buzzard's Bay. The big social gathering of the weekend was a cocktail party given by C.C.'s folks, a fund-raiser for New Bedford mayoral candidate John Bullard. (New Bedford is the nearest city to tiny Marion.) C.C. did not have her checkbook with her, and she very much wanted to contribute to Bullard's campaign, so I very innocently wrote out a check for two hundred dollars, in my name, but on C.C.'s behalf.

Within days, news of my "contribution" had reached ABC, via a small item in *The New Bedford Standard Times*. Within weeks, it became the first shrill note in the disharmonic convergence that ultimately cost me my job.

Enter Marilyn Monroe. My friend and colleague Sylvia Chase, working with producers Ene Riisna and Stanhope Gould, had spent the last three months (and approximately one hundred fifty thousand dollars in network funds) reporting a blockbuster segment on the late, great sex goddess of the silver screen. The piece was the buzz of the newsroom and promised hard proof of Monroe's affairs with President John Kennedy, and later with his brother, then Attorney General Robert Kennedy. Working with journalist Anthony Summers, who was about to publish his book, *Goddess: The Secret Lives of Marilyn Monroe,* Sylvia and team had unearthed telephone records of calls from Monroe to Robert Kennedy's Justice Department during the week she died. There were also allegations of mob surveillance and blackmail plots, but the central revelations revolved around the romantic relationships behind Camelot's closed doors. It sounded like pure dynamite— the stuff of great ratings—and it was slated to be the lead piece for the program's fall season debut.

On a Monday afternoon, three days before the segment was

scheduled to air, my secretary Jo-Ann Torres walked into my office and dropped the bombshell that would send me spiraling into the most damaging controversy of my career. Jo-Ann had been with me since September 1979, and she knew that what she had to say would set me off. "They're giving Sylvia a hard time on the Monroe story," she said.

"What kind of hard time?"

"Word is they might not run it at all."

"Shit."

The office was pulsing with the sudden rocky road encountered by what was to have been a major, headline-making coup. Sylvia and team had been asked to edit their forty-minute piece to twenty-five minutes, and now it appeared the segment would be shelved indefinitely. What the hell was going on? I looked to Sylvia and Stanhope for answers, but they were as much in the dark as anyone else. "What happened?" I asked.

"Ask Arledge," Stanhope replied.

Roone Arledge had been dodging my calls for two years; there was no reason to expect he would respond to a query over an issue like this one. Instead, I confronted Av Westin, who had himself signed off on the piece without reservations, and learned from him that Roone and his senior aide David Burke had termed the piece "sleazy." I had not yet screened the segment, but I knew from reputation that the work of Sylvia, Stanhope, and Ene would be as far from sleazy as mine would ever be from conventional. The real reason the piece was being quashed, I was slow to realize, was cronyism. Roone was a longtime friend of Ethel Kennedy; David Burke had once been a high-level staffer for Senator Ted Kennedy and a veteran of the Chappaquiddick fiasco. (Burke would later go on to be president of CBS News.) There was every evidence to support the theory that these two family friends were too close and tied in to air a report so potentially damaging to the Kennedy legend. Worse, I allege, they tried to cover up their cover-up. The two men had thrown the unit's professionalism into question, and then, to avoid the appearance of conflict, removed themselves from the editorial process. They appointed news executive Bob Siegenthaler, a man with no apparent Kennedy connection, to make the final decision to air the piece, but the strategy backfired when Siegenthaler unexpectedly approved the original piece for air. It was not at all the decision Roone had anticipated, and our compromised leader was left to make the final call on his own.

With the fate of the piece still uncertain, Sylvia and team cut the piece a third time, to just thirteen minutes, in a last-ditch effort to salvage their work and their reputations. It was not enough that Roone had spiked the piece, but he had impugned the good names of these good people in the process.

Right up until taping began that Thursday, no one was sure whether the piece would air, or, if it did, in what form. Sylvia was actually in makeup when Roone's final decision came down: Officially, he announced that the piece was not yet ready for air; unofficially, and more accurately, it was spiked, dead.

I was incensed, and reacted with every inch of righteous indignation I could muster. Even though the Monroe piece was not my story, I looked on *20/20* as my show, and I did not like anyone, even Roone, tampering with it. We were a news program, and this was news. We were not in the business of shielding friends and relations from the harsh light of press scrutiny. This was the second *20/20* story on the Kennedys to bear Roone's fingerprints. The first, in 1978, was to have been a revealing second look at Chappaquiddick, which Roone had also found reason to bury. I could not sit idly by and watch the same thing happen again. As one of the newsmagazine's three senior producers, I felt an obligation to champion the work of my less powerful colleagues. On a less lofty plane, the crisis loomed as the chance to make Roone pay publicly for his refusal to deal with me on other, more personal matters.

Meanwhile, allegations about the Monroe/Kennedy connection were breaking all over the country. Spurred by Sylvia's shelved report, and by the prepublication swirl surrounding Summers's book, Los Angeles officials were making public various documents that appeared to verify some of the story's claims. Leaks about the silenced *20/20* report began to spring from our newsroom, adding current heat to the old controversy; soon, media watchers were talking about Sylvia's report as if its censoring was more newsworthy than the allegations it contained.

I went to the two on-air colleagues with more clout than I— cohosts Barbara Walters and Hugh Downs—to enlist their outrage and support. When I arrived in the studio later that Thursday to tape my own segment, Hugh allowed that he had contacted his Rogers and Cowan press agents and was prepared to speak out on the issue; Barbara stated that she, too, intended to voice her objections. The three of us promised to do what we could to restore the credibility sacrificed to Roone's parochial whim, and to see that Sylvia's piece made it to air in something at least resembling its original form. To me, these vows were marching orders for an all-out campaign against a Mickey Mouse news decision. To Hugh and Barbara, understandably, they suggested something less.

I committed professional suicide later that evening in a telephone interview with syndicated columnist Liz Smith. She called me around midnight, tipped that I would talk about the handling of the Monroe story. I stood in my kitchen and made headlines. Stoked with moral fury, I charged Roone with cronyism and censorship, and questioned his journalistic integrity. In the process, I burned the already rickety bridge connecting me with my onetime friend and longtime employer.

BARBARA WALTERS: Geraldo had a very emotional relationship with Roone. They were close, in a way that I'm not sure that I understand. I don't know whether it was a father and son relationship, although Roone isn't that much older, or whether it was brother-brother. But somehow the relationship had deteriorated. And my feeling is that Geraldo felt he could not get to Roone, that he had somehow lost Roone, and that this was Geraldo's way of saying, "I'm not somebody you can push around." Geraldo was like a child trying to get attention, and he got it. I thought he had great courage to take the stand that he did, but I think it had a lot more to do with his personal feelings about Roone than his feelings about the piece.

HUGH DOWNS: ABC publicity advised us to keep a low profile on this, and I stayed out of it until it appeared in print that Roone had called the piece sleazy. So I contacted the *Times* and said, "Look, I don't work with sleazy journalists. This is a better-documented piece than anything I saw on Watergate." I just did not want the accusation to stand. Geraldo went a little further. He is easily outraged by injustice and it's a measure of the man that he gets more outraged about injustice against somebody else than against himself.

I sounded off with impunity, fully expecting my voice to blend in with the chorus of condemnation. But, apart from some carefully chosen and politically correct statements from Hugh and Barbara, I was singing solo. That was okay, though. There is safety in numbers, but there is no courage there. I actually enjoyed trashing Roone to the press. It felt right, and good. It was not until after I had said my piece that I realized ABC had yet to deliver my new contract for signature. I do not think I would have done anything differently, had this occurred to me before speaking out, but I was nevertheless alarmed.

And so, with this slip to my firm footing, C.C. and I left the next morning for Los Angeles, and a much-needed weekend with Gabriel.

> October 4, 1985. JFK, en route LAX, to see the kid. It means far more to me than I ever expected. I miss him hugely. Thinking about the recent cascade of events, I realize how little time there is for reflection and reaction. So many canons fired, so little time to analyze causes championed, or courses run. It is exhilirating, though, to challenge at this level. I enjoy talking to people like Liz Smith about Roone's dilemma, and his failure. Also, I am energized about my work. It is so uniformly good and strong and real. Can life stay this good for long?

When I checked into the Bel Air Hotel there were messages waiting from a dozen news organizations—*Newsweek, Variety, People,* the Associated Press, and the *Hollywood Reporter,* among others. I did not return any of the calls, but I did take a call the following morning from a West Coast *People* reporter. Again, I attacked Roone and ABC News without a thought for my own ass. I still had not seen Sylvia's piece, but was certain that Roone had crossed the line to where his personal relationships clouded his news sense.

From Los Angeles, I traveled to western Tennessee, for an investigation of an allegedly corrupt county sheriff, back to New

York, and then on to Philadelphia, to begin taping an extended report on the tragic and fiery aftermath of the MOVE confrontation, between dangerously eccentric cult members and city officials. At every stop, beginning Monday morning, October 7, there was a message from Roone. I was in no hurry to get back to him.

SYLVIA CHASE: I was out on another assignment, somewhere in the flats of New Jersey, and I asked the cameraman and the producer to stop so I could make a phone call. Geraldo was off somewhere on his own story, and we had an appointment to talk on the phone. I can remember the phone booth, and the gray light at the filling station. Everything was concrete and marshlands. And I remember saying to Geraldo, "Listen, I want you to be careful because this doesn't have anything to do with you. I would be really unhappy if you caused yourself any agony over this." We were like a couple of turf lords talking. I told him I could handle myself. "I can do this. Don't do anything to jeopardize your career because I'm not going to do anything to jeopardize my career."

The first indication that my public stand against Roone Arledge would cost me my job came from Bob Siegenthaler, who called me into his office during my short stopover in New York.

"I want to talk to you about this campaign contribution," he started in.

"What campaign contribution?" I honestly had no idea.

"The two hundred dollars, to the guy running for mayor, on the Cape."

"Oh," I said, catching on. "That. What about it?"

"Well," he stated, matter-of-factly and as if it were rehearsed, "we have to treat you in exactly the same manner we have treated other people who have become involved in politics." Siegenthaler, who went on to run the Bureau of Operations and Engineering at ABC, is a tall, angular, bespectacled guy; at the time, he was acting as Roone's deputy henchman. As he spoke, it became clear he was setting me up to be fired.

I never let him get to the punchline. "This is bullshit," I fumed. "How dare you come to me with something like this!" I shouted at this guy, called him a lackey, told him there was no way they were firing me over a piece of shit charge like that. "You tell Roone that if he tries to breach our contract over an insignificant event like this in a nonpartisan election, I'll drag him into court," I railed.

Siegenthaler was clearly flustered by my tirade, and he seemed to shrink under the attack. I left for Philadelphia understanding for the first time that battle lines had been drawn and, without a signed contract, I was critically unarmed for what lay ahead. I was exposed, vulnerable to management retaliation. When inquiries about my contract were referred by the staff attorneys (who normally handled such routine matters) to Irwin Weiner (who normally did not), I knew I was in serious trouble.

And it got worse. C.C. called me in Philadelphia later that week with devastating news. "Your worst nightmare has been realized," she said when I picked up the phone.

Indeed it had. In the most awful coincidence of my life, C.C. was caught dispatching an ABC messenger to pick up an ounce of marijuana from a friend of hers at CNN. The dope was for a friend of C.C.'s, and it was concealed in a package with videocassettes. The messenger, allegedly suspicious (or, according to C.C., acting on instructions from one of Roone's men), reached to open the package, whereupon C.C.'s CNN source grabbed it back and fled. The messenger reported the incident to his boss, who reported it to his boss, until news of the incident had reached Roone.

My world was spinning out of control. I returned to New York later that night to assess the damage. I was furious with C.C. for exposing me in this way. The drugs had nothing to do with me, but I knew that because of C.C.'s involvement they would be seen as having everything to do with me. That I had been out of town and ignorant of the transaction, I knew, was irrelevant. I was already being tried and judged guilty by association.

I stopped in on Av Westin, to gauge management reaction to the fiasco. Av said people were questioning whether the package, which was never relocated, contained marijuana or cocaine.

"Av, what the fuck are you talking about?" I said. "There is absolutely no similarity between a vial of cocaine and an ounce of marijuana. What are you talking about?"

"I'm just telling you what Roone had heard," he said.

This was the last thing I needed. And, it was so unfair. Let me state the extent of my drug history unambiguously. I have honestly chronicled my earlier marijuana use, my membership on the board of NORML (I resigned seven years before this incident), and my one-time-only hit of acid in 1969. That was it. I have never abused cocaine and, though I have no moral objection to adult marijuana use, I had virtually stopped smoking grass by the late 1970s. Like most people I know, I have on occasion accepted a party toke, but I would never buy or possess, or condone my partner's buying or possessing the stuff. The stakes are too high.

And so I spent a long, worried, and tearful night with C.C. She felt horrible and ashamed. We made love. I comforted her and assured her we would be together always.

Roone finally reached me the next morning. I took the call in my kitchen, appropriately dressed for battle in my workout clothes. The sun shone through the windows of our penthouse apartment. I had a grim idea what was about to pass between us.

"I want you to quit," Roone announced, clipped, impersonal.

"Bullshit," I said. "I'm not quitting."

"You can't continue," he said, "not after this."

"I have a contract."

"You have no contract."

"Yes, I do have a contract. Irwin and I have shaken hands. We have a deal and you have to live with it."

"There's no deal," he insisted. "And the drug thing?"

"That has nothing to do with me and you know it."

"It's relevant here. The police are going to investigate."

"Let the police investigate. I have nothing to hide. What, C.C.'s the only one that ever bought marijuana in the news business?" I held the phone in my left hand and jabbed with my right every time I made a point.

"That's for the police to determine."

"Listen, Roone, I'm an investigative reporter. You want a full report on everybody at ABC, and I mean everybody, who has ever used or is using drugs?"

"What I want is your resignation."

"You're not getting my resignation. We have a contract."

"Show me the contract, Geraldo. We have no contract. Show me the contract."

It was an ugly, hateful conversation. I was sweating by the time I got off the phone. I left off declaring war on my former friend, telling him he would rue the day he ever tried to fire me. And then

I called Jim Griffin at William Morris and told him I changed my mind about representation.

Word of C.C.'s transgression spread like a brushfire, and with it came charges of my own drug use. I have always suspected, and in some respects have since confirmed, that these drug rumors were fueled by my enemies in news management. Given my recent, outspoken stand against management's handling of the Monroe piece, I was certain the network was out to destroy me with whatever dirt it could find.

I was fighting for my life. I worked the phones tirelessly, speaking to every reporter who had challenged me on the drug issue. "I was out of town," I explained. "You can't smear me with this brush. This is bullshit. I'll take a drug test to prove it." Eventually, the drug rumors died down, but the damage had been done. C.C. resigned, immediately, and disappeared to her parents' home in Marion. I hired a lawyer and threatened to sue ABC if they tried to fire me. In strict legal terms, I was advised, there was indeed no contract, even though I had been working under this new agreement since September 16. Still, I resolved to ride out the storm. I had no other choice.

On the night after my screaming phone conversation with Roone, I looked to one of my most enduring allies. I had started seeing Marian Javits again during this unsettled period and, since C.C. and I were living together in Manhattan, most of our dangerous liaisons were on the road. We traveled together to San Francisco, where we were linked socially (although not romantically) in Herb Caen's *Chronicle* column. We went to L.A., staying in separate suites at the Bel Air; she also accompanied me on a trip to Geneva. Now, confronting my professional ruin, I took her to dinner at Elaine's, the high-profile literary hangout on Second Avenue and Eighty-eighth Street. It was twelve years after we'd first met; Marian was sixty-one, and she was still sexier than most coeds, at least in my eyes. I had no qualms about cheating on C.C.; she was out of town, out of mind, and out of favor in the wake of her catastrophic foul-up. I was, I thought, entitled to this.

As we ate, and talked, a half-dozen plugged-in acquaintances (writer Pete Hamill among them) approached our table and offered me their sympathies and support. My confrontation with Roone was widely known in news circles, and "Page Six" of the *New York Post* had already hinted at C.C.'s scandal. "Don't worry about it," I would say, in rushed thanks. "It's not as bad as you hear." Marian had no clue what the steady interruptions were about, and I did not want to spoil our evening by telling her.

We spent the night together and I forgot my troubles in her arms. It was like old times, but it also symbolized an earlier, more certain time in my career. I actually separated myself from the scene enough to wonder if my desire for Marian was not propelled as much by a professional nostalgia as a personal one.

Next morning, the fallout from my conversation with Roone and the accompanying gossip were all over the papers. Marian was furious. "How could you use me like that?" she demanded.

"What are you talking about?" I said.

"You should have told me about all this," she said, "before we were out in public together."

"You're right," I allowed, "I should have told you. I'm sorry."

Then, pacified, she said, "What about this woman? I suppose you'll leave her now." I had no idea what my next move would be concerning C.C., but before I could answer, Marian caught herself and said, "Actually, you can't leave her now. Do you love her?"

"Yes," I said. "I'm afraid I do."

"Then you can't leave her. She needs you more than ever."

It was the last time Marian and I were ever together, and the encounter resonates with her insight, compassion, and generosity. Her simple proclamation crystallized my thinking, and I knew C.C. and I would get past even this disaster.

Still, the standoff with Roone consumed me. I continued to work, during this uncertain period, while Jim Griffin negotiated my leave-taking. ABC was anxious to reach a cash settlement, to make the mess go away. And I was so wounded by C.C.'s mistake that I was unable to rally my allies to protect my own hide. Anyway, I told myself, if these guys did not want me, then fuck them. I'll go to work for the competition. The network offered me two hundred fifty thousand dollars to leave quietly. Jim talked them up to five hundred thousand dollars, and I insisted they let me wrap the half dozen or so pieces I was still working. The "MOVE" story, which was to be my last piece for *20/20*, was shaping up as an explosive indictment against the city of Philadelphia and Mayor Wilson Goode, and I was not about to let another correspondent shepherd it to air.

In technical terms, I was not fired; effectively, of course, I was. Both sides agreed to state for the record that I was resigning; I further agreed to refrain from disclosing details surrounding my resignation—including the cash settlement and my heated discussions with Roone—for two years. I negotiated a press release, which the network's publicity department used in announcing my departure: "After fifteen years of hard, honorable work with ABC, Geraldo Rivera has told us that he wishes to leave to pursue other opportunities. Although we sincerely regret his decision, ABC does not wish to stand in the way of his future plans. We wish him well in those endeavors, including the possibility of future work for ABC on a free-lance basis."

I sat in my apartment as word spread on the wires, thinking about the way things were, and the way they might have been.

November 1, 1985. En route New York to LAX. How disastrous this month has been, nerve-racking, embarrassing, painful, worried. Announcement generated some nice comment; the process of change, some excitement. Still, it is deeply upsetting to be fired. Couple that with C.C.'s ridiculous gambit and you see the threat it poses to my reputation and you see why I worry.

November 4, 1985. Back in the office after weekend in California. Got the bad news on *60 Minutes*. [Don Hewitt was not interested in hiring me.] Trying to deal with an uncertain future and the whole idea of scrambling for business. I am reasonably confident it will work. The question is how big? And how important? And starting when?

November 12, 1985. En route New York to Philadelphia. I am sick in my heart and my gut. The world has collapsed and there is not yet a firm foundation on which to rebuild it. I am anxious and I need help.

At one point, before my final broadcast on Thanksgiving evening, David Burke called Jim Griffin and asked him if there was any way

I might consider returning to the fold. "Can we just forget the whole thing," Burke reportedly said. "What's the chance of that?" All along, I am sure, Burke had been egging Roone on about letting me go, and now, suddenly, Roone must have panicked at the possible backlash—Puerto Rican demonstrators, a tell-all book or, simply, a *20/20* lineup without his star correspondent. But I had gone too far to go back. I had silenced the drug rumors and professed public relief to be free from the weekly grind of the newsmagazine business. I was looking forward to an extended hiatus. I worried what a return would do to my image and credibility. The moment was too dramatic to let go. There was no way I could not leave at this point. I had painted myself into a romantic corner. I was gone.

And so, on Thursday, November 21, after presenting my last story, I signed off with the following words:

"Sixteen years ago, I was a long-haired storefront lawyer challenging the system on behalf of my clients. It was exciting, frustrating, passionate stuff and I expected it to be my life's work. Then something totally unexpected happened. I got discovered. Standing on a ghetto street representing a group of demonstrators, I was approached by a reporter who told me ABC was actually interested in putting me on the air, making me a newsman. Two thousand stories and a lifetime later, I've come to the point where it's time for another change. For now at least, I'm going to be leaving *20/20*. As one of the founding members of this wonderful program, this is one of the toughest decisions I have ever made. But, it's time to go. I've always been sort of a square peg trying to squeeze into the round hole of network news. Sometimes that friction has been hard on me. I'm leaving with a bag filled with memories, like swimming with the whales and running from the bulls. I've covered eleven wars on four continents, but I am proudest of the stories right here at home, the reports that have made a positive difference in people's lives. Other than the fact that I'm going to take my first real vacation, I have no set plan for the future. Maybe I'll do what my buddy Hugh Downs did when he was my age and go sailing off after the sunset. Eventually, he came back. So will I."

They were the last words I ever spoke as a network newsman.

November 23, 1985. En route JFK to LAX. So, the last report
has aired and I have already explained what I plan on doing next.
Out of work. Out of sight, and not yet out of hope, but hurt.
Now I need genius again.

December 5, 1985. My first entry written in my own apartment.
I am incredibly depressed about this professional swamp that
leads nowhere and holds the promise of more frustration as time
goes by. I am four days into my inheritance and no closer to
anything than I was two months ago. There are surely ways
through it, but they are elusive, and very difficult to navigate.

December 23, 1985. 11:30 A.M. Sitting in a bar on Seventh
Avenue waiting for some wimp PBS bureaucrat to get back so
our eleven o'clock meeting can take place. Two days before a
holiday I hate and the blues are as malignant as ever. Now
Sidney Lumet wants me to be in a Jane Fonda movie, and maybe
I'll do the damn thing. Shit! It's not as if anything better has
come along.

December 25, 1985. Still sitting by the window of the apartment,
working on a plan of attack for life. One good line I remember
from *The Last Unicorn*: "A hero's job is to be a hero."

January 6, 1986. The new year is here and ticking. The
prospects? Oh, shit, who cares? The news is how empty the days
are even when they are full. They are empty compared with the
incredible stimulation of my other life, and yet in some ways,
my mind is more active now. I am forced to assess my life.
Watching these turkeys pontificate on air, I am furious they
have cut me out. I can out-report the best of them most of the
time.

January 8, 1986. In Jim Griffin's office, waiting while he talks on
the phone about some local performer of news and a deal he's
not even making. I sit and wait and listen and dream of the good
old days.

January 14, 1986. Two weeks into the new year and things do
not go well. In fact, they still go badly. I hate how fast the time
goes. I miss the boy. And not having a job is getting increasingly
worrisome. The space reporter news started breaking today, and

at least it deflects some of the hurtful attention C.C.'s trauma still generates.

A sobering and depressing reminder of my out-of-work status surfaced in my active application to NASA's Journalist in Space program. I had applied, along with hundreds of my colleagues, to train for a future shuttle launch; I had even survived the first few cuts, but now my efforts were suddenly hobbled. I made the Northeast finals, based on an essay I had written, and I traveled to the campus of Penn State shortly after my dismissal from ABC, to appear before a selection panel made up mostly of small-town print reporters and academicians. My application had survived to this point in the intense competition, despite the burden of my controversial reputation; now, I also had to shoulder the fact of my unemployment. The reporter's end of the bargain, naturally, was to write about, or broadcast an account of the space experience; without a job, as far as NASA was concerned, I could hardly be considered a journalist.

"Where will you put this?" one of the panelists grilled.

"I don't know," I replied. "I'll figure that out."

"It's something we have to think about now," I was told.

"I'll get it on," I said. "Somewhere. It's not a problem."

But it was a problem. For the first time in a decade and a half, I had no corporate flag to wrap myself in. I felt naked without it, incomplete. The free-lancer label also inhibited my other major project during this period—the effort to obtain funding for a documentary chronicling a *New Wave* voyage to Cuba, through war-torn, dope-riddled Central America and into Panama. PBS expressed lukewarm interest in airing the completed piece, but was unwilling to subsidize production costs. Potential sponsors, understandably, were reluctant to kick in funds without any founded hope that the documentary would reach even a small-scale audience. And, most troubling of all, our efforts to obtain the necessary visas and clearances were slowed without the portfolio of ABC News to move things along.

The only conventional work available to me was an occasional gig substitute-hosting CNN's *Larry King Live,* which I seized for the opportunity to keep myself sharp and in the public eye, but it, too, reinforced the downturn of my career. Only five years earlier, the same cable network had offered me millions to anchor their prime-time newscasts; now, after a few successful pinch-hitting appearances, they offered me two hundred thousand dollars a year, as a morning talk-show host. It was a lot of money, to be sure, but it was also less than ten percent of the initial offer, when I was at full strength, and far less than I needed to support my high-ticket lifestyle.

The most lucrative unconventional offer, as I described in the prologue of this book, was a fifty-thousand-dollar one-shot deal hosting the live excavation of the basement of Chicago's long dormant Lexington Hotel, believed to house the private vaults of Depression-era mobster Al Capone.

I took what I could get.

January 15, 1986. *20/20*'s ratings continue unaffected by my absence. If anything, they are better, which is extremely troubling and leads to the disturbing possibility that David Burke is right, I do turn people off. To be fair to myself, there are also thousands of people who tell me they miss me. Thinking now about the legal profession. Saw these ads on TV and I know I would have a tremendous impact on that market. I would have to do it with care, and dignity, but also with fire. It could be fantastic fun, and extremely profitable. . . . Must call the *Miami Vice* producer. (I had written a script for an episode. It was later rejected.)

January 19, 1986. En route New Orleans to Newark. Coming home after sitting in for Larry King on CNN and my first-ever NATPE convention. Trying to do business with a class of people made hungry by their independence and competition. It is a bit humiliating for someone so long protected from the hum and hubris of big business, but perhaps it will make me stronger.

January 23, 1986. D.C. Working at CNN is a funny contradiction. It seems a small-time shop, but significant because of the people who watch or at least have made it a point to watch me. All I ask is an even chance. That would be plenty. *Newsweek* is indicative of the fundamental inability of the establishment to give me an even break. [What *Newsweek* said was that if I got to be the first reporter in space then it would prove the effect of weightlessness on weightlessness. Clever, and hurtful.] I have no doubt most of Washington will read only *Newsweek*'s opinion of me. Anyway, I feel better, and maybe I'll sleep tonight without dreams. Praise the Lord and my beautiful boy.

January 25, 1986. En route Sarasota to Key West, on board *New Wave*. I have waited a long time to be able to say that and I leave at a time when fortune seems finally to have turned. We have done well with our little sortie into cable. I belive the market is really there. And the other projects: *Miami Vice,* PBS . . . Things are beginning to happen. I managed to fool myself again into thinking the world would realize its awful mistake and take me back. What is clear is the world doesn't even think about me or Marilyn Monroe or Roone Arledge or anybody.

The entire Marilyn Monroe incident was the most painful and devastating of my career. Would I play it out the same way all over again? Maybe. Maybe not. Roone was my friend. He put me on the air. If things had been different between us, I could have vented my disagreement with him in a more personal forum and remained with ABC News, perhaps until this very day. But our relationship had broken down—beyond repair, I thought at the time—and there was nothing for me to do but to make him answer publicly for his behavior.

I paid the terrible price for my convictions, but I also made Roone Arledge pay for the extraordinary lapse of his. The quashed Monroe story has become his Achilles heel. Any assessment of his career (and there is no denying that he will be regarded as one of the most important men in the history of television) will turn up this black mark on his record. And, there will be the vindication on mine that I put it there. Still, he was my friend, and I miss him.

BELIZE

Craig, C.C., cameraman Carl Hersh, a few friends, and myself were due to set sail on the *New Wave* at the end of January 1986,

without funding for our planned documentary. I financed the
journey, and hoped to recoup at least production-related costs at a
later date. The trip promised at high adventure and escape, and
teased at a provocative example of alternative journalism. It only
half delivered.

> February 1, 1986. January is history. Still no job. But the
> crushing negativity that was squeezing the life out of me is well
> gone. It was the oppression born of doing functionary work that
> in my previous life was left to people whose job it was to make
> my life run as smoothly as possible. Today it is irrelevant. We
> are at sea and flying downwind. I love this boat. It is my magic
> carpet—clean, pretty, and rugged enough for anything but the
> ocean's profound anger.

The journey did not get off to the smoothest start. Even the
weather was against us. We slammed into a polar cold front before
we even left the coast of Florida, en route to Key West. The boat
was rocked by forty-knot winds, and bathed by ten-foot swells. We
made Key West a day late, and battered. We were without television
and radio, untethered to the news of the world, and as an old
seadog helped us to repair the *New Wave*'s balky navigational
equipment, he tipped us to a national tragedy.

"A shame about that shuttle, ain't it?" he said. He tossed the
words over his shoulder, without looking up from his work.

"What about it?" I asked quickly.

I sat down heavily at the news. The space shuttle *Challenger*
had blown up, her mission tragically aborted before it even got
started. Weeks later, in Mexico, we would finally see the taped
replay of the disaster, but for now we had only the imagined
images of that awful explosion.

We sailed for Cuba as soon as the storm was quieted and our
equipment repaired. It had taken more than two months to arrange
for visas from our suspicious Communist neighbors. We arrived
off the Cuban coast a half-hour before dawn and anchored just
outside the breaking surf, off the once plush beach resort of
Veradero, fifty miles east of Havana. A few minutes after sunrise,
the official Cuban greeting party came steaming over the eastern
horizon in a heavily armed gunboat. We had been told by the
Cubans that we better be at that exact rendezvous, with the same

boat and precise crew members we had specified, or there would be trouble. We followed our powerful escort into Veradero harbor, whereupon our hosts gave our vessel a thorough going-over. Carl Hersh recorded the bizarre scene as paranoid Cuban military, customs, health, and agricultural officials searched *New Wave*'s every nook and cranny. They confiscated all of our fresh meat, fruit, and vegetables. I cringed at the loss of our limes (an essential ingredient for gin and tonics), but was silently relieved that the authorities had failed to locate our most precious and (in this case) dangerous cargo: our weapons. The *New Wave* was heavily armed, our pieces well-wrapped and stowed in the bowels of the boat. Man should not journey through these war-torn waters with only limes for cover.

Once in Cuba, our principal objective was to interview Fidel Castro, but on this trip our timing could not have been worse. Castro was said to be ill, and Cuban officials were busy staging his third Communist Convention, playing host to more than two thousand prominent Socialists from all over the world. Our camera crew made do with an escorted tour of Havana, although Carl managed to steal a few shots of the lines outside the food and clothing stores, and the Russian ships at anchor in the city's harbor. In many ways, and despite the shortages, Cuba seemed to have changed for the better since my last visit nine years earlier; her people were better off in material ways. And yet, the country seemed stifled, without color; its soul seemed to have shrunken, its Latin passion cut out.

Carl, Sydney Weinberg (C.C.'s lifelong friend and for a brief time her successor as my *20/20* assistant), and sailing-mate Andy McMaster left our crew in Havana, flying out on the same charter flight to Florida that brought another friend, a well-traveled playboy named Tak Konstantinou, in from Miami. It was the first of the many crew changes we had planned for the journey down the Central American isthmus.

Once clear of Cuba, in blustery seas on the three-hundred-mile trip to Isla Mujeres in the Yucatan, my attention drifted back to the reality of being unemployed.

Undated entry. Talked with Jim Griffin on the ship-to-shore radio today. He did not have much to say. Unless I am there and

involved, I fear not much is going to happen. At least there is
this voyage. It offers the illusion of work. When we get back, I
must go on a tear. I am in the hole seven hundred thousand
dollars, with only nine months to make some deals. And then
there is next year. And et cetera.

We took about two weeks to sail gently down the Caribbean
coast of the Yucatán, with stops on hot and funky Isla Mujeres,
Cancun, and Cozumel, where we were joined by six-year-old
Gabriel and his traveling companion, my good friend and former
cameraman Anton Wilson. From there, we worked our way
through a severe storm and a boat-killing barrier reef to the tiny
nation of Belize, once known as the colony British Honduras.
What a crazy, exotic place! We used our rubber dinghy to motor
up the river that defined the harbor of Belize City, and were it not
for the black skins and English tongues of the natives, we might
as well have been cruising in Asia. Rickety houseboats, barely
floating, lined both sides of the heavily polluted waterway; reggae
music, bare-assed kids, and untended livestock crowded their
decks. To protect itself against the expansionist impulses of its
Spanish-speaking Guatemalan and Honduran neighbors, the
Belizean army had stationed three PT-boats along the river,
manned by pinkly sunburned British sailors. And, to complete the
panoply, we looked across the harbor to a spectacular, twenties-era
yacht, immaculately maintained; the vessel was as out of place in
this sewer as the *Love Boat* on the Harlem river.

The yacht, we quickly learned, belonged to the actor Harrison
Ford, who was anchored in this toilet of a town to film the movie
The Mosquito Coast. Wisely warned against staying in one of the
city's two colorful hotels, he and his wife, the screenwriter Melissa
Mathison, were living out in the harbor roads on board his *Mariner
III* motor yacht. It was a fit home for a movie hero. He invited us
aboard, for a tour and a drink, and Gabriel was hugely impressed
at the chance encounter with Indiana Jones. I was more interested
in the boat than the man, at least initially.

The next day, a Sunday, we all spent the day with Harrison and
family—diving, snorkeling, and spearfishing at English Cay, a rich
reef about ten miles southeast of the harbor. He had been holed

up in this place for months, and he was happy for the company; even our happy band of out-of-touch travelers was a welcome relief to the strange tedium of this place. Harrison and Melissa were fun and gracious hosts, down to earth, confident, and adventurous. Back on the *Mariner III,* we passed around a joint offered by one of the Belizean mates. (This was one of those rare party exceptions to my drug-free rule.) After only a couple tokes we were all buzzed. At one point, it was decided we were going to resume diving later that afternoon, but we could neither find a needed spear gun, nor concentrate on the search. We had also been drinking Belizean rum and sitting in the hot shade of the boat's covered fantail. Finally, Harrison volunteered to go below to fetch the spear gun. He was gone for nearly fifteen minutes before he poked his head through the hatch, looked at us with a mock-innocent Indiana Jones grin and asked, "What did I go down there for?"

As the sun set, we said our good-byes. *Mariner III* steamed back up to Belize City. We up anchored to continue south on our long run down to the Panama Canal. Later that night, at a remote and stormy anchorage off a dark jungle coast, we had the most anxious moment of the voyage. There were five of us on board: Anton and Craig were sleeping in the main salon; Gabriel was bedded down in the small forward cabin; C.C. and I were in the cabin aft. I heard Anton's shout first, followed immediately by the high-pitched whine of a small outboard motor. I leapt out of bed and poked my head through the big rear hatch. There was a military-style dinghy bobbing in the surge about twenty feet away. The night was bright enough to reveal four black men, each wearing a beret and armed with a machine gun.

One of the men was shining a powerful light in our direction. "We're going to board," he shouted.

"Who the hell are you?" I yelled back.

I did not wait for an answer. I ducked my head back into the boat and pulled the double-barreled Rossi & Overland shotgun from its hiding place behind my bunk. Amidships, Anton stood guard with our .357 Smith & Wesson revolver. Craig drew the mini-14, semiautomatic rifle. If our visitors were pirates, or dopers, it would be a fair fight.

I returned to the hatch. "Who the hell are you?" I tried again.

"We're the Belizean Defense Forces," the leader hollered back.

The wind was blowing hard from the east, and the four men in the dinghy were soaked to the bone. They were also angry. Apparently, people did not question authority in these parts. I told them there was a woman and a child on board, and, while we had nothing to hide, nobody was going to board my vessel unless they could prove who they were. (We had been warned pirates were common in these waters; they boarded sailboats, killed their crews, and used the vessels for drug runs.)

After some tense shouting, the dinghy sped away. When it returned, ten minutes later, we turned our searchlight on them. The leader ordered me to go below and turn on our radio. I did. I spoke to a British voice belonging to a man identifying himself as Left-tenant Somebody, the commander of the PT-boat *Toledo*. He reported that his vessel, the dinghy's mothership, was just a few hundred yards away. In a polite, but scolding voice, he said we had no choice but to allow his men to board. It was to be a standard customs check for drugs; in recent years, Belize had also become a major transshipment point for the international drug trade. When I asked if it could wait until daylight, he refused, but very reasonably offered to send just one unarmed man on board to conduct the search. I could not refuse.

C.C. tucked the weapons behind her pillow, while I went above to join Craig and Anton. It was a curious, comic scene. After the radioed back-and-forthing, the lead soldier in the rubber boat was now refusing to board until I apologized for my initial rudeness. My efforts did not satisfy him, and so I went back below and called the patrol boat commander.

"It seems I've hurt your man's feelings," I said, enjoying this uniquely British Catch-22.

After several minutes of coaxing from me and his commanding officer, the lead soldier agreed to look past my manners to board and search the *New Wave*.

Gabriel—my dear, sweet six-year-old, who would learn to tie a bowline on this trip—awoke the next morning, annoyed that he had slept through the excitement.

Following the coast of Central America, we next visited Guatemala and the fabulous Rio Dulce. Sweet River. It is appropriately named. A tropical fjord, it cuts through sheer jungle canyons and leads, finally, to a vast and glorious inland lake. The entrance to the lake is protected by the ruins of an ancient Spanish fort. This was the first place it really hurt to leave behind. After Belize, and the call to arms, it was a slice of paradise, an exotic place where all the residents were running from something or someone.

Anton and Gabriel flew home from our next stop, the Bay Islands of Honduras. We sailed on to the Colombian island of San Andrés. A week later, we were in Panama, and for me the long sailboat journey was over. Craig and C.C. would take the *New Wave* through the Canal and wait for a new crew. C.C. would then join me in Chicago, while Craig would stay on board to take the *New Wave* to her new home off the coast of southern California, in Marina del Rey, where she would remain as my West Coast home for the next two years.

I was heading back to *terra firma,* while the ground beneath my feet was anything but steady.

CHICAGO

"The Mystery of Al Capone's Vault"—the live, syndicated special that signaled a new chapter in my broadcasting career—was developed by Doug Llewelyn (better known as Judge Wapner's *People's Court* reporter) and free-lance producer John Jocelyn, and peddled to the Chicago-based Tribune Entertainment Company, part of Tribune Broadcasting, one of the country's leading syndicators and independent television station groups. Before I joined the project, the actor Robert Stack was signed to be the host, and I remember thinking the transition ironic—one *Untouchable* being moved aside to make room for another.

SHELDON COOPER (former president, Tribune Entertainment): As we talked about it, the show began to grow into a live event, rather than a documentary. And then we realized we had the wrong host. Robert Stack would have been terrific for something written, and preproduced and packaged. But we needed someone who could walk and talk and think on his feet, and interview. And then I remembered there was this guy ABC had just released, and as far as I knew he was not doing anything.

I disappeared on the New Wave just after agreeing to host the program, with the understanding that I would return to Chicago by the first week in March, in time for five weeks of preproduction. Still, I began receiving urgent radio messages at sea, from Tribune execs anxious to keep tabs on me, and to drag me back to dry land as soon as possible.

I had begun to look on the Capone show as a paycheck and a lifeline, both. It was the only thing I had going, and it was everything. It was my one chance back. When I finally did arrive at the Hyatt Regency in Chicago, my body was calloused and sunbeaten from more than a month at sea; my hair was long, tangled and out-of-control; a full beard masked my tentative enthusiasm.

We began our documentary fieldwork the next day, reporting various sidebar stories to complement the live excavation of the hotel basement. The show was scheduled at two hours, and half of that time was to be filled with packaged pieces to fill the spaces between blastings and diggings. I traveled the country to interview Capone's surviving friends and enemies. I interviewed mob experts and Depression-era historians. I talked to Internal Revenue Service agents who had placed a lien on the property in the hopes of collecting the nearly one million dollars in back taxes and penalties owed by Capone. I examined virtually every square foot of the Lexington Hotel, until I was as knowledgeable about its structure as any landmarks preservationist.

The hectic prebroadcast days were filled also with a carnivorous press tour to promote the show. During one of these publicity sessions, I made a bet with a Chicago reporter, in cocksure answer to a too-common question: What would I do if our excavation yielded little more than dirt and rubble? The more we researched the history of the hotel, and the comings and goings of Capone and his gang, the more I became convinced that fear was groundless. Surely, these long-sealed vaults contained fascinating relics—bootlegging equipment, weapons, documents, cash, or even the massacred remains of the mob's ill-fortuned enemies— and would reveal astonishing truths about the Capone legend. The press, though, was not as certain, and so, to silence the skeptics, I vowed to sing—live, and effortlessly off-key, to untold millions of viewers, in 181 American television markets and seven foreign countries—if our search turned up empty.

A crisis surfaced several weeks into our preproduction to nearly derail the entire effort. I had been enthusiastic about the Capone show up until this time, and excited about the possibility of future projects with Tribune. (After all, the company was the only one to offer me real work since ABC; it seemed only natural I would want to pursue more of the same.) In fact, I began to talk in broad, general terms about follow-up specials, although there were no offers on the table to continue our collaboration beyond this one-shot broadcast. On March 19, however, I confronted the harsh possiblity that no such offers would be forthcoming. I was in Los Angeles to visit Gabriel, when the slow fallout from C.C.'s months-ago scandal reached me in front of the Bel Air Hotel. I happened to run into Bill Murray, the actor-comedian, in the hotel parking lot, and he and I started to chat. As we spoke, we saw Jim Dowdle, the chief executive officer of Tribune Broadcasting. Bill Murray was also from Chicago, and in fact used to date Dowdle's niece back in high school, so the three of us had a nice, informal talk. After a while, Murray disappeared to keep an appointment, and Dowdle took me aside for a more serious conversation.

"Geraldo," he said, "I'm not going to beat around the bush with you because that's not my style." Jim is a big, hulking sweetheart of a guy, and he seemed embarrassed and uncomfortable with what he had to say. He put his hands in his pockets.

"I'm listening," I said.

"I hear you've got a problem with cocaine," he announced.

"What?" I stammered.

"Well," he said, "that's what I've been hearing. I've been hearing that's the real story behind your departure from ABC." He skipped a beat, and then continued: "Look, Geraldo. I don't know you too well, we've only worked together a couple weeks, but I need to know if there's any truth to these stories. There's no other way to ask than to just ask."

"Jim," I started in, as calmly as my seething rage would allow, "that's an absolute, fucking lie."

"It is?" he said, awash in relief.

"I'll go down and take a drug test right now. I've never used cocaine. It's absolute bullshit."

"I can't tell you how glad I am to hear that," he said, extending his meaty palm.

I shook his hand thinking, Jesus, when is this thing going to go away? and thanking the gods of syndicated television that I had partnered with a group of people so willing to believe in me, despite the vicious innuendo.

The moments leading up to our live broadcast on April 27, 1986, were charged with adrenaline and drama. The stakes were enormous. Everything hinged on my performance, and on my ability to sustain viewer interest, which was expected to be high. There is a certain opening-night urgency, a palpable nervousness, to any live broadcast, even a newscast, but especially a prime-time extravaganza. My butterflies, as I have mentioned, typically take the form of cold hands; here, as the world waited and my future hung in the balance, my anxiety moved to other extremities. My cold feet were, I think, understandable. Viewer projections promised a huge audience, and it was my job to hold their attention until we determined what, if anything, was entombed behind the sealed walls that had possibly been used by a legendary mob figure.

Despite my nervousness, I had more fun during the first hour of this show than I have ever had in this business. It was thrilling, edge-of-the-seat stuff, and I was ringmaster to a mass of frenzied activity. We were blowing up walls and sifting through rubble. A small Bobcat tractor roared around, carting away the debris. We had various experts on hand to provide commentary to my play-by-play; we even dragged the city medical examiner down to the hotel basement to examine any bones we might uncover.

Initially, things went well, but about an hour and a half into the program I began to realize we were coming up empty. Our excavators had dug up nothing of prurient, or even collectible value, apart from two 1920s Gilbeys gin bottles, and an old road sign. We were blasting, digging, and scraping and still, we had found nothing.

C.C., who had joined me in Chicago after leaving the *New Wave* with Craig and the new crew, tried to put a smile on the situation during one of our second-half commercial breaks. "This is the most exciting television I have ever seen," she enthused, handing me a cup of water. "I love this."

"Don't you realize?" I said sternly. "Don't you see what's happening? We haven't found anything. We won't find anything. This could be the end of my career."

I had been talking, in booming broadcasting tones, for nearly two hours, and my voice was hoarse. For the past half hour our blasts had produced nothing but dirt. We had reached a dead end. There was nothing left to do but fold up our tent. I finished the show by honoring the losing end of my bargain with the local reporter, and broke into what I could recall of "Chicago": "My kind of town . . ."

In substantive terms, "The Mystery of Al Capone's Vault" seemed to have played out as a colossal failure. Nobody would remember the documentary, I felt sure. I wanted to hide. I retreated into my dressing room. I wanted to be alone, with C.C. and a bottle of Cuervo Gold, but I still had some motions to go through. The first of these was a mandatory stop at the Conrad Hilton Hotel, for a wrap party with Tribune executives and their spouses. I wanted to be anywhere else in the world, but propriety (and the hope of someday again doing business with these people) mandated an appearance. By the time I arrived, an hour after our broadcast, the grand ballroom had thinned; only the midlevel sales types remained. The most notable absence was Jim Dowdle, and I took his early exit as the worst possible sign: The higher-ups were running for cover. The mood of the room was a lot like election night in a losing candidate's campaign headquarters. The two hundred party-goers still there knew they had put on a good show; they knew the company had made a ton of money (due to upfront sales, with no guarantees); and, they also knew that they would not be made to answer for the disappointment of the search. It was my credibility on the line, not theirs. I was the one who was going to take the fall.

I shook some hands and beat it out of there as fast as I could. I was obviously subdued. C.C. was on one arm, and she was almost propping me up. We disappeared to a catfish bar on Chicago's

South Side, about a block west of the Lexington Hotel. I had promised the construction guys I would meet them for a drink; I was more comfortable with them in my crisis than I was with the suits at the Hilton. These guys had worked their asses off and were ready to celebrate. To them, the show was a lark, a nice payday and a rare chance to appear on television; they had no idea what the broadcast had meant to me, or what I had lost with its failure. If I was going to anesthetize myself against what happened, these were the guys I wanted to do it with. I ordered a bottle of Cuervo and tried to forget.

When C.C. and I finally found our way back to the Hyatt, I collapsed on the bed. In my stupor, I barely noticed the stacks of message slips. I did register the constant bleat of the telephone, which I tried to ignore, until finally telling the hotel operator to hold all calls. I slept like a dead man.

The first contact with the outside world was with my parents, calling from Sarasota, Florida, where they were living in the RV I had bought for them. The operator had the kind sense to put them through. "Everybody's talking about the show," my mother announced, with misplaced glee.

It was the worst possible news. I knew the show would pull through-the-roof numbers in Chicago, where it was a local phenomenon, but the only way I had gotten from last night to this morning was in convincing myself that the interest would be diluted throughout the rest of the country. Without the local spin, I hoped/prayed, there would be no compelling reason for people to tune in. Maybe the damage to my reputation would be confined to one city. I hurried through our small talk; the effort to sound cheerful, and pleasant, was too much for me that morning, even with my dear parents. When I was about to hang up, Mama's voice called me back. "I'm afraid there's something else," she said. "I'm afraid I have some bad news."

I thought she had already delivered her bad news. But this sounded like something personal. Something worse. I dread these moments in long distance phone calls. "What?" I demanded. "What? Tell me." I wanted to hear it, whatever it was, as quickly as possible.

"It's Frankie DeCecco," she said.

Frankie? Jesus. "What happened?"

"He's dying," Mama said. "Cancer. He only has a few days left."

I was already beaten down by the developments of the night before. And now this. Frankie. One of my oldest friends. True, the pulls of our lives had taken us along different paths and we were no longer close, but we kept tabs on each other through our families and I still thought of him as one of the handful of special people in my life. The idea of losing him, on top of everything else, was almost too much to bear.

I hung up with my folks and called Frankie's ex-wife Jolene. "How could you not tell me?" I shouted through my tears.

"Frank didn't want you to know," she explained. "He didn't want you running to him now just because he's dying."

I asked to speak to my godson Frankie, Jr. At seventeen, he was the same age his father and I were when we'd first met. Where does the time go? Frankie, Jr., and I shared our grief, and reminisced. Two weeks earlier, he told me, his father had gotten off his deathbed to marry the woman he had lived with for the past seven years.

My next call was to Frankie. Marianne, Frankie's new wife, answered the phone. She confirmed that he was dying of a rare form of thyroid cancer and was not expected to live out the week. She put Frankie on the line, warning me not to keep him too long. His voice was noticeably weak, but wrenchingly familiar. He asked how I was doing and joked about Capone. How am I doing? Who the hell cares how I'm doing? When he was too weak to speak, he handed the phone back to his wife, and I made arrangements with Marianne to come back to Long Island to see my old friend.

Now I had a second, more pressing reason to get out of Chicago as quickly as possible.

I was startled from my melancholy by a knock on the door from the room service waiter, with breakfast. I put on my bathrobe to answer it, and found an elderly, rail-thin black man, his wiry arms sticking from his too-short white coat. He reminded me of a Pullman porter. The man recognized me, and his face lit up like a pinball machine. The news about Frankie was still sinking in for me; I was also hung over, both from the drink and the embarrassing broadcast; my despair was obvious.

The old man put one of his long arms around me and said, "Man, you feelin' bad?"

"Yeah," I said, "I'm feeling pretty bad."

"About that program?"

"That," I allowed, "and other things."

"Well, shoot," he said, "don't be feelin' bad about that program. Not your fault there was nothin' there." And then he patted me on the back, wheeled his cart into place, and left.

The exchange brightened my mood considerably, and distracted me from Frankie. Maybe the response to the show would not be what I feared. Maybe I was not the laughingstock I thought I was. Maybe the silent majority of television viewers would not blame the messenger for the bad news.

When the old man left, I saw the dozens of message envelopes piled by the door. I was too scared to open them, but collected them and set them aside. C.C. and I looked at the pile all during breakfast. I began to think that the messages contained the keys to my future, that they would tell me whether or not I would ever work again. And, underneath this overwhelming professional anxiety, I was thinking about my old friend Frankie.

We were interrupted by another knock on the door. C.C. went to answer it. It was Doug Llewelyn. The hotel operator would not put him through, so he came calling. "I know he's not taking any calls," Doug said, as C.C. fumbled for some excuse why I could not see him. "It's okay," he said, "just give him this." He handed her a slip of paper. "Make sure he sees it. Tell him in a week nobody will remember the damn thing was empty."

C.C. sat back down and handed me the paper. The overnight ratings. The numbers eclipsed any I had ever seen attached to a single television program. New York: fifty share. Los Angeles: sixty-five share. Chicago: eighty-two share. Eighty-two percent of all Chicagoans watching television last night were watching our program! It was a staggering number. (Matched only by the Chicago Bears when they won the Super Bowl.) C.C. was reading over my shoulder, and then we looked at each other and started laughing. We nearly choked, we laughed so hard. Half that rating would have been a smash hit. We were delirious.

The moment, displacing what only seconds before had been seen as an unqualified disaster and coming on the heels of some devastating personal news, was rich. It was like reading the returns from an election rout. I was transformed, instantly, from a has-been to a hot property. My career was not over, I knew, but had just begun. And all because of a silly, high-concept stunt that failed to deliver on its titillating promise. I had done better work, but never before such a vast audience. Whatever our winged-monster of a program turned out to be, it crapped on the networks. We absolutely crushed the competition in the ratings, benefiting from a wind of hype and a high-voltage combination of substance and live theater. The thrill of commercial victory was made even richer against the overwhelmingly negative reviews, and the embarrassment of digging for a vault that turned out to be virtually nonexistent.

In the final tally, available the next day, the show checked in with a 34.2 national rating, representing more than thirty million households. It was, and remains, the highest-rated syndicated special in the history of television, by a significant margin. What made the numbers even more remarkable was that the show was aired on a makeshift network of independent stations; in many markets, we were carried on weak-signaled UHF stations.

My air had been cut off, and now, suddenly, I was breathing sweet oxygen. Again. I forgot about Frankie, and about the disappointments of the night before, and soaked in the numbers. C.C. and I tore into the stack of message envelopes like kids at Christmas. The envelopes contained congratulations from every Tribune executive, and from friends, family, and former colleagues. And, buried in the pile were twelve job offers, from every television syndicator in the business: Paramount, Viacom, Columbia, King World, Taft, Group W . . . Twelve job offers! I could not believe the sudden turn, but then I understood it for what it was. Everything follows success in Hollywood, and I was the glamour boy of the moment.

I immediately called Jim Griffin in New York, who was also besieged with inquiries. Together, we talked to Bob Crestani, in William Morris's West Coast office; Bob was the agency's syndication authority, and the three of us schemed a strategy to handle the turnabout. The reversal of my professional fortunes was dramatic and complete.

On the day after the Capone special, as I flew to New York to see Frankie, Bob established the ground rules for any companies wanting to negotiate for my services. He decreed that any project under consideration had to guarantee me at least one million dollars in the first year, before William Morris would even present it to me. A few of the syndicators choked on the fee and dropped from the chase, but to my delight, and surprise, several checked in with their seven-figure offers.

But I was not thinking about Bob Crestani's strategy as I picked up Frankie, Jr., and he drove with me to his father's new home outside of Center Moriches, on Long Island. Looking at the kid was like looking back in time to the father. I was a teenager again, tooling around the neighborhood with my friend. I felt a sudden, happy nostalgia for a lost and (relatively) innocent time.

I went in to see Frankie alone. His body looked wasted and spent. I lied that he did not look so bad. He joked that I was late, as usual. And then we started the hard process of saying hello again, and good-bye. He died three days later.

HOUSTON

The post-Capone tumult continued, despite Frankie's death, and I allowed myself to be swept away by it all. At every turn, there was something new to divert me from the tragedy.

Critics, cartoonists, comics, and commentators began roasting me mercilessly. The lampooning continued for weeks. (I still deal with the residue of those barbs, even five years later.) I became everyone's punchline, and some of it was pretty funny stuff. Andy Rooney joked on *60 Minutes* that he was planning a live, television spectacular around the excavation of the space behind his office wall. *Saturday Night Live* reported that my next project would be the exhumation of the Tomb of the Unknown Soldier. And Johnny Carson suggested I unearth the cement-encased Chernobyl reactor when it cooled in the next century.

Behind the laugh lines, Bob Crestani was positioning me for the long haul. With his encouragement, I decided I would no longer be a salaried player in the television news business. I wanted an equity position in whatever offer I decided to accept. I wanted to become an entrepreneur.

Paramount and Tribune leapfrogged to the head of the pack with similar offers: a series of specials, leading up to a regular series. My instincts screamed Tribune. I was hugely impressed with the way they turned a nonevent like the opening of a would-be vault into a happening. And I will never forget the way Jim Dowdle found the courage to confront me on those drug rumors, and the way he was quick to accept the truth. I was also leery of the Hollywood mentality, a mindset that Paramount seemed to symbolize. (The parent company, Gulf&Western, was nicknamed "Engulf and Devour.") The Tribune executives were not like any other executives. They were all Notre Dame, blockhead good guys from the Midwest, with square shoes and sincere smiles. You could take their promises to the bank.

And so I went with my gut. Tribune would pay my million-dollar salary, in return for which I would develop, produce, and host a series of prime-time, syndicated specials; we would also produce a pilot for a syndicated strip (five days a week) series, to be ready to bring to the next NATPE convention in January 1987, for launch the following September.

SHELDON COOPER: Ever since Phil Donahue left us, we had been looking for someone to replace him with on a daytime talk show. Someone who could play morning, afternoon, whatever. Geraldo seemed like a good fit, and I talked to everybody about it, and everybody got excited about it. Everybody except Geraldo. He wasn't too sure, I think, at first. And I said to Geraldo, you know, there's nothing to invent here except to do it in your style. The format has already been invented by Phil, and he's done very well with it, and now Oprah's doing very well with it. But you do it in your own style.

I was not at all sure about a daytime talk show. Students, housewives, shift workers . . . these people were not my traditional audience. I did not think they were interested in the news of the day, or in compelling social issues. A daytime talk show seemed the least likely vehicle for me. It seemed to me like I was finally allowed back in the ring, and being made to fight with one hand tied behind my back. I had made my reputation doing great adventure stories, investigative pieces, or confrontational interviews, and these things had little place on daytime television.

What I wanted was to do another version of *Good Night America*, to turn myself into a hip late-night cross between Ted Koppel and Tom Snyder. But the more I heard about daytime, the more I warmed to it. The Tribune executives—Jim Dowdle, Don Hacker, Sheldon Cooper, and Peter Marino—convinced me it was possible to be fresh, and hard-hitting in the land of soap operas and game shows.

Once I was sold on that notion, there was no stopping me.

We produced two pilots in the next several months—one of them using the single-topic format we would later adopt, the other relying on multiple topics to fill the hour. We initially called the show *Geraldo Live*. We shot the pilots at WGN-TV in Chicago, the Tribune-owned superstation there. I tried to woo my old friend and producer Marty Berman from his post at *Hour Magazine* to sign on to produce the shows, but he could not break away. George Merlis, one of my former producers at *Good Morning America*, handled the chores instead.

Surrounding production of the two pilots, I commenced work on my second prime-time special, "American Vice: The Doping of a Nation," and signed on as a regular contributor to the syndicated program *Entertainment Tonight*. I also enjoyed a brief love match with tennis great Chris Evert Lloyd, a graceful athlete and a beautiful lady. We met in Florida, at a celebrity tennis tournament. C.C. was with me at the time, but Chrissie was flirtatious just the same. At the end of the event, one of her girlfriends slipped me Chrissie's phone number. It came in handy a few weeks later, when I was making plans to visit Florida, sans C.C., in preparation for the upcoming drug special. I called Chrissie, told her I was coming to town on a shoot, and set up a date for dinner.

I had watched Chrissie play tennis for years, and I always thought she looked great in those short tennis skirts, lunging for a drop shot. She had the cutest buns in women's sports. She was alone at the time, going through the last of a painful divorce to John Lloyd. I was, of course, still passionately linked to C.C., but not so entwined that I could let an opportunity like this pass me by. And so Chrissie and I went out for a romantic dinner in Ft. Lauderdale. It was clear to each of us that the meal would only be the appetizer.

Chrissie was charming and sweet. She was also incredibly smart.

She was not looking for any kind of commitment from me, although I like to think she would have welcomed one if I'd thought to offer it. She knew about C.C. She'd done her homework on me before I showed up. In fact, she was curious about C.C. and asked a lot of questions. I was candid about the relationship. There was no bullshitting Chrissie; she was too bright for that.

I made a second trip to Florida a few weeks later, and Chrissie and I picked up where we'd left off. By this time, my appetite was well-whetted, and I started to think about where this casual affair might lead. Not only was this woman attractive, accomplished, and successful, but she was also relaxed and confident around me, as I was around her. The thought never even occurred to me to leave C.C. to take up with Chrissie, but I would have liked to see where our budding affair might lead. Trouble was, after our two times together, Chrissie started to make herself unavailable to me. Maybe she was put off by the resilience of my relationship with C.C., or maybe she had sampled the goods and decided not to make the purchase. Whatever it was, her initial eagerness cooled, and my occasional attempts to resurrect our passion went nowhere.

Still, I called. I was drawn by Chrissie's energy, and excitement, and by the thrill of the chase. C.C. would be in New York, and I would be in Los Angeles, aboard the *New Wave,* and as I dialed Chrissie's number I would stop to figure what the hell I was doing. It was like C.C. and Sheri all over again. Am I going to fuck this up? I wondered. Where is this going to end? I later learned that Chrissie had taken up with skier Andy Mill, the man she would later marry, and that that was the reason she kept putting me off. She was looking for someone to love and she could not find him in me.

The "American Vice" special was memorable for other reasons. It was noteworthy for its subject matter, and for the fact that it was my first major effort following Capone. "American Vice," broadcast live on December 2, 1986, was born of simple (and selfish) motives; the best way I could think to combat the drug rumors that continued to plague me was to confront them directly, and the show, I thought, would do just that. It was designed to inform viewers, in two hours, of every aspect of the drug plague gripping our society. We traveled the globe, tracing cocaine and heroin to their sources; we monitored international airports and seaports, to examine the ways drugs were smuggled into this country. The program was conceived with two, high-concept hooks. The first: I planned to take a drug test, live, on national television, and to administer the same to our studio audience. The second: We arranged with law enforcement officials in four different cities to record actual drug raids live, as they happened.

The show was produced by Malcolm Barbour and John Langley, two then struggling (now prosperous and colorful) independent producers with a thing for cops and robbers; we became great friends and they would stay on to produce all of my subsequent specials. "American Vice" was the most technologically ambitious independent television project ever mounted. We had eight live remotes. The finished product was exciting as hell, and more in keeping with my earlier work than the Capone special. (With the cooperation of police, I went undercover to make a drug buy; during the tense, high-risk exchange, the seller turned to me and said, "You know, you look like that guy, Geraldo Rivera.") This was news, not theater. It was also a high-stakes enterprise, and it generated even more controversy than any of us had anticipated. Critics jumped all over us for broadcasting the live busts, alleging that we were infringing on the rights of the accused with the glare of our television cameras. But these were real cops, making real arrests, pursuant to real warrants. Local news programs put this stuff on everyday, long before the innocence or guilt of the subject is determined, but they are never made to shoulder the kind of criticism launched at "American Vice."

The international fieldwork for these two hours was laced with high adventure. I traveled with Craig, C.C., and Carl Hersh to La Paz, Bolivia, to look at the coca plantations there. We rode with the Tiger Battalion of the Bolivian army, in Israeli-supplied helicopters, as they raided coca leaf processing plants. For a trip over the Andes from Lima, Peru, to a small Peruvian town in the Amazon jungle known as Tinga Maria, we chartered a single-engine Cesna piloted by two inept Lima city policemen, who overloaded the plane with guns they were smuggling to their jungle contacts; we were so weighted down by their illicit cargo that we barely cleared the mountain peaks.

"American Vice" pulled a 17.2 national rating, far less than the Capone special but still enough to place it among the top five specials ever syndicated. The strong ratings, though, were not gained without cost. One of the live drug raids, in a Houston suburb, resulted in a thirty-million-dollar lawsuit against me, Maravilla, Tribune, and local police, and a backlash of bad press that diminished the program's impact and almost stalled the momentum of my new career in syndicated television. A twenty-eight-year-old woman named Terry Rouse claimed she was a house painter who happened to be working in a targeted house at the time of the police raid; the initial cocaine possession charge against Rouse was dismissed by a state district judge after she spent two days in jail. She came after us upon her release, listing defamation, invasion of privacy, false imprisonment, malicious prosecution, and conspiracy among her charges.

Rouse's charges were picked up by the press and given far more play than my initial report had received. The suit dragged on for several years, and was finally settled out of court in the summer of 1990. Despite the settlement, I still champion our efforts in that program.

The fallout from Rouse's lawsuit occurred at the worst possible time for the talk show. It made headlines just as we were gearing up to take the pilot to NATPE, to try to convince local station owners to carry the program on a daily basis beginning in September.

December 16, 1986. The pressure is unrelenting. The critics have seized on the live bust. I am surrounded by pussies-turned-tigers. The only choice is to fight back. The only hope: that the crowd stays with me. Pray that the junkyard dog (me) wins. My side has the greater motivation. Theirs is avarice and opportunism. Mine is life. Dig in or die.

I deflected the constant criticism (or, at least, ignored it) by burying myself in my new role at *Entertainment Tonight*, where I was given license to investigate stories of my own choosing, provided they were in some way connected to a celebrity. The weekly exposure on *Entertainment Tonight* did a great deal to restore my familiarity and credibility; too, the prime time specials were so sporadic that I welcomed the regular outlet for my work. (The ironic aspect to my *ET* assignment is that it put me back on my mother-station, New York's WABC-TV, Channel 7; in a way,

I had bypassed Roone Arledge just as I had bypassed Bill Sheehan more than ten years earlier with *Good Night America*.)

My *ET* stories drifted to the harder edge of the soft-news program. I looked at the dangers posed to Hollywood stuntmen, and the tragedy of AIDS in the fashion industry. Wherever possible, I borrowed material from my syndicated specials and gave them a Hollywood spin. For example, in researching "Innocence Lost: The Erosion of American Childhood," my next special following "American Vice," I discovered a sidebar story on the runaway teenagers flocking to Los Angeles in search of fame and fortune and turned it into a multipart series for *ET*.

But even with the heightened exposure from *ET*, and a critic-proof special on lost American youth, sales of the talk show lagged below expectations.

> February 24, 1987. Problems continue in launching this ad-hoc talk show. Another war, and I'm still in it. I won't let them kill me. I have not given up. Things anguish me. Personal life still unsettled, even though it appears stable. Professionally, much remains in doubt. But I'm still in it. Dig in or die.

While reporting "Innocence Lost," and shouldering the uncertain launch of the talk show, I fell off the love wagon, heavily. Driven perhaps by boredom and insecurity, I abandoned the relative fidelity that characterized this period, and began a series of high-risk one-night stands. The ensuing mess nearly cost me C.C., but in a strange way led to the catharsis that allowed me finally to clean up my act.

In Montgomery, Alabama, after working a couple long days and nights on the special, Craig and I partied at a country-western bar with some local ladies who had been especially helpful in our reporting. I ended up spending the night with a pretty blonde who also happened to be married. Word of my Alabama fling tailed me to New York, in the form of a love letter, triple-sealed and marked "urgent" and "personal." With packaging like that, C.C. naturally looked inside. Like most cheats, when caught, I cried, moaned and begged forgiveness.

> March 15, 1987. How *Geraldo Live* will do is really the biggest unknown, rather than whether it will get on. KCBS [the L.A. CBS

station] is a no-go so far, so it looks as if we will go on the air with no owned and operated stations. Makes it tough to plan ahead, which makes it unpleasant, and tentative, and leaves my psyche somewhat vulnerable. Can't be weak now. Dig in or die. That's got to continue to be this year's operating philosophy.

My troubles with C.C. continued. Another one-night stand, this one from Texas, made herself known through a phone call to the office. Despite all my entreaties not to get in touch with me, the woman placed an agitated call on the morning after "Innocence Lost" was broadcast to mediocre ratings (but relatively good reviews). The girls at the front desk put the call through to C.C., who had been working with me as one of my producers since Capone.

Again, I begged and moaned.

April 21, 1987. Darling, how can I put into words the terror I feel at the prospect of losing you? My dear darling, love of my life. You have been my middle life. My passion. My heat. My drama. My girl.

C.C. left, but after several terrible nights away she came back. Two months later, a final affair (this one in Los Angeles) revealed itself. I was leaving clues everywhere. This time, C.C. found a damning picture.

June 24, 1987. C.C. is gone without a trace. Now I face the world alone, during a perilous time. What to do? What to tell the boy? Where to go? Woe. Woe.

(I really wrote that . . ."Woe. Woe.")
It slowly dawned on me that I was destroying my only hope at long-term love and domestic tranquillity. How could I cause such pain to a woman who had done nothing but love me? How could I be so self-destructive? So obsessive? I was like the goldfish who eats himself to death because food is available. Or the drunk . . . Or the junkie . . . I will not use the lame excuse that I was ill. That would be no admission; it would be cowardice. I screwed all those women because it felt better than self-denial. I was a pig—a grunting, voracious pig in heat—who finally realized he had to

choose between the decency he preached and the indecency he practiced.

In an X-rated impression of Jimmy Stewart about to jump off the bridge in *It's a Wonderful Life,* I had another, final epiphany. I decided, on the farfetched chance she would have me, to ask C.C. to marry me. I swore on my soul and everything I saw as clean and sacred that if C.C. married me I would never have sex with another woman.

MARION, MSSACHUSETTS

When I finally proposed to C.C., she was understandably noncommittal. She did, however, agree to a July vacation in a house we had rented in her hometown of Marion, on Buzzard's Bay. Gabriel came east, and we began a tense holiday. As the days passed, I proposed again, swore my fidelity again, begged again. C.C. warmed slightly to the idea. I took signs of encouragement where I could find them. By the July 4 weekend, we were making secret plans to marry. We told no one.

We were scheduled to leave for Europe on the evening of July 18, to continue production on my next live special, a program on the current state of organized crime that I had been working on for the last two months. Time was becoming extremely tight. We went to the local clinic for our blood tests, and worried about leaks when we applied at the tiny town hall for a marriage license. We made arrangements with Reverend Ernie Cockrell, the family's longtime minister, to conduct the ceremony. And we set the date: July 11, 1987 . . . seven/eleven would be my lucky numbers.

Rumors circulated in the Boston newspapers that we were shopping local antique stores for a ring. Still, our families were unaware of our plans. I invited my parents and all my siblings up for what we said was to be a big reunion clambake. C.C.'s parents, three sisters and brother (and their respective spouses) all showed up, ready for a party on the beach. As the clambake cooked, and people swam and frolicked in the surf, I called my dad, Gabriel, and my brothers Willie and Craig aside to break the great news. They were all ecstatic. Everyone in my family loved C.C., and recognized what a wonderful, positive, and tolerant partner she had been to me. I asked Gabriel to be my best man. He happily agreed and then raced to call his mother on the phone with the news. ("Mom," he began, "do I have news for you.")

When Reverend Ernie showed up, the assembled clan rejoiced at the truly surprising news. After a wedding rehearsal conducted in wet bathing suits, we all retired into the house to dress for the ceremony. The afternoon was fresh and golden in the way the Cape can be in early summer; the wind was modest, the blue-green water of the bay sparkling and magnificent. We were married on the lawn, with the sea behind us. We made the familiar pledges and, for the first time, I have had the honor of keeping them. It was simple and glorious.

The impromptu celebration was fueled by my frozen margarita machine, and we all enjoyed a traditional Rivera/Dyer celebration. For the first time in a long time, we joined in a cherished family ritual; we Rivera boys tossed Pop back and forth between us, the way he had "played catch" with us as kids.

The week immediately following the emotional wedding was hectic and intense, and effectively stalled our joyous celebration. The next morning, with virtually no sleep and a margarita hangover to end all, I was on my way to New Orleans for a series of interviews in preparation for the live Mafia special. (With a nod toward my old pal Capone, we christened the new show, "The Sons of Scarface: The New Mafia.")

From the Crescent City, it was on to Vegas, and then Los Angeles, filming with cops or cons at each stop. In Los Angeles, I announced our nuptials on *Entertainment Tonight*; cohosts John Tesh and Mary Hart were gracious enough not to mention that it was my fourth time out. After interviewing jailed members of the Mexican Mafia, I took the red-eye to New York and proceeded directly to a Nassau County jail, to interview a Mafia squealer. The next day, we raided numbers parlors in Harlem, with cameras rolling. One of the managers, apoplectic with rage at our trespass, told me my ass was grass. I told him to go fuck himself. That night, I interviewed former-*Deep-Throat*-star-turned-suburban-housewife Linda Lovelace about Mafia control of the pornography business.

Afterwards, I finally flew back to idyllic Marion and my waiting family. Exactly a week after our beachfront ceremony, I was home. But not for long. The next afternoon, C.C. and I were off to Rome and Sicily for more work on the special. All thoughts of a more traditional honeymoon, or even a period of reflection, were placed on hold. We were running on adrenaline, too busy to look back. Gabriel broke my heart as we took off on this latest leg of the production. "Dad," he said, "you are always leaving."

The trip to Sicily was one of the strangest honeymoons on record. We spent it covering the so-called "Maxi-trial" of over 350 local mafiosi, and by traveling to the mountain city of Corleone, made infamous by the *Godfather* saga. The most memorable moment of our trip came when police discovered the decapitated head of a local informant, placed on the front seat of a car parked across from the courthouse. As I was soon to discover personally, these racket guys can't take a joke.

Cheech and his new wife Patti, and their great kid, one-year-old Joey Dee, came to stay with us on the eve of the live broadcast of "Scarface." I loved having my old friend around. When an interviewer asked Cheech during this period why our friendship had endured, he replied, "Geraldo and I got married together. Had kids together. Our wives went to the same divorce lawyers. So, we got screwed together. Our careers went up and down together. And we got married again together. Plus, we both have that crazy Latin streak. He's my brown-brother."

The two-hour broadcast went well. (It was our first in Times Square Studios, a rehabilitated facility on Forty-third Street, smack in the rotten core of the Big Apple; the talk show later originated from this same facility for three seasons, and the running jokewas that there was a season's worth of topics within one block of our studio.) Trouble began later that evening, after a post-special celebration at SoHo's Odeon restaurant, although I did not find out about it until the next morning. Tony, the flirtatious and charming Puerto Rican doorman working the night shift in our Ninety-sixth Street building, pulled me aside as I went off to work and told me he had been visited at two o'clock in the morning by three older guys in a black Cadillac. The driver stayed in the car, while the other two got out and walked up to Tony. They looked Italian, he said. One of them leaned in and stage-whispered, "Tell Geraldo we know where he lives."

I walked to my car, a 1983 El Dorado convertible parked a block away, and reviewed the special in my head. Who had sent the thugs to the apartment? I wondered. It had to be John Gotti. I had embarrassed the Godfather in the special, chasing him down the streets of Little Italy with cameras rolling. I had also embarrassed his otherwise effective lawyer Bruce Cutler, surprising him with a live confrontation with a stool pigeon who had some nasty things to say about his client. Yes. It had to be Gotti. I was worried, I admit, but my concern turned to anger when I got to my car. The convertible had been trashed. The windows were smashed, the ragtop slashed, and the dashboard torn off. Worse, nothing was taken. It was not a robbery. It was another heavy-handed warning.

I turned around, ran home, and called the office. I was not going to be scared in private. I alerted *Entertainment Tonight* to send up a camera crew, and filmed a story about the post-show events. I contacted the federal prosecutor's office and filled in a couple print and television reporters on these latest developments. Gotti, reached through a well-connected criminal lawyer, claimed no part in the incident, but I was not convinced. The prosecutor's office in the Eastern District later told me that wiretaps had intercepted several mentions of my name in angry conversation at Gotti's base of operations, the Ravenite Social Club in Little Italy. Gotti was heard telling his consorts to leave me alone, that I was not worth the heat actions against me would bring. My own theory, developed later but confirmed with the years, was that the culprits were amateurs, fans of Gotti's enraged to see their icon humiliated.

As the September debut of the talk show approached, I developed an occasional tick in my left eye. "There can be no doubt it is caused by stress," I wrote in my notebook. "Also, my vision is clearly fading. Maybe I'll be wearing reading glasses before long." (Note: I do.)

I was as thrilled with the success of my marriage as I was nervous over the success of the new show. After a life of promiscuity and a notoriously short attention span, I was feeling an uncontrolled tingle toward my wife. It was more than passion or affection. It was more like religion. For the first time, all the love-song clichés made sense. C.C. was part of me.

The theme of our first talk show, carried initially on approximately sixty stations across the country, was intentionally righteous. The star guest was Marla Hanson, the razor-slashed model. C.C., who produced that segment, managed to convince the beautiful woman whose face had been mutilated on orders from an unrequited lover to appear on our show first, soon after the highly publicized court case in which her attackers were finally sent to prison. Our intention was not merely to tell Marla Hanson's frightening story, but also to editorialize about the need for our criminal justice system to be more sensitive to and protective of the rights of crime victims. It would become a recurring theme on the show.

No matter what we put on the air, the critics were poised to attack me. "A television critic's worst nightmare has become reality," *The Los Angeles Times* began its review, which went on to describe me as "a highly theatrical journalist . . . despised by much of the press." *The New York Times* checked in with this: "Mr. Rivera has won many top broadcast journalism awards but almost never the fond embrace of television critics, who have frequently sneered at his signature style of swashbuckling bravado, naked emotion, and show-biz glitz."

Although many producers complain that their new shows are not given enough time to find a niche in a crowded TV marketplace, my feeling was that we would know in days whether or not the talk show was going to work. In fact, we knew by that Wednesday, September 9, that we would be at least a moderate success. With occasional exceptions, like the week I had the rumble with the neo-Nazis, that level of achievement—a moderate success—has been our basic performance ever since.

And so, as Rand Corporation analyst Francis Fukuyam said after the tumbling of the Berlin Wall and the turning of the Soviet Union to a market economy, it was the end of history. My talk show's sustained success, and the sustained success of my marriage, mark the end, at least, of my history. In substance, I am now the man I was in the fall of 1987. Of course, there have been some unexpected twists, turns, triumphs, and tragedies, some shattering disappointments, exhilirating victories, violent encounters, and terrible losses.

And C.C. and I are living happily ever after.

EPILOGUE

ROUGH POINT

We gave up on Manhattan in February of 1989. Though sometimes chatted about (" . . . wouldn't it be nice to live in the country?"), the actual decision to leave New York was sudden. It came on a Saturday morning after a particularly brutal crime. A pregnant young doctor, serving her residency at Bellevue Hospital, apparently had been raped and murdered by a psychotic homeless man posing as a hospital employee. A person on the threshold of a wonderful and useful life was snuffed out in a heartbeat. "That's it, we're going," I said to C.C., even as I crumpled in disgust *The New York Times* that had just yielded the dreadful news.

The city had changed, we reasoned. There had always been

problems (crime, poverty, pollution), and infinite inconveniences, but they seemed outweighed by New York's indisputable assets. This was the exciting capital of the Western World, the center of culture, commerce, and communications. In the immediate aftermath of the Bellevue doctor's murder, none of that mattered. Crack cocaine, the migratory homeless, and the escalating and random nature of gun-related violence had changed the landscape. While I once felt like the King of New York, I was now frightened by the danger the city posed to my family, and I was exhausted by daily exposure to problems I felt powerless to effect.

Coming as it did after years of watching the exodus of the city's middle class with derision bordering on contempt, guilt was one of the emotions that greeted the decision to flee. The other was anticipation. I have dealt with the guilt by continuing to base my professional life in the city, and by continuing our extensive involvement in New York-based charities and causes. For example, in 1989, I "adopted" a class of eighth-graders at a junior high school in "El Barrio," Spanish Harlem, and eventually established The Maravilla Foundation for them. Facing a dropout rate that exceeded sixty percent, I promised the twenty-eight youngsters that if they finished high school, I would subsidize their college tuitions. Two years later, we have lost only four of the kids. We are working with the class on a weekly basis to encourage the remaining twenty-four to stick it out. C.C. and I have decided that the profits from this book will be used to fund the foundation that will see them through school.

We searched all the traditional suburbs to find our dream house, but to no avail. Would we ever find our suburban paradise, on the water, where our three dogs could walk themselves, and I could efficiently get to work? Then C.C. got a call from her favorite aunt, Peter Sorensen. (I've discovered that WASPs often give their girls boys' names and vice versa.) "Why don't you come down to Monmouth County?" said Aunt Peter. "There's a wonderful old house for sale on the Navesink River."

"The what river?" I asked. C.C. explained that Monmouth, in an affluent corner of coastal New Jersey, was where her family had lived for generations before moving to Massachusetts. She is the only one of the five Dyer kids not born there.

We fell in love with the house, a Victorian, built in 1893, hard by the banks of the Navesink. I loved its name, Rough Point. I loved the idea that the house *had* a name. I now commute into Manhattan either by ferry, helicopter, or, during summers, by my own speed boat, which I christened *Bubba/Jersey*. Looking out the window of my third-floor study, the *New Wave* swings on her Navesink mooring, and I dream of far horizons. Although it has principally been a time of consolidation, the last four years have not lacked drama. Aside from the talk show generating ratings sufficient to sustain its long and prosperous run, several significant things happened that fall of 1987.

They closed Willowbrook. Forty-two years after they opened that dungeon, and fifteen years after my initial exposé, New York's governor Mario Cuomo presided over a closing ceremony on the lovely grounds, already in the process of being converted into a college campus. Bernard Carabello and I were among the honored guests. After receiving a hero's welcome from many of the assembled parents, I was shocked by what I perceived to be jabs thrown my way by the governor. After crediting *The Staten Island Advance* with technically breaking the story (as if their small efforts would have made any substantive difference), he compounded the insult by referring to me as a "television celebrity," rather than a journalist.

True, television makes celebrities, whether we star on sitcoms, sell beer, or do the news. But the Willowbrook saga was nothing if not advocacy journalism at its finest, or at least most effective. Screw Cuomo, I decided. Anyway, Bernard saved the day, urging the crowd to give me a rousing cheer. His tortured, but impassioned words about me were worth a million speeches by any mere politician. Over the years, we had become best friends and blood brothers. These days, in the words of Pittsburgh Pirates All-Star Willie Stargell, "We are family."

Another noteworthy event during this period was my rapprochement with Jerry Weintraub. I had seen Jerry only once, since leaving him for Jon Peters. One day, he and his wife Jane were driving down Pacific Coast Highway in an antique Dodge convertible. Driving past in my treasured old Jaguar XK120, I waved as all vintage car owners tend to do. After a second look,

Jerry and I noticed each other, pulled over, and had a nice, polite chat. But that was years before the extravagant fiftieth birthday bash Jane threw for him at their magnificent Malibu oceanfront estate, sweetly called, My Blue Heaven. Every mogul, movie star, crooner, and producer imaginable was there. Among others, the guest list included Elvis's reclusive manager Colonel Tom Parker, Bob Dylan, Frank Sinatra, Neil Diamond, Sidney Poitier, Olivia Newton-John, Frankie Valli, Ed McMahon, Jacqueline Bisset, and Alexander Gudunov. Jane invited me as a surprise for Jerry. At this landmark birthday, she wanted friends and associates representing all the significant chapters of his life. Waiting our turn on the receiving line, C.C. and I happened to be standing next to Johnny Carson and his new wife Alexis. For the last several years, at least, I had been a staple in Carson's monologue. He had gotten several hundred laughs from the Al Capone special alone. After we exchanged greetings, he put his arm around C.C. and said, "Please don't ever let anything happen to Geraldo. If you do, I'll be out of material." I still repeat it whenever anyone asks me why I tend to attract far more heat and critical attention than my talk show rivals. Carson's quip is the key. At some point in my *20/20* years, I passed into the lexicon, a caricature for columnists, cartoonists, and commentators seeking a shorthand way of describing all that ails the popular culture. Want to get an easy laugh or start a cocktail party argument? Just mention *Geraldo.*

The most profound event that fall was the death of my father. Let me start at the end, with my sister Sharon's call from Florida. "Geraldo," she said, "Poppa is dead!" The news had been half expected. At seventy-two-years old, Poppa had never recovered from the stroke he'd suffered during bypass surgery in Sarasota the month before. Still, there was a physical reaction to Sharon's sorrow-filled news. Later, sitting at my office desk, I deflated, my head collapsing into the shelter of my arms. My longtime assistant, Jo-Ann Torres Conte, hearing my sobs, came quickly into the office. She comforted me with the rhythmic sounds of sympathy Puerto Rican women use at times of tragedy, *Ah Dios mio . . . pobrecito.* (Oh, my God . . . you poor thing.)

Reflecting on his life in the aftermath of his death, I retrieved mixed memories. Most of the sad stuff was restricted to the period immediately following his bankruptcy in 1966. Dreaming always of the treasure just over the horizon, he went from one menial job to the next. Working as a uniformed night watchman at the mall, or as the counterman at Frankie's deli, he seemed to grow old before his time.

In the 1970s, a wonderful thing happened. His adoring children began finding their way. After raising four of her own children, my older sister Irene went to college, became a teacher, and later a school principal. Willie married, had a lovely daughter, and got a good-paying union job as a steamfitter (those are the guys who install sprinkler systems in high-rise buildings). Sharon, who like Dad and me had always been a semiwild soul, settled down with a stable guy, had three great kids, and started a successful business as a party planner (if you're interested, she's listed in the phone book, in Lakewood, New Jersey). Craig grew up big and handsome (*The New York Post* calls him my " . . . younger, taller, better-looking brother"), and came to work as an on-camera reporter, first on *Inside Edition,* later with me on *Now It Can Be Told.*

With money no longer a problem, Dad also prospered socially and intellectually. I named him president of my newly formed production company. His basic job perfectly suited his expansive charm and engaging personality. He became my liaison to various community groups, a kind of public relations ambassador whose special turf was the Hispanic community. He and Mom attended functions I couldn't, gave interviews to the Spanish-language press, and just generally chatted with anyone with a problem. Irene and I joked during this period that he could converse with equal confidence with Kissinger, Qaddafi, a pregnant teenager, or a precocious three-year-old. To everyone, he became known as Poppa.

But he was also restless. Despite being ill with diabetes and heart disease, he was always dreaming of this idea or that to better use his tireless energy. "Let's buy a building," he would say. "I could be the super." Or, "Why don't we start a business? I could run it for you." Busy with my professional life, and unwilling to be distracted, I would humor him until the scheme-of-the-moment died of inertia. After his death, the fact that I never took a chance on him was the one thing that haunted me.

Time had rescued me from his ambition. After he reached retirement age, Mom and Pop hit the road. In a succession of ever-larger trailers and motorhomes, the two crisscrossed the nation. At campgrounds from New England to New Mexico, Mom would swap pictures of grandchildren, while Poppa shared his global philosophy and expansive dreams with the guys. When advancing illness wrecked his vision and made the highways inaccessible, they settled in Sarasota, Florida. In early 1987, on Craig's initiative, we bought them a swell condo in a building called, Whispering Sands, right on the Gulf in the best part of town. They loved it, and so did their children and grandchildren. Sarasota seemed as if it would become the setting for the next generation of family reunions. To make the picture even rosier, C.C.'s parents wintered barely a mile down the road. When he wasn't entertaining family or friends, Pop would sit in his balcony easy-chair for hours, watching the dolphins and the sunsets, all the time dreaming.

In the second month of the talk show, my parents flew up from Florida to appear as guests on a program we were taping about coping with heart disease. As it turned out, he was not coping all that well. Walking the long block from our office on Eighth Avenue to the studio on Broadway, he collapsed. The experts assembled for the show advised him to undergo extensive diagnostic evaluation. Eager to get back to Florida, my parents decided to have the work done there. Should I have insisted that they stay in New York? Another guilt that plagued me. In any case, the news from Florida was bad. I had just returned from an overnight flight from Los Angeles, when Mom called to tell me he had to have a quintuple bypass.

Craig was with him when the operation began at seven the next morning. The rest of us were on the way. When C.C. and I got to the hospital, my big, loving lug of a brother embraced us crying. Pop was in critical condition, after suffering a stroke during the operation. Irene, Sharon, and Willie were there within hours. The five of us comforted each other and Mom, who was frantic with worry. The irony of this happening when everything was going so well was not lost on any of us.

With Poppa still unconscious, Craig and I had to shoot over to Houston to fulfill a long-scheduled taping. When we got back to

Sarasota the next day, Poppa was conscious and out of intensive
care. "Where you boys been?" he asked as we walked in the door.
My heart soared with joy. For the rest of the month, at least one
of the kids was by his side. His recovery was agonizingly slow.
Sharon proved the strongest among us. She took the place of the
regular night-nurse, staying with him from sunset to sunrise. As
soon as his school schedule allowed, Gabriel joined us in Florida. I
cried when the eight-year-old climbed up on his grandfather's bed
to wish him well. But no amount of love could reverse Dad's
decline. He developed a blood clot in one of his legs, and we waited
grimly as they amputated it. I was in New York and planning on
spending the next day, Thanksgiving 1987, back in Florida, when
Sharon called with the dreadful news.

After making the funeral and travel arrangements, I told Gabriel
his grandfather had passed away. We were on my apartment
balcony, looking out at the city lights. The November night was
uncharacteristically fair and still. As I struggled through tears to
explain to my son what made my father so special, he put his arms
around me.

When I next saw my father, he was lying all dressed up in his
open casket. He looked noble, proud, and accomplished. He could
have been secretary-general, or president of someplace. How we
kids cried. We embraced each other and Mom, alternately consoling
and being consoled. There would be a full-blown memorial service
arranged by Irene's husband Howard, an Army major, at their
home base, Fort Hamilton, New York. But for Mom and the kids,
farewell to Poppa was a private affair down in Florida.

My father had requested that his ashes be scattered in the Gulf.
Maybe he was just an armchair sailor, but he wanted his remains
to sail the Seven Seas. After downing a couple of tear-filled
margaritas, Craig, Willie, and I chartered a yacht. Accompanied by
a Baptist preacher who had been a great comfort to us during the
last days, the family set sail. In keeping with the ecumenical
nature of the clan, a priest and a rabbi had also been present at
times in the hospital, but the fire-and-brimstone preacher seemed
to reach Dad the most. So he was with us, as we sailed out into
the Gulf. Standing in the surf, C.C.'s parents and some other
friends tossed flower petals into the sea as we cruised past

Whispering Sands. The skipper of the vessel sounded one long, mournful blast of the boat's horn.

At my mother's request, the captain turned off the engine when we were about a mile out, directly opposite her now widow's apartment. With the vessel drifing, we said our good-byes. Mine was a poem. Reading it now, it seems awkward and naive, but Mom said he would have loved it. The last stanza reads:

> Sailing past his widow's walk
> to bid bon voyage to his ash and bone,
> we say farewell to our seafaring man.
> Dad, your ship's come home.

SAN QUENTIN

In some ways, 1988 was one of the most commercially successful and critically controversial years of my life. With the talk show beginning to spin off the kinds of profits that make a man forget ever working for a salary again, I scored an exclusive interview with Charles Manson. It was part of "Murder: Live from Death Row," the fifth, and highest-rated, of the live, two-hour syndicated specials produced by my company, the Investigative News Group. The hook for the show was to be live, satellite interviews with condemned men and women sitting on death rows around the country. While that aspect of the program was certainly compelling, it was the bizarre and confrontational prison interview with Manson, conducted on March 11, 1988, that really put this one over the top.

It had been nineteen years since we'd first heard of Charles Manson, the weird little man with the unforgettable satanic gleam in his eyes, the man responsible for creating a national paranoia, a dread that absolutely nobody was safe from mayhem and murder. In the exclusive Los Angeles home of film director Roman Polanski, on a hot summer night in 1969, Manson had masterminded the massacre of Polanski's pregnant wife, the actress Sharon Tate, coffee heiress Abigail Folger, friends Jay Sebring and Voityck

Fryowski, and neighbor Steven Parent. The next night, Manson's "family" butchered supermarket tycoon Leno LaBianca and his wife Rosemary in the same ritualistic way.

Arranged by John Langley and Malcolm Barbour, my skilled colleagues on the West Coast, this was only Manson's second national television interview since his conviction and death sentence, later commuted to seven life sentences. (Tom Snyder, another underrated broadcast outlaw had landed the first interview back in 1981.) Frequently asked, Manson said yes to me because he was a regular viewer of my show. I later discovered mine was the number-one rated talk show in San Quentin.

After initially agreeing to the interview, Manson tried to hold us up for money. When we explained that paying him would be illegal, he reduced his demands to a guitar, and later to a red cloth bandanna. I brought the ninety-eight-cent bandanna into the prison with me. When asked directly by the institution's staff whether I was carrying anything for Charlie, I confessed and had to turn the item over to the guards. Waiting for the celebrated monster, I had a feeling of anticipation and revulsion. I knew I would hate him, and yet, I was fascinated by the opportunity to match wits with the founding father of ritual murder. They brought him down a long corridor, his ankles and wrists shackled. He was in a bad mood.

"Are you going to unhook me?" he railed. "Unhook me, then, dammit." The shackles removed, I gave Charlie a release to sign. He refused until I read a four-page, handwritten manifesto he had prepared. It was his plan for cleaning up the environment. I scanned through it, then told him he could tell me about it on camera. He agreed, and for the next hour he phased in and out of sanity like a drunken cameraman fooling with the focus. He would speak rationally for a couple of minutes, then jump up and begin chanting and waving his arms about, his eyes glazed over and a scary grin on his face.

When he did speak, there was diabolical substance in what he had to say: "Yeah, I chopped up nine hogs [the seven Tate/La Bianca victims, plus two separate homicides], and I'm going to chop up some more of you motherfuckers. I'm going to kill as many as I can. I'm going to pile you up to the sky. I figure about fifty million, if I could get about fifty million of you, I might be able to save my trees and my air and my water and my wildlife."

"You want to kill fifty million people?" I asked.

"Well," he said, "that's just a drop in the bucket to what's really coming."

At the end of our interview, as Charlie was being reshackled, he seemed both angry with my taunting attitude, and sorry that the encounter was over. "There ain't too many things in the whole world you can't do, but there's one thing you can't do," he declared.

"What's that, Charlie?"

"You can't break a man's soul. . . . We talked about what I did, you want to talk about what I could do? I could do just about anything I want on my row [cellblock]. I could send for your head and put it in a box, if I wanted."

"If anything happens to me, Charlie, the Mexicans in here will light you on fire again," I answered. Charlie had recently had an incident in which fellow inmates had squirted him with lighter fluid and then thrown a match into his cell. I wanted him to think they were friends of mine. I didn't want him to know that I was unnerved by his threat.

THE 21 CLUB

The murder special was a triumph. Its 20.1 national rating placed it third on the all-time list of syndicated specials (after "Capone" and a Telly Savalas show that opened another vault, this one from the sunken luxury liner, the *Andrea Doria*), and it provided the daytime talk show with a week's worth of related topics. It also brought me back to network television. The unprecedented success of these syndicated specials was obviously coming at the expense of the networks' prime-time programs. At a William Morris Agency cocktail party held at "21," Robert Wright, NBC's new president, approached Lee Stevens and Jim Griffin and asked if I would be interested in doing one or more of the two-hour extravaganzas on his air. He told the agents that if I was able to garner big numbers on an ad hoc network of weak stations, imagine what I would do on a "real" network like NBC. I was excited by the idea. It was my ticket back to the big time. The problem was *Tribune*. I was under exclusive contract with the boys from Chicago and needed their permission to go elsewhere. After several conversations about how good the heightened visibility would be for all our mutual projects, they consented.

Enter Brandon Tartikoff, the wunderkind president of NBC Entertainment. In our only conversation before production began, we discussed, then agreed on a topic from the three I proposed. My NBC special would investigate the occult. (Two others suggested had been the secret world of private investigators and exposing the hidden network of child molesters.) I don't know what Tartikoff had in mind, but my plan was to tear the wraps off what my team and I perceived to be a huge underground of ritual criminals. The operating thesis was that Manson was not alone; from kids who dabble in satanic rituals, to heavy-metal devotees who self-mutilate, to cults that kill, devil worship is a reality involving tens of thousands of Americans in wildly varying degrees. It was a topic I knew going in would be ridiculed by the sophisticated elite, but compelling television to everyone else.

For the actual production, we traveled the country, interviewing a dozen murderers who claimed that the devil made them do it. One stop was Carl Junction, Missouri, population 4,000, in the heart of the Bible Belt. Late one night in December 1987, four teenagers who had been dabbling in satanism carried baseball bats, a cat, and a length of rope to an isolated spot. By the time the night was over, the cat had been mutilated and one of the boys beaten to death. I interviewed one of the perpetrators, a good-looking, fresh-faced seventeen-year-old kid named Pete Rolland, now serving a life sentence without possibility of parole. We also broadcast his never-before-seen confession tape, in which he claimed, ". . . I didn't feel like I was the master of my own body, like something else kind of took over within the inside of my mind." He later identified the "something," as the devil.

With anecdotes like that one, a never-before-broadcast exorcism (three years before *20/20*'s widely acclaimed similar effort), a live satellite interview from London with heavy-metal rocker Ozzie Osborne (godfather of satanic graffiti artists everywhere), and with a panel of experts who painted a scary picture of ritual criminals on the loose, our broadcast was the stuff of nightmares. But it was also responsibly reported, and fully supported by the facts. The public was fascinated by it.

"World Series numbers!" Tartikoff exclaimed in a phone conversation the morning after our October 25, 1988 broadcast. "Hell, it's bigger than the Series."

Aired opposite ABC's then powerful Tuesday night lineup, the "Devil Worship" program handed Roseanne Barr her one and only ratings defeat that season. With a 21.8 national rating, "Exposing Satan's Underground" became the highest-rated multihour documentary in the history of network television. I looked forward to doing lots more of them with NBC. It never happened.

The critics savaged the report. In an editorial, not a review, an unprecedented editorial about a television program, *The New York Times* said " . . . it was pornography masquerading as journalism." My old nemesis Tom Shales of *The Washington Post* went even further, saying I " . . . plumbed uncharted depths in dirty-minded teleporn . . . inexcusable slop." I could take the heat, Tartikoff could not. He immediately backed away from me and the program, apologizing for its content, while emphasizing how NBC and I had many creative disagreements during production, and how the network had only screened the on-location pieces at the eleventh hour. Ever clever, Tartikoff donned priestly garb to swear to critics assembled in Los Angeles that he would never, ever hire me to do another special.

I was angry, rather than hurt. Despite our tacit agreement to exaggerate our creative differences in order to hype the broadcast in the days leading up to air, in reality, there were virtually no substantive disagreements between NBC's supervising producers and my staff. NBC had gotten the hypocritical best of both worlds. They had distanced themselves from the special, while taking full advantage of its extraordinary performance.

But I got the last laugh, or at least grim smile. Several months after the special aired to widespread professional disbelief and ridicule, a devil-worshipping cult was discovered in Matamoros, Mexico, just across the border from Brownsville, Texas. Cult members had dismembered nine people, including two Americans. Buried in the text of its extensive article covering the ritual horrors, *The New York Times* article stated how this type of crime was first brought to the public's attention, " . . . in Geraldo Rivera's recent special."

TIMES SQUARE STUDIOS

The special and its accompanying controversy were forgotten a couple of weeks later, when I got into a knock-down-drag-out rumble with a gang of neo-Nazis in my talk show studio. What would become the most notorious brawl in the history of broadcasting, began as all our shows do, with the weekly story conference. Our office, at the time, a penthouse overlooking Eighth Avenue and the rest of Times Square, featured one large, loft-type space, divided by partitions. If a producer absolutely needed privacy on a phone call, he or she could barely achieve it, by sort of crouching below the level of the partitions. For our weekly story conferences, everyone sat on the desks, above the partitions, and the room became a common space. I would direct the meeting, gruff and playful ("C'mon, Jay. Don't waste my time with bullshit!"), going from one producer to the next for an idea. Often, an idea would evolve into an assigned story with a specific angle in the ebb and flow of these unstructured, organic meetings.

At the meeting in question, someone suggested doing a program on the spread of neo-Nazism in America. Five years before, I had collaborated with producer Bob Lange for a major *20/20* investigation we called "Seeds of Hate." The focus of that piece was the growth in influence of white supremacy groups among a significant minority of those farmers who, at the time, were in economic distress. The story, which aired on August 15, 1985, was condemned by many farm groups, but honored at a dinner for major contributors to the B'nai B'rith. Indeed, even before that broadcast, my hostile, confrontational relationship with the neo-Nazis, and their allied groups the KKK and the White Aryan Nation, had been long-established by previous work on *Good Morning America,* and the evening news.

"Let's focus on the younger generation, the young hatemongers," suggested producer Bill Flohr, one of our best. I agreed. My specialty is less doing totally original stories, than in taking totally original approaches to otherwise familiar stories. (Roone taught me that.) Marilyn Kaskel, who happened to be Jewish, was assigned to escort the young neo-Nazis, after their arrival at JFK from the West Coast. She got them under her wing and into town, but that first talk show, booked for early October, never happened. The local chapter of the Jewish Defense Organization (the JDO), under the direction of Mordechai Levy (a radical from the Meir Kahane school), had somehow gotten word of our scheduled taping. His gang surrounded Times Square Studios and refused to allow the neo-Nazis to enter. They believed these Hitler youth so heinous that the Bill of Rights did not apply to them: "We are Jews! We couldn't be prouder! And if you can't hear us, we'll shout a little louder." I shouted back that even hatemongers deserved a chance to be knocked around by me. My arguments were to no avail. The Nazis never got close to the building. Upon hearing of the demonstrators, they beat a hasty retreat out of town.

Two weeks later, on November 3, 1988, knowing it would be a hot show, we coaxed them back to New York. Our pledge was to keep their movements and taping time confidential. We tried. It leaked out, necessitating some extraordinary security measures. For one thing, we booked them into the Novotel in Times Square, instead of the Omni, our usual guest accommodations farther uptown on Seventh Avenue. (The Omni would end its relationship with the talk show soon after, annoyed by the picketing.) Then, we taped the show earlier than we usually do, allowing us to get our guests, and the two hundred-odd audience members, inside the studio building before the JDO demonstrators could regroup. Although we usually tape two shows a day, on this day, we scheduled three, on the contingency the neo-Nazis would chicken out again, leaving us high and dry without a show.

We advised our regular security contingent, comprised entirely of retired NYPD detectives, armed and confident, that trouble was a real possibility. Although I later told the media that physical violence was totally unexpected, I do not make that claim here. In fact, my instructions to the studio team were just a slight modification of the rule I had expressed to my camera crews for years. The head of the security detail, white-haired, mustachioed, slickly dressed, former Brooklyn detective Bobby Merz, was told to

pass the word: In the event of trouble, he and the boys were to
stay out of it, unless it looked like the audience members were in
danger, or that I was losing. Agitated both by recent hate crimes,
and a deep-seated loathing of these creepy crawlers, I was looking
to kick some butt.

The stage was set for violence, and it almost erupted before the
first segment was over. I asked, "Recently, in California, a group
of skinheads, racist skinheads slit the throat of a young Hispanic
woman. They wanted to make a point and to scare minority people.
Do you endorse that activity?" Knowing that it would tweak me to
the core, the director of the White Aryan Resistance Youth, a
blond, smallish, twenty-five-year-old named John Metzger,
answered, "Why are you beating around the bush, Gerry? Look—"
I cut him off. "What did you say?" As I walked toward him, he
responded, "Gerry King. That's your former name, wasn't it?"
King? I was seething. I leaned my right arm heavily on his left
shoulder, bent toward him, and said in my most malevolent voice,
"It wasn't, and I really recommend that you don't push me too
hard, pal." *Playboy* later described the encounter as "a moment of
'macho frisson,' a flash of the essential Geraldo, scarily telegraphing
his urge to surge . . . "

The actual surge came about fifteen tension-packed minutes
later, when a woman in the audience, frustrated by the skinheads'
refusal to answer questions about their educational backgrounds,
or criminal records, asked, "If you have true belief in your
convictions and your movement is as good and as powerful as you
say it is, why are you afraid to let other people speak, why are you
not like other minorities and allow other people to pursue whatever
happiness they find in whatever religion they find? . . . What are
you afraid of?"

Metzger answered, "The reason why I do that is because I get
sick and tired of seeing Uncle Tom here (he pointed to one of our
other panelists, Roy Innis, the chairman of the Congress of Racial
Equality), sucking up, trying to be a white man."

With that, the fiercely proud Mr. Innis stood up and began to
move toward the three skinheads seated across the stage from him.
"Go ahead, Roy," I said. Looking back on the moment, I have no
idea whether I meant, "go ahead and whack him," or, "go ahead
and respond." In either case, Roy clenched his right fist and

grabbed Metzger by the collar. All hell broke loose. Instantly, the six or eight skinheads seated in the audience charged the stage. After the close encounter at the top of the show, they must have been waiting for this contingency. I was hit in the face by the thrown chair in the first five seconds of the melee. In brawls of this nature, although you register the fact of a blow, you don't really feel it. All I wanted to do was single out my assailant and make him pay.

A big, 230-pounder, wearing a bold plaid shirt, he was hard to miss. Fortunately for me, throwing the chair had cost him his balance, so as he stumbled, it was relatively easy for me to put on a headlock and twist him off the elevated stage. The celebrated video of the Riot-Shown-Round-the-World reveals the audience, at this point, running for cover. I never saw them. My full attention was locked on Mr. Fat 'n' Plaid. As soon as we were off the stage, I released the headlock. Remember, street fights are over in seconds, you can't waste time with wrestling holds. He was still bent over, his shirt now pulled half up around his head, when I started swinging rights and lefts, hitting his head as if it were the heavybag. Unable to prevent or respond to the blows, he finally tackled me. We rolled into the now-vacated audience seats, where Bobby and the boys broke it up.

The riot aftermath built streamroller momentum within the hour. Based just blocks away, a squad from the Midtown North Precinct had responded immediately. Heeding the direction of our security guards, who had rounded up and were holding all the skinheads in a separate room, the cops ushered the Nazis out of the building and right to the airport. Shaken by the encounter, and frantic over spending the night in mongrel and angry New York, the skinheads needed no encouragement.

As soon as things calmed a bit, I discovered my nose was broken. It had happened before, and there was no mistaking the sickening "click" it made when I bent it back and forth. Still, I had two more shows to do that night. I took a shower, then Diane Jones, my makeup lady, did her best to cover the great gash on my nose. As the storm of publicity began to build outside the studio, I managed to get through the two tapings. One was a show of ordinary people who turn to "Sex for Survival." The other was an interview with Paula Parkinson, a pretty blonde Washington lobbyist who admitted sleeping with various well-connected members of Congress to get her point across.

By the time the tapings were over, the studio was crawling with reporters, attracted to the scene by the police response, and by the efforts of Jeff Erdel, my longtime, ever-vigilant publicist. Tom Brokaw broadcast a two-minute clip of the riot on NBC *Nightly News*. By eleven that night, all the TV stations and CNN were running with the riot. "Isn't this awful?" asked the commentators. "It's so awful, why don't we see it again, this time in slow motion?" It was shown repeatedly over the next few days, not only in America, but around the world. I later received newspaper clippings from France, Australia, Holland, Japan, and Argentina. The next Monday, the day before the presidential election, *Newsweek* put me on its cover. I guess my riot was bigger news than George Bush's coming rout of Michael Dukakis. The headline screamed, "Trash TV—From the Lurid to the Loud, Anything Goes." Like the rest of the media *Newsweek* had condemned me, while simultaneously profiting by prominently displaying that which offended them. (Isn't he awful? Buy this magazine and read all about it.)

The surgery to repair the torn cartilage in my nose would have been straightforward, but I took advantage of the opportunity to ask my doctor, the eminent plastic surgeon James Smith, if he wouldn't mind giving me an upgrade. The proud bearer of a prominent proboscis, I would have never had the guts to get a cosmetic nose job, but, I thought, hey as long as they're fixing it anyway. . . . So, Dr. Smith took a little off the bottom and straightened it a bit. When the wraps came off a week later, I liked my new look. Sadly, it was short-lived. My nose's second violent encounter of the month was unpublicized. It happened up in Marion, during a vigorous doubles game of paddle tennis. I was at the net and made the mistake of looking back at C.C. just as she was returning a lob. A strong woman, once ranked number one on the NYU tennis team, my wife rocketed a shot squarely off the tip of my newly straightened nose, instantly returning it to its former, swollen, and meandering shape. There, it remains.

We broadcast the "Young Hate Mongers" show in mid-November, to coincide with the fiftieth anniversary of *Kristallnacht,* the night the Nazis destroyed thousands of German-Jewish synagogues and businesses. And although I have taken considerable heat for the studio violence, I think it is fair to say that the program accomplished its substantive purpose. It focused the nation's attention on the rapid growth and spreading influence of neo-Nazism. It is from that date that law enforcement increased its scrutiny of the violent actions of the racist groups, and it is from that date that various legal actions were initiated, slowing the fascists' evil momentum. It was also great television. When broadcast, it achieved a national rating of 13.1, for a very short time, the highest rated daytime talk show ever. (Oprah broke the record the next week, when she unveiled her dramatically (and temporarily) slimmed body. "Diet Dreams Come True," she called it.) Nazis and diets have since become talk show staples.

The fallout from the riot was noisy, but mixed. The professionals generally regarded it as grandstanding. ". . . what you noticed most in the video replay was the look on his face (before and after the chair hit it), his sheer determination to be on camera. Whether it means standing watch for two days at Al Capone's secret vault or uncovering satanic rituals in suburbia, you can't keep this guy off TV. Period," wrote Bill Thomas in *The Washington Post*. Most of the audience had a different read. They admired the fact that I had taken the physical risk of standing up to obnoxious, hateful bullies.

That audience approval showed up long-term in the ratings. In the months following the brawl, mine became the fastest growing daytime talk show. By the time of the next NATPE convention, held in Houston, in January 1989, my partners at *Tribune,* along with Paramount, the company that at the time distributed the program, decided to capitalize on its surging popularity and move the show out of its mostly morning time-periods, and into the afternoon. Since more people watch TV in the afternoons, the potential audiences are larger, and so are the fees charged the stations who carry the show. The stakes are higher, and the competition is tougher.

By the fall of 1989, *Geraldo* was an essentially afternoon talk show, up against *Oprah* and/or *Donahue* in virtually every major market. Driven by my own commercial insecurities, I almost committed professional suicide (for the second time) that November. To attract people away from Phil and Oprah, I resorted to every tried-and-true ratings-grabber in the business. My best (read worst) idea was "Bad Girls Week," five programs on such topics as "Mothers Who Murder" and "Women Who Fake Orgasms." By the middle of the next week, national advertisers were fleeing the broadcast, and our affiliated station managers, particularly in Bible Belt centers like Dallas, were up in arms over the flack they were receiving from irate citizens. Admittedly, I had brought most of these problems on myself, but I was still curious as to why my offerings had generated so much negative attention. After all, my programming mix was different only by degrees from that of the competition. (Indeed, if you compare my show at its worst, with Sally Jesse Raphael's show today ("Mothers Who Became Hookers," Transsexual Lesbians," and "Men Who Pay to Watch Women Fight"), mine seems relatively conservative.

My brother Craig provided the answer to the puzzle of the militant reaction. The anti-Geraldo campaign was being orchestrated by burly, boozing Roger King, the bear-sized man who, with his brother Michael, runs King World, the company that syndicates *Oprah*, along with *Wheel of Fortune, Jeopardy*, and *Inside Edition*. Craig was working as a reporter on *Inside Edition* at the time. Roger grabbed him at a party and said, "Tell your brother I'm coming after him. Tell him I'll have him off the air in a year." King World wanted my time slots and they wanted to eliminate Oprah's toughest competition. They nearly succeeded. Roger took out two- and three-page ads in all the trade publications, proclaiming King World's "Clean Air Act," their campaign to rid the airwaves of undesirable programs (like mine). They also faxed my titles to all station reps, advertisers, and station managers, under the title "Geraldo Pulls Out All the Stops."

Alerted by Craig, I began a counteroffensive, granting interviews about the irony of Roger King, a man recently convicted on a cocaine-possession rap, as the champion of public morality. It is a ". . . Hot Air Act," I told the press. I also pledged to forsake titillating topics, and to make mine the most mainstream of the daytime shows. I met with advertisers and with station managers and pleaded with them to give me another chance. I was a man transformed, I told them. I was also a man hanging onto his show by his fingertips.

At the next NATPE, in January 1990 (ironically, held in New Orleans, the scene of my first convention), the buzz was that I would not be around in September. Bull, I told the press. Compare what I'm doing with the crap the others are putting on. Who really is doing trash TV? I worked that convention like a man possessed, shaking hands, granting interviews, challenging any allegation that my show was somehow unfit. It was a close call, but by the end of the convention, Tribune Entertainment V.P. (now president) Don Hacker would say, ". . . You really turned this convention around."

More than the convention, I had really turned myself around. At the height of my excesses, the talk show had become a psychic burden. I was embarrassing myself, to the point where I had lost the desire and energy to leave the makeup room and run out on-stage. For the first (and only) time of my professional life, I had crossed the line from outlaw-eccentric to panderer. It is good to be back. It is not that my show had become some puritanical public-service hour. It is just that now, our topic mix and story selection comes much more from the mainstream of life, than from the polluted shallows.

The biggest fallout from the King World campaign was to force the *Geraldo* show basically back to its original morning time periods. It is an arena in which I feel comfortable, and gladly sacrifice the added visibility and profit of the afternoons, for the relative quiet and commercial stability of the mornings.

Sitting at my desk, watching the *New Wave* buck on her mooring to the rhythms of a brisk southwest wind, I have been reviewing this two years in the writing, forty-seven years in the living, life story. I started with the intention of writing an absolutely revealing autobiography, a kind of *Confessions of a Rock 'n' Roll Newsman* that would be toughest on me. The trouble with tell alls is that, in addition to the life of the author, they inevitably affect the lives of the other people portrayed. So, I've pulled some punches, and changed some names. Still, this is an honest chronicle of the meandering course of a fast-flowing and controversial life. Because the outcome is uncertain, I haven't talked about my return to investigative reporting with *Now It Can Be Told,* or about my recent debut as a newspaper publisher, with the purchase of a small, New Jersey weekly called *The Two River Times.*

The most important omission concerns the so-far unsuccessful attempts by C.C. and me to make a baby. For a long time, we wouldn't discuss our infertility problem publicly. Like most couples in this situation, we felt it was too painful. We want to have a baby. We are not sure we'll be able to, and the last couple of years of alternating hope and despair has been a tremendous strain. It is almost as if I've been cursed for all the previous excesses. We are asked every month for updates from concerned family and friends ("any news?").

We decided to go public last fall, to give some comfort to others in the same situation. Now, I have fans writing in every month asking for updates. C.C. did get pregnant in January 1991, but our boundless joy was stifled when she miscarried two months later. Still, since she can get pregnant, we remain hopeful, and passionately involved in bringing all our goals to successful conclusions. In the meantime, as a rock 'n' roll newsman used to say, peace and good night America.

ABOUT THE AUTHOR

GERALDO RIVERA is host of his own talk show, *Geraldo,* and anchor of the syndicated news program. *Now It Can Be Told.* He has received more than 150 awards in his twenty-plus years as a broadcast journalist, including three national and seven local Emmy Awards, two Columbia Du Pont journalism awards, two Scripps Howard journalism awards, and the George Foster Peabody Award. During his fifteen-year career at ABC-TV, he worked as a special correspondent for *20/20, World News Tonight,* and *Good Morning America,* and as a local reporter for the network's New York station, WABC-TV. He was also the host of his own late-night talk show, *Good Night America,* from 1974–1976. His articles have appeared in *The New York Times, Esquire, New York* magazine, the *Village Voice,* and several other publications. He is also the author of four previous books, including *Willowbrook: A Report on How It Is and Why It Doesn't Have to Be That Way* (1972) and *A Special Kind of Courage: Profiles of Young Americans* (1976).

DANIEL PAISNER is the author of several books of nonfiction, including *The Imperfect Mirror: Reflections of Television Newswomen* and *Heartlands: An American Odyssey.* He is also the author of a novel, *Obit.* His articles have appeared in the *New York Times Magazine, People, Entertainment Weekly,* and many other publications. He is currently completing a book about the television industry.